ANNALS OF ENGLISH DRAMA

Previous Publications

MIDDLETON'S TRAGEDIES (1955)
THE BLOODY BANQUET (1962)
in an edition for the Malone Society

ANNALS
OF ENGLISH DRAMA

975–1700

AN ANALYTICAL RECORD
OF ALL PLAYS, EXTANT OR LOST,
CHRONOLOGICALLY ARRANGED AND INDEXED
BY AUTHORS, TITLES, DRAMATIC COMPANIES, &c.

BY ALFRED HARBAGE
REVISED BY S. SCHOENBAUM

METHUEN & CO LTD
11 NEW FETTER LANE · LONDON EC4

CONTENTS

PREFACE TO REVISED EDITION

SIX YEARS AGO, while in London on a Guggenheim Fellowship, I was invited by Professor Alfred Harbage to undertake a revision of his *Annals of English Drama*. The book had been, in my own experience, one of the most useful of reference works: remarkable for the way in which comprehensiveness was allied with economy of presentation. Yet it had been out of print for some years, and was almost impossible to come by on the secondhand-book market; several great reference collections were without a copy. Moreover, since 1940, when the book was published, there had appeared the monumental works of Greg, on the English printed drama to the Restoration, and Bentley, on the Jacobean and Caroline stage. For the Restoration period, Woodward and McManaway's *Check List of English Plays* was now available. A number of important editions, monographs, and articles had been published. Brought up to date with the aid of these new tools, the *Annals* would, I felt, be even more helpful than before. So I did not hesitate to set aside for a year (as I then thought) my own work on Thomas Middleton, and begin at once the labour of revision.

The task has proved more arduous than I anticipated, and one year has stretched to six. The original plan to reprint by photo-offset, with such corrections as could not be made in the text relegated to an appendix, had ultimately to be abandoned, along with the apparatus I had devised for the purpose. As my work progressed, several ways of including additional information without sacrifice of conciseness occurred to me, and these innovations were adopted. The titles listed in the second column of the Chronology now appear in more complete form, without omission of articles, etc. In the Limits column the month and day of first performance are provided in a great many instances where formerly only the year was given; here, too, I have used Henslowe's *Diary* to fuller advantage, and supplied dates for the purchase of plays. In the Type column I have not exempted from classification translated or adapted works. I have made the bibliographically important distinction between edition and issue in the Earliest Texts column. The final column (Last Edition) is now documented, and I have appended a list of doctoral thesis editions. Approximately one hundred new entries, including about a dozen plays extant in manuscript, have been added to the Chronology and supplements. The indexes have been made fuller and more detailed (there are some six hundred additions to the Index of English Plays). In the Appendix I have given the new catalogue numbers assigned by the Folger Shakespeare Library to their manuscripts. Where necessary, I have described these changes more fully in the Introduction.

In a book of this scope, extending as it does from the Middle Ages to the close of the Restoration period, errors and omissions on my part are inevitable, although I have not spared myself effort to avoid them. Moreover, scholarly investigation will not cease, of course, to bring to light facts previously unnoted, or to replace old interpretations with new. It is my expectation, as it was that of the original compiler, to take note of advances in knowledge, and also to record mistakes and omissions brought to my attention. I hope to assemble this information from time to time, and to make it freely available, in the form of supplements, to users of this book, who need only inform me of their wish to be recipients.

Friends and colleagues have once again demonstrated the essential unselfishness of scholarly enterprise by generously sharing their knowledge, and it is a pleasure for me to express my appreciation. Professor Harbage supplied me at the outset with a number of corrections, and he was a faithful correspondent as problems arose. Professor Arnold Williams looked at the medieval section, and made a number of suggestions from which I have, I trust, profited. Dr James G. McManaway was good enough to show me his own annotated copy of the *Check List of English Plays,* and also his personally corrected copy of the *Annals.* Professor Emmett L. Avery not only examined my notes for the Restoration years but also placed at my disposal a draft of his forthcoming volume for *The London Stage, 1660–1800*; as a result, I was able to provide more accurate limits for a number of Restoration plays. Many others have helped by volunteering information, or by answering queries. I wish particularly to thank W. A. Armstrong, Lester A. Beaurline, Arthur Brown, Giles Dawson, G. Blakemore Evans, Mrs Inga-Stina Ewbank, R. A. Foakes, Arthur Freeman, Richard Hosley, George Hunter, S. F. Johnson, R. J. Kaufmann, J. W. Lever, Robert J. Lordi, James M. Osborn, William A. Ringler, Jr, I. A. Shapiro, and John Hazel Smith. With characteristic generosity, the late Professor F. P. Wilson offered several corrections and suggestions. I am obliged to Mrs Ann G. Larson, my typist, for excellent work on a difficult assignment. Mr Clive Burch assisted with the proof-reading. My wife, as always, gave invaluable support from beginning to end.

Work on this book has been facilitated by a leave of absence from Northwestern University for the autumn of 1960, and by grants for summer study from the Huntington Library and the Newberry Library. To the staffs of these institutions, as well as to the librarians and assistants at the British Museum, the University of London Library, the Folger Shakespeare Library, and the English College in Rome, I am grateful for many courtesies. Northwestern University helped also to defray clerical and other research costs. Mr A. P. Riemer saved me many hours of labour by assisting with the compilation of the list of editions in Section IV. To Mr Peter Wait at Methuen I am much indebted for his unfailing kindness and patience.

S. S.

12 *August* 1963

PREFACE TO FIRST EDITION

THE NATURE OF THIS BOOK – its method, purpose, and defects – is explained in the Introduction. I wish to reserve this space for a request that I be sent notice of errors and omissions. It is part of my plan to bring together, a year or two after my list has been exposed to view, as much corrective material as possible, and to publish it, with acknowledgements, in the 'Comment and Criticism' section of *PMLA*. Such material, transferred to individual copies, should increase the usefulness of the book. Its pages are intended for marginal notation, and I have petitioned for paper that would take ink.

For their interest and encouragement I am deeply indebted to Dr Joseph Quincy Adams and to Professor Albert C. Baugh. I wish also to thank, for their good offices, the Secretary and the Committee of Research Activities of the Modern Language Association, and the Secretary for Grants and the Jury of Award of the American Council of Learned Societies.

A. H.

July 1940

INTRODUCTION

[As far as possible I have retained the arrangement and language of the Introduction to the 1940 edition. Additions and alterations were required, however, to bring up to date the section on Sources of the Information, to describe changes and innovations in the plan of the work, and to provide a few further explanatory remarks for the guidance of the user. (S.S.)]

THIS BOOK contains a list of plays, masks, and other dramatic or quasi-dramatic representations devised in England, or by Englishmen abroad, from the time of the first recorded *Quem Quaeritis* until the year of the death of John Dryden. Included are plays in Latin and French as well as in English, lost as well as extant, unacted as well as acted, translated or adapted as well as original, the only limit to inclusion being that the work should be of known title or subject matter. Also listed are descriptions of royal receptions and entertainments (such as Henry Roberts's two accounts of the reception of Christian IV of Denmark in 1606), although such descriptions are themselves narrative rather than dramatic. The reviser has, however, eliminated several pieces included in the 1940 edition: e.g. *Necromantia* (1525); *Seven Dialogues* (1530); *Flowers for Latin Speaking* (1533); speeches made to General Monk on behalf of the Livery Companies in 1660; *Women, in Defence of the Sex* (1691). These, for the most part, are literary dialogues; thus, *Necromantia* is merely a parallel text verse translation of Lucian. Admit this piece and the others, and it is difficult to justify exclusion of *The Shepherd's Calendar*. Comprehensiveness has been sought, but a line had to be drawn somewhere as a matter of practical necessity.

The items are arranged chronologically, at first by centuries,* later by years, and a minimum of essential information is provided with each. A series of indexes gives access to the list. The aim of the book is to facilitate the study of English drama by supplying a convenient supplementary means of reference. It is compiled chiefly from authoritative historical works and from articles in scholarly journals, but in the course of revision such primary materials as manuscripts, early editions, etc., have been consulted frequently, and they have provided corrections and new facts. It was possible, thus, to add to the Chronology the anonymous Caroline comedy *Wit's Triumvirate, or The Philosopher*, extant in a British Museum manuscript but not listed by Bentley or, apparently, any other stage historian. However, the book attempts to present no original interpretation of contemporary evidence, but to render its service solely through inclusiveness, condensation, and arrangement.

Even a compiler must exercise certain discretionary powers, for he must weigh inferences as well as record facts. Old records are incomplete, and modern scholars disagree. The plan of the present book required that I come to at least tentative conclusions about the date and authorship of a large number of plays still subject to dispute, and I have tried to make my conclusions reflect the most conservative opinions of the most reliable authorities. (For a discussion of the problem and statement of principles regarding authorship questions, see S. Schoenbaum, 'Internal Evidence and the Attribution of Elizabethan Plays', *Bull. of the N.Y. Public Library*, LXV [1961], 102–24.) By a liberal use of interrogation points in the Author column, and by indicating alternative possibilities of date, I have tried to do justice to divergent opinion and to give flexibility to an arrange-

* Originally my plan was to begin with the year 1495. Medieval drama does not lend itself to the type of listing attempted here: the chronology is vague and the record fragmentary and confusing when the survey is confined to a single nation. Although the pages devoted to medieval drama will not prove very lucid, I have included them in order to preserve distinctions when my index is used as a finding list.

ment otherwise too rigid. An ultimate refinement of facts cannot, of course, be achieved in a book of this kind. Frequently, on my pages, only an interrogation point marks the place where learned conflicts have been waged.

The list is unannotated and, in any true sense, undocumented, and it may seem that a large measure of trustfulness on the part of the reader is implied. Such is not intended. The lack of documentation limits the usefulness of the book, but was unavoidable if its present scope and arrangement were to be retained. A great deal of time and care have been expended on the list, and I believe that it is trustworthy in the main. Yet it must contain errors – not only in respect to the preponderance of the best current opinion but also, probably, in respect to clearly demonstrable fact. In extenuation one can only say that many thousands of facts have been recorded, and that these facts have been extracted from the most copious and confusing body of discussion in the realm of literary scholarship. Analytical lists of this kind have limitations that are too well known to require enumeration here, and the research worker will seek his information in more detailed works than the present book; but he may find it useful sometimes in assisting his memory in the peripheral regions of his immediate problem. The chronological and tabular arrangement has the advantage of making quickly accessible related bodies of information.

The list is intended not only for the historian but also for the librarian, and for the teacher, the student, the ordinary reader of early English drama: these will not resent its attempt at simplification. It may not be amiss to suggest some of the uses to which the book may be put. The exhaustiveness of the contents, together with the fact that subtitles and alternative titles are included in it, should make the index of plays a useful finding list. The author index should prove helpful to those not primarily interested in drama but anxious to discover quickly what slight attention some poet or scholar conceded to the type. Foreign influences are suggested by the later indexes; some of the relations between early and late drama by the method of indicating adaptations. I should like to think that, by ascertaining easily what is known and conjectured about a particular play, a reader will get to his reading more quickly. The list, in fact, may be used to plan a course of reading, where it is desirable to trace for oneself the evolution of English drama, of a dramatic type, of the plays produced by a particular group of authors, or presented by a particular dramatic company. Where extensive reference facilities are not available, it will provide the necessary clue as to the accessibility of a play, and whether the particular edition available may have been superseded. The book ignores the terminal points usually forced upon historians of drama, and a playwright's complete canon (except in the case of some of the later Restoration writers) can readily be extracted from it. Simply leafing the pages should prove suggestive, for a great deal of dramatic history in outline will unfold.

Finally, and it was for this purpose that the book was originally planned, it will aid the student in determining immediately the approximate *environment* of any given play. In reading a play we often wish to know what other new plays were being performed at the same time, the few years before, the few years after, by the same company, by a competing company, or by all companies. The question cannot be answered precisely in all periods, the records being what they are, but this book makes what may prove to some a welcome attempt.

Sources of the Information

Certain older play-lists cover the entire period treated in the present book; although superseded in the main, they have not, I have found, entirely lost their usefulness. They are: Gerard Langbaine, *An Account of the English Dramatick Poets*, 1691; *Biographia Dramatica*, ed. D. E. Baker, I. Reed, S. Jones, 4 vols., 1812; J. O. Halliwell[-Phillipps], *A Dictionary of Old English Plays*, 1860; W. C. Hazlitt, *A Manual for the Collector and Amateur of Old English Plays*, 1892.

For medieval and early Tudor drama I have used primarily E. K. Chambers, *The Mediaeval Stage*, 2 vols., 1903; F. S. Boas, *University Drama in the Tudor Age*, 1914; G. C. Moore Smith, *College Plays*, 1923; *A Short-Title Catalogue of Books . . ., 1475–1640*, comp. A. W. Pollard, G. R. Redgrave, et al., 1926; A. W. Reed, *Early Tudor Drama*, 1926; A. J. Mill, *Mediaeval Plays in Scotland*, 1927; K. Young, *The Drama of the Medieval Church*, 2 vols., 1933; G. M. Sibley, *The Lost Plays and Masques, 1500–1642*, 1933; J. E. Wells, *A Manual of Writings in Middle English, 1050–1400*, 1916, 1st–9th Supp., 1919–51; E. K. Chambers, *English Literature at the Close of the Middle Ages*, 1945; C. J. Stratman, C. S. V., *Bibliography of Medieval Drama*, 1954; H. Craig, *English Religious Drama of the Middle Ages*, 1955; G. Wickham, *Early English Stages, 1300 to 1660*, Vol. I (to 1576), 1959. Also useful were two recent Malone Society *Collections* volumes: III (1954), *A Calendar of Dramatic Records in the Books of the Livery Companies of London, 1485–1640*, and V (1959 [1960]), containing extracts from the records of the academic drama in Oxford.

For the Elizabethan period more than elsewhere I have used articles in learned journals. My basic books were: F. E. Schelling, *Elizabethan Drama, 1558–1642*, 2 vols., 1908; E. K. Chambers, *The Elizabethan Stage*, 4 vols., 1923; E. K. Chambers, *William Shakespeare*, 2 vols., 1930; W. W. Greg, *A Bibliography of the English Printed Drama to the Restoration*, 4 vols., 1939–59. (In dating Shakespeare's plays I have followed Chambers, with a few modifications; here I have found useful a comparative table by R. A. Law, 'On the Dating of Shakespeare's Plays', *Shakespeare Assoc. Bull.*, XI [1936], 46–51, and J. G. McManaway's supplement to Chambers, 'Recent Studies in Shakespeare's Chronology', *Shakespeare Survey 3* [1950], 22–33.) The *Elizabethan Bibliographies* of Samuel A. and Dorothy R. Tannenbaum proved helpful despite their limitations.

For the Jacobean and Caroline periods more than elsewhere I have consulted books on, and editions of, individual dramatists, but the principal work used was G. E. Bentley, *The Jacobean and Caroline Stage*, 5 vols. (to date), 1941–56. Other general works – aside from Greg's *Bibliography*, previously cited – were W. W. Greg, *A List of English Plays, written before 1643 and printed before 1700*, 1900; W. W. Greg, *A List of English Masques, Pageants, &c.*, 1902; W. W. Greg, *Pastoral Poetry and Pastoral Drama*, 1906; P. Reyher, *Les Masques anglais*, 1909; J. Q. Adams, *The Dramatic Records of Sir Henry Herbert*, 1917; M. S. Steele, *Plays and Masques at Court*, 1926. It is perhaps impossible to ignore entirely F. G. Fleay, *A Biographical Chronicle of the English Drama, 1559–1642*, 2 vols., 1891, and H. Dugdale Sykes, *Sidelights on Elizabethan Drama*, 1924; but the shadow cast by these fantastics has, it is hoped, been shortened.

For the period of the Restoration I have used chiefly M. Summers, *A Bibliography of the Restoration Drama*, n.d.; M. Summers, *The Playhouse of Pepys*, 1935; *A Check List of English Plays, 1641–1700*, comp. G. L. Woodward and J. G. McManaway, 1945, supp. F. Bowers, 1949; A. Nicoll, *Restoration Drama, 1660–1700* (*A History of English Drama*, Vol. II), 4th ed., rev., 1952. The existence of the above books rendered Genest of little use for my particular purpose, but I have been able to alter some of the dates of first performance by putting articles to use, notably one by S. Rosenfeld, 'Dramatic Advertisements in the Burney Newspapers, 1660–1700', *PMLA*, LI (1936), 123–52. Many of the Restoration adaptations are noted in H. Spencer, *Shakespeare Improved*, 1927, and A. C. Sprague, *Beaumont and Fletcher on the Restoration Stage*, 1926.

For the dramatic companies, besides the works of Chambers and Bentley already cited, I have used: J. T. Murray, *English Dramatic Companies*, 2 vols., 1910; L. Hotson, *The Commonwealth and Restoration Stage*, 1928; E. Nungezer, *A Dictionary of Actors*, 1929; and for the playhouses, besides the works cited, J. Q. Adams, *Shakespearean Playhouses*, 1917.

The works listed above represent a very small fraction of those I have actually consulted. Most of them are comprehensive in nature and themselves contain play-lists. Omitted are the many recent works on individual authors and the many editions of individual plays, with their informative prefaces. Omitted also are the periodical articles laid under contribution. My method has been to select basic books for each period (chiefly those of Chambers and Bentley for the period ending 1642), and to consult only the periodical literature appearing after the publication of these basic books. In this part of my task the Modern Humanities Research Association's *Annual Bibliography of English Language and Literature*, 1920–21 to date, *The Year's Work in English Studies*, Oxford University Press, 1921 to date, and the annual bibliography of *Literature of the Renaissance* appearing in *Stud. in Philol.*, 1922 to date, have proved invaluable. I have not consulted all articles, but I believe I have missed few that are to my purpose. The correspondence columns of *The Times Literary Supplement* have supplied a surprising amount of factual material. Among the more onerous tasks I have undertaken has been to go through all available catalogues in search of manuscript plays. I have also found it necessary to go through Hall's *Chronicle* (edition of 1809) to supplement available lists of early Tudor entertainments at Court. I have not entirely shunned primary sources of information, and have turned frequently to the Stationers' Register, transcribed by Arber and Eyre, and (in extract) by Greg; the Term Catalogues, transcribed by Arber; the Revels documents, edited by Feuillerat; and Henslowe's *Diary* and papers, edited by Greg (1904–8) and by Foakes and Rickert (1961). A list of all the works consulted in preparing my play-list would be long, yet inadequate as a bibliography of early English drama, and, in view of the bibliographical facilities already available, not very useful. Authors of works used but not cited will forgive the omission; the greater injustice is to those whose contributions I have neglected to use.

Arrangement and Abbreviations

The Chronology and tabulation is arranged after 1495 according to modern calendar years, with each play placed in that year when it was most probably first presented. Using 1 January as the point of division creates an awkward split in several instances, since winter festivities at the Court and in the schools tended to extend from before Christmas until after Twelfth Night. However, no other arrangement was practical, and since the dramatic activities of professional companies in former times were more continuous than at present, there would be little point in keeping the winter seasons intact, even had it been possible. Within each year the plays are listed alphabetically by author; where there is more than one entry for the same author within a given year, the sequence is alphabetical by title. Anonymous plays are listed alphabetically by title at the end of each year.

The Chronology contains seven columns, and for each of these a word of explanation will be necessary.

FIRST COLUMN: This column is devoted to the names of authors. When the play is a work of collaboration the collaborators are indicated simply thus: *Day; Dekker; Chettle*. To indicate that Fletcher had the main hand in a play on which Beaumont collaborated and on which Massinger may have collaborated, the arrangement might be thus: *Fletcher, with Beaumont (and Massinger?)*. The term 'Anonymous' is used in all cases where authorship is unknown, whether or not the author's name was consciously withheld. Authors assigned to anonymous plays and generally accepted are indicated thus: *Fletcher, J.; Massinger, P.*; authors assigned and pretty generally accepted, thus: *Heywood, Thomas (?)*; authors assigned and not generally accepted, thus: *Anon. (Peele, G.?)*, or *Anon. (Marlowe? Kyd? Greene?)*, or simply *Anon.* Inverted commas about an author's name indicate that a contemporary attribution of authorship is now held in question. In a few instances of Tudor and Stuart entertainments, where more than one description is extant, the names of the describers are separated by a diagonal (/) rather than a semicolon, to distinguish these entries from collaborations; for example, *The Queen's Visit to Tilbury* (1588), described independently by Aske and by Deloney, is entered thus: *Aske, James / Deloney, Thomas (describers)*.

SECOND COLUMN: This column is devoted to titles. Some of these are condensed, but fuller titles are given in the play index. (A number of the designations, such as those for early Tudor entertainments known only from Revels documents and contemporary descriptions, are of course not true titles, but merely convenient descriptive phrases.) Beside the title, in round brackets, are placed alternative titles, from licensing records, running-titles, etc. All titles are given in modern spelling.[1] At the expense of strict logic, advantage has often been taken of the space afforded by this column, the widest of the seven, to give cross-references, to provide information about revival or revision, to cite the author and title of parent plays in cases of adaptation or translation, and to supply other kinds of miscellaneous information which otherwise could not have been included.

THIRD COLUMN: This supplies the limits of date. When the year of first performance is conclusively known there will be in this column a single date coinciding with that of the year in which the play is grouped. Where greater refinement is possible a more exact date is given – the licensing date for all plays where the licensing record has survived, the day of first performance for many masks, entertainments, and civic pageants, and the month or day of first performance for most of the Restoration plays. When the date of first performance of a Restoration play derives from Pepys's *Diary* it is followed by his name in round brackets. Where the date supplied for a Restoration play is that of the licence for printing, the abbreviation *imprim.* for *imprimatur* follows in round brackets. When the date of first performance is not conclusively known the forward and backward limits are indicated thus: *1622–1630*, or thus: *c. 1600–1610*, the latter meaning that the play in all probability was performed first before 1610 but not much before 1600. Henslowe's plays presented special problems. Where Henslowe gives the date of first performance, this information is supplied, but where he is wrong, Greg's corrections are inserted in square brackets[2]; thus the date given for *The Tanner of Denmark* (1592) is *23 [26] May*. For a number of other Henslowe plays, where the date of first performance is unavailable, the dates of payments to dramatists or of expenditures for properties have been provided. An initial *P* in round brackets follows dates of payments made to playwrights; the abbreviation *prop.* for *property*, also in round brackets, signifies the purchase of stage properties. For example, the entry for *Damon and Pythias* (1600) is *16 Feb.–27 Apr./6 May (P)*, and means that Henslowe made his first payment to Chettle for the play on 16 February and his last between 27 April and 6 May. (Sometimes the year in which a play has been placed is merely a median point between a forward and a backward limit, but usually there are better reasons for its chronological position than this.)

FOURTH COLUMN: This supplies a rough classification of the play: *Mask, History, Tragedy, Latin Comedy*, etc. Unless otherwise indicated, the play is in English.

FIFTH COLUMN: This supplies the auspices of first production; that is, the name of the professional company performing the play, such as *Strange's, Queen's Revels*, or *King's*: or the place where the play was performed if the production was amateur or by an unknown company, such as *London; King's College, Camb.; Middle Temple;* or *Court*. Plays not intended for performance are here marked *Closet*; those possibly intended for performance but evidently not performed are marked *Unacted*; a few early Elizabethan interludes printed with such legends as 'Six may easily play' are marked *Offered for acting*; the word *Unknown* needs no explanation.

SIXTH COLUMN: This gives the date of the first edition of printed plays, or the information that the play has come down to us in manuscript, or both. For medieval plays, the approximate date of the manuscript is supplied in this column. The present location of any play manuscript may be determined by consulting the catalogue in the Appendix. Square brackets about a date mean that the title page of the edition is undated. A single asterisk (*) after the date means that the first is the only early edition. By 'early' is meant before 1700 for plays written before 1660, and before about 1750 for plays written between 1660 and 1700. A double asterisk (**) following the date signifies that there was only one early edition, but two or more issues of that edition. (For an explanation of the distinction between edition and issue, see Greg, *Bibliography*, IV, xxxv–xxxvi.) An initial *F* in this column means that a manuscript or early edition, usually the first, has been reproduced in photographic facsimile. To illustrate: *1594 & MS* should be interpreted thus: the first edition of the play appeared in 1594, but there are later early editions, and also an early manuscript copy. Or, to take an impossibly complicated case: [*c. 1580*]***F & MSS* (*frags.*) should be interpreted thus: the play was published in a single early edition, of which there was more than one issue, about the year 1580 with no date on the title page; this edition has been reproduced in photographic facsimile, and there exist in addition two or more early manuscript fragments, for the location of which see the Appendix. (It is necessary only to add that such entries as *Hall, 578*, which appear a number of times in the sixth column for the early Tudor period, refer to a page number in the 1809 edition of Hall's *Chronicle*, where a description of the entertainment in question may be found; citations – less frequent – of the *Great Chronicle* refer to *The Great Chronicle of London*, ed. A. H. Thomas and I. D. Thornley, 1938.)

SEVENTH COLUMN: This gives the date of the latest modern edition of the play. (It is perhaps unnecessary to caution the reader that although the most satisfactory edition is very often the most recent, this is not always the case.) Popular paperback editions, not ordinarily preserved in libraries, have gone unrecorded; in only one case, that of Leo Kirschbaum's edition of *The Plays of Christopher Marlowe* (1962) for Meridian Books, did there seem cause to regret the omission. The editions prepared by French scholars for Aubier's *Collection bilingue*, too often unregarded, have been included. An obelisk (†) after the date means that there is only the one modern edition. By modern is meant, with one or two exceptions, nineteenth and twentieth centuries. Initials are used to indicate certain standard collections usually found in college libraries: *E* (publications of the *Early English Text Society*); *D* (W. C. Hazlitt's edition of Dodsley's *Old English Plays*, 15 vols., 1874–76); *M* (the *Mermaid Series*); *B* (*Materialien zur kunde des älteren englischen Dramas*, W. Bang, gen. ed.; New Series, H. de Vocht, gen. ed.); *G* (the *Malone Society Reprints*, W. W. Greg, gen. ed., 1906–39; F. P. Wilson, gen. ed., 1948–61; Arthur Brown, gen. ed., 1960–). When the initial, unembraced in round brackets, follows a date, the latest edition is in the series indicated; the initial within brackets means that the series includes the play, but there is a later edition. The initial *A*, always in round brackets, means that the play has been printed in at least one, usually several, popular anthologies, such as the *World's Classics* volumes in Great Britain, and the college textbook collections in the United States (e.g. *English Drama, 1580–1642*, ed. C. F. T. Brooke and N. B. Paradise, 1933). The distinguishing line between a popular anthology and a more – or less – scholarly collection is sometimes difficult to draw; perhaps certain decisions will seem arbitrary, but thought at least has been given to the matter. Thus J. Q. Adams's *Chief Pre-Shakespearean Dramas* (1924), addressed by the editor to students and scholars alike, was treated as a collection of separate editions in the unrevised *Annals*, but here becomes a popular anthology – a status which the expurgation of texts in that volume seemed alone sufficient to justify. An initial *T* (for *thesis*) in round brackets following a date indicates that the play has been edited as a doctoral dissertation; a finding list for these thesis-editions is provided in Section 3 of this book. To illustrate, then: *1915B†* means that the only modern edition of the play appeared in Bang's *Materialien* in 1915; *1933G* (*DM*) means that the play was last edited in the *Malone Society Reprints* in 1933, and that it also appears in Hazlitt's *Dodsley* and in the *Mermaid Series*. For several of the *Malone Society Reprints* a discrepancy exists between the year for which the play was assigned and the actual year of publication. In such instances the year of publication, in round brackets, follows the year to which the reprint was allocated; thus, *1940* (*1947*)*G* means that a play for 1940 was actually distributed in 1947. What to do with the seventh column in the case of Shakespeare's plays presented a problem; simply to give the latest edition would be pointless, but to discriminate would be dangerous. In casting about for some useful bit of information I could convey here, I decided to tell which of Shakespeare's plays have appeared in the *New Variorum Shakespeare*, and which are in progress. I have supplied the dates and the initial *V*. Where the space is left blank, the reader can supply the date of his favourite modern edition. The initial *V* is also used to designate the twenty plays issued under the general editorship of A. H. Bullen in the *Variorum Beaumont and Fletcher*, most of which appeared concurrently with A. Glover and A. R. Waller's complete edition of 1905–12. The superior figures following dates are intended to direct the reader to Section 2, the *List of Editions*, where information is supplied to make the editions more readily accessible.

OTHER ABBREVIATIONS: Abbreviations not mentioned in the foregoing explanation are, for the most part, self-explanatory. Generally used are *a.* for *after*; *adapt.* for *adaptation*; *add.* for *addenda* (referring to additional plays grouped in the fifteenth century and in the years 1570 and 1599); *b.* for *before*; *c.* for *circa*; *C.* or *Col.* for *College*; *Co.* for *Company*; *d.* for *died*; *descrip.* for *description*; *ed.* for *edition*; *Epil.* for *Epilogue*; *Lat.* for *Latin*; *lic.* for *licensed*; *ment.* for *mentioned*; *perf.* for *performance*; *poss.* for *possibly*; *prob.* for *probably*; *prog.* for *progress*; *Prol.* for *Prologue*; *Pt.* for *Part*; *pub.* for *published*; *S.R.* for *Stationers' Register*; *Supp. I*, or *Supp. II, a*, etc. (referring to the supplementary lists following the Chronology); *t.p.* for *title page*; and *trans.* for *translation*. Several of these abbreviations, not ordinarily admitted, have been employed in the interest of conciseness.

NOTES

1. Exceptions are made, however, for certain proper names, where a difference of pronunciation is implied, e.g. *Bristow* (rather than *Bristol*), *Feversham* (rather than *Faversham*).

2. But see Henslowe's *Diary*, ed. R. A. Foakes and R. T. Rickert (Cambridge, 1961), pp. xxvi–xxix.

I

CHRONOLOGY AND INFORMATION

DATE AUTHOR	TITLE	LIMITS
Tenth century		
Aethelwold, Bishop of Winchester (adapter)	*Quem Quaeritis* (of Easter), or *Visitatio Sepulchri* (Included in the *Regularis Concordia*, appended to the *Rule* of St Benedict. The *Concordia* contains also directions for the quasi-dramatic ceremonies, *Adoratio Crucis*, *Depositio Crucis*, and *Elevatio Crucis*. Directions for, or descriptions of, these ceremonies at Sarum and Durham occur between the 13th and the 16th centuries, and examples are printed severally by Chambers, Adams, and Young.)	965–975 (?)
Anon.	*Quem Quaeritis* (of Easter) in the *Winchester Troper*, otherwise known as the *Aethelred Troper*.(For the relations of this trope with the more advanced form in the *Regularis Concordia*, see Chambers, *M.S.*, II, 12–15.)	978–980 (?)
Eleventh century		
Geoffrey, afterwards Abbot of St Albans	*St Katherine (Ludus de Sancta Katerina)*	*c.* 1090–*c.* 1119
Twelfth century		
Hilarius (poss. English)	*The Raising of Lazarus (Suscitacio Lazari)*	*c.* 1120–*c.* 1130
Hilarius (with others)	*Daniel (Historia de Daniel Repraesentanda)*	*c.* 1120–*c.* 1130
Hilarius	*St Nicholas (The Image of St Nicholas. Ludus super Iconia Sancti Nicolai)*	*c.* 1120–*c.* 1130
Anon.	*Adam (Le Mystère d'Adam. Repraesentatio Adae)* (Poss. Norman rather than Anglo-Norman.)	*c.* 1146–*c.* 1174
Anon.	'Lundonia . . . ludos habet sanctiores, repraesentationes miraculorum quae sancti confessores operati sunt, seu repraesentationes passionum quibus claruit constantia martyrum.'	*c.* 1170–1182 (ment. by Fitzstephen)
Anon.	*Pastores*; *Quem Quaeritis* (of Easter); *Peregrini*	1188–*c.* 1300
Thirteenth century		
Anon.	'. . . et verbis et actu fieret repraesentatio Dominicae resurrectionis.'	*c.* 1220 (ment.)
Anon.	*Stella* (?) ('coronae ad repraesentationes faciendas')	1222 (ment.)
Anon.	'Actiones' at the churches of the parish	1220–1228 (ment.)

TYPE	AUSPICES	EARLIEST TEXTS	LAST ED.	DATE
			Tenth century	
Latin Liturgical Drama	Winchester Cathedral	MS (*c.* 1025) & MS (*c.* 1000?)	1953[1]	
Latin Trope	Winchester Cathedral	MS (978–980?) & MS (*c.* 1050)	1933[2]	
			Eleventh century	
Latin or French Miracle	Dunstable, Bedfordshire	Lost		
			Twelfth century	
Latin and French Semi-liturgical Drama	France	MS (12th cent.)	1933[2]	
Latin Semi-liturgical Drama	France	MS (12th cent.)	1933[2]	
Latin and French Semi-liturgical Drama	France	MS (12th cent.)	1933[2] (A)	
Anglo-Norman or Norman Mystery	Unknown	MS (12th cent.) (frag.)	1918[3] & 1926[4] (trans.)	
Miracles and Mysteries	London	Lost		
Latin Liturgical Dramas	Lichfield Cathedral	Lost		
			Thirteenth century	
Latin Liturgical Drama (?)	Beverley Minster, Yorkshire	Lost		
Latin Liturgical Drama (?)	Salisbury Cathedral	Lost		
Miracles and Mysteries (?)	Shipton, Oxfordshire	Lost		

DATE	AUTHOR	TITLE	LIMITS
	Anon.	'Miracula' ordered suppressed by Bishop Grosseteste	c. 1244
	Anon.	*The Harrowing of Hell* (Non-dramatic, but apparently influenced by mystery plays.)	c. 1200–c. 1250
	Anon.	*St Nicholas Play*	c. 1250 (ment.)
	Anon.	*Pastores*; *Stella, or Tres Reges*	c. 1255 (ment.)
	Anon.	'. . . comedendo, bibendo, ludendo, ioculando seu quod cumque ystrionatus officium exercendo . . .'	1286 (condemned by Bishop of Hereford)
	Anon.	*La Seinte resureccion* (*La Résurrection du Sauveur*)	b. c. 1275

Fourteenth century

DATE	AUTHOR	TITLE	LIMITS
	Anon.	*Dux Moraud* (One speaker's part in a play on the story of the Incestuous Daughter.)	c. 1300–c. 1400
	Anon.	*Caiphas* (Ceremonial verses, in Latin and English, for Palm Sunday.)	c. 1300–c. 1325
	Anon.	*Interludium de Clerico et Puella*	c. 1290–c. 1335
	Anon.	*Shrewsbury Fragments: Pastores* (*Officium Pastorum*); *Quem Quaeritis* (of Easter), or *Visitatio Sepulchri* (*Officium Resurrectionis*); *Peregrini* (*Officium Peregrinorum*) (Fragments, consisting of one actor's part and cues in the three plays.)	Late 13th–early 14th cent.
	Anon.	*Stella, or Tres Reges*	1317–1318 (1st ment.)
	Anon.	*St Thomas* (from *Peregrini*?)	1321–1322 (1st ment.)
	Anon.	*Origo Mundi*; *Passio Domini*; *Resurrexio Domini* (*The Creation of the World*) (Fifty episodes divided into three groups, for performance on three separate days.) See also 1611, 1695.	c. 1300–c. 1325
	Anon.	*Ipswich Corpus Christi Procession* (and *Plays*?) (In charge of Corpus Christi Guild.)	1325 (Guild formed); laid aside, 1531
	Anon.	*Quem Quaeritis* (of Easter), or *Visitatio Sepulchri* (Included in the MS are directions for the quasi-dramatic ceremonies, *Depositio Crucis* and *Elevatio Crucis*.)	1300–1400
	Anon.	*Bury St Edmunds Fragment* (French and English versions of a single stanza.)	Early 14th cent.
	Anon.	*Ludi Domini Regis* (First recorded disguising at Court.)	Xmas, 1347
	Anon.	*Ludus Filiorum Israelis*	1350 (ment.)

TYPE	AUSPICES	EARLIEST TEXTS	LAST ED.	DATE
Miracles or Mysteries, or both	Lincoln Diocese	Lost		
Dialogue	Unacted	MSS (c. 1325)	1927[5] (E)	
Miracle	Unknown	Lost		
Latin Liturgical Dramas	York Minster	Lost		
Festival Play (?)	Hereford, Herefordshire	Lost		
Anglo-Norman Mystery	Unknown	MSS (frags.)	1931[6] & 1943[7]	

			Fourteenth century	
Miracle (of Virgin ?)	Unknown	MS (c. 1300–1325)	1907[8] (A)	
Latin and English Dramatic Monologue and Song	Wells Cathedral	MS (c. 1300–1325)	1913[9]	
Interlude (?)	Unknown	MS (c. 1290–1335) (frag.)	1951[10] (A)	
Liturgical Plays in Latin and English	Lichfield Cathedral (?)	MS (c. 1400–1425) (frag.)	1933[2] (E)	
Latin Liturgical Drama	Lincoln Cathedral	Lost		
Latin Liturgical Drama	Lincoln Cathedral	Lost		
Cornish Cosmic Cycle of Mystery Plays	Penrhyn (?), Cornwall	MS (1400–1500)	1859† (whole cycle)[11] & 1955 (trans.)[12]	
Procession, and later a Play	Ipswich, Suffolk	Lost		
Latin Liturgical Drama, and Ceremonials	Church of St John the Evangelist, Dublin	MSS (1300–1400)	1933[2]	
Mystery	East Midlands	MS (1370) (frag.)	1921[13]	
Disguising or Mumming	Court	......		
Mystery (?)	Cambridge, Cambs.	Lost		

DATE	AUTHOR	TITLE	LIMITS
	Anon.	*York Plays* (*Corpus Christi Plays*) (Forty-eight plays and a fragment in present form, at one time fifty-seven; acted on pageants at stations in the city.)	*c.* 1352–b. 1376 (originated); 1376 (1st ment.); played until *c.* 1568
	Katherine of Sutton (adapter ?)	*Quem Quaeritis* (of Easter), or *Visitatio Sepulchri*; also *Depositio Crucis*; *Elevatio Crucis*	1363–1376
	Anon.	*The Visit to Richard II* (First Court disguising recorded in detail.)	1 Feb. 1377
	Anon.	*Beverley Plays* (*Corpus Christi Plays*) (Consisted in 1490 of thirty-eight plays.)	1377 (1st ment.); played until *c.* 1555
	Anon. (conceivably Higden, R.)	*Chester Plays* (*Whitsun Plays. Corpus Christi Plays*) (Consist of banns and twenty-five plays, acted on pageants at stations in the city.)	*c.* 1377–1382 (?) (originated); 1462 (1st ment.); played until 1575
	Anon.	*Pater Noster Play* (On the triumph of the virtues over the vices, performed at stations in the city by a guild formed to perpetuate it.)	1378 (1st ment.); played until 1572
	Anon.	*St Paul's Old Testament Plays*	1378 (ment.)
	Anon.	*Skinners' Well Plays* (Of a cyclical character, given by the London clerks in minor orders.)	1384 (1st ment.); played until a. 1442
	Anon.	*St Thomas the Martyr*	1385–1386
	Anon.	*Pater Noster Play*	1397 (1st ment.); played until 1521
	Anon. (revised by Croo, R., 1534)	*Coventry Plays* (*True Coventry Plays. Corpus Christi Plays*) (Of the cycle, only two plays survive: the *Shearmen and Tailors' Pageant* of the Annunciation, Nativity, and Shepherds; and the *Weavers' Pageant*, of the Magi, Herod, the Massacre, and the Flight to Egypt. Cycle was acted on ten or twelve pageants at stations in the city.)	1392 (1st ment.); played until 1580
	Anon.	*Abraham and Isaac* (Brome.)	*c.* 1375–*c.* 1400
	Anon.	*Interludium de Corpore Christi* (Performed by the Corpus Christi Guild.) Pageants (for mysteries ?) by the craft guilds are mentioned below, 15th cent.	1389 (ment.)
	Anon.	*Hedon Plays*	1389–1390 (1st ment.)
	Anon.	*Annunciation Play* (?) ('pro Salutacione')	1390–1391 (1st ment.)

TYPE	AUSPICES	EARLIEST TEXTS	LAST ED.	DATE
Cosmic Cycle of Mystery Plays	York, Yorkshire	MS (*c.* 1475 & 1558)	1885† (whole cycle)[14] & 1957† (trans. whole cycle)[15]	
Latin Liturgical Drama, and Ceremonials	Nunnery of Barking, near London	MS (1363–1376)	1933[2]	
Disguising or Mumming	Court	......		
Cosmic Cycle of Mystery Plays	Beverley, Yorkshire	Lost		
Cosmic Cycle of Mystery Plays	Chester, Cheshire	MS (1475–1500) (frag.) Other MSS, 1591, etc.	1893 E, 1916 E (whole cycle), & 1958 (trans. 16 plays)[15a]	
Morality	York, Yorkshire	Lost		
Mysteries	St Paul's, London	Lost		
Mysteries	Skinners' Well, London	Lost		
Miracle	King's Lynn, Norfolk	Lost		
Morality	Lincoln, Lincolnshire	Lost		
Cosmic Cycle of Mystery Plays	Coventry, Warwickshire	MS (1534) (*Shearmen Pageant* destroyed 1879)	1902 E	
Mystery	Unknown	MS (*c.* 1470–1480)	1909 E (A)	
Mystery	Bury St Edmunds, Suffolk	Lost		
Mysteries (?)	St Augustine's Church, Hedon	Lost		
Latin Liturgical Drama	Lincoln Cathedral	Lost		

DATE	AUTHOR	TITLE	LIMITS
	Maydiston, Richard (describer)	*Richard II's Reconciliation with the City of London*	21 Aug. 1392
	Anon.	*St Katherine*	1393
	Anon.	*Wells Plays*	1394 (1st ment.)
	Anon.	*Wakefield Plays* (*Towneley Plays. Woodkirk* or *Widkirk Plays. Corpus Christi Plays*) (Consists of thirty-two plays, including the *Suspencio Iude*, which is in a different hand and may not be a play. Several of the plays are taken from the *York Cycle*, others resemble York plays, especially a homogeneous group usually credited to an unknown 'Wakefield Master'; in the latter group is the play variously called *Secunda Pastorum, The Second Shepherd's Play*, or *Mak*.)	*c.* 1390–1410 (?) (originated); work of Wakefield Master may have begun *c.* 1435 and extended to *c.* 1450
	Anon.	*The Pride of Life*	Late 14th cent.

Fifteenth century

DATE	AUTHOR	TITLE	LIMITS
	Anon.	*Corpus Christi Procession* (and *Plays*?)	*c.* 1400–*c.* 1462
	Anon.	*The Castle of Perseverance* (One of the *Macro Morals*.)	1405–1425
	Anon.	*St George, St Thomas a Becket*, and *Corpus Christi Processions*	15th and 16th cent.
	Anon.	*The Reception of Henry V, Returning from France*	23 Nov. 1415
	Chamberleyn, Thomas	*Rubum Quem Viderat* (Part of an *Ordo Prophetarum*?)	1420
	Anon.	*Noah Play* (By Guild of Master Mariners and Pilots.)	1421 (?)– *c.* 1529
	Anon.	*Newcastle Plays* (*Corpus Christi Plays*) (Consisted of twenty-two plays, of which only one, *Noah's Ark*, is extant.)	1426 (1st ment.); played until 1567– 1568
	Anon.	*St Clotilda*	1429
	Lydgate, John	*A Mumming at Eltham*	1427–1430
	Lydgate, John	*A Mumming at Hertford*	*c.* 1430 (?)
	Lydgate, John	*The Mumming at Bishopswood*	*c.* 1430 (?)
	Lydgate, John	*A Mumming at London* (*A Mumming before the Great Estates of the Land*)	1427–1430
	Lydgate, John	*A Mumming at Windsor*	1427–1430
	Lydgate, John	*A Mumming for the Goldsmiths of London*	1427–1430
	Lydgate, John	*A Mumming for the Mercers of London*	1427–1430
	Lydgate, John (describer)	*The Reception of Henry VI, Returning from France*	21 Feb. 1432
	Anon.	*Passion and Resurrection Play*	*c.* 1428–*c.* 1560

TYPE	AUSPICES	EARLIEST TEXTS	LAST ED.	DATE
Pageants and Speeches	London	MSS	1835†[15b] & 1959 (extracts)[16]	
Miracle	London	Lost		
Liturgical Plays	Wells	Lost		
Cosmic Cycle of Mystery Plays	Wakefield, Yorkshire	MS (1450–1500)	1897 E (whole cycle), 1958 (6 plays),[16a] & 1961 (trans. whole cycle)[17]	
Morality	Kent (?)	MS (1400–1425) (frag.)	1909 E	
			Fifteenth century	
Cosmic Cycle (?)	King's Lynn, Norfolk	Lost		
Morality	Lincolnshire (?)	MS (c. 1440) F	1904 E	
Guild Processions	Norwich, Norfolk	......		
Royal Reception	London	*Great Chronicle*, 93–94		
Liturgical Drama (?)	Lincoln Cathedral	Lost		
Mystery	Hull, Yorkshire	Lost		
Cosmic Cycle of Mystery Plays	Newcastle-on-Tyne	Lost MS (1425–1450)	1931[18] (E)	
Miracle	Acted at Court	Lost		
Verses, for Mumming	Court	MSS	1934 E	
Verses, for Mumming	Court	MSS	1934 E	
Verses, for Mumming	Court	MS	1934 E	
Verses, for Mumming	London	MSS	1934 E	
Verses, for Mumming	Court	MSS	1934 E	
Verses, for Mumming	London	MSS	1934 E	
Verses, for Mumming	London	MSS	1934 E	
Pageants and Speeches	London	MS	1934 E	
Mysteries	New Romney, Kent	Lost		

DATE	AUTHOR	TITLE	LIMITS
	Anon.	*The Burial and Resurrection of Christ* (*Christ's Burial and Resurrection*) (In Two Parts: I for Good Friday, II for Easter.)	c. 1430–c. 1450
	Anon.	*Hereford Plays* (*Corpus Christi Plays* or *Dumb Shows*.)	1440 (1st ment.); ceased b. 1548
	Anon.	*Aberdeen Plays* (*Haliblud* or *Passion Play* on Corpus Christi Day, *Nativity Play* on Candlemas Day, and also *St Nicholas Day Ride*, with Robin Hood, Maid Marian, etc.)	1440–1442 (1st ment.); played until early 16th cent.
	Anon.	*Ludus Coventriae* (*Corpus Christi Plays. Hegge Plays. N. Town Plays*) (Consists of forty-two plays, variously considered an amalgam for reading, a travelling cycle, or an adaptation for acting on a fixed stage.) See *The Assumption or Coronation of the Virgin*, and *Lincoln Plays*, below.	c. 1400–c. 1450
	Anon.	*St Laurence*	1441–1442 (ment.)
	Anon.	*The Welcome for Margaret of Anjou* (Pageant of St Margaret.)	28 May 1444
	Anon.	*Eglemour and Degrebelle*	30 June 1444 (acted)
	Anon.	'a knight cleped Florence'	Aug. 1444 (acted)
	Anon.	*Corpus Christi Procession*	c. 1444–c. 1544
	Anon.	*Creed Play* (Stationary play, acted about 1 Aug., every tenth year.)	1446 (1st ment.); played until 1535
	Anon.	*St Susannah*	1447–1448 (ment.)
	Anon.	*Abraham and Isaac* (Dublin.)	c. 1445–c. 1450
	Anon.	*King Robert of Sicily*	1447–1453 (ment.)
	Laingby, Robert (?)	*St Dionysius*	1455 (ment.)
	Anon.	*St Clara*	1455–1456 (ment.)
	Anon.	*St George*	1456 (ment.)
	Anon.	*The Assumption or Coronation of the Virgin* (Prob. represented in Play XLI of *Ludus Coventriae*, above.)	1458–1459 (1st ment.)
	Anon.	*Mankind* (One of the *Macro Morals*.)	1465–1470
	Anon.	*Worcester Plays* (*Corpus Christi Plays*) (Consisted of five plays.)	1467 (1st ment.); played until a. 1559

TYPE	AUSPICES	EARLIEST TEXTS	LAST ED.	DATE
Liturgical Drama	Unknown (Northern)	MS (*c.* 1430–1450)	1896 E	
Cosmic Cycle	Hereford, Herefordshire	Lost		
Processions with Mystery and Folk Plays	Under direction of Abbot of Bon Accord, Aberdeen	Lost		
Cosmic Cycle of Mystery Plays	Lincoln (?)	MS (1468)	1922 E (whole cycle)	
Miracle	Lincoln, Lincolnshire	Lost		
Royal Reception	London	*Great Chronicle*, 177–8		
Romance (?)	St Albans	Lost		
Romance (?)	Bermondsey	Lost		
Guild Procession	Coventry, Warwickshire	......		
Morality	York, Yorkshire	Lost		
Miracle	Lincoln, Lincolnshire	Lost		
Mystery	Northampton (?)	MS (*c.* 1458)	1909 E	
Miracle	Lincoln, Lincolnshire	Lost		
Miracle	York, Yorkshire	Lost		
Miracle	Lincoln, Lincolnshire	Lost		
Miracle	Lydd, Kent	Lost		
Latin and English Semi-liturgical Drama	Lincoln Cathedral	Lost (?)		
Morality	Norfolk (?)	MS (1450–1500) F	1907[19] (EA)	
Mystery Cycle	Worcester, Worcestershire	Lost		

DATE	AUTHOR	TITLE	LIMITS
	Anon.	*Pater Noster Play* (Consisted of eight pageants devoted severally to eight vices, presented by craft guilds at stations in the city.)	1469 (ment.)
	Anon.	*Belial* (*Ludus de Bellyale*)	1471 (ment.)
	Anon.	*Lincoln Plays* (*Corpus Christi Plays*, so called, but acted on St Anne's Day [26 July]. In 1483 Lincoln Cathedral Chapter voted to add *The Assumption of the Virgin* [in vernacular?] to the citizens' plays [a new departure?]. The *Assumption*, perhaps all the plays, to be performed in the nave of the Cathedral. See *The Assumption or Coronation of the Virgin*, and *Ludus Coventriae*, above.)	1472 (1st ment.); played until 1555
	Anon.	*Mind, Will, and Understanding* (*The Wisdom That Is Christ*) (One of the *Macro Morals*.)	1450–1500
	Anon.	*Robin Hood Plays*	1473
	Anon.	*Robin Hood and the Sheriff of Nottingham*	*c.* 1473
	'R.C.' (scribe?)	*The Sacrament* (*The Croxton Play of the Sacrament*)	1461–1500
	Anon.	*Bury St Edmunds Plays* or *Dumb Shows*	Old in 1477
	Anon.	*Leicester Passion Play*	1477 (ment.)
	Anon.	*Norwich Plays* (*Whitsun Plays*) (Consisted of at least twelve plays; only the Grocers' play survives: *Adam and Eve*, or *The Creation of Eve, with the Expelling of Adam and Eve out of Paradise* [two versions].)	1478 (1st ment.); played until *c.* 1565
	Anon.	*Sleaford Ascension Play*	1480 (ment.)
	Anon.	*Quem Quaeritis*	1482 (ment.)
	Anon.	*Henry VII's Provincial Progress*	1486
	Anon.	*Descensus Christi ad Inferos*	1486
	Anon.	*Quem Quaeritis*	1487 and later
	Anon.	*St Katherine*	1490–1491
	Anon.	*St George*	1490–a. 1497
	Anon.	*The Conversion of St Paul* (A *Digby* 'Mystery'.)	*c.* 1480–1520
	Anon.	*Mary Magdalene* (A *Digby* 'Mystery'.)	*c.* 1480–1520
	Parfre, John (scribe?)	*The Massacre of Innocents* (*Candlemas Day and the Killing of the Children of Israel*) (A *Digby* 'Mystery', part of a cycle.)	*c.* 1480–*c.* 1490
	Anon.	*Quem Quaeritis* (*Play* or *Puppet Show*.)	1491 (1st ment.)
	Anon.	*Abraham and Isaac*	1491–1520
	Anon. (Cornish, W.?)	*St George and the Castle*	6 Jan. 1494

TYPE	AUSPICES	EARLIEST TEXTS	LAST ED.	DATE
Morality	Beverley, Yorkshire	Lost		
Mystery, or Morality (?)	Aberdeen	Lost		
Mysteries	Lincoln, Lincolnshire	Lost		
Morality	West Midlands (?)	MSS (1450–1500) F	1904 E	
Folk Plays	At Sir John Paston's	Lost		
Folk Play	At Sir John Paston's (?)	MS (c. 1475–1476) (frag.) F	1908 G (A)	
Miracle	Croxton (Norfolk?)	MS (1461–1500) F	1909 E (A)	
Cosmic Cycle (?)	Bury St Edmunds	Lost		
Mystery	Leicester, Leicestershire	Lost		
Cosmic Cycle of Mystery Plays	Norwich, Norfolk	Lost MSS (1533 & 1565)	1909 E (A)	
Mystery	Sleaford, Lincolnshire	Lost		
Liturgical Play (?)	Bath, Somersetshire	Lost		
Pageants	York, Hereford, Worcester, and Bristol	MS (descrip.)	1774[20] & 1939 (1947) (extract)[21]	
Mystery	Court	Lost		
Liturgical Play (?)	Magdalen Col., Oxford	Lost		
Miracle	Coventry, Warwickshire	Lost		
Miracle	New Romney, Kent	Lost		
Miracle–Mystery	East Midlands (?)	MS (c. 1480–1520)	1882 E (A)	
Miracle–Morality	Lynn, Norfolk (?)	MS (c. 1480–1520)	1896 E (A)	
Mystery	East Midlands (?)	MS (1512)	1896 E	
Liturgical Play (?)	Leicester Churches	Lost		
Mystery	St Dunstan's Church, Cant.	Lost		
Disguising	Court	*Great Chronicle*, 251–2		

DATE	AUTHOR	TITLE	LIMITS
	Anon.	*Canterbury Plays* (*Corpus Christi Plays*)	1500 (revived)

Additional lost plays of traditional character mentioned at various times after 1495:

St James (15th cent., Lincoln); *Shrewsbury Plays* (1st ment. 1495; *Sts Feliciana and Sabina*, 1516, *Three Kings of Cologne*, 1518); *Midsummer Show* (1498–1678, Chester); *Robin Hood Play* (ment. 1498, Wells, Somerset); *Corpus Christi Procession*, including shows on *Arthur and His Knights* and *Nine Worthies* (1st ment. 1498, Dublin); *St George Pageant* (contemporary with preceding? Dublin); *Adam and Eve, Kings of Cologne*, etc. (1499–1535, Reading); *Three Kings of Cologne* (ment. 1503, Canterbury); *St Thomas à Becket Pageant* (1st ment. 1504, Canterbury); *St Mary Magdalene* (ment. 1503–1504, Thetford Priory, Norfolk); *St Mary Magdalene* (ment. 1506, Oxford); *St Christian* (ment. 1504–1505, Coventry); *Easter Play* (1505–1565, Kingston-on-Thames); *Corpus Christi Pageant* (1514–1591, Bungay, Suffolk); *Easter Play* (16th cent., Morebath, Devonshire); *Corpus Christi Play* (1516–1532, Heybridge, Essex); *Corpus Christi Play* (1526–1546, Dunmow, Essex); *St Erasmus* (1518, Aberdeen); *St Christina* (1522, Bethersden, Kent); *Nativity Play* and *Resurrection Play* (played until at least 1522, Earl of Northumberland's Chapel); *St Swithin* (1523, St Michael's Church, Braintree, Essex); *St Andrew* (1525, same as preceding); *St Eustace* (1534, same as preceding); *King Robert of Sicily* (1529, Chester); *Corpus Christi Play*, distinct from Chester cycle (1544–1547, Chester); *Midsummer Watch* (played until 1538, and once revived in 1548, London); '*Fisher Play*' (recorded 1540 in Court Rolls of Doncaster, Rossington, Hexthorpe, and Long Sandall); *Three Kings of Cologne* (1548, Holbeach, Lincolnshire); *St George Riding* (old in 1554, York); *Passion Play* (1557, Greyfriars, London); *St Olave's Play* (1557, St Olave's Church, London); *Corpus Christi Play* (1562–1574, Chelmsford, Essex: wardrobe of this play was hired by the following towns: Baddow, Billericay, Boreham, Braintree, Brentford, Burnham, Colchester, Hanningfield,

TYPE	AUSPICES	EARLIEST TEXTS	LAST ED.	DATE
Cosmic Cycle	Canterbury, Kent	Lost		

C

DATE	AUTHOR	TITLE	LIMITS
		High Easter, 'Lanchire', Little Baddow, Maldon, Nayland, 'Sabsford', Saffron Walden, Stapleford, Woodham, Walter, Witham, Writtle); *Tobias* (1564, Lincoln); *Corpus Christi Play* (1575–1612, Kendal, Westmorland); *Corpus Christi Play* (played until *c.* 1576, Doncaster); '*King Play*' (1579, Hascombe, Surrey); *Manningtree Moralities* (played until 1612, Manningtree, Essex); *St Tewdricus* (ment. 1701, Carnarvon, Bangor); *St Obert* (b. 1575, Perth, Scotland).	
1495	Medwall, Henry More, Thomas Anon.	*I & II Nature* '*Comoediolae*' *The Summoning of Every Man* (*Every Man. A Treatise How the High Father of Heaven Sendeth Death to Summon Every Creature*) (Adapt. *Elckerlijc* of Dorlandus?)	*c.* 1490–*c.* 1501 *c.* 1491–*c.* 1499 *c.* 1495–1500
1496			
1497	Medwall, Henry	*I & II Fulgens and Lucrece* (*Fulgens, Senator of Rome*) (Adapt. of a tale by Bonaccorso through French and English intermediaries.)	*c.* 1490–*c.* 1501
1498			
1499			
1500			
1501	Cornish, W., and others	*The Marriage of Prince Arthur* (Pageants of castle, ship, and mount, prob. by Cornish, on 19 Nov.)	Nov.
1502	Fox, Richard (?)	*The Welcome for Katherine of Aragon* (Pageants, with speeches, of St Katherine, and St Ursula; the Castle of Portcullis, with Policy, Nobleness, and Right; Raphael, Alphonso, Job, and Boethius; the Sphere of the Sun; the Temple of God; Honour and the Seven Virtues.)	12 Nov.
1503	Dunbar, William (?) Anon.	*The Droichis* [*Dwarf's*] *Part of the Play* (*The Manner of the Crying of a Play*) (A part of the following?) *The Welcome for Princess Margaret*	1503 (?) 7 Aug.

TYPE	AUSPICES	EARLIEST TEXTS	LAST ED.	DATE
Moral Interlude	Morton's House (?)	[1530–34 ?]* F	1907[19] (B)	**1495**
Interludes (?)	Unknown	Lost		
Morality	Unknown	[1510–19 ?] F	[1953][22] (DBA)	
				1496
Romantic Interlude	Morton's House (?)	[c. 1512–16]* F	1926[20] (A)	**1497**
				1498
				1499
				1500
Tilt and Disguising	Westminster and Richmond	MS (descrip.); cf. also Hall, 493–4	1809[24]	**1501**
Pageantry	London	MSS (descrip.); cf. also *Great Chronicle*, 297–310, & Hall, 493	1808[25]	**1502**
Banns for May Game	Edinburgh	MSS	1932[26]	**1503**
Pageantry	Edinburgh	......		

DATE	AUTHOR	TITLE	LIMITS
1504	Hadton, 'Dominus'	*The Life of St Meriasek, Bishop and Confessor*	1504
	Skelton, John	*The Nigramansir* [*Necromancer*] (Poss. a fabrication, by Warton.)	*c.* 1504
1505			
1506			
1507	Anon.	*The Joust of the Wild Knight and the Black Lady*	June
	Anon.	*The Jousts of the Months of May and June*	May, June
1508	Anon.	*The World and the Child* (*Mundus et Infans*)	*c.* 1500–1522
1509	Anon.	*The Coronation Triumph of Henry VIII*	24 June
	Anon.	*The Scholars of Dame Pallas and Knights of Diana*	June
1510	Anon.	*Almains and Spaniards*	14 Nov.
	Anon.	*The Entertainment of the Ambassadors*	10 Feb.
	Anon. (Rastell, J.?)	*The Nine Hierarchies of Angels*	1510
	Anon.	*Robin Hood's Men*	1510
1511	Hobarde, John	*St George* (For other miracles of 16th cent., see 15th cent. add.)	20 July
	Anon.	*The Four Chevaliers of the Forest Salvigny*	13 Feb.
	Anon.	*The Garden of Pleasure*	14 Feb.
	Anon.	*A Pageant of a Mountain*	6 Jan.
	Anon.	*The Ship of Fame*	1 May
	Anon.	*The Welcome for Queen Margaret*	May
1512	Anon.	*The Castle Dangerous*	1 Jan.
	Anon.	*The Dolorous Castle*	June
	Anon.	*An Epiphany Mask*	6 Jan.
1513	Arduenna, Remaclus	*Palamedes* (By a foreigner, living in London.)	*c.* 1513 (pub.)
	Anon.	*Beauty and Venus*	1513–1514
	Anon.	*Hick Scorner* (*Hycke Scorner*)	*c.* 1513–1516
	Anon.	*The Mask at Tournay*	18 Oct.
	Anon.	*The Rich Mount*	6 Jan.
1514	Cornish, William	*The Triumph of Love and Beauty* (Prob. a Collier forgery.)	6 Jan.
	Medwall, Henry	*The Finding of Troth* (Prob. a Collier forgery.)	6 Jan.
1515	Skelton, John	*Achademios*	*c.* 1504–1523
	Skelton, John	*Good Order* (*De Bono Ordine*) (Poss. same as *Old Christmas*, 1533.)	*c.* 1504–1529

TYPE	AUSPICES	EARLIEST TEXTS	LAST ED.	DATE
Cornish Miracle	Camborne (?), Cornwall	MS	1872†[27]	**1504**
Interlude	Court at Woodstock	Lost		
				1505
				1506
Tilt	Scottish Court	......		
Tilt	English Court	[c. 1508]* (descrip.)	1866[28]	**1507**
Moral Interlude	Unknown	1522* F	1905[29] (D)	**1508**
Pageantry	London and Westminster	Hall, 507–13		**1509**
Disguising and Tilt	Court	Hall, 511–12		
Disguising	Court	Hall, 516		**1510**
Disguising	Court	Hall, 513–14		
Pageant for King	Coventry	......		
Disguising	Court	Hall, 513		
Miracle	Bassingbourne, Cambridgeshire	Lost		**1511**
Disguising and Tilt	Court	Hall, 517		
Disguising	Court	Hall, 518–19		
Entertainment	Court	Hall, 516–17		
Setting for Tilt	Court	Hall, 520		
Pageants	Aberdeen	......		
Disguising and Tilt	Court	Hall, 526		**1512**
Disguising and Tilt	Court	Hall, 533–4		
Mask	Court	Hall, 526		
Latin Comedy	Closet	[c. 1513]		**1513**
Interlude	Court	Lost		
Moral Interlude	Unknown	[1515–16?] F	1905[29] (D)	
Mask	Court at Tournay	Hall, 566		
Disguising	Court	Hall, 535		
Interlude	Chapel at Court	'Lost'		**1514**
Interlude	Court Interluders	'Lost'		
Comedy	Unknown	Lost		**1515**
Moral Interlude (?)	Unknown	Lost (?)		

DATE	AUTHOR	TITLE	LIMITS
	Skelton, John	*Magnificence*	1515–1523
	Skelton, John	*Virtue (De Virtute)*	*c.* 1504–1523
	Anon.	*The Place Perilous (Wild Men)*	6 Jan.
	Anon.	*Robin Hood's Feast*	1 May
1516	Anon.	*The Eltham Pageant of a Castle*	6 Jan.
	Anon.	*Troilus and Pander*	6 Jan.
1517	Cornish, William (?)	*The Garden of Esperance*	6 Jan.
	Rastell, John	*The Nature of the Four Elements (Natura Naturata)*	*c.* 1517–*c.* 1518
1518	Anon.	*The Entertainment of the French Ambassadors*	Oct.
	Anon.	*A Mask of Palmers*	1518
	Anon.	*The Rock of Amity* (With speeches in French.)	8 Oct.
	Anon.	*St Erasmus*	1518 (acted)
1519	Heywood, John (?)	*The Pardoner and the Friar, the Curate, and Neighbour Pratte*	1513–1521
	Anon.	*The Entertainment of the Hostages*	7 Mar.
	Anon.	'Revels called a Maskalyn'	1519
1520	Heywood, John	*The Four P's*	*c.* 1520–1522
	Heywood, John (?)	*Johan Johan the Husband, Tib His Wife, and Sir Johan the Priest (Johan Johan)* (Adapt. *Farce du Pasté.*)	1520–1533
	Anon.	*Andria (Terence in English)*	1516–1533
	......	*The Field of the Cloth of Gold*	9–24 June
	Anon.	*Johan the Evangelist*	*c.* 1520–*c.* 1557
	Anon.	*A Pageant of a Wagon*	1 Feb.
	Anon.	'Summer and Lust', etc.	1520
	Anon.	*Youth*	1513–1529
1521	Anon.	*The Entertainment of the Emperor's Ambassadors*	1521–1522
1522	Cornish, William	*Friendship, Prudence, and Might (The Triumph of Amity)*	15 June
	Lyly, W.; Rastell; and others	*The Welcome for Emperor Charles V* (Pageants, with Latin verses, of Jason and Medea; Charlemagne; John of Gaunt; the Four Cardinal Virtues; King Alphonsus; the Apostles [by Rastell].)	6 June
	Anon.	*The Conquest of Lady Scorn*	4 Mar.

TYPE	AUSPICES	EARLIEST TEXTS	LAST ED.	DATE
Moral Interlude	Unknown	[1530?]* F	1906 E	
Moral Interlude	Unknown	Lost		
Disguising	Court	Hall, 580		
Maying	Court	Hall, 582		
Disguising	Court	Hall, 583		**1516**
Romantic Interlude	Chapel at Court	Lost		
Disguising	Court	Hall, 585–6		**1517**
Didactic Interlude	Unknown	[c. 1526–30]* (frag.) F	1905[29] (D)	
Mask	Wolsey's House	Hall, 594–5		**1518**
Mask	Court	Lost		
Allegorical Show	Court	Hall, 595		
Miracle	Aberdeen	Lost		
Comic Interlude	Unknown	1533* F	1937[30] (DA)	**1519**
Disguising	Court	Hall, 597		
Mask	Court	Lost		
Comic Interlude	Unknown	[1541–47] F	1937[30] (DA)	**1520**
Comic Interlude	Unknown	1533* F	1937[30] (A)	
Comedy	Closet	[1516–33]*		
Disguising and Tilt	Court at Guisnes	Hall, 610–20		
Moral Interlude	Unknown	[c. 1550?]* F	1907[19] (G)	
Disguising and Tilt	Court	Hall, 600–1		
Interlude	Chapel at Court	Lost		
Moral Interlude	Unknown	[1530–35] F	1906[29] (DB) & 1922 (trans.)[31]	
Disguising	Court	Hall, 628		**1521**
Political Moral	Boys at Court	Cf. *State Papers Spanish*; also Hall, 641		**1522**
Royal Entertainment	London	MS (descrip.) & Hall, 637–40	1918 (excerpts)[32] & 1936[32a]	
Disguising and Tilt	Wolsey's House	Hall, 631		

DATE	AUTHOR	TITLE	LIMITS
1523			
1524	Anon.	*The Entertainment of the Scottish Ambassadors*	28 Dec.
1525	Artour, Thomas	*Microcosmus*	1520–1532
	Artour, Thomas	*Mundus Plumbeus*	1520–1532
	Bourchier, John	*Ite in Vineam, or The Parable of the Vineyard*	1525
	Anon.	*The Golden Fleece*	2 Feb.
1526	Roo (or Rho), John	*Lord Governance and Lady Public Weal*	Xmas (acted)
1527	Rastell, John	*Love and Riches (The Father of Heaven)*	5 May
	Rastell, John (?)	*Calisto and Melebea (Celestina. The Beauty and Good Properties of Women)* (Adapt., through Italian intermediary, of part of the *Celestina* of de Rojas.)	*c.* 1527–1530
	Rastell, J. (?) (Heywood, J., also suggested)	*I & II Gentleness and Nobility*	*c.* 1527–1530
	Ritwise, John	*Dido*	1522–1532
	Ritwise, John (?)	*Heretic Luther (The Deliverance of the Pope)* (In Latin and French.)	10 Nov.
	Anon.	*Godly Queen Hester*	1525–1529
	Anon.	*The Mask for the French Ambassadors*	10 Nov.
	Anon.	*A Mask of Venus, Cupid, Six Damsels, and Six Old Men*	3 Jan.
	Anon.	*The Visit of Henry VIII to Wolsey*	5 May
1528	Heywood, John	*The Play of the Weather*	1525–1533
	Anon.	*Adam and Eve* (by Tailors), *Bacchus* (by Vintners), *Ceres* (by Bakers), *Crispin and Crispinianus* (by Shoemakers), *The Deaths of the Apostles* (by Priors), *Joseph and Mary* (by Carpenters), *The Passion of the Saviour* (by Priors), *Vulcan* (by Smiths)	1528 (ment.)
	Anon.	*Religion, Peace, and Justice*	7 Jan.
1529			
1530	Anon.	*Pater, Filius, et Uxor, or The Prodigal Son* (Adapt. Textor's *Juvenis, Pater, Uxor.*)	*c.* 1530–1534 (?)
1531			
1532	Anon.	*The Triumph at Calais and Boulogne*	11–29 Oct.

TYPE	AUSPICES	EARLIEST TEXTS	LAST ED.	DATE
				1523
Mask and Tilt	Court	Hall, 688–90		**1524**
Latin Tragedy or Comedy	St John's Col., Cambridge	Lost		**1525**
Latin Tragedy or Comedy	St John's Col., Cambridge	Lost		
Interlude	At Calais	Lost		
Pageant or Interlude (?)	Cappers of Canterbury	Lost		
Political Moral	Gray's Inn	Lost		**1526**
Pageant and Dialogue	Chapel at Court	Lost		**1527**
Romantic Interlude	Rastell's stage (?)	[c. 1527–30]* F	1908 G (D)	
Dialogue	Rastell's stage (?)	[c. 1527–30]* F	1949 (1950) G	
Latin School Play	Paul's at Wolsey's	Lost		
Anti-Protestant Interlude	Paul's at Court	Lost		
Biblical Interlude	Unknown	1561*	1906[33] (B)	
Mask	Court at Greenwich	Hall, 735		
Mask (Latin Speeches)	At Wolsey's	Cf. *State Papers Venetian*		
Mumming	At Wolsey's	Hall, 724		
Comic Interlude	Unknown	1533 F	1905[34] (A)	**1528**
Popular Plays on classical and religious subjects	Guilds of Dublin	Lost		
Latin Political Interlude	At Wolsey's (by Paul's ?)	Cf. *State Papers Venetian*		
				1529
Interlude	Unknown	[1530–34 ?]* (frag.)	1907 G†	**1530**
				1531
Pageantry and Mask	Court abroad	[1532] (descrip.) & Hall, 793–4	1903[35]	**1532**

DATE	AUTHOR	TITLE	LIMITS
1533	Heywood, John	*A Play of Love* (Perf. during Xmas 1528–1529, conjectured.)	1533–1534 (pub.)
	Heywood, John	*Witty and Witless* (*Wit and Folly*)	c. 1520–c. 1533
	Udall, N., with Leland, J.	*The Coronation Triumph of Anne Boleyn*	31 May
	Anon.	*Against the Cardinals*	1533
	Anon. (Skelton, J. ?)	*Old Christmas, or Good Order* (Poss. same as *Good Order*, 1515.)	1533 (pub.)
	Anon.	*Old Custom*	c. 1520–1550
1534	Udall, Nicholas (?)	*Placidas, alias Sir Eustace*	1534
1535	Anon.	*Temperance and Humility* (*Disobedience, Temperance, and Humility*)	c. 1521–1535
	Anon.	*The Lord Mayor's Show* (Installation ceremonies were revived in or just before this year, after suppression since 1481. Shows will be listed below when descriptions are extant.)	29 Oct.
1536	Bale, John	*The Life of John the Baptist*, in 14 books (*Vitam D. Ioannis Baptistae*); *Christ and the Doctors* (*De Christo Duodenni*); *I & II The Baptism and Temptation* (*De Baptismo et Tentatione*); *The Raising of Lazarus* (*De Lazaro Resuscitato*); *The Council of Bishops* (*De Consilio Pontificum*); *Simon the Leper* (*De Simone Leproso*); *The Lord's Supper and Washing the Feet* (*De Coena Domini et Pedum Lotione*); *I & II The Passion of Christ* (*De Passione Christi*); *I & II The Burial and Resurrection* (*De Sepultura et Resurrectione*)	c. 1530–1539
	Bale, John	*On the Seven Sins* (*De Septem Peccatis*) (Distinct from following ?)	c. 1530–1539
	Bale, John	*Pater Noster Play* (?) (*Super Oratione Dominica*)	c. 1530–1539
1537	Bale, John	*Against Adulterators of the Word of God* (*Contra Adulterantes Dei Verbum*)	c. 1536–1539
	Bale, John	*I & II Against Momi and Zoili* (*Erga Momos et Zoilos. Against Scoffers and Backbiters*)	c. 1536–1539
	Bale, John	*I & II On Sects among the Papists* (*De Sectis Papisticis*)	c. 1538–1548
	Bale, John	*I & II Treacheries of the Papists* (*Proditiones Papistarum*)	c. 1538–1548
	Bale, John	*I & II Upon Both Marriages of the King* (*Super Utroque Regis Coniugio*)	1533–1539

TYPE	AUSPICES	EARLIEST TEXTS	LAST ED.	DATE
Disputation	Inns of Court (?)	1534 (i.e. 1533/34) F	1944[36]	**1533**
Dialogue	Closet (?)	MS (frag.) F	1937[30]	
Pageantry	London	[1533] (descrip.) & MS (frag.)	1903[35]	
Anti-Catholic Interlude	Court	Lost		
Moral Interlude	Unknown	1533 (frag.) F	1956 G	
Interlude	Unknown	Lost		
Neo-Miracle	Braintree, Essex	Lost		**1534**
Moral Interlude	Unknown	[1521–35]* (frag.)	1909 G†	**1535**
Civic Pageant	London	Lost		
Mystery Cycle adapted to anti-Catholic purposes (?)	Thorndon, Suffolk (?); later (1538–1540) St Stephen's, Canterbury (?). The plays were written, says Bale, for the Earl of Oxford.	Lost		**1536**
Anti-Catholic Moral (?)	Same as above (?)	Lost		
Anti-Catholic Moral (?)	Same as above (?)	Lost		
Anti-Catholic Interlude	Unknown	Lost		**1537**
Anti-Catholic Interlude	Unknown	Lost		
Anti-Catholic Interlude	Unknown	Lost		
Anti-Catholic Interlude	Unknown	Lost		
Anti-Catholic Interlude	Thorndon, Suffolk (?); later (1538–1540) St Stephen's, Canterbury (?). The play was written, says Bale, for the Earl of Oxford.	Lost		

DATE	AUTHOR	TITLE	LIMITS
	Udall, Nicholas (?)	*Thersites* (Adapt. Textor.)	12–24 Oct.
	Wylley, Thomas	*Against the Pope's Councillors*	1535–*c.* 1537
	Wylley, Thomas	*A Reverent Receiving of the Sacrament*	1537
	Wylley, Thomas	*A Rude Commonalty*	1537
	Wylley, Thomas	*The Woman on the Rock*	1537
	Anon.	*Albion Knight*	*c.* 1537–1566
1538	Bale, John	*God's Promises* (*The Chief Promises of God unto Man. De Magnis Dei Promissionibus*)	1538
	Bale, John	*The Image of Love* (*Amoris Imago*)	*c.* 1538–1548
	Bale, John	*John Baptist's Preaching in the Wilderness* (*De Predicatione Ioannis*)	1538
	Bale, John	*I & II King John* (*De Ioanne Anglorum Rege*)	A-version: 1538; B-revision: 1558–1562 (?)
	Bale, John	*The Knaveries of Thomas Becket* (*De Imposturis Thomae Becketi*)	*c.* 1536–1539
	Bale, John	*I, II, III, & IV Pammachii* (Adapt. Kirchmayer's *Pammachius.*)	1538–1548
	Bale, John	*The Temptation of Our Lord and Saviour Jesus Christ by Satan* (*De Christi Tentatione*)	1538
	Bale, John	*Three Laws of Nature, Moses, and Christ, Corrupted by the Sodomites, Pharisees, and Papists* (*Corruptiones Legum Divinarum*)	1538; revised *c.* 1547; again in 1562
	Lindsay, David	*The Welcome for Marie de Lorraine*	10 June; July
1539	Heywood, John	*King Arthur's Knights*	1539
	Hoker, John	*Piscator sive Fraus Illusa*	1535–1543
	Redford, John	*Courage, Kindness, Cleanness*	1531–1547
	Redford, John	*D, G, and T[om]*	1531–1547
	Redford, John	*Wit and Science*	1531–1547
	Spencer, ——	*The Sacrament of the Altar*	*c.* 1539
	Udall, Nicholas	*De Papatu* (Poss. identical with following.)	*c.* 1537–1548
	Udall, Nicholas	*Ezekias* (Poss. same as above.)	1537–1556
1540	Grimald, Nicholas	*Christus Nascens*	*c.* 1540 (?)
	Grimald, Nicholas	*Christus Redivivus*	*c.* 1540
	Lindsay, David	*A Satire of the Three Estates* (The following titles have sometimes been assigned to separate parts: *The Poor Man and the Pardoner; The Three Vices Overcome Truth and Chastity; The Sermon of Folly; The Punishment of the Vices; Humanity and Sensuality; Auld Man and His Wife; Flattery, Deceit, and Falsehood Mislead King Humanity.*)	6 Jan. (Version I); 7 June 1552 (Version II); 12 Aug. 1554 (Version III)

TYPE	AUSPICES	EARLIEST TEXTS	LAST ED.	DATE
Interlude	Eton Boys (?)	[1561–63]* F	1905[29] (D)	
Anti-Catholic Moral	Yoxford (?)	Lost		
Lenten Play	Before Cromwell	Lost		
Moral Interlude (?)	Yoxford (?)	Lost		
Unknown	Closet	Lost		
Moral Interlude	Unknown	[c. 1565]* (frag.)	1909 G	
Anti-Catholic Mystery	St Stephen's, Canterbury	[c. 1547–48] F	1907[37] (D)	**1538**
Didactic Interlude (?)	Unknown	Lost		
Anti-Catholic Mystery	St Stephen's, Canterbury	[c. 1547–48]* (now lost)	1907[37]	
Anti-Catholic History	St Stephen's, Canterbury	MS (1560–63) F	1931 G	
Anti-Catholic History	Unknown	Lost		
Anti-Catholic Neo-moral	Closet (?)	Lost		
Anti-Catholic Mystery	St Stephen's, Canterbury	[c. 1547–48]* F	1907[37]	
Anti-Catholic Moral	St Stephen's, Canterbury	[c. 1547–48] F	1907[37]	
Pageants	St Andrews, and Edinburgh	Lost		
Mask	Court	Lost		**1539**
Latin Play	Magdalen Col., Oxford	Lost		
Moral Interlude	Paul's (?)	MS (frag.)	1951 G†	
Interlude	Paul's (?)	MS (frag.)	1951 G†	
Moral Interlude	Paul's (?)	MS (frag.) F	1951 G (A)	
Anti-Catholic Moral	Unknown	Lost		
From a Latin Tragedy	Trans. for Katherine Parr	Lost		
Biblical Interlude	Eton Boys (?) (King's C., Camb., in 1564)	Lost		
Latin Neo-miracle	Brasenose Col., Oxford (?)	Lost		**1540**
Latin Neo-miracle	Brasenose Col., Oxford	1543*	1925 (text & trans.)[38]	
Political-Religious Moral	Before James V at Linlithgow (Version I); Castle Hill, Cupar, Fifeshire (Version II); Calton Hill, Edinburgh (Version III)	MS (Version I, descrip. only), MS (Version II, extracts), 1602** (Version III)	1931 (all versions)[39] & 1954 (Version III)[40]	

DATE	AUTHOR	TITLE	LIMITS
	Palsgrave, John	*Acolastus* (Trans. de Volder.)	1540
	Watson, Thomas	*Absalom* (Prob. same as *Absalom* of MS Stowe 957.)	*c.* 1535–1544
	Wedderburn, James	*The Beheading of John the Baptist*	1539–1540
	Wedderburn, James	*Dionysius the Tyrant*	1539–1540
1541	Buchanan, George	*Baptistes sive Calumnia* (Prob. same as *John Baptist* acted at Trinity Col., Camb., in 1562–1563.)	1540–1545
	Anon.	*The Nine Worthies*	1541
1542	Buchanan, George	*Jephthes sive Votum*	1540–1545
	Anon.	*The Four Cardinal Virtues* (Related to *Temperance and Humility*, 1530.)	1537–1547
1543	Ascham, Roger	*Philoctetes* (Trans. Sophocles.)	1543
	Buchanan, George	*Alcestis* (Trans. Euripides.)	1543 (?)
	Buchanan, George	*Medea* (Trans. Euripides.)	1543
	Anon.	*A Mask of Almains*	1543
	Anon.	*A Mask of Mariners*	1543
	Anon.	*A Mask of Women*	1 Jan.
1544	Christopherson, John	*Jephthes*	*c.* 1539–*c.* 1544
1545	Anon.	*A Mask of Egyptian Women*	1545–1546
	Anon. (Bale, J. ?)	*The Resurrection of Our Lord* (*Christ's Resurrection*) (Poss. a part of Bale's *Burial and Resurrection*, 1536.)	*c.* 1530–*c.* 1560
1546	Radcliffe, Ralph	*De Ioannis Huss Bohemie Noti Condemnatione*; *De Iobi Iusti Afflictionibus*; *De Iona a Deo ad Niniuitas Ablegati Defectione*; *De Iudith Bethuliensis Incredibili Fortitudine*; *De Lazaro a Diuitis aedibus Abacto*; *De Sodomo et Gomorre Incendio*; *De Susanne per Iudices Iniquos ob Lese Pudicitie Notam Diuini Liberatione*	1546(?)–1556 (Bale gives 1538 for Radcliffe's plays, but Radcliffe went to Hitchin in 1546)
	Radcliffe, Ralph	*The Melibeus of Chaucer* (*De Melibaeo Chauceriano*)	1546(?)–1556
	Radcliffe, Ralph	*The Most Firm Friendship of Titus and Gisippus* (*De Titi et Gisippi Firmissima Amicitia*)	1546(?)–1556
	Radcliffe, Ralph	*The Rare Patience of Chaucer's Griselda* (*De Griseldis Chauceriane Rara Patientia*)	1546(?)–1556
	Anon.	*The Market of Mischief*	1546–1547

TYPE	AUSPICES	EARLIEST TEXTS	LAST ED.	DATE
Neo-moral Latin Biblical Play	Closet St John's Col., Cambridge	1540* MS (?)	1937 E†	
Anti-Catholic Tragedy	Playfield, Dundee	Lost		
Anti-Catholic Comedy	Playfield, Dundee	Lost		
Latin Political Allegory	Guyenne Col., Bordeaux	1577	1907 (trans.)[41]	**1541**
Pageant (?)	Dublin	Lost		
Latin Biblical Play	Guyenne Col., Bordeaux	1554	1906 (trans.)[42]	**1542**
Moral Interlude	Unknown	[1541–47]* (frag.)	1956 G†	
Latin Tragedy	Closet (?)	Lost		**1543**
Latin Tragedy	Guyenne Col., Bordeaux	1556		
Latin Tragedy	Guyenne Col., Bordeaux	1544		
Mask	Court	Lost		
Mask	Court	Lost		
Mask	Court	Lost		
{ Greek Biblical Play	Trinity Col., Cambridge (?)	MSS	1928† (text	**1544**
{ Latin version of same	Trinity Col., Cambridge (?)	MS	& trans.)[43]	
Mask	Court	Lost		**1545**
Protestant Mystery	Unknown	MS (frag.)	1912 G†	
Tragedies (except for *De Lazaro*, a Comedy). Prob. in Latin, and poss. anti-Catholic.	Radcliffe's School at Hitchin	Lost		**1546**
Comedy (English ?)	Radcliffe's School at Hitchin (?)	Lost		
Comedy (English ?)	Radcliffe's School at Hitchin (?)	Lost		
Comedy (English ?)	Radcliffe's School at Hitchin (?)	Lost		
Moral Interlude (?)	Queen's Men at Norwich	Lost		

DATE	AUTHOR	TITLE	LIMITS
1547	Grimald, Nicholas	*Archipropheta* (Adapt. Schoepper's *Decollatus.*)	1546–1547
	Grimald, Nicholas	*Athanasius sive Infamia*	c. 1540–c. 1547
	Grimald, Nicholas	*Fama*	c. 1540–c. 1547
	Grimald, Nicholas	*Protomartyr*	c. 1540–c. 1547
	Grimald, Nicholas	*Troilus, from Chaucer (Troilus ex Chaucero)*	c. 1540–c. 1547
	Grimald, Nicholas	'De Puerorum in Musicis Institutione'	c. 1540–c. 1547
	Anon.	*The Coronation of King Edward VI*	19 Feb.
	Anon.	*Impatient Poverty*	c. 1547–1558
	Anon.	*A Mask of Prester John*	Xmas, 1547–1548
	Anon.	*The Story of Orpheus*	9 Mar.
1548	Edward VI	*De Meretrice Babylonica (The Whore of Babylon)*	1548
	Anon.	*A Mask of Men*	1548
	Anon.	*A Mask of Young Moors*	12 Feb.
	Anon.	*The Tower of Babylon*	Xmas, 1547–1548
	Anon.	*Two Masks of Women*	1548
1549	Anon.	*Jube the Sane* (i.e. *Job the Saint*?)	1547–1553
	Anon.	*A Mask of Almains*	Xmas, 1548–1549
1550	Hoby, Thomas	*Free-Will* (Trans. Bassano's *Tragedia del libero arbitrio.*)	1550
	Key, or Caius, Thomas	*Tragedies of Euripides* (Trans. Euripides.)	c. 1540–1572
	Wever, R.	*Lusty Juventus*	1547–1553
	Anon.	*Love Feigned and Unfeigned*	c. 1540–c. 1560
	Anon.	*Nice Wanton* (Adapt. Macropedius's *Rebelles.*)	1547–1553
	Anon.	*Somebody, Avarice, and Minister (Somebody and Others, or The Spoiling of Lady Verity)*	1547–1550(?)
1551	Anon.	*A Mask of Amazons, Women of War*	Xmas, 1551–1552
	Anon.	*A Mask of Argus*	Xmas, 1551–1552
	Anon.	*A Mask of Moors and Amazons*	Xmas, 1551–1552
1552	Chaloner, Thomas (?)	*Riches and Youth*	6 Jan.
	Udall, Nicholas	*Ralph Roister Doister (Roister Doister)*	1545–1552
	Anon.	*Aesop's Crow*	Xmas, 1552–1553

TYPE	AUSPICES	EARLIEST TEXTS	LAST ED.	DATE
Latin Biblical Tragedy	Christ Church or Exeter, Oxford	1548* & MS	1925† (text & trans.)[38]	**1547**
Latin Play	Brasenose, Merton, or Christ Church, Oxford	Lost		
Latin Play	Same as above	Lost		
Tragedy (Latin ?)	Same as above	Lost		
Comedy	Same as above	Lost		
Comedy	Unknown	Lost		
Pageantry and Masks	London and Westminster	MS (descrip.)	1774†[20]	
Moral Interlude	Offered for acting	1560 F	1911 B	
Mask	Court	Lost		
Play or Mask	Court	Lost		
Anti-Catholic Interlude	Unknown	Lost		**1548**
Mask	Court	Lost		
Mask	Court	Lost		
Biblical Interlude	Court	Lost		
Masks	Court	Lost		
Biblical Interlude (?)	Court (?)	Lost		**1549**
Mask	Court	Lost		
Anti-Catholic Moral	Closet	Lost		**1550**
Latin Tragedies	Closet (?)	Lost		
Anti-Catholic Moral Interlude	Offered for acting	[c. 1565 ?] F	1905[45] (D)	
Interlude	Unknown	MS (frag.)	1907 G	
Anti-Catholic Moral Interlude	Unknown	1560 F	1905[45] (D)	
Anti-Catholic Moral Interlude	Unknown	[c. 1547–50 ?]* (frag.) F	1931 G	
Mask	Court	Lost		**1551**
Mask	Court	Lost		
Mask	Court	Lost		
Dialogue	Court	Lost		**1552**
Comedy	Unknown	[c. 1567]	1939 B (DGA)	
Anti-Catholic Interlude	Court Interluders	Lost		

D

DATE	AUTHOR	TITLE	LIMITS
	Anon.	*A Drunken Mask*	2 Jan.
	Anon.	*A Mask of Babions* (i.e. *Baboons*)	Xmas, 1552–1553
	Anon.	*A Mask of Covetous Men*	Xmas, 1552–1553
	Anon.	*A Mask of Matrons*	Xmas, 1552–1553
	Anon.	*A Mask of Men*	6 Jan.
	Anon.	*A Mask of Polanders*	Xmas, 1552–1553
	Anon.	*A Mask of Soldiers*	Xmas, 1552–1553
	Anon.	*A Mask of Women of Diana*	Xmas, 1552–1553
	Anon.	*Self Love*	1551–1553
1553	Baldwin, William (?) ('set out' by)	*The State of Ireland*	Easter & May Day
	Howard, G. (?) or Ferrers, G. (?)	*Cupid, Venus, and Mars*	6 Jan.
	Robinson, Nicholas	*Strylius*	1553
	Stevenson, W. (?) (revised by Bridges, J. ?)	*Gammer Gurton's Needle* (*Diccon of Bedlam, etc.*)	*c.* 1552–1563
	Anon.	*Anglia Deformata et Anglia Restituta*	Xmas, 1553–1554
	Anon.	*Genus Humanum*	Xmas, 1553–1554
	Anon.	*A Mask of Bagpipes*	Easter & May Day
	Anon.	*A Mask of Cats*	Easter & May Day
	Anon.	*A Mask of Greek Worthies*	Easter & May Day
	Anon.	*A Mask of Medioxes*	Easter & May Day
	Anon.	*A Mask of Tumblers*	Easter & May Day
	Anon. (Udall, N. ?)	*Respublica*	Xmas
1554	Lauder, William	*The Entertainment for Queen Mary*	Dec.
	Udall, N. (?) or Hunnis, W. (?)	*Jacob and Esau*	*c.* 1550–1557
	Anon.	*A Mask of Arcules* (i.e. *Hercules*), *with Mariners*	St Andrew's Tide
	Anon.	*A Mask of Mariners* (Same as above ?)	Hallowtide
	Anon.	*A Mask of Venetian Senators*	Xmas, 1554–1555

TYPE	AUSPICES	EARLIEST TEXTS	LAST ED.	DATE
Mask	Court	Lost		
Mask	Court	Lost		
Mask	Court	Lost		
Mask	Court	Lost		
Mask	Court	Lost		
Mask	Court	Lost		
Mask	Court	Lost		
Mask	Court	Lost		
Moral Interlude (?)	Court Interluders	Lost		
Interlude	Court	Lost		**1553**
Comedy (?)	Court	Lost		
Latin Comedy	Queens' Col., Cambridge	Lost		
Comedy	Christ's Col., Cambridge	1575 F	1920[46] (DA)	
Show	Trinity Col., Cambridge	Lost		
Moral Interlude	Chapel at Court	Lost		
Mask	Court	Lost		
Mask	Court	Lost		
Mask	Court	Lost		
Mask	Court	Lost		
Mask	Court	Lost		
Anti-Protestant Moral Interlude	Boys, at Xmas, London	MS F	1952 E	
'Farce and Play'	Edinburgh	Lost		**1554**
Biblical Interlude	Unknown (boys)	1568* F	1956 G (D)	
Mask	Court	Lost		
Mask	Court	Lost		
Mask	Court	Lost		

DATE	AUTHOR	TITLE	LIMITS
	Anon.	*A Mask of Venuses with Cupids*	Xmas, 1554–1555
	Anon.	*Wealth and Health*	1554–*c.* 1555
1555	Hutton, Matthew (?)	*De Crumena Perdita (Crumenaria)*	1555
	Worseley, Ralph	*Synedrii sive Concessus Animalium* (and *Synedrium*, an incomplete prose version of *Synedrii*.)	1554–1555
	Anon.	*Jack Juggler* (Adapt. Plautus's *Amphitruo*.)	*c.* 1553–*c.* 1558
	Anon.	*A Mask of Goddesses, Huntresses, with Turkish Women*	24–26 Feb.
	Anon.	*A Mask of Turks Magistrates with Turks Archers*	24–26 Feb.
1556	Baldwin, William	*The Way to Life* (*A Discourse of the World*)	1556–1557
	Foxe, John	*Christus Triumphans*	1556
	Anon.	*The Hatfield Mask for the Princess Elizabeth* (See following.)	1554 or 1556
	Anon.	*Holophernes* (Authenticity of these Hatfield performances is questioned.)	1554 or 1556
1557	Anon.	*A Great Mask of Almains, Pilgrims, and Irishmen*	25 Apr.
	Anon.	*The Sackful of News*	Aug. (suppressed)
	Anon.	*The Six Worthies* (See *The Nine Worthies*, 1541.)	1557
1558	Browne, Thomas	*Thebais* (Trans. Seneca.)	*c.* 1550–*c.* 1559
	Lauder, W.; Adamson, W.	*The Marriage of Queen Mary*	July
	Lumley, Jane	*Iphigenia in Aulis* (Trans. Euripides.)	1549–1577
	Wager, Lewis	*The Life and Repentance of Mary Magdalene*	*c.* 1550–1566
1559	Heywood, Jasper	*Troas* (Trans. Seneca.)	1559
	Phillip, John	*Patient and Meek Grissil*	1558–1561
	Wager, W.	*The Longer Thou Livest the More Fool Thou Art*	*c.* 1559–1568
	Anon.	*The Coronation Triumph of Queen Elizabeth*	14 Jan.
	Anon.	*A Mask of Almains and Palmers*	1559 (?)
	Anon.	*A Mask of Astronomers*	24 May
	Anon.	*A Mask of Conquerors*	1558–1559
	Anon.	*A Mask of Fishermen, Fishwives, and Market-wives*	7 Feb.
	Anon.	*A Mask of Hungarians*	1558–1559
	Anon.	*A Mask of Mariners*	1558–1559
	Anon.	*A Mask of Moors*	1558–1559

TYPE	AUSPICES	EARLIEST TEXTS	LAST ED.	DATE
Mask	Court	Lost		
Moral Interlude	Court Interluders (?)	[c. 1565?]* F	1922[47] (G)	
Latin Play	Trinity Col., Cambridge	Lost		**1555**
Latin 'Beast Drama'	Closet (?)	MS		
Comedy	Offered for acting	[c. 1562] F	1936 G (D)	
Mask	Court	Lost		
Mask	Court	Lost		
Moral Comedy	Inns of Court, or Court	Lost		**1556**
Latin Religious Play	Trinity Col., Camb., in 1562–1563	1556 & MS		
Mask	Hatfield	Lost		
Interlude	Hatfield	Lost		
Mask	Court	Lost		**1557**
Popular Comedy	Boar's Head Inn	Lost		
Popular Show	Dublin	Lost		
Tragedy	King's Col., Cambridge (?)	Lost		**1558**
'Triumph and Play'	Edinburgh	Lost		
Tragedy	Closet (?)	MS	1910[48] (G)	
Moral–Biblical Interlude	Offered for acting	1566–67* F	1904[49]	
Tragedy	Closet	1559	1927[50] (B)	**1559**
Comedy	Offered for acting	[1566?]*	1909 G (T)	
Protestant Moral	Offered for acting	[c. 1569]* F	1900†[51]	
Pageant	London	1558[59] (descrip.) F	1903[35]	
Mask and Tilt	Court	Lost		
Mask	Court	Lost		
Mask	Court	Lost		
Mask	Court	Lost		
Mask	Court	Lost		
Mask	Court	Lost		
Mask	Court	Lost		

DATE	AUTHOR	TITLE	LIMITS
	Anon.	*A Mask of Nusquams, with Turkish Commoners*	1559–1560
	Anon.	*A Mask of Shipmen and Country Maids*	Aug.
	Anon.	*A Mask of Swart Rutters*	5 Feb.
	Anon.	*A Mask of Turks*	1558–1559
	Anon.	*Papists*	6 Jan.
1560	Alley, William (?)	*Aegio*	c. 1560–1565
	Heywood, Jasper	*Thyestes* (Trans. Seneca.)	1560
	Ingelend, Thomas	*The Disobedient Child*	c. 1559–1570
	Wager, W.	*Enough Is as Good as a Feast*	c. 1559–c. 1570
	Anon.	*A Mask of Actaeons*	1559–1560
	Anon.	*A Mask of Barbarians*	1 Jan.
	Anon.	*A Mask of Clowns*	1559–1560
	Anon.	*A Mask of Diana and Six Nymphs Huntresses*	1560
	Anon.	*A Mask of Italian Women*	6 Jan.
	Anon.	*A Mask of Patriarchs*	6 Jan.
	Anon.	*Robin Hood* (*Robin Hood and the Friar. Robin Hood and the Potter*)	1560
	Anon.	*Sapientia Solomonis* (Adapt. Sixt Birck.)	1560
	Anon.	*Tom Tyler and His Wife*	1558–1563
1561	Ashton, Thomas	*The Passion of Christ*	25 May
	Buchanan, George	*Apollo et Musae Exules*	Oct. (?)
	Elizabeth I	*Hercules Oetaeus* (Trans. pseudo-Seneca.)	1561–c. 1570
	Heywood, Jasper	*Hercules Furens* (Trans. Seneca.)	1561
	Preston, Thomas	*Cambises* (Same as *Huff, Suff, and Ruff*, below?)	c. 1558–1569
	Anon.	*Huff, Suff* [sic], *and Ruff* (Same as *Cambises*, above?)	Xmas, 1560–1561
	Anon.	*A Mask of Wise and Foolish Virgins*	25–28 Oct.
	Anon.	*The Pedlar's Prophecy*	1561–c. 1563
	Anon.	*Romeo and Juliet*	c. 1560–1562
	Anon.	*The Welcome for Queen Mary*	2 Sept.
1562	Norton, T.; Sackville, T.	*Gorboduc* (*Ferrex and Porrex*)	28 Jan.
	Anon.	*Devices for Nottingham Castle*	May
	Anon.	*Julius Caesar* (Poss. not a play.)	1562
	Anon.	*The Marriage Entertainment for Lord James Stuart*	8 Feb.
	Anon.	*The Two Sins of King David*	1562 (S.R.)
1563	Croston, W.; Man, —	*Aeneas and Queen Dido*	27 June
	Neville, Alexander	*Oedipus* (Trans. Seneca.)	1563
	Wager, W.	*'Tis Good Sleeping in a Whole Skin*	c. 1560–c. 1565
	Anon.	*Six Shepherds*	11 Jan.

TYPE	AUSPICES	EARLIEST TEXTS	LAST ED.	DATE
Mask	Court	Lost		
Mask	West Horseley	Lost		
Mask	Court	Lost		
Mask	Court	Lost		
Anti-Catholic Farce	Court Interluders (?)	Lost		
Interlude	Unknown	1565* (frag.)		**1560**
Tragedy	Closet	1560	1927[50] (BA)	
Interlude	Offered for acting	[c. 1569?]* F	1905[45] (D)	
Protestant Moral	Offered for acting	[c. 1565–70]* F		
Mask	Court	Lost		
Mask	Court	Lost		
Mask	Court	Lost		
Mask	Court	Lost		
Mask	Court	Lost		
Mask	Court	Lost		
May Game Play	Offered for acting	[c. 1560]	1908 G (A)	
Latin Biblical Play	Trinity Col., Cambridge	Lost		
Domestic Interlude	Chapel (?) Paul's (?)	1661** F	1910 G	
Biblical Play	Shrewsbury	Lost		**1561**
Latin Mask	Scottish Court	1584 (verses)		
Tragedy	Closet	MS (frag.)	1806[52]	
Tragedy	Closet	1561	1927[50] (B)	
Tragedy	Court (?)	[c. 1569] F	1898[53] (DA)	
Comedy (?)	At Court	Lost (?)		
Mask	Court	Lost		
Protestant Moral	Unknown	1595* F	1914 G†	
Tragedy	Unknown	Lost		
Royal Reception	Edinburgh	MSS (descrip.)	1927[54]	
Tragedy	Inner Temple	1565 F	1912[55] (A)	**1562**
Moral Mask	Projected for meeting of Elizabeth and Mary	MS (design)	1897[56]	
Classical History (?)	At Court (?)	Lost		
Mask (?)	Scottish Court	Lost		
Biblical History	Unknown	Lost		
Show	Chester	Lost		**1563**
Tragedy	Closet	1563	1927[50]	
Interlude (?)	Unknown	Lost		
Pastoral Mask (?)	Scottish Court (Marriage of Commendator of St Colm's Inch)	Lost		

DATE	AUTHOR	TITLE	LIMITS
1564	B[ower ?], R[ichard ?]	*Appius and Virginia*	1559–1567
	Buchanan, G., & another	*Cupid, Chastity, and Time*	13–15 Feb.
	Halliwell, Edward	*Dido*	7 Aug.
	Jeffere, John (?)	*The Bugbears* (Adapt. Grazzini's *La Spiritata.*)	1563–*c.* 1565
	Anon.	*Ajax Flagellifer* (Trans. Sophocles.)	9 Aug. (projected)
	Anon.	*Holofernes* (Prob. a traditional play.)	*c.* 1563–1565
	Anon.	*'Mock Mass'*	10 Aug.
1565	Buchanan, George	*Pompae Deorum in Nuptiis Mariae*; *Pompae Equestres*	29 July
	Edwards, Richard	*Damon and Pithias*	1565 (?)
	Wager, [W. ?]	*The Cruel Debtor*	*c.* 1560–1565
	Anon.	*Juno and Diana* (*Diana, Pallas*)	4–6 Mar.
	Anon.	*King Darius*	1565 (pub.)
	Anon.	*A Mask of Hunters and the Nine Muses*	18 Feb.
	Anon.	*A Mask of Satyrs and Tilters*	4–6 Mar.
	Anon.	*Massinissa and Sophonisba*	1565
1566	Ashton, Thomas	*Julian the Apostate*	1556–1566
	Buchanan, George	*Pompae Deorum Rusticorum*	17 Dec.
	Calfhill, James	*Progne* (Adapt. Corraro.)	5 Sept.
	Edwards, Richard	*I & II Palamon and Arcite* (Trans. from Latin ?)	Pt. I: 2 Sept.; Pt. II: 4 Sept.
	Gascoigne, George	*Supposes* (Trans. Ariosto's *I Suppositi.*)	1566
	Gascoigne, G.; Kinwelmershe, F.	*Jocasta* (Trans. Dolce's *Giocasta.*)	1566
	Nuce, Thomas	*Octavia* (Trans. Seneca.)	1566 (S.R.)
	Pound, Thomas	*The Radcliffe Wedding Mask*	1 July
	Pound, Thomas	*The Southampton Wedding Mask*	Feb.
	Studley, John	*Agamemnon* (Trans. Seneca.)	1566
	Studley, John	*Hercules Oetaeus* (Trans. pseudo-Seneca.)	1566 (S.R.)
	Studley, John	*Medea* (Trans. Seneca.)	1566
	Wilmot, R.; Stafford; Hatton; Noel; Al., G.	*Gismond of Salerne* (Revised by Wilmot in 1591 as *Tancred and Gismund.*)	1566 or 1568
	Anon.	*Far Fetched and Dear Bought Is Good for Ladies*	1566 (S.R.)
	Anon.	*Marcus Geminus*	1 Sept.
	Anon.	*Sapientia Solomonis* (Adapt. Sixt Birck.)	17 Jan.
1567	Pickering, John	*The Interlude of Vice* (*Horestes*)	1567 (S.R.)
	Studley, John	*Hippolytus* (Trans. Seneca.)	1567 (S.R.)
	Wager, W. (?)	*The Trial of Treasure*	1567 (pub.)

TYPE	AUSPICES	EARLIEST TEXTS	LAST ED.	DATE
Classical Moral	Westminster Boys (?)	1575* F	1911 G (D)	**1564**
Banquet Show	Scottish Court	MS (Ital. & Lat. verses)	1845[57]	
Latin Tragedy	King's Col., Cambridge	Lost		
Comedy	By 'Boys'	MS	1911[58]	
Latin Tragedy	Cambridge	Lost		
Interlude	Donington, Lincolnshire	Lost		
Anti-Catholic Burlesque	Cambridge students at Hinchinbrook	Lost		
Latin Masks	Scottish Court	1584 (verses)		**1565**
Tragicomedy	Chapel	1571 F	1957 G (DAT)	
Interlude	Unknown	[c. 1566]* (frag.)	1911 G & 1923 G	
Disputation	Gentlemen of Gray's Inn	Lost		
Protestant Moral	Offered for acting	1565 F	1906[59]	
Mask	Court	Lost		
Mask	Court	Lost		
Latin (?) Tragedy	At Court	Lost		
Neo miracle	Shrewsbury	Lost		**1566**
Latin Mask	Scottish Court	1584 (verses)		
Latin Tragedy	Christ Church, Oxford	Lost		
Tragedy	Christ Church, Oxford	Lost		
Comedy	Gray's Inn	1573	1957[60] (A)	
Tragedy	Gray's Inn	1573 & MS	1912[55]	
Tragedy	Closet	[c. 1566]	1927[50]	
Wedding Mask	Before Elizabeth	MS (frag.)		
Wedding Mask	Before Elizabeth	MS (frag.)	1812† (excerpts)[61]	
Tragedy	Closet	1566	1927[50] (B)	
Tragedy	Closet	1581*	1927[50]	
Tragedy	Closet	1566	1927[50] (B)	
Senecan Tragedy	Inner Temple	MSS F & 1591–92* F	1912[55] & 1915 G (D)	
Comedy (?)	Unknown	Lost		
Latin Comedy	Christ Church, Oxford	Lost		
Latin Biblical Play	Westminster Boys	MSS	1938† (text & trans.)[62]	
Moral Interlude	Rich's, or Boys, at Court (?)	1567* F	1962 (1963) G	**1567**
Tragedy	Closet	1581*	1927[50]	
Moral Interlude	Offered for acting	1567* F	1906[59] (D)	

DATE	AUTHOR	TITLE	LIMITS
	Anon.	*As Plain as Can Be*	1567–1568
	Anon.	*The College of Canonical Clerks*	1566–1567 (S.R.)
	Anon.	*Jack and Jill*	1567–1568
	Anon.	*The Painful Pilgrimage*	1567–1568
	Anon.	*Prodigality* (Same as *The Contention between Liberality and Prodigality*, 1601 ?)	1567–1568
	Anon.	*Samson*	1567
	Anon.	*Six Fools*	1567–1568
	Anon.	*Wylie Beguylie*	3 Jan.
1568	Cheke, Henry	*Free-Will* (Trans. Bassano's *Tragedia del libero arbitrio*.)	*c.* 1565–*c.* 1572
	Fulwell, Ulpian	*Like Will to Like*	1562–1568
	Anon. (Hunnis, W. ?)	*The King of Scots*	1567–1568
	Anon.	*The Marriage of Wit and Science* (Same as following ?)	b. 1569 (S.R.)
	Anon.	*Wit and Will* (Identical with above ?)	1567–1568
1569	Garter, Thomas	*The Most Virtuous and Godly Susanna*	1563–1569 (S.R.)
	Anon.	*The Destruction of Thebes* (*The Contention between Eteocles and Polynices*)	15 May (projected)
1570	Rudd, A. (?) Richards, T. (?) Johnson, L. (?)	*Misogonus* ('Laurentius Barjona' on t.p. prob. Laurence Johnson.)	*c.* 1560–1577
	Anon.	*The Castle* (or *Cradle*) *of Security*	1565–1575
	Anon. (Preston, T. ?)	*Clyomon and Clamydes*	*c.* 1570–1583
	Anon.	*Juli and Julian*	*c.* 1570 (?)
1570 ADDENDA	Anon.	The following plays cannot be dated with any approximation to accuracy, but all seem to belong to the period of the popularity of the moral interlude: *Dives and Lazarus, The Dialogue of Dives*, and *The Devil and Dives* are titles mentioned satirically in Greene's *Groatsworth of Wit*, in *Sir Thomas More*, and in *Histriomastix*, all referring perhaps to a popular moral stemming from Radcliffe's *Dives and the Devil*; *Delphrygus and the King of Fairies, The Highway to Heaven, Man's Wit*, and *The Twelve Labours of Hercules* are mentioned in *Groatsworth of Wit*; *Hit Nail o' the Head*, in *Sir Thomas More*; *Craft upon Subtlety's Back*, in S.R., 1609; *Joseph's Afflictions, Manhood and Misrule* (*Manhood and Wisdom*), *Susanna's Tears*, and *Nineveh's Repentance*, in the play-lists of 1656 and 1661.	......

TYPE	AUSPICES	EARLIEST TEXTS	LAST ED.	DATE
Comedy (?)	Rich's, or Boys, at Court	Lost		
Interlude	Unknown	Lost		
Comedy (?)	Rich's, or Boys, at Court	Lost		
Moral Interlude (?)	Rich's, or Boys, at Court	Lost		
Moral Interlude (?)	Rich's, or Boys, at Court	Lost (?)		
Biblical History (?)	At Red Lion Inn	Lost		
Moral Interlude (?)	Rich's, or Boys, at Court	Lost		
Comedy	Merton Col., Oxford	Lost		
Anti-Catholic Moral	Closet	[1573 ?]* & MS		**1568**
Moral Interlude	Offered for acting	1568 F	1906[63] (D)	
Tragedy	Chapel at Court	Lost		
Moral Interlude	At Court (?)	[c. 1569]* F	1960 (1961) G (DA)	
Moral Interlude	At Court	Lost (?)		
Moral Interlude	Offered for acting	1578*	1936 G†	**1569**
Latin(?) Play	Christ Church, Oxford	Lost		
Comedy	Cambridge (?)	MS	1911[58]	**1570**
Moral Interlude	At Gloucester	Lost		
Heroical Romance	Revived by Queen's (?)	1599* F	1913 G	
Comedy	Unknown	MS	1955 G†	
......	Unknown	Lost		**1570** ADDENDA

DATE	AUTHOR	TITLE	LIMITS
1571	Davidson, John	*The Siege of Edinburgh Castle*	July
	Anon.	*Iphigenia*	28 Dec.
	Anon.	*Lady Barbara*	27 Dec.
	Anon.	*New Custom (Nugize, i.e. New Guise)*	1570(?)–1573
1572	Gascoigne, George	*The Mask for Lord Montacute (The Montague Mask)*	1572
	Goldingham, William	*Herodes*	*c.* 1570–*c.* 1575
	Woodes, Nathaniel	*The Conflict of Conscience*	1570–1581
	Anon.	*Ajax and Ulysses*	1 Jan.
	Anon.	*Chariclea (Theagenes and Chariclea)*	1572–1573
	Anon.	*Cloridon and Radiamanta*	17 Feb.
	Anon.	*A Double Mask [of Fishermen and Fruit-wives?]*	1572–1573
	Anon.	*Fortune*	Xmas, 1572–1573
	Anon.	*A Mask of Apollo, the Nine Muses, and Lady Peace*	15 June
	Anon.	*Narcissus*	6 Jan.
	Anon.	*Paris and Vienne*	19 Feb.
1573	Anon.	*Alcmaeon*	27 Dec.
	Anon.	*Mamillia*	28 Dec.
	Anon.	*A Mask of Janus*	1 Jan.
	Anon.	*A Mask of Lance Knights*	27 Dec.
	Anon.	*Predor and Lucia*	26 Dec.
1574	Authinleck, Patrick	*The Forlorn Son*	1 Aug.
	Churchyard, T.; Roberts, J.	*The Queen's Entertainment at Bristow*	13–21 Aug.
	Anon.	*Herpetulus the Blue Knight and Perobia*	3 Jan.
	Anon.	*An Interlude of Minds* (Trans. Niclaes's *Ein Gedicht des Spels van Sinnen.*)	*c.* 1574
	Anon.	*A Mask of Foresters, or Hunters [with Wild Men?]*	1 Jan.
	Anon.	*A Mask of Seven Ladies*	23 Feb.
	Anon.	*A Mask of Seven Warriors*	23 Feb.
	Anon.	*A Mask of Six Pedlars*	1574–1575
	Anon.	*A Mask of Six Sages*	6 Jan.
	Anon.	*A Mask of Six Virtues*	2 Feb. (projected)
	Anon.	*Panecia*	Xmas, 1574–1575
	Anon.	*Perseus and Andromeda*	23 Feb.
	Anon.	*Phedrastus*	Xmas, 1574–1575 (projected)

TYPE	AUSPICES	EARLIEST TEXTS	LAST ED.	DATE
Polemical Show	St Leonard's Col., St Andrews	Lost		**1571**
Tragedy	Paul's at Court	Lost		
Romance (?)	Lane's at Court	Lost		
Protestant Moral	Offered for acting	1573* F	1906[59] (D)	
Wedding Mask	At Lord Montacute's	1573	1907[64]	**1572**
Latin Tragedy	Trinity Col., Camb. (?)	MS		
Protestant Moral	Offered for acting	1581** F	1952 G (D)	
Classical Legend	Windsor Boys at Court	Lost		
Heroical Romance (?)	At Court	Lost		
Heroical Romance (?)	Lane's at Court	Lost		
Mask	Court	Lost		
Moral Interlude (?)	At Court	Lost		
Mask	Court	Lost		
Classical Legend	Chapel at Court	Lost		
Heroical Romance (?)	Westminster at Court	Lost		
Classical Legend (?)	Paul's at Court	Lost		**1573**
Romance (?)	Leicester's at Court	Lost		
Mask	Court	Lost		
Mask	Court	Lost		
Romance (?)	Leicester's at Court	Lost		
Biblical Interlude	St Andrews School	Lost		**1574**
Royal Reception	Bristol	1575	1867[65]	
Heroical Romance	Clinton's at Court	Lost		
Protestant Moral	Closet	[c. 1574]*		
Mask	Court	Lost		
Mask	Court	Lost		
Mask	Court	Lost		
Mask	Court	Lost		
Mask	Court	Lost		
Mask	Court	Lost		
Romance (?)	Leicester's at Court	Lost		
Classical Legend	Merchant Taylors Boys at Court	Lost		
Romance (?)	Sussex's at Court	Lost		

DATE	AUTHOR	TITLE	LIMITS
	Anon.	*Phigon and Lucia*	Xmas, 1574–1575 (projected)
	Anon.	*Philemon and Philecia*	21 Feb.
	Anon.	*Pretestus*	Xmas, 1574–1575
	Anon.	*Quintus Fabius*	6 Jan.
	Anon.	*Timoclea at the Siege of Thebes by Alexander*	2 Feb.
	Anon.	*Truth, Faithfulness, and Mercy*	1 Jan.
1575	Gascoigne, George	*The Glass of Government*	1575
	Gascoigne; with Hunnis; Ferrers; Goldingham, H.; Badger; Paten (?); Mulcaster (?)	*The Princely Pleasures at Kenilworth* (*Zabeta* [projected]; *Silvanus* [27 July]; *The Savage Man and Echo* [1 July], by Gascoigne: *The Lady of the Lake* [18 July], by Hunnis, Ferrers, Goldingham: Speeches, by the others: Hock-Tuesday play also performed [17 July].)	9–27 July
	Gascoigne, G. (?) or Lee, H. (?)	*The Queen's Entertainment at Woodstock* (Consisted of various 'conceiptes', some poss. by Lee; an extant allegorical tale, *Hemetes the Hermit*, later translated into Latin, Italian, and French by Gascoigne; and as sequel to the tale, an extant brief comedy of Occanon and Caudina [acted 20 Sept.], poss. by Gascoigne.)	Sept.
	Golding, Arthur	*Abraham's Sacrifice* (Trans. Beza's *Abraham Sacrifiant*.)	1575
	Wyatt, R.; Heywood, T.	*The Entertainment at Worcester*	Aug.
	Anon.	*King Xerxes*	6 Jan.
	Anon.	*Processus Satanae*	c. 1570–1575
1576	Wapull, George	*The Tide Tarrieth No Man*	1576 (pub.)
	Anon.	*The Collier*	30 Dec.
	Anon.	*Common Conditions*	1576 (S.R.)
	Anon.	*The Painter's Daughter*	26 Dec.
	Anon.	*The Red Knight*	25 July–5 Aug.
	Anon.	*Tooly*	27 Dec.
1577	Campion, Edmund	*King Saul*	1577
	Gosson, Stephen	*Captain Mario* (First acted in 1581–1582.)	1576–1577
	Gosson, Stephen	*Praise at Parting* (First acted in 1581–1582.)	1576–1577
	Lupton, Thomas	*All for Money*	1559–1577
	Anon.	*Cutwell*	1576–1577
	Anon.	*The Cynocephali* (*The History of the Cenofalles*)	2 Feb.
	Anon.	*The History of Error* (Adapt. Plautus's *Menaechmi*?)	1 Jan.

TYPE	AUSPICES	EARLIEST TEXTS	LAST ED.	DATE
Romance	Sussex's at Court	Lost		
Romance	Leicester's at Court	Lost		
Romance (?)	Clinton's at Court	Lost		
Classical History	Windsor Boys at Court	Lost		
Classical History	Merchant Taylors Boys at Court	Lost		
Moral Interlude	Westminster at Court	Lost		
Moral Allegory	Closet	1575** F	1910[64]	**1575**
Royal Entertainment	Host: Leicester	1576* (lost) & 1587*	1910[64]	
Royal Entertainment	Court	1579 (& MSS) & 1585* (frag.)	1910[64] & 1910[66]	
Tragedy	Closet	1577[k]	1907[67]	
Royal Entertainment	Worcester	Lost		
Classical History (?)	Windsor Boys at Court	Lost		
Neo-miracle	Unknown	MS (actor's part)	1931 G†	
Moral	Offered for acting	1576* F	1907[68]	**1576**
Comedy (?)	Leicester's at Court	Lost		
Heroical Moral	Offered for acting	[c. 1576]	1915[69]	
Romance (?)	Warwick's at Court	Lost		
Heroical Romance	Sussex's at Bristol	Lost		
Unknown	Howard's at Court	Lost		
Latin Tragedy	At Prague	Lost		**1577**
Comedy	Leicester's at Theatre (?)	Lost		
Moral	Leicester's at Theatre (?)	Lost		
Satirical Moral	Unknown	1578* F	1904[70]	
Unknown	Tried at Court	Lost		
Pseudo-history (?)	Sussex's at Court	Lost		
Comedy (?)	Paul's at Court	Lost		

DATE	AUTHOR	TITLE	LIMITS
	Anon.	*The Irish Knight*	18 Feb.
	Anon.	*A Mask of Boys*	19 Feb.
	Anon.	*Mingo* (or *Myngs*)	13–19 Oct.
	Anon.	*Mutius Scaevola*	6 Jan.
	Anon.	*The Solitary Knight*	17 Feb.
	Anon.	*Titus and Gisippus*	19 Feb.
1578	Campion, Edmund	*Nectar et Ambrosia* (*St Ambrose and Emperor Theodosius*)	1578
	Churchyard; Garter, B.; Goldingham, H.	*The Entertainment at Norwich*	Aug.
		The Entertainment in Norfolk and Suffolk	Aug.
	Gosson, Stephen	*Catiline's Conspiracies*	1576–1579
	Sidney, Philip	*The Lady of May* (*The Entertainment at Wanstead*)	1578–1582
	Whetstone, George	*I & II Promos and Cassandra*	1578
	Anon.	*The Blacksmith's Daughter*	1576–1579
	Anon.	*The Court of Comfort*	1578 (acted)
	Anon.	*The Cruelty of a Stepmother*	28 Dec.
	Anon.	*The Jew* (*The Practice of Parasites*)	1576–1579
	Anon.	*Ptolome* (Same as *Telemo* of 1583?)	1576–1579
	Anon.	*The Queen of Ethiopia* (*Chariclea* of 1572?)	1578 (acted)
	Anon.	*Quid pro Quo*	1578–1579
	Anon.	*The Three Sisters of Mantua*	26 Dec.
	Anon.	*What Mischief Worketh in the Mind of Man*	6–12 July
1579	Churchyard, Thomas	'The devices of war and a play at Osterley'	1579 (?)
	Fraunce, A. (?) or Hickman, H. (?)	*Hymenaeus*	Mar.
	Merbury, Francis	*A Marriage between Wit and Wisdom* (Date on MS may be interpreted as either 1570 or 1579. Same as *The Marriage of Mind and Measure*, below?)	1579 (or 1570)
	Peele, George	*Iphigenia* (Trans. Euripides.)	1576–1580
	Wilson, Robert	*Short and Sweet* (Poss. descrip. rather than title.)	c. 1578–1579
	Anon.	*Alucius*	27 Dec.
	Anon.	*The Duke of Milan and the Marquis of Mantua*	26 Dec.
	Anon.	*A Greek Maid*	4 Jan.
	Anon.	*The Knight in the Burning Rock*	1 Mar.
	Anon.	*Loyalty and Beauty*	2 Mar.
	Anon.	*The Marriage of Mind and Measure*	1 or 4 Jan.
	Anon.	*A Mask of Amazons*	11 Jan.
	Anon.	*A Mask of Knights*	11 Jan.
	Anon.	*A Morris Mask*	3 Mar.
	Anon.	*Murderous Michael*	3 Mar.
	Anon.	*The Rape of the Second Helen*	6 Jan.
	Anon.	*The Welcome for James VI*	30 Sept.

TYPE	AUSPICES	EARLIEST TEXTS	LAST ED.	DATE
Heroical Romance	Warwick's at Court	Lost		
Mask	Court	Lost		
Unknown	Leicester's at Bristol	Lost		
Classical Legend	Chapel and Windsor at Court	Lost		
Heroical Romance	Howard's at Court	Lost		
Comedy	Paul's at Court	Lost		
Latin Tragedy	At Prague	Lost		**1578**
Entertainment	Norwich	[c. 1578]	1823†[71]	
Entertainment	Norfolk and Suffolk	[c. 1578]*		
Didactic History	Leicester's at Theatre (?)	Lost		
Royal Entertainment	Host: Leicester	1598 & MS	1922[72] (A)	
Comedy	Unacted (?)	1578* F	1958[60]	
Heroical Romance	Leicester's at Theatre (?)	Lost		
Moral (?)	Sheffield's at Bristol	Lost		
Tragedy (?)	Sussex's at Court	Lost		
Satirical Comedy (?)	At the Bull Inn	Lost		
Pseudo-history (?)	At the Bull Inn	Lost		
Heroical Romance	Howard's at Bristol	Lost		
Comedy or Moral (?)	Bath's at Bristol	Lost		
Comedy (?)	Warwick's at Court	Lost		
Moral	Berkeley's at Bristol	Lost		
Royal Entertainment	Host: Thomas Gresham	Lost		**1579**
Latin Comedy	St John's Col., Cambridge	MSS	1908†[73]	
Moral Interlude	Offered for acting	MS F	1908[74]	
Latin (?) Tragedy	Christ Church, Oxford (?)	Lost		
Classical History (?)	Unknown	Lost		
Unknown	Chapel at Court	Lost		
Romance (?)	Sussex's at Court	Lost		
'Pastorell'	Leicester's at Court	Lost		
Heroical Romance (?)	Warwick's at Court	Lost		
Moral (?)	Chapel at Court	Lost		
Moral	Paul's at Court	Lost		
Mask	Court	Lost		
Mask	Court	Lost		
Mask	Prepared for Court	Lost		
Realistic Tragedy (?)	Sussex's at Court	Lost		
Classical Legend (?)	Sussex's at Court	Lost		
Royal Reception	Edinburgh	MS (descrip.)	1927[54]	

E

DATE	AUTHOR	TITLE	LIMITS
1580	Legge, Thomas	*Richardus Tertius*	Mar.
	Puttenham (Rich. ?, or George ?)	*Gynaecocratia*	*c.* 1570–1589
	Puttenham (Rich. ?, or George ?)	*Lusty London*	*c.* 1570–1589
	Puttenham (Rich. ?, or George ?)	*The Wooer*	*c.* 1570–1589
	Sidney, Philip	*A Dialogue between Two Shepherds* (*Pastoral Dialogue*)	1577–1583
	Anon.	*Calistus* (Same as *Calisto and Melebea*, 1527 ? *Celestina*, S.R., 1598 ?)	*c.* 1576–1580
	Anon.	*Delight* (Same as *The Play of Plays and Pastimes*, 1582 ?)	26 Dec.
	Anon.	*The Four Sons of Fabius* (*The Fabii*)	1 Jan.
	Anon.	*Portio and Demorantes*	2 Feb.
	Anon.	*Publii Ovidii Nasonis Meleager*	1570–1590
	Anon.	*Sarpedon*	16 Feb.
	Anon.	*Scipio Africanus*	3 Jan.
	Anon.	*The Soldan and the Duke of* —	14 Feb.
1581	Forsett, Edward	*Pedantius* (Formerly attrib. to A. Wingfield.)	6 Feb. (?)
	Goldwell, Henry (describer)	*The Fortress of Perfect Beauty*	15–16 May
	Newton, Thomas	*Thebais* (Trans. Seneca.)	1581
	Peele, George	*The Arraignment of Paris*	*c.* 1581–1584
	Watson, Thomas	*Antigone* (Trans. Sophocles.)	1581 (pub.)
	Wilson, Robert	*The Three Ladies of London*	*c.* 1581
	Anon.	*Caesar and Pompey* (Poss. same as *Pompey*, below.)	1576–1582
	Anon.	*Cupid and Psyche*	*c.* 1580–1582
	Anon.	*Hugh Aston's Mask*	1581 (?)
	Anon.	*London against the Three Ladies*	1581–1582
	Anon.	*Pompey* (Poss. same as *Caesar and Pompey*, above.)	6 Jan.
1582	Edes, Richard	*Caesar Interfectus* (Epil. extant.)	Feb.
	Fraunce, Abraham	*Victoria* (Adapt. Pasqualigo's *Il Fedele*.)	1580–1583
	Gager, William	*Meleager*	Feb.
	Hutton, Leonard	*Bellum Grammaticale sive Nominum Verborumque Discordia Civilis*	*c.* 1578–1591
	Murgetrode, Michael (?)	*Puer Vapulans*	1581–1582
	Anon.	*Beauty and Housewifery*	27 Dec.
	Anon.	*A Game of the Cards*	26 Dec.
	Anon. (poss. Lodge, T.)	*The Play of Plays and Pastimes* (Same as *Delight*, 1580 ?)	1580–1582
	Anon. (Munday, A. ?)	*The Rare Triumphs of Love and Fortune*	30 Dec.
	Anon.	*Solymannidae*	5 Mar.

TYPE	AUSPICES	EARLIEST TEXTS	LAST ED.	DATE
Latin Tragedy	St John's Col., Cambridge	MSS	1875[75] (T)	**1580**
Comedy	Unknown	Lost		
Interlude	Unknown	Lost		
Interlude	Unknown	Lost		
Dialogue	In show at Wilton	1613	1922[72]	
'Tragical comedie'	At the Theatre (?)	Lost (?)		
Comedy	Leicester's at Court	Lost		
Classical Pseudo-history (?)	Warwick's at Court (and Theatre?)	Lost		
Romance (?)	Sussex's at Court	Lost		
Tragedy	Paul's	Lost		
Classical Legend	Sussex's at Court	Lost		
Classical History	Paul's at Court	Lost		
Heroical Romance	Derby's at Court	Lost		
Latin Satirical Comedy	Trinity Col., Cambridge	1631* & MSS	1905 B†	**1581**
Tilt and Entertainment	Court	[1581]*	1823†[71]	
Tragedy	Closet	1581*	1927[50]	
Classical Legend (Pastoral)	Chapel at Court	1584*	1910 G (AT)	
Latin Tragedy	Cambridge in c. 1583	1581*		
Moral	Unknown	1584 F	1874 D	
Classical History	At the Theatre (?)	Lost		
Classical Legend	Paul's (?)	Lost		
Mask	Unknown	Lost		
Moral	Unknown	Lost		
Classical History	Paul's at Court	Lost		
Latin Tragedy	Christ Church, Oxford	Lost		**1582**
Latin Comedy	St John's Col., Cambridge (?)	MS	1906 B†	
Latin Tragedy	Christ Church, Oxford	1592*		
Latin Allegory	Christ Church, Oxford, in 1592	1635*	1908†[76]	
Latin Comedy	Jesus Col., Cambridge	Lost		
Comedy	Hunsdon's at Court	Lost		
Moral (?)	Chapel at Court	Lost		
Moral (defending plays)	At the Theatre	Lost		
Mythological Moral	Derby's at Court	1589*	1930 G (DT)	
Latin Tragedy	Unknown	MS		

DATE	AUTHOR	TITLE	LIMITS
1583	Gager, William	*Dido*	12 June
	Gager, William	*Rivales* (Prol. extant.)	11 June
	Anon.	*Ariodante and Genevora*	12 Feb.
	Anon.	*A History of Ferrar*	6 Jan.
	Anon.	*A Mask of Ladies and Boys*	5 Jan.
	Anon.	*A Mask of Six Seamen*	1583
	Anon.	*Telomo* (Poss. same as *Ptolome*, 1578.)	10 Feb.
1584	Gager, William	*Oedipus*	*c.* 1577–1592
	Grafton, John	*Midsummer Show*	23 June 1584 & 1585
	Harrison, John	*Philomathes' Dream* (Title assigned.)	11 Feb.
	Legge, Thomas	*The Destruction of Jerusalem*	*c.* 1580–1598
	Lyly, John	*Campaspe* (*Alexander, Campaspe, and Diogenes*)	1580–1584
	Lyly, John	*Sappho and Phao*	1582–1584
	Smythe, John	*The Destruction of Jerusalem*	1584
	Anon. (poss. De Vere, E.)	*Agamemnon and Ulysses*	27 Dec.
	Anon. (Munday, A. ?)	*Fedele and Fortunio* (*Two Italian Gentlemen*) (Trans. Pasqualigo's *Il Fedele*.)	1579–1584
	Anon.	*Phyllida and Corin*	26 Dec.
1585	Lyly, John	*Gallathea* (*Titirus and Galathea*, S.R., 1585 ?)	1584–1588
	Peele, George	*The Pageant before Woolstone Dixie*	29 Oct.
	Anon.	'Antic Play and a Comedy'	23 Feb.
	Anon.	*Felix and Philiomena*	3 Jan.
	Anon. (Tarlton, R. ?)	*Five Plays in One* (Revived as *I The Seven Deadly Sins, c.* 1590 ?)	6 Jan.
	Anon. (Tarlton, R. ?)	*Three Plays in One* (Revived as *II The Seven Deadly Sins*, by Strange's, *c.* 1590, and as *Four Plays in One*, 6 Mar. 1592 ?)	21 Feb. (projected)
1586	Harrison, John	*Philomathes' Second Dream* (Title assigned.)	Feb.
	Nashe, T. (?) & another	*Terminus et Non Terminus*	1580–1588
	Peele, George	*The Hunting of Cupid*	1581–1591
	Wotton, Henry	*Tancredo*	1586–1587
	Anon.	*Duns Furens*	1580–1587
	Anon. (Tarlton ? Rowley, S. ?)	*The Famous Victories of Henry V*	1583–1588
	Anon.	*The Forces of Hercules*	23 Apr.
	Anon.	*Tararantantara turba*	*c.* 1581–1586
	Anon.	*Timon*	*c.* 1581–1590 (?)
1587	Churchyard, Thomas	*Leicester's Service in Flanders*	1587 (?)
	Greene, Robert	*Alphonsus, King of Aragon*	1587–1588

TYPE	AUSPICES	EARLIEST TEXTS	LAST ED.	DATE
Latin Tragedy	Christ Church, Oxford	MS & MS frag.	1858 (frag.)[77]	**1583**
Latin Comedy	Christ Church, Oxford	Lost		
Romance (?)	Merchant Taylors Boys at Court	Lost		
Unknown	Sussex's at Court	Lost		
Mask	Court	Lost		
Mask	Prepared for Court	Lost		
Unknown	Leicester's at Court	Lost		
Latin Tragedy	Christ Church, Oxford (?)	MS	1949†[78]	**1584**
Show	York, Yorkshire	Lost		
Dialogue	St Paul's School	MS	1954 G†	
Tragedy	Unacted (?)	Lost		
Classical Legend (Comedy)	Oxford's Boys	1584	1933 G (A)	
Classical Legend (Comedy)	Oxford's Boys	1584	1902[79]	
Biblical History	Coventry	Lost		
Classical Legend	Oxford's Boys at Court	Lost		
Comedy	At Court	1585*	1909 G (T)	
Pastoral	Queen's at Court	Lost		
Classical Legend (Comedy)	Paul's (revived 1588?)	1592	1902[79]	**1585**
Civic Pageant	London	1585*	1952[80]	
Comedy	Queen's at Court	Lost		
Romance	Queen's at Court	Lost		
Moral	Queen's at Court	Lost		
Moral	Queen's at Court	MS ('plot' of *The Seven Deadly Sins*, c. 1590) F	1931[81]	
Dialogue	St Paul's School	MS	1954 G†	**1586**
Satirical Show	St John's Col., Cambridge	Lost		
Pastoral (Play?)	Unknown	(Lost ed., c. 1591)	1952[80] (G) (frags.)	
Latin (?) Tragedy	Queens' Col., Oxford	Lost		
Latin Satirical Comedy	Peterhouse, Cambridge	Lost		
History	Queen's at Bull Inn	1598 F	1962[60] (AT)	
Athletic Show	For Leicester at Utrecht	Lost		
Satirical Comedy	Clare Hall, Cambridge (?)	Lost		
Tragedy	Cambridge (?)	MS	1875[75]	
Show	Unknown	Lost		**1587**
Heroical Romance	Unknown	1599*	1926 G (M)	

DATE	AUTHOR	TITLE	LIMITS
	Greene, Robert (?)	*Job*	1586–1593 (?)
	Kyd, T. (revised by Jonson, B.)	*The Spanish Tragedy (Hieronimo Is Mad Again)* (Revised *c.* 1597? and 1601–1602.)	1582–1592
	Marlowe, Christopher	*I Tamburlaine the Great*	1587–1588
	Marlowe, C.; Nashe, T.	*Dido, Queen of Carthage* (1591 recently urged.)	*c.* 1587–1593
	Peele, George	*The Love of King David and Fair Bethsabe*	*c.* 1581–1594
	Anon.	*The Mad Priest of the Sun* (Same as *Heliogabalus*, 1594?)	1587–1588
1588	Aske, James/ Deloney, Thomas (describers)	*The Queen's Visit to Tilbury (Elizabetha Triumphans)*	8–9 Aug.
	Hughes, T.; with Bacon; Trotte; Fulbeck; Lancaster; Yelverton; Penroodock; Flower	*The Misfortunes of Arthur (Certain Devices and Shows Presented to Her Majesty)*	28 Feb.
	James I	*An Epithalamion on the Marquis of Huntly's Marriage*	21 July
	Kyffin, Maurice	*Andria* (Trans. Terence.)	1588
	Kyffin, Maurice (?)	*Eunuchus* (Trans. Terence.)	1587–1597
	Lateware, Richard	*Philotas*	*c.* 1588–1596
	Lodge, Thomas	*The Wounds of Civil War, or Marius and Scilla* (i.e. *Sulla*)	1587–1592
	Lyly, John	*Endymion, the Man in the Moon*	2 Feb. (?)
	Marlowe, Christopher	*II Tamburlaine the Great*	1587–1588
	Peele, George	*The Pageant for Martin Calthrop*	29 Oct.
	Peele, George	*The Turkish Mahomet and Hiren the Fair Greek* (Poss. same as *Mahomet*, or *The Love of a Grecian Lady* [*The Grecian Comedy*]; see 1599 add.)	1581–1594
	Porter, Henry	*I The Two Angry Women of Abingdon*	*c.* 1585–1589
	Wilson, Robert	*The Three Lords and Three Ladies of London*	1588–1590
	Anon.	*Sylla Dictator (Catiline)*	16 Jan.
	Anon.	*I Tamar Cham* (See 1596.)	*c.* 1587–1592
	Anon. (Peele, G.?)	*I & II The Troublesome Reign of King John*	*c.* 1587–1591
	Anon.	*The Wars of Cyrus* (Based on play by Farrant, *c.* 1578?)	1587–1594
1589	Greene, Robert	*Friar Bacon and Friar Bungay*	*c.* 1589–1592
	Kempe, William	*Rowland (Rowland and the Sexton)*	*c.* 1589
	Lyly, John	*Midas*	1589–1590
	Lyly, John	*Mother Bombie*	1587–1590
	Marlowe, C. (revised by Heywood, T., *c.* 1632?)	*The Jew of Malta*	*c.* 1589–1590

TYPE	AUSPICES	EARLIEST TEXTS	LAST ED.	DATE
Biblical History	Unknown	Lost		
Tragedy	Strange's (by 1592); (Admiral's in 1597)	[c. 1592]	1959[82] (DGA)	
Heroical Romance	Admiral's	1590	1930[83] (MA)	
Classical Legend (Tragedy)	'Chapel'	1594* F	1930[83]	
Biblical History	Unknown	1599*	1912 G (A)	
Romance (?)	Unknown	Lost		
Royal Entertainment	Tilbury Camp	1588/[1588]	1823[71]/ 1912[84]	**1588**
Tragedy	Gray's Inn at Court	1587[88]* F	1912[55] (D)	
Wedding Mask	Scottish Court	MSS	1958[85]	
Comedy	Closet	1588*		
Comedy	Closet	Lost		
Tragedy	St John's Col., Oxford	Lost		
Classical History	Admiral's (by 1594)	1594*	1910 G (D)	
Classical Legend (Comedy)	Paul's at Court	1591	1902[79] (A)	
Heroical Romance	Admiral's	1590	1930[83] (MA)	
Civic Pageant	London	Lost		
Heroical Romance	Unknown (Admiral's in 1594?)	Lost		
Comedy	Admiral's	1599 F	1912 G (DMA)	
Moral	Queen's (?)	1590* F	1874 D	
Classical History	Gray's Inn	Lost		
Heroical Romance	Strange's or Admiral's	See 1596		
History	Queen's	1591 F	1962[60]	
Classical History	'Chapel'	1594* F	1942[86]	
Comedy	Strange's (by 1592)	1594 F	1952[87] (MGAT)	**1589**
Jig	Unknown	Lost		
Comedy	Paul's	1592	1902[79] (A)	
Comedy	Paul's	1594	1939 (1948) G (A)	
Tragedy	Strange's (by 1592)	1633*	1931[83] (MA)	

DATE	AUTHOR	TITLE	LIMITS
	Munday, Anthony	*John a Kent and John a Cumber*	*c.* 1587–1590
	Peele, George	*The Battle of Alcazar* (Poss. same as *Muly Molloco*, 1599 add.)	1588–1589
	Anon. (poss. Kyd, T.)	*Hamlet*	*c.* 1587–*c.* 1590
	Anon.	*King Ebrauk with All His Sons*	1589
	Anon. (poss. Shakespeare, W.)	*The Taming of a Shrew*	*c.* 1588–1593
1590	Greene, Robert	*The Scottish History of James IV*	*c.* 1590–1591
	Greene, Robert (?)	*George a Greene, the Pinner of Wakefield*	1587–1593
	Greene, R.; Lodge, T.	*A Looking Glass for London and England*	1587–1591
	Herbert, Mary	*Antonius* (*Antony*) (Trans. Garnier's *Marc-Antoine.*)	1590
	Lee, H.; Peele, G.	*Polyhymnia* (Directed by Lee; described by Peele.)	17 Nov.
	Lyly, John	*Love's Metamorphosis*	*c.* 1588–1590
	Nelson, Thomas	*The Pageant for John Allot*	29 Oct.
	Peele, George	*The Old Wives Tale* (Revised for provincial perf. ?)	*c.* 1588–1594
	Salterne, George	*Tomumbeius sive Sultanici in Aegypto Imperii Eversio*	*c.* 1580–1603
	Wilson, Robert	*The Cobbler's Prophecy*	*c.* 1589–1593
	Anon.	*The Dead Man's Fortune*	*c.* 1590–1591
	Anon. (Shakespeare in part ?)	*Edward III* [Shakespeare Apocrypha]	*c.* 1590–1595
	Anon. (Wilson, R. ?)	*Fair Em, the Miller's Daughter* [Shakespeare Apocrypha]	*c.* 1589–1591
	Anon.	*King Leir*	*c.* 1588–1594
	Anon.	*Mucedorus* (*and Amadine*) [Shakespeare Apocrypha]	1588–1598 (revised 1610)
	Anon.	*Rowland's Godson*	*c.* 1590
	Anon. (Kyd, T. ?)	*Soliman and Perseda* (*Zulziman*)	*c.* 1589–1592
	Anon.	*The Welcome for Queen Anne*	19 May
1591	Breton, N. (& Lyly, J. ?)	*The Entertainment at Elvetham*	20–23 Sept.
	Fraunce, Abraham	*Phillis and Amyntas* (*Ivychurch. Amyntas' Pastoral*) (Trans. Tasso.)	1591
	Greene, R. (& Rowley, S. ?)	*Orlando Furioso* (Same as *Brandimer*, 1599 add. ?)	1588–1592
	Peele, George	*Descensus Astraea*	29 Oct.
	Peele, George	*Edward I*	1590–1593
	'W.S.' (Peele ? Greene ?)	*Locrine* (Collier [forgery ?] calls *Elstrid* and assigns to G. Buck, and C. Tilney, who d. 1586.) [Shakespeare Apocrypha]	1591–1595

TYPE	AUSPICES	EARLIEST TEXTS	LAST ED.	DATE
Pseudo-history	Admiral's (?) Strange's (?)	MS F	1923 G (T)	
Foreign History	Admiral's (by 1594)	1594* & MS ('plot') F	1961[80] (G) & 1931 ('plot')[81]	
Tragedy	Chamb.'s & Adm.'s (by 1594)	Lost		
Show	Chester	Lost		
Comedy	Queen's (?) ('Pembroke's' on t.p., 1594)	1594 F	1957[88]	
History	Queen's (?)	1598*	1921 G (MA)	**1590**
Romantic Comedy	Sussex's (by 1593)	1599* F	1911 G (MA)	
Biblical Moral	Queen's (?)	1594 F	1932 G (M)	
Tragedy	Closet	1592	1897†[89]	
Tilt	Court	1590 & MS	1952[80]	
Pastoral	Paul's	1601*	1902[79]	
Civic Pageant	London	1590*	1960[60]	
Romance	Queen's	1595*	1916[90] (GAT)	
Latin Tragedy	Unknown	MS		
Comedy	At Court (?)	1594* F	1914 G (T)	
Romantic Comedy	Admiral's (?)	MS ('plot') F	1931[81]	
History	Unknown	1596 F	1908[91] (A)	
Romantic Comedy	Strange's	[1593 ?] F	1927 G (T)	
Legendary History	Queen's (?)	1605* F	1914[92] (G)	
Romantic Comedy	Unknown (King's in 1610)	1598 F	1908[91] (DA)	
Jig	Unknown	MS	1929[93]	
Tragedy	Unknown	[c. 1592] F	1901[94] (DT)	
Royal Reception	Edinburgh	1590* (descrip.)	1927[54]	
Royal Entertainment	Host: Edward Seymour	1591 (2nd ed. lost)	1902[79]	**1591**
Pastoral	Closet	1591*		
Romantic Comedy	Queen's and Strange's	1594 & MS (frag. of Orlando's part) F	1922 G (M) & 1931[81] (G) (Orlando's part)	
Civic Pageant	London	[1591]*	1952[80]	
History	Queen's (?)	1593	1961[80] (G)	
Pseudo-history	Unknown	1595 F	1908 G	

DATE	AUTHOR	TITLE	LIMITS
	Shakespeare, William	*II Henry VI* (*I The Contention betwixt the Two Famous Houses of York and Lancaster*)	*c.* 1590–1592
	Shakespeare, William	*III Henry VI* (*The True Tragedy of Richard Duke of York*)	*c.* 1590–1592
	Anon. (Kyd, T. ?)	*Arden of Feversham* [Shakespeare Apocrypha]	1585–1592
	Anon. (Lyly, J. ?)	*The Entertainment at Cowdray*	14 Aug.
	Anon.	*A Fig for a Spaniard* (Poss. not a play title.)	*c.* 1578–1592
	Anon.	*Jack Straw*	1590–1593
	Anon.	*Octavia*	1590(?)–1591
	Anon. (Peele ? Lyly ?)	*The Queen's Welcome at Theobalds*	10–20 May
	Anon.	*The True Tragedy of Richard III*	1588–1594
1592	Alabaster, William	*Roxana* (Adapt. Groto's *La Dalida.*)	1590–*c.* 1595
	Edes, R. (& Lee, H. ?)	*The Second Woodstock Entertainment*	20 Sept.
	Gager, William	*Panniculus Hippolyto Assutus*	8 Feb.
	Gager, William	*Ulysses Redux*	6 Feb.
	Greene, Robert (?)	*I Selimus* (Second part unknown.)	1586–1593
	Greene, R. (?); Chettle, H. (prob. reviser rather than collab.)	*John of Bordeaux, or The Second Part of Friar Bacon*	1590–1594
	Herbert, Mary	*Thenot and Piers in Praise of Astraea* (*The Royal Entertainment at Ramsbury*)	1592 (?)
	Marlowe, C. (& Rowley, S. ?)	*Doctor Faustus* (1588–1589 recently urged again.) (Additions by W. Bird and S. Rowley in 1602.)	1588–1592
	Marlowe, Christopher	*Edward II*	1591–1593
	Nashe, Thomas	*Summer's Last Will and Testament*	1592
	Shakespeare, William	*The Comedy of Errors*	*c.* 1590–1594
	Shakespeare, William	*I Henry VI*	3 Mar.
	Warner, William	*Menaechmi* (Trans. Plautus.)	1592(?)–1594
	Anon. (Lyly, J. ?)	*The Entertainment at Bisham*	21 Aug.
	Anon. (Lyly, J. ?)	*The Entertainment at Rycote*	10, 11 Sept.
	Anon. (Lyly, J. ?)	*The Entertainment at Sudeley*	28 Sept.; 1, 2 Oct.
	Anon. (Kempe ? Peele ? Wilson ?)	*A Knack to Know a Knave*	10 June
	Anon.	*I Richard II, or Thomas of Woodstock* (*Woodstock*)	1591–1595
	Anon.	*II Tamar Cham* (See 1596.)	28 Apr.
	Anon.	*The Tanner of Denmark* (i.e. *Tamworth* ?) (Part basis of *Edward IV*, 1599 ?)	23 [26] May
	Anon.	*Titus and Vespasian*	11 Apr.

TYPE	AUSPICES	EARLIEST TEXTS	LAST ED.	DATE
History	Strange's (?) Pembroke's (?)	1594 F		
History	Strange's (?) Pembroke's (?)	1595 F		
Realistic Tragedy	Unknown	1592 F	1950[94a] (GA)	
Royal Entertainment	Host: Anthony Browne	1591 (2nd ed lost)	1902[79]	
Unknown	At the Bull Inn	Lost		
History	Unknown	1593 (coloph. 1594) F	1957 G (D)	
Latin (?) Play	Christ Church, Oxford	Lost		
Royal Entertainment	Host: Wm. Lord Burghley	MSS (frags.) (extant ?)	1902[79]	
History	Queen's	1594*	1929 G	
Latin Tragedy	Trinity Col., Cambridge	1632 & MSS		1592
Royal Entertainment	Court	MSS (frags.)	1902[79]	
Latin Additions to Seneca	Christ Church, Oxford	1592*		
Latin Tragedy	Christ Church, Oxford	1592*	(T)	
Heroical Romance	Queen's	1594**	1908[91] (G)	
Comedy	Strange's (?)	MS	1952[87] (G)	
Pastoral Dialogue	Host: Pembroke	1602	1931–32[95]	
Tragedy	Admiral's (by 1594)	1604 F	1962[96] (MA)	
History	Pembroke's	1594	1933[83] (MGA)	
Comedy	Whitgift's household (?)	1600*	1905[97] (D)	
Comedy	Strange's (?)	1623 F	V (in prog.)	
History	Strange's	1623 F	V (in prog.)	
Comedy	Closet	1595*	1957[60]	
Royal Entertainment	Host: Edward Hoby	1592*	1902[79]	
Royal Entertainment	Host: Henry Lord Norris	1592*	1902[79]	
Royal Entertainment	Host: Giles Brydges	1592*	1902[79]	
Comedy	Strange's	1594* F	1874 D (T)	
History	Unknown (later Chamberlain's ?)	MS (last leaf missing)	1946[98] (G)	
Heroical Romance	Strange's	Lost		
History (?)	Strange's	Lost		
Classical or British History	Strange's	Lost		

DATE	AUTHOR	TITLE	LIMITS
1593	Attowell, George	*Attowell's Jig* (*Francis and Richard*)	*c.* 1590–1595
	Daniel, Samuel	*Cleopatra*	1593 (revised 1607)
	Lyly, John	*The Woman in the Moon*	1590–1595
	Marlowe, Christopher	*The Massacre at Paris*	30 [26] Jan.
	Marlowe, C.; Day, J.(?)	*The Maiden's Holiday* (S.R., 1654, & Warburton.)	1586(?)–1593(?)
	Shakespeare, William	*Richard III*	*c.* 1591–1597
	Shakespeare, William	*The Two Gentlemen of Verona*	*c.* 1590–1598
	Anon.	*The Jealous Comedy* (See *Cosmo*, 1599 add. Also conjectured basis of *The Merry Wives of Windsor*, 1601.)	5 Jan.
	Anon. ('B.J.' on t.p.)	*Guy Earl of Warwick* (See also 1620.)	b. 1642
1594	Bacon (?); Campion; Davison; etc.	*Gesta Grayorum* (Narrative of a series of entertainments, including *The Amity of Graius and Templarius*, followed by speeches of six 'Councellors', prob. written by F. Bacon, 3 Jan. 1595; *Knights of the Helmet*, a Mask, 6 Jan. 1595; *Proteus and the Rock Adamantine*, a Mask, written by Campion and Davison, 3 Mar. 1595.)	1594 and 1595
	Cecil, Robert	*The Queen's Entertainment at Theobalds*	13–23 June
	Kyd, Thomas	*Cornelia* (*Pompey the Great His Fair Cornelia's Tragedy*) (Trans. Garnier's *Cornélie.*)	1594 (pub.)
	Kyd, Thomas	*Portia* (Trans. Garnier's *Porcie.*) (Projected only ?)	1594
	Shakespeare, William	*The Taming of the Shrew*	*c.* 1594–*c.* 1598
	Shakespeare, William (reviser ?)	*Titus Andronicus* (Related to *Titus and Vespasian*, 1592 ?) (Poss. originally written in 1589–1590.)	23 [24] Jan.
	Yarington, Robert	*Two Lamentable Tragedies*	1594–*c.* 1598
	Anon. (Peele, G. ?)	*Alphonsus, Emperor of Germany* (Ascribed in S.R., 1653, to John Peele, and on t.p. to Chapman.)	b. 1604 (?) (revised, *c.* 1630 ?)
	Anon.	*The Baptism of Prince Henry*	30 Aug.
	Anon.	*Bellendon* (i.e. *Belin Dun*) (Same as *King Rufus* [i.e. *Henry*] *I, with the Life and Death of Belyn Dun*, S.R., 1595 ?)	8 [10] June
	Anon.	*I Caesar and Pompey*	8 Nov.
	Anon. (Dekker, T. ?)	*Diocletian* (Basis of *The Virgin Martyr*, 1620?)	16 Nov.
	Anon.	*Galiaso*	26 [28] June
	Anon. (Heywood, T. ?)	*II Godfrey of Boulogne* (Related to *Jerusalem*, 1599 add., and *The Four Prentices of London*, 1600? Prob. same as 'interlude' of *Godfrey of Boulogne, with the Conquest of Jerusalem*, S.R., 1594.)	19 July

TYPE	AUSPICES	EARLIEST TEXTS	LAST ED.	DATE
Jig	Strange's (?)	[1595?]*	1929[95] (A)	**1593**
Tragedy	Closet	1594	1911 B (T)	
Comedy	Unknown	1597*	1902[79]	
Foreign History	Strange's	[1594?]* & MS (frag.)	1931[83] (G)	
Comedy	Unknown	Lost		
History	Strange's (?) Pembroke's (?)	1597 F	1908 V	
Comedy	Unknown (later Chamberlain's)	1623 F		
Comedy	Strange's	Lost		
Heroical Romance	'King's' (II Derby's Men in 1618?)	1661*		
Royal Entertainment	Gentlemen of Gray's Inn	1688* & MSS (frags.)	1921[99] (G)	**1594**
Royal Entertainment	Host: Wm. Lord Burghley	MS (frag.)	1823[71]	
Tragedy	Closet (?)	1594**	1901[94] (D)	
Tragedy	Closet (?)	Lost		
Comedy	Sussex's (?) Chamberlain's (?)	1623 F		
Tragedy	'Pembroke's', Sussex's	1594 F & MS (frag.)	V (in prog.)	
Tragedy	Admiral's (?)	1601* F	1883†[100]	
Tragedy	Unknown (later King's)	1654* F	1910[101]	
Royal Entertainment	Stirling Castle	1594 (descrip.)		
History	Admiral's	Lost		
Classical History	Admiral's	Lost		
Classical History (?)	Admiral's	Lost		
Unknown	Admiral's	Lost		
Heroical Romance (?)	Admiral's	Lost		

DATE	AUTHOR	TITLE	LIMITS
	Anon.	*Heliogabalus* (Same as *The Mad Priest of the Sun*, 1587?)	1594 (S.R.)
	Anon.	*John of Gaunt* (Poss. not a play.)	1594 (S.R.)
	Anon. (Munday? Heywood?)	*A Knack to Know an Honest Man*	22 [23] Oct.
	Anon.	*The Love of an English Lady*	24 [25] Sept.
	Anon.	*The Merchant of Emden*	30 July
	Anon.	*Palamon and Arcite*	17 [18] Sept.
	Anon. (poss. Dekker, T.)	*Philipo and Hippolito* (Basis of Massinger's *Philenzo and Hippolyta*, 1620?)	9 July
	Anon.	*Robin Hood and Little John*	1594 (S.R.)
	Anon.	*The Set at Maw*	14 Dec.
	Anon. (revised by Dekker, 1602)	*Tasso's Melancholy*	11 [13] Aug.
	Anon. (James I & Fowler, W.?)	*The Three Christians* (Part of baptismal celebrations.)	23 Aug.
	Anon.	*The Venetian Comedy*	25 [27] Aug.
	Anon.	*The Wise Man of West Chester* (Related to *John a Kent*, 1589?)	2 [3] Dec.
1595	Dekker, Thomas (?)	*Disguises, or Love in Disguise, a Petticoat Voyage* (Author and double title given by Hill; see Supp. II, m. Henslowe mentions only *The Disguises*, 1595, without naming an author.)	2 Oct.
	Kempe, William (?)	*The Broom-Man*	b. 1595
	Kempe, William (?)	*The Kitchen Stuff Woman*	b. 1595
	Kempe, William (?)	*Singing Simpkin* (*A Soldier, and a Miser, and Sym the Clown*)	b. 1595
	Munday; Dekker; Chettle; Heywood (?); Shakespeare (?)	*Sir Thomas More* (Revision of play originally composed *c.* 1590–1593.) (1600–1601 also urged for revision.) [Shakespeare Apocrypha]	*c.* 1593–*c.* 1601
	Peele, George (describer)	*Anglorum Feriae*	17 Nov.
	Phillips, Augustine (?)	*The Slippers*	b. 1595
	Shakespeare, William	*Love's Labour's Lost* (Recently urged that play was originally written *c.* 1588–1589, poss. for Paul's, and revised *c.* 1596–1597.)	*c.* 1588–1597
	Shakespeare, William	*A Midsummer-Night's Dream*	1594–1598
	Shakespeare, William	*Richard II*	1594–1595
	Shakespeare, William	*Romeo and Juliet*	1591–1597
	Anon.	*Barnardo and Fiammetta*	28 [30] Oct.
	Anon.	*II Caesar and Pompey*	18 June
	Anon.	*Caesar and Pompey, or Caesar's Revenge*	*c.* 1592–*c.* 1596
	Anon.	*Crack Me This Nut*	5 Sept.

TYPE	AUSPICES	EARLIEST TEXTS	LAST ED.	DATE
Romance (?)	Unknown	Lost		
History	Unknown	Lost		
Tragicomedy	Admiral's	1596* F	1910 G†	
Comedy (?)	Admiral's	Lost		
Realistic Tragicomedy (?)	Admiral's	Lost		
Tragedy (?)	Admiral's	Lost		
Tragicomedy (?)	Admiral's	Lost		
'Pastoral Comedy'	Unknown	Lost		
Comedy (?)	Admiral's	Lost		
Tragedy (?)	Admiral's	Lost		
Mask	Stirling Castle	Lost		
Comedy	Admiral's	Lost		
Pseudo-history (?)	Admiral's	Lost		
Comedy (?)	Admiral's	Lost		**1595**
Jig	Strange's and Chamberlain's (?)	Lost		
Jig	Strange's and Chamberlain's (?)	Lost		
Jig	Strange's and Chamberlain's (?)	[1655?]	1932[102]	
History	Unknown (Chamberlain's?)	MS F	1954[103] (GT)	
Tilt	Court	MS	1952[80]	
Jig	Strange's and Chamberlain's (?)	Lost		
Comedy	Unknown (later Chamberlain's)	1598 F	1904 V	
Comedy	Chamberlain's	1600 F	1895 V	
History	Chamberlain's	1597 F	1955 V	
Tragedy	Chamberlain's (?)	1597 F	1871 V	
Romance (?)	Admiral's	Lost		
Classical History	Admiral's	Lost		
Tragedy	Trinity Col., Oxford	[c. 1606]** F	1911–12[104] (G)	
Comedy (?)	Admiral's	Lost		

DATE	AUTHOR	TITLE	LIMITS
	Anon.	*Edmond Ironside, or War Hath Made All Friends*	*c.* 1590–1600
	Anon.	*The French Comedy*	11 Feb.
	Anon.	*Henry V*	28 Nov.
	Anon.	*I Hercules*	7 May
	Anon.	*II Hercules*	23 May
	Anon.	*Judith* (Trans. Schonaeus's *Judithae Constantia.*)	1595–*c.* 1600
	Anon.	*Laelia* (Adapt. *Gl'Ingannati* through Estienne's *Le Sacrifice* [*Les Abusez*].) (Revival of play performed at Queens' Col., 1546?)	1 Mar.
	Anon.	*Long Meg of Westminster*	14 (?) Feb.
	Anon.	*Longshanks* (Poss. a revision of Peele's *Edward I*; see also *The Welshman*, 1599 add.)	29 Aug.
	Anon. (Bacon? Essex?)	*Love and Self-Love* (*The Essex Entertainment*)	17 Nov.
	Anon.	*The Mack*	21 Feb.
	Anon.	*The New World's Tragedy*	17 Sept.
	Anon.	*Ninus and Semiramis* (Poss. not a play.)	1595 (S.R.)
	Anon.	*Seleo and Olympio* (Prob. same as *Olympio and Heugenyo* [*Eugenio*].)	5 Mar.
	Anon.	*I The Seven Days of the Week*	3 June
	Anon.	*A Toy to Please Chaste Ladies*	14 Nov.
	Anon.	*Valentine and Orson* (Basis of *Valentine and Orson*, 1598?)	1595 (S.R.)
	Anon.	*The Wonder of a Woman* (Poss. basis of *A New Wonder, a Woman Never Vexed*, 1609.)	15 [16] Oct.
1596	Burton, William	*Amores Perinthi et Tyantes*	1596
	Chapman, George	*The Blind Beggar of Alexandria* (*Irus*)	12 Feb.
	Greville, Fulke	*Mustapha*	*c.* 1594–*c.* 1596
	Jonson, Ben	*A Tale of a Tub* (Substantially new when lic., 7 May 1633?)	1596–1633
	Shakespeare, William	*King John*	1591–1598
	Shakespeare, William	*The Merchant of Venice*	1594–1597
	Anon. (Heywood, T., in part?)	*Captain Thomas Stukeley* (Revised *c.* 1599?)	11 [10] Dec.
	Anon.	*Chinon of England*	3 Jan.
	Anon.	*Julian the Apostate*	29 Apr.
	Anon.	*Nebuchadnezzar*	19 [18] Dec.
	Anon.	*Paradox*	1 July
	Anon.	*Phocasse* (*Focas*)	19 [20] May
	Anon.	*Pythagoras*	16 Jan.
	Anon.	*II The Seven Days of the Week*	22 [23] Jan.
	Anon.	*I Tamar Cham* (New version of play? See 1588.)	6 [7] May
	Anon.	*II Tamar Cham* (New version of play? See 1592.)	11 June
	Anon.	*That Will Be Shall Be*	30 Dec.

TYPE	AUSPICES	EARLIEST TEXTS	LAST ED.	DATE
History	Unknown	MS	1927 G† (T)	
Comedy	Admiral's	Lost		
History	Admiral's	Lost		
Classical Legend	Admiral's	Lost		
Classical Legend	Admiral's	Lost		
Sacred Comedy	Closet	MS (frag.)	1917†[105]	
Latin Comedy	Queens' Col., Cambridge	MS	1910†[106]	
Comedy (?)	Admiral's	Lost		
History	Admiral's	Lost		
Royal Entertainment	Court	MSS (frags.)	1861†[107]	
Comedy (?)	Admiral's	Lost		
Tragedy	Admiral's	Lost		
'Tragedie'	Unknown	Lost		
Classical Legend	Admiral's	Lost		
Moral (?)	Admiral's	Lost		
Comedy	Admiral's	Lost		
Romance	Queen's	Lost		
Comedy (?)	Admiral's	Lost		
Latin Play	Unacted	Lost		**1596**
Comedy	Admiral's	1598*	1928 G	
Tragedy	Closet	1609 & MSS	1939[108]	
Comedy	Admiral's (?)	1640	1927[109] (B)	
History	Chamberlain's	1623 F	1919 V	
Comedy	Chamberlain's	1600 F	1888 V	
History	Admiral's	1605* F	1878†[110]	
Heroical Romance	Admiral's	Lost		
Classical History	Admiral's	Lost		
Biblical History	Admiral's	Lost		
Comedy (?)	Admiral's	Lost		
Classical History (?)	Admiral's	Lost		
Classical Biography (?)	Admiral's	Lost		
Moral (?)	Admiral's	Lost		
Heroical Romance	Admiral's	Lost MS ('plot' of 1602)	1931[81]	
Heroical Romance	Admiral's	Lost		
Unknown	Admiral's	Lost		

F

DATE	AUTHOR	TITLE	LIMITS
	Anon.	*The Tinker of Totness*	18 [23] July
	Anon.	*Troy*	22 [25] June
	Anon.	*Vortigern* (*Valteger*) (See *Hengist*, 1599 add.)	4 Dec.
1597	Chapman, George	*An Humorous Day's Mirth* (*The Comedy of Humours*)	11 May
	Jonson, Ben	*The Case Is Altered* (Interpolations later.)	1597–1598
	Morrell, Roger (?)	*Hispanus*	Mar.
	Nashe, T. (& others ?)	*The Isle of Dogs*	July
	Shakespeare, William	*I Henry IV*	*c.* 1596–1598
	Shakespeare, William	*II Henry IV*	*c.* 1597–*c.* 1598
	Wiburne, Nathaniel	*Machiavellus*	9 Dec.
	Anon.	*Alexander and Lodowick*	14 Jan.
	Anon.	*Alice Pierce*	8–10 Dec. (prop.)
	Anon.	*Black Joan*	1597(?)
	Anon.	*Branhowlte* (*Brunhild*)	26 Nov. (prop.)
	Anon.	*The Cobbler* (*of Queenhithe*)	21 (or 23) Oct. (P)
	Anon.	*Five Plays in One*	7 Apr.
	Anon.	*Frederick and Basilea*	3 June
	Anon.	*The French Comedy*	18 Apr.
	Anon.	*Friar Spendleton*	31 Oct.
	Anon.	*Guido*	19 [21] Mar.
	Anon.	*Henry I* (Basis of *The Famous Wars of Henry I*, 1598 ?)	26 May
	Anon.	*Martin Swart*	30 June
	Anon. (poss. Dekker, T.)	*Pontius Pilate* (Prol. and Epil. in 1601 by Dekker.)	*c.* 1597–1601
	Anon. (Rollinson, F. ?)	*Silvanus*	1597–1598
	Anon.	*Uther Pendragon* (Basis of *Merlin*, 1608 ?)	29 Apr.
	Anon.	*A Woman Hard to Please*	27 Jan.
1598	Bernard, Richard	*Terence in English*: *Andria, Eunuchus, Adelphi, Heautontimorumenus, Hecyra, Phormio* (Trans. Terence.)	1598 (pub.)
	Brandon, Samuel	*The Virtuous Octavia*	1598
	Chapman, George	*The Fount(ain) of New Fashions* (*The Ill* [*Jill* ?] *of a Woman*)	16 May–12 Oct. (P)
	Chettle, Henry	*II The Conquest of Brute* (Prob. same as *Brute Greenshield*, 1599.)	12–22 Oct. (P)
	Chettle, Henry	*'Tis No Deceit to Deceive the Deceiver* (Not completed ?)	25–28 Nov. (P)
	Chettle, Henry (reviser ?)	*Vayvode* (An old play revised ?)	29 Aug. (P)
	Chettle, Henry	*The Woman's Tragedy* (Not completed ?)	14 July (P)

TYPE	AUSPICES	EARLIEST TEXTS	LAST ED.	DATE
Comedy (?)	Admiral's	Lost		
Classical Legend	Admiral's	Lost		
History	Admiral's	Lost		
Comedy	Admiral's	1599*	1937 (1938) G	**1597**
Comedy	Unknown (later Queen's Revels)	1609	1927[109]	
Latin Comedy	St John's Col., Cambridge	MS		
Satirical Comedy	Pembroke's	Lost		
History	Chamberlain's	[1598] F	1936 V (Suppl. 1956)	
History	Chamberlain's	1600 F	1940 V	
Latin Comedy	St John's Col., Cambridge	MS		
Romance (?)	Admiral's	Lost		
History	Pembroke's and Admiral's	Lost		
Tragedy (?)	Pembroke's (?) (Admiral's in 1598)	Lost		
Tragedy (?)	Pembroke's (?) and Admiral's	Lost		
Comedy (?)	Pembroke's and Admiral's	Lost		
Unknown	Admiral's	Lost		
Romance	Admiral's	MS ('plot') F	1931[81]	
Comedy	Admiral's	Lost		
Comedy (?)	Pembroke's and Admiral's	Lost		
Unknown	Admiral's	Lost		
History	Admiral's	Lost		
History	Admiral's	Lost		
Biblical History	Pembroke's (?)	Lost		
Latin Comedy	St John's Col., Cambridge	MS		
Pseudo-history	Admiral's	Lost		
Comedy	Admiral's	Lost		
Comedies	Closet	1598		**1598**
Tragicomedy	Closet	[1598]** F	1909 G†	
Comedy	Admiral's	Lost		
Pseudo-history (?)	Admiral's	Lost		
Comedy (?)	Admiral's	Lost		
Foreign History (?)	Admiral's	Lost		
Tragedy	Admiral's	Lost		

DATE AUTHOR	TITLE	LIMITS
Chettle; Dekker; Drayton	*The Famous Wars of Henry I and the Prince of Wales* (*The Welshman's Prize*)	13–13/20 (?) Mar. (P)
Chettle; Dekker; Drayton; Wilson	*I Black Bateman of the North*	2/9–22 May (P)
Chettle; Dekker; Drayton; Wilson	*I & II Earl Godwin and His Three Sons*	25 Mar.– 10 June (P)
Chettle; Dekker; Drayton; Wilson	*Pierce of Exton* (Not completed?)	30 Mar./ 7 Apr. (P)
Chettle; Drayton; Munday; Wilson	*The Funeral of Richard Cœur de Lion*	13–26 June (P)
Chettle; Jonson; Porter	*Hot Anger Soon Cold*	18 Aug. (P)
Chettle, H.; Munday, A.	*The Death of Robert, Earl of Huntingdon* (*II Robin Hood*)	20 Feb.– 8 Mar. (P)
Chettle, H.; Munday, A.	*The Downfall of Robert, Earl of Huntingdon* (*I Robin Hood*)	15 Feb. (P)
Chettle, H.; Wilson, R.	*Catiline's Conspiracy* (*Catiline*) (Not completed?)	21–29 Aug. (P)
Chettle, H.; Wilson, R.	*II Black Bateman of the North*	26 June– 14 July (P)
Chettle or Dekker; Drayton; Munday; Wilson	*Chance Medley*	19–24 Aug. (P)
Day, J. (prob. completed by Chettle, H.)	*I The Conquest of Brute*	30 July– 16 Sept. (P)
Dekker, Thomas	*Phaeton* (Basis of *The Sun's Darling*, 1624?)	8–15 Jan. (P)
Dekker, Thomas	*The Triangle* (or *Triplicity*) *of Cuckolds*	1 Mar. (P)
Dekker, T.; Drayton, M.	*I, II, & III The Civil Wars of France*	29 Sept.– 30 Dec. (P)
Dekker, T.; Drayton, M.	*Connan, Prince of Cornwall*	16–20 Oct. (P)
Dekker, T.; Drayton, M.	*[II] Worse (A)feared Than Hurt* (*II Hannibal and Hermes*)	30 Aug.– 4 Sept. (P)
Dekker; Drayton; Wilson	*[I] Hannibal and Hermes* (*[I] Worse (A)feared Than Hurt*)	17–27 July (P)
Dekker; Drayton; Wilson	*The Madman's Morris*	31 June [1 July]– 10 July (P)
Dekker; Drayton; Wilson	*Pierce of Winchester*	28 July– 10 Aug. (P)
Drayton, M.; Munday, A.	*Mother Redcap*	22 Dec. 1597– 5 Jan. 1598 (P)
Hathway, Richard	*Arthur, King of England*	11–12 Apr. (P)
Hathway, R.; Munday, A.	*Valentine and Orson* (Based on *Valentine and Orson*, 1595?)	19 July (P)
Haughton, William	*Englishmen for My Money, or A Woman Will Have Her Will*	18 Feb.– 2/9 May (P)
Jonson, Ben	*Every Man in His Humour*	1598
Porter, Henry	*Love Prevented*	30 May (P)
Rankins, William	*Mulmutius Dunwallow* (Poss. an old play.)	3 Oct. (P)

TYPE	AUSPICES	EARLIEST TEXTS	LAST ED.	DATE
History	Admiral's	Lost		
Tragedy (?)	Admiral's	Lost		
History	Admiral's	Lost		
History	Admiral's	Lost		
History	Admiral's	Lost		
Comedy	Admiral's	Lost		
History	Admiral's	1601* F	1874 D (T)	
History	Admiral's	1601* F	1874 D (T)	
Classical History	Admiral's	Lost		
Tragedy (?)	Admiral's	Lost		
Comedy	Admiral's	Lost		
Pseudo-history (?)	Admiral's	Lost		
Classical Legend	Admiral's	Lost		
Comedy	Admiral's	Lost		
Foreign History	Admiral's	Lost		
History	Admiral's	Lost		
Unknown	Admiral's	Lost		
Unknown	Admiral's	Lost		
Comedy (?)	Admiral's	Lost		
Unknown	Admiral's	Lost		
Comedy (?)	Admiral's	Lost		
Pseudo-history	Admiral's	Lost		
Romance	Admiral's	Lost		
Comedy	Admiral's	1616 F	1917[111] (DG)	
Comedy	Chamberlain's	1601 F	1928[109] (BMA)	
Unknown	Admiral's	Lost		
Pseudo-history (?)	Admiral's	Lost		

DATE	AUTHOR	TITLE	LIMITS
	Shakespeare, William	*Love's Labour's Won* (Same as *The Taming of the Shrew*, 1594, or *Much Ado about Nothing*, below?)	*c.* 1590–1598
	Shakespeare, William	*Much Ado about Nothing*	1598–1600
	Anon.	*Astiages*	1597–1598
	Anon.	*Celestina* (Trans. or adapt. de Rojas.)	1598 (S.R.)
	Anon.	*Dido and Aeneas* (Poss. an old play.)	8 Jan. (acted)
	Anon. (Lyly, J. ?)	*The Entertainment at Mitcham* (*Poet, Painter, and Musician*)	13 Sept.
	Anon.	*The Fair Maid of London*	1598 (lic.)
	Anon.	*A Mask of the Nine Passions*	6 Jan.
	Anon. (Lee, Robert, payee)	*The Miller* (Poss. an old play.)	22 Feb. (P)
	Anon.	'*Pope, Cardinals, Friars*'	July
	Anon.	*Sturgflaterey* (i.e. *Stark Flattery*? *Strange Flattery*?)	1598 (listed)
	Anon.	*The Wooing of Nan*	*c.* 1590–*c.* 1600
1599	Chapman, George	*All Fools but the Fool* (Title altered from *The World Runs on Wheels*. Basis of *All Fools*, 1604?)	22 Jan.– 2 July (P)
	Chapman, George	*The Four Kings*	18/22 Mar. (lic.)
	Chapman, George	*A Pastoral Tragedy* (Not completed?)	17 July (P)
	Chettle, Henry	*Troy's Revenge, with the Tragedy of Polyphemus*	16–27 Feb. (P)
	Chettle, H.; Dekker, T.	*Agamemnon* (Same as *Orestes' Furies*, below?)	2(?)–30 May (P)
	Chettle, H.; Dekker, T.	*The Stepmother's Tragedy*	23 Aug.– 14 Oct. (P)
	Chettle, H.; Dekker, T.	*Troilus and Cressida*	7–16 Apr. (P)
	Chettle; Dekker; Jonson (& Marston?)	*Robert II, King of Scots* (*The Scot's Tragedy*)	3–27 Sept. (P)
	Chettle, H.; Haughton, W.	*Arcadian Virgin* (Not completed?)	13–17 Dec. (P)
	Chettle, H.; Porter, H.	*The Spencers*	4–22 Mar. (P)
	Day, J.; Haughton, W.	*Cox of Collumpton* (*John Cox*)	1–14 Nov. (P)
	Day, J.; Haughton, W.	*Thomas Merry* (*Beech's Tragedy*)	21 Nov– 6 Dec. (P)
	Dekker, Thomas	*Bear a Brain* (Title altered from *Better Late Than Never*.) (Poss. same as *The Shoemakers' Holiday*, below; or *Look about You*, below.)	1 Aug. (P)
	Dekker, Thomas	*The First Introduction of the Civil Wars of France*	20 Jan. (P)
	Dekker, Thomas	*Old Fortunatus* (See *I Fortunatus*, 1599 add.)	9–30 Nov. (P)
	Dekker, Thomas	*The Shoemakers' Holiday, or The Gentle Craft*	15 July (P)
	Decker, T. (& Chettle, H.?)	*Orestes' Furies* (*Furens*?) (Same as *Agamemnon*, above?)	2 May (P)
	Dekker, T.; Jonson, B.	*Page of Plymouth*	10 Aug.– 2 Sept. (P)

TYPE	AUSPICES	EARLIEST TEXTS	LAST ED.	DATE
Comedy	Chamberlain's (?)	Lost (?)		
Comedy	Chamberlain's	1600 F	1899 V	
Latin (?) Tragedy	St John's Col., Oxford	Lost		
Romance	Closet (?)	Lost		
Classical Legend	Admiral's	Lost		
Royal Entertainment	Host: Dr Julius Caesar	MS	1953†[112]	
Romance (?)	Unknown	Lost		
Mask	Middle Temple at Court	Lost		
Comedy (?)	Admiral's	Lost		
Protestant Comedy	High School, Edinburgh	Lost		
Unknown	Admiral's	Lost		
Jig	Unknown	MS	1929[93]	
Comedy	Admiral's	Lost		**1599**
Unknown	Admiral's	Lost		
Tragedy	Admiral's	Lost		
Classical Legend	Admiral's	Lost		
Classical Legend	Admiral's	Lost		
Tragedy	Admiral's	Lost		
Classical Legend	Admiral's	MS ('plot' frag.) F	1931[81]	
History	Admiral's	Lost		
Pastoral (?)	Admiral's	Lost		
History	Admiral's	Lost		
Tragedy	Admiral's	Lost		
Tragedy	Admiral's	Lost		
Comedy	Admiral's	Lost (?)		
History	Admiral's	Lost		
Comedy	Admiral's	1600*	1953[113] (MA)	
Comedy	Admiral's	1600	1953[113] (MA)	
Classical Legend	Admiral's (?)	Lost		
Tragedy	Admiral's	Lost		

DATE	AUTHOR	TITLE	LIMITS
	Drayton, Michael	*William Longbeard* (i.e. *Longsword*?) (Not completed?)	20 Jan. (P)
	Drayton; Hathway; Munday; Wilson	*I Sir John Oldcastle* [Shakespeare Apocrypha]	16 Oct. (P)
	Haughton, William	*The Poor Man's Paradise* (Not completed?)	20–25 Aug. (P)
	Hawkesworth, Walter	*Leander* (Adapt. Della Porta's *La Fantesca.*) (Revised when revived in 1602.)	7 Jan. (MS date)
	Heywood, Thomas	*Joan as Good as My Lady*	10–12 Feb. (P)
	Heywood, Thomas	*War without Blows and Love without Suit* (or *Strife*)	6 Dec. 1598– 26 Jan. 1599 (P)
	Heywood, T. (?), and others (?)	*I & II Edward IV* (See *The Siege of London*, 1599 add., and *The Tanner of Denmark*, 1592.)	1592–1599
	Jonson, Ben	*Every Man out of His Humour*	1599
	Marston, John	*Antonio and Mellida*	1599–1600
	Marston, J. (reviser [of Chapman, G. ?])	*Histriomastix, or The Player Whipped* (Based on play of *c.* 1589?) (The following titles, some no doubt fictitious, are mentioned in the above play: *A Knot of Knaves, Lady Nature, The Lascivious Knight, The Prodigal Child, A Proud Heart and a Beggar's Purse, A Russet Coat and a Knave's Cap, The Widow's Apron Strings.*)	1589–1599
	Porter, Henry	*II The Two Angry Women of Abingdon* (See following.)	22 Dec. 1598– 12 Feb. 1599 (P)
	Porter, Henry	*Two Merry Women of Abingdon* (Not completed? Or same as preceding?)	28 Feb. (P)
	Ruggle, George (?)	*Club Law*	1599–1600
	Ruggle, George (?)	*Re Vera, or Verily*	*c.* 1598–1620
	Shakespeare, William	*As You Like It*	1598–1600
	Shakespeare, William	*Henry V*	1599
	Shakespeare, William	*Julius Caesar*	1598–1600
	Wilson, Robert	*II Henry Richmond* (No first part known.)	8 Nov. (P)
	Anon.	*Friar Fox and Gillian of Brentford*	10 Feb. (P)
	Anon.	*A Larum for London, or The Siege of Antwerp*	*c.* 1598–1600
	Anon. (poss. Chettle, Dekker, or Wadeson)	*Look about You* (Poss. same as *Bear a Brain*, above.)	*c.* 1598–1600
	Anon. (Gwyn, O., in part?)	*The Pilgrimage to Parnassus*	1598–1599
	Anon. ('John Webster and William Rowley' on t.p. rejected)	*The Thracian Wonder*	1590–*c.* 1600
	Anon.	*Tristram de Lyons* (A revised older play?)	13 Oct. (P)
	Anon.	*Turnholt*	1598–1599
	Anon. (Heywood, T. ?)	*A Warning for Fair Women*	*c.* 1598–1599
	Anon.	*The Wisdom of Doctor Dodypoll*	1599–1600

TYPE	AUSPICES	EARLIEST TEXTS	LAST ED.	DATE
History	Admiral's	Lost		
History	Admiral's	1600 F	1908 G	
Comedy (?)	Admiral's	Lost		
Latin Comedy	Trinity Col., Cambridge	MSS (both versions)		
Comedy	Admiral's	Lost		
Comedy (?)	Admiral's	Lost		
History	Derby's	1599 F	1874[114] (T)	
Comedy	Chamberlain's	1600 F	1927[109] (BG)	
Tragicomedy	Paul's	1602	1934[115] (G)	
Comedy	Paul's (?)	1610* F	1939[115]	
Comedy	Admiral's	Lost		
Comedy	Admiral's	Lost		
Satirical Comedy	Clare Hall, Cambridge	MS	1907†[116]	
Satirical Comedy	Clare Hall, Cambridge (?)	Lost		
Comedy	Chamberlain's	1623 F	1890 V	
History	Chamberlain's	1600 F	V (in prog.)	
Tragedy	Chamberlain's	1623 F	1913 V	
History	Admiral's	Lost		
Comedy	Admiral's	Lost		
History	Chamberlain's	1602* F	1913 G	
Comedy	Admiral's	1600* F	1913 G (D)	
Satirical Comedy	St John's Col., Cambridge	MS F	1949[117]	
Comedy	Unknown	1661*	1857[118]	
Romance	Admiral's	Lost		
Topical Play	Unknown	Lost		
Tragedy	Chamberlain's	1599* F	1878[110]	
Comedy	Paul's	1600* F	1884†[100]	

DATE AUTHOR	TITLE	LIMITS
1599 ADDENDA	The following plays are known only through revivals, in the years 1592–1600, by Henslowe's groups. The year of the revival is here given as the posterior limit, followed by the month and day in round brackets; the company is that of the revival.	
Anon.	*Abraham and Lot*	c. 1580–1594 (9 Jan.)
Anon.	*Antony and Vallia* (Poss. basis by Dekker of Massinger's *Antonio and Vallia*, S.R., 1660, and Warburton's list.)	c. 1590(?)–1595 (4 Jan.)
Anon.	*Bendo* (or *Byndo*) *and Richardo*	c. 1580–1592 (4 Mar.)
Anon.	*Brandimer* (Same as *Orlando Furioso*, 1591?)	1588(?)–1592 (6 Apr.)
Anon.	*Buckingham* (Poss. same as *The True Tragedy of Richard III*, 1591.)	1591(?)–1593 (30 [29] Dec.)
Anon.	*Burbon* (i.e. *Bourbon*?)	c. 1580–1597 (2 Nov.)
Anon.	*Clorys and Orgasto* (i.e. *Ergasto*?)	c. 1580–1592 (28 Feb.)
Anon.	*Constantine*	c. 1580–1592 (21 Mar.)
Anon.	*Cosmo* (Poss. *The Jealous Comedy*, 1593.)	1593(?)–1593 (12 [11] Jan.)
Anon.	*Cutlack* (i.e. *Guthlac*?)	c. 1580–1594 (16 May)
Anon.	*Don Horatio* (*Jeronimo. Spanish Comedy*)	c. 1584–1592 (23 Feb.)
Anon.	*The Fair Maid of Italy*	c. 1580–1594 (12 Jan.)
Anon.	*I Fortunatus* (Basis of *Old Fortunatus*, 1599?)	c. 1580–1596 (3 Feb.)
Anon.	*The French Doctor* (Same as *The Venetian Comedy*, 1594?)	1594(?)–1594 (18 [19] Oct.)
Anon.	*Friar Francis*	c. 1580–1594 (7 Jan.)
Anon.	*God Speed the Plough*	c. 1580–1593 (27 [26] Dec.)
Anon.	*Hardicanute* (*Canute*)	c. 1580–1597 (20–30 Oct.)
Anon.	*Harry of Cornwall*	c. 1580–1592 (25 Feb.)
Anon.	*Hengist* (Same as *Vortigern*, 1596, and basis of *Hengist, King of Kent*, 1618?)	1596(?)–1597 (22 June)
Anon.	*Hester and Ahasuerus*	c. 1580–1594 (3 [5] June)
Anon.	*Huon of Bordeaux*	c. 1580–1593 (28 [27] Dec.)

TYPE	AUSPICES	EARLIEST TEXTS	LAST ED.	DATE
				1599
				ADDENDA
Biblical History	Sussex's	Lost		
Romance (?)	Admiral's	Lost		
Comedy	Strange's and Admiral's	Lost		
Romantic Comedy (?)	Strange's and Admiral's	Lost (?)		
History	Sussex's	Lost (?)		
Foreign History (?)	Admiral's and Pembroke's	Lost		
Pastoral (?)	Strange's and Admiral's	Lost		
Classical or English History	Strange's and Admiral's	Lost		
Comedy (?)	Strange's and Admiral's	Lost		
Tragedy (?)	Admiral's	Lost		
Comedy	Strange's and Admiral's	Lott		
Comedy (?)	Sussex's	Lost		
Romantic Comedy	Admiral's	Lost		
Comedy (?)	Admiral's	Lost		
Realistic Tragedy (?)	Sussex's	Lost		
Comedy (?)	Sussex's	Lost		
History	Pembroke's and Admiral's	Lost		
History	Strange's and Admiral's	Lost		
History	Admiral's	Lost		
Biblical History	Admiral's or Chamberlain's	Lost		
Romance	Sussex's	Lost		

DATE	AUTHOR	TITLE	LIMITS
	Anon.	*Jerusalem* (Related to *Godfrey of Boulogne*, with the Conquest of *Jerusalem*, S.R., 1594, and *II Godfrey of Boulogne*, 1594?)	*c.* 1580–1592 (22 Mar.)
	Anon.	*King Lud*	*c.* 1580–1594 (18 Jan.)
	Anon.	*Like unto Like* (Same as *Like Will to Like*, 1568?)	*c.* 1568–1600 (28 Oct.)
	Anon.	*The Love of a Grecian Lady* (*The Grecian Comedy*) (Same as *The Turkish Mahomet*, 1588, and *Mahomet*, below?)	1588(?)–1594 (4 [5] Oct.)
	Anon.	*Machiavel*	*c.* 1580–1592 (2 Mar.)
	Anon.	*Mahomet* (Same as *The Love of a Grecian Lady*, above, and *The Turkish Mahomet*, 1588?)	1588(?)–1594 (14 [16] Aug.)
	Anon.	*Muly Molloco* (Poss. same as *The Battle of Alcazar*, 1589.)	*c.* 1588–1592 (20 [21] Feb.)
	Anon.	*Osric*	*c.* 1580–1597 (3 Feb.)
	Anon.	*Pope Joan*	*c.* 1580–1592 (1 Mar.)
	Anon.	*The Ranger's Comedy*	*c.* 1580–1594 (2 Apr.)
	Anon.	*Richard the Confessor*	*c.* 1580–1593 (31 Dec.)
	Anon.	*Roderick*	*c.* 1580–1600 (29 Oct.)
	Anon.	*The Siege of London* (Part basis of *Edward IV*, 1599?)	*c.* 1580–1594 (26 [27] Dec.)
	Anon.	*Sir John Mandeville*	*c.* 1580–1592 (24 Feb.)
	Anon.	*Time's Triumph and Fortus* (i.e. *Fortune's?*)	*c.* 1580–1597 (13 Apr.)
	Anon.	*Warlamchester*	*c.* 1580–1594 (28 Nov.)
	Anon.	*The Welshman* (Same as *Longshanks*, 1595?)	1595(?)–1595 (29 Nov.)
	Anon.	*William the Conqueror* (Same as *Fair Em*, 1590?)	*c.* 1590(?)–1594 (4 Jan.)
	Anon.	*The Witch of Islington*	*c.* 1580–1597 (14 July)
	Anon.	*Zenobia*	*c.* 1580–1592 (9 Mar.)
1600	Boyle, William	*Jugurth, King of Numidia*	9 Feb. (P) (re-lic. 3 May 1624)

TYPE	AUSPICES	EARLIEST TEXTS	LAST ED.	DATE
Heroical Romance (?)	Strange's	Lost		
History	Sussex's	Lost		
Unknown	Pembroke's	Lost		
Heroical Romance (?)	Admiral's	Lost		
Foreign History (?)	Strange's and Admiral's	Lost		
Heroical Romance (?)	Admiral's	Lost		
Foreign History	Strange's	Lost		
Unknown	Admiral's	Lost		
Foreign Pseudo-history	Strange's and Admiral's	Lost		
Comedy	Queen's and Sussex's	Lost		
History	Sussex's	Lost		
History (?)	Pembroke's	Lost		
History	Admiral's	Lost		
Romantic Comedy (?)	Strange's and Admiral's	Lost		
Moral (?)	Admiral's	Lost		
History (?)	Admiral's	Lost		
History (?)	Admiral's	Lost		
Romantic Comedy (?)	Sussex's	Lost (?)		
Realistic Tragedy (?)	Admiral's	Lost		
Classical History	Strange's and Admiral's	Lost		
Tragedy (?)	Admiral's	Lost		**1600**

DATE	AUTHOR	TITLE	LIMITS
	Chettle, Henry	*Damon and Pithias*	16 Feb.– 27 Apr./ 6 May (P)
	Chettle, Henry	*The Wooing of Death* (Not completed?)	27 Apr.– 6 May (P)
	Chettle; Day; Dekker	*Cupid and Psyche* (*The Golden Ass*)	27 Apr./ 6 May– 14 May (P)
	Chettle; Day; Dekker; Haughton	*The Seven Wise Masters*	1–8/10 Mar. (P)
	Chettle; Day (& Haughton?)	*I The Blind Beggar of Bednal Green* (*I Tom Strowd*)	26 May (P)
	Chettle; Dekker; Haughton	*Patient Grissil*	16 Oct./ 1 Nov.– 29 Dec. (P)
	Day, John	*The Italian Tragedy of —* (Not completed?)	10 Jan. (P)
	Day; Dekker; Haughton (& Marston?)	*The Spanish Moor's Tragedy* (Prob. same as *Lust's Dominion,* below.)	13 Feb. (P)
	Dekker, Thomas	*The Fortewn Tenes* (i.e. *Fortune's Tennis?*) (Revision of *II Fortune's Tennis,* 1597?)	6 Sept. (P)
	Dekker, Thomas	*Truth's Supplication to Candlelight* (Basis of *The Whore of Babylon,* 1606?)	18–30 Jan. (P)
	Dekker; Drayton; Hathway; Munday; Wilson	*I Fair Constance of Rome*	3–14 June (P)
	Drayton; Hathway; Munday; Wilson	*II Sir John Oldcastle* (Additions by Dekker in 1602.)	16 Oct.– 19/26 Dec. (P)
	Drayton; Hathway; Munday; Wilson	*Owen Tudor* (Not completed?)	10/18 Jan. (P)
	Greville, Fulke	*Alaham*	*c.* 1598–*c.* 1600
	Hathway, R.; & others	*II Fair Constance of Rome* (Not completed?)	20 June (P)
	Haughton, William	*The English Fugitives* (Not completed?)	16–24 Apr. (P)
	Haughton, William	*Ferrex and Porrex*	18 Mar.– 3/13 Apr. (P)
	Haughton, William (revised for press by 'I.T.')	*The Devil and His Dame* (Prob. same as *Grim the Collier of Croydon,* or *The Devil and His Dame,* pub. 1662.)	6 May (P)
	Haughton, W.; Pett, [Peter?]	*Strange News out of Poland*	17 May (P)
	Heywood, Thomas	*The Four Prentices of London* (Related to *Jerusalem,* 1599 add., and *II Godfrey of Boulogne,* 1594?)	1592–*c.* 1600
	Marston, John	*Antonio's Revenge* (*II Antonio and Mellida*)	1599–1601
	Marston, John	*Jack Drum's Entertainment* (*Katherine and Pasquil*)	1600
	Shakespeare, William	*The Merry Wives of Windsor* (First perf. 23 Apr. 1597 recently urged again.)	1597–1602
	Shakespeare, William	*Twelfth Night, or What You Will*	1600–1602

TYPE	AUSPICES	EARLIEST TEXTS	LAST ED.	DATE
Tragicomedy (?)	Admiral's	Lost		
Tragedy (?)	Admiral's	Lost		
Classical Legend	Admiral's	Lost		
Tragicomedy (?)	Admiral's	Lost		
Comedy	Admiral's	1659* F	1902 B	
Comedy	Admiral's	1603* F	1953[113]	
Tragedy	Admiral's	Lost		
Tragedy	Admiral's	1657** (?)	1961[114] (BD) (?)	
Unknown	Admiral's	Lost		
Allegorical History (?)	Admiral's	Lost (?)		
Classical History (?)	Admiral's	Lost		
History	Admiral's	Lost		
History	Admiral's	Lost		
Tragedy	Closet	1633* & MS	1939†[108]	
Classical History (?)	Admiral's	Lost		
Topical Play (?)	Admiral's	Lost		
Tragedy (?)	Admiral's	Lost		
Comedy	Admiral's (?)	1662* F (?)	1908[74] (D) (?)	
Foreign History	Admiral's	Lost		
Heroical Romance	Admiral's	1615	1874[114]	
Tragedy	Paul's	1602	1934[115] (G)	
Domestic Comedy	Paul's	1601 F	1939[115]	
Comedy	Chamberlain's	1602 F		
Comedy	Chamberlain's	1623 F	1901 V	

DATE	AUTHOR	TITLE	LIMITS
	Anon. (poss. Chapman, G.)	Charlemagne, or The Distracted Emperor (Same as The Fatal Love, below ?)	1584–c. 1605
	Anon.	Cloth Breeches and Velvet Hose	1600 (S.R.)
	Anon.	Give a Man Luck and Throw Him into the Sea	1600 (S.R.)
	Anon.	The Lost Muse	16 June
	Anon. ('Christopher Marlowe' on t.p.; by Day; Dekker; Haughton ? [& Marston ?])	Lust's Dominion, or The Lascivious Queen (Prob. same as The Spanish Moor's Tragedy, above.)	13 Feb. (P)(?)
	Anon. (Day ? Lyly ?)	The Maid's Metamorphosis	1599–1600
	Anon. (Gwyn, O., in part ?)	I The Return from Parnassus	1599–1601
	Anon.	The Tartarian Cripple, Emperor of Constantinople (Poss. non-dramatic.)	1600 (S.R.)
	Anon. (by 'W.S.')	Thomas Lord Cromwell [Shakespeare Apocrypha]	c. 1599–1602
	Anon. (Dekker, T., in part ?)	The Weakest Goeth to the Wall	c. 1599–1600
1601	Bird; Haughton; Rowley, S.	Judas (Prob. same as Judas begun in 1600 by Haughton.)	27 May 1600– 24 Dec. 1601 (P)
	Chettle, Henry	All Is Not Gold That Glisters	31 Mar.– 6 Apr. (P)
	Chettle, Henry	The Life of Cardinal Wolsey	5 June– 18 Aug. (P)
	Chettle, Henry	The Orphans' Tragedy (Not completed ?)	10 Nov. 1599– 24 Sept. 1601 (P)
	Chettle, H.; Dekker, T.	Sebastian, King of Portugal (Poss. the basis of Believe as You List, 1631.)	1601
	Chettle; Drayton; Munday; Smith, Went.	The Rising of Cardinal Wolsey	24 Aug.– 12 Nov. (P)
	Day, J.; Haughton, W.	II The Blind Beggar of Bednal Green (II Tom Strowd)	29 Jan.– 5 May (P)
	Day, J.; Haughton, W.	III The Blind Beggar of Bednal Green (III Tom Strowd)	21 May– 30 July (P)
	Day, J.; Haughton, W.	Friar Rush and the Proud Woman of Antwerp ('Mended' by Chettle, Jan. 1602.)	4 July– 29 Nov. (P)
	Day, J.; Haughton, W.	The Six Yeomen of the West	20 May– 8 June (P)
	Day, J.; Haughton, W.	II Tom Dough (II The Six Yeomen of the West ?)	30 July– 11 Sept. (P)
	Day; Haughton; Smith, Went.	The Conquest of the West Indies	4 Apr.– 1 Sept. (P)
	Dekker, T. (with Marston, J. ?)	Satiromastix, or The Untrussing of the Humorous Poet	1601
	Dymock, John (?)	Il Pastor Fido, or The Faithful Shepherd (Trans. Guarini.)	1601 (S.R.)
	Dymock, Tailbois	The Death of the Lord of Kyme	31 Aug.

TYPE	AUSPICES	EARLIEST TEXTS	LAST ED.	DATE
Tragedy	Unknown	MS	1937 G	
Comedy (?)	Chamberlain's	Lost		
Jig (?)	Unknown	Lost		
Mask	Court's visit to Blackfriars	Lost		
Tragedy	Admiral's (?)	1657**	1961[113] (BD)	
Comedy	Paul's	1600* F	1902[79]	
Satirical Comedy	St John's Col., Cambridge	MS F	1949[117]	
'Tragical History'	Unknown	Lost		
History	'Chamberlain's'	1602 F	1908[91]	
Pseudo-history	Oxford's	1600 F	1912 G	
Biblical History	Admiral's	Lost		**1601**
Comedy (?)	Admiral's	Lost		
History	Admiral's	Lost		
Tragedy	Admiral's	Lost		
Foreign History	Admiral's	Lost		
History	Admiral's	Lost		
Comedy	Admiral's	Lost		
Comedy	Admiral's	Lost		
Comedy (?)	Admiral's	Lost		
Comedy (?)	Admiral's	Lost		
Comedy (?)	Admiral's	Lost		
History	Admiral's	Lost		
Comedy	Chamberlain's and Paul's	1602*	1953[113] (B)	
Pastoral	Closet (?)	1602		
Topical Satire	'May Pole Green', Lincoln	Lost		

G

DATE	AUTHOR	TITLE	LIMITS
	Greville, Fulke	*Antony and Cleopatra*	*c.* 1600–1601
	Hathway; Haughton; Smith, Went.	I *The Six Clothiers*	12–22 Oct. (P)
	Hathway; Haughton; Smith, Went.	II *The Six Clothiers* (Not completed?)	3/8 Nov. (P)
	Hathway, R.; Rankins, W.	*The Conquest of Spain by John of Gaunt* (Not completed.)	24 Mar.– 16 Apr. (P)
	Hathway, R.; Rankins, W.	*Hannibal and Scipio*	3–12 Jan. (P)
	Hathway, R.; Rankins, W.	*Scogan and Skelton*	23 Jan.– 8 Mar. (P)
	Haughton, William	*Robin Hood's Pennyworths* (Not completed? Or completion of *The English Fugitives*, 1600?)	20 Dec. 1600– 13 Jan. 1601 (P)
	Jonson, Ben	*Cynthia's Revels, or The Fountain of Self-Love*	1600–1601
	Jonson, Ben	*Poetaster, or The Arraignment*	1601
	Marston, John	*What You Will*	1601
	Mitchell, Francis	*Michael and Frances*	1601–1602
	Percy, William	*Arabia Sitiens, or A Dream of a Dry Year* (*Mahomet and His Heaven, or Epimethea, Grand Empress of the Deserts of Arabia, or A Dream of a Dry Summer, or The Weather-Woman*)	1601
	Percy, William	*The Cuckqueans and Cuckolds Errants, or The Bearing Down the Inn* (*Change Is No Robbery, or The Bearing Down of the Inn*)	1601
	Shakespeare, William	*Hamlet*	1599–*c.* 1601
	Wadeson, Antony	*The Humorous Earl of Gloucester, with His Conquest of Portugal* (Not completed?)	13 June– 23/25 July (P)
	Anon. (Middleton? Dekker?)	*Blurt, Master Constable, or The Spaniard's Night Walk*	1601–1602
	Anon.	*The Contention between Liberality and Prodigality* (Revival of *Prodigality*, 1567?)	22 Feb. (acted)
	Anon.	*George Scanderbarge*	1601 (S.R.)
	Anon. (Heywood? Chettle?)	*The Trial of Chivalry* (*This Gallant Cavaliero Dick Bowyer*)	1599–1603
1602	Chapman, George	*The Gentleman Usher* (*Vincentio and Margaret*)	*c.* 1602–1604
	Chapman, George	*May-Day*	1601–1609
	Chapman, George	*Sir Giles Goosecap*	1601–1603
	Chettle, Henry	*A Danish Tragedy*	7 July (P)
	Chettle, Henry	*Hoffman, or A Revenge for a Father*	29 Dec. (P)
	Chettle, Henry	*Tobias*	16 May– 27 June (P)
	Chettle; Dekker; Heywood; Smith, Went.; Webster	I *Lady Jane* (*The Overthrow of Rebels*) (Parts of I & II *Lady Jane* may be incorporated in *Sir Thomas Wyatt*, 1604.)	15–21 Oct. (P)

TYPE	AUSPICES	EARLIEST TEXTS	LAST ED.	DATE
Tragedy	Closet	Lost		
Unknown	Admiral's	Lost		
Unknown	Admiral's	Lost		
History	Admiral's	Lost		
Classical History	Admiral's	Lost		
Comedy (?)	Admiral's	Lost		
Comedy (?)	Admiral's	Lost		
Comedy	Chapel	1601 F	1932[109] (MB)	
Comedy	Chapel	1602	1934 B (M)	
Comedy	Paul's (?)	1607	1938[115]	
Jig	Strollers in Yorkshire	MS F	1936†[119]	
Tragicomedy	Privately acted (?)	MSS		
Comedy	Privately acted (?)	MSS	1824†[120]	
Tragedy	Chamberlain's	1603 F	1877 V	
History	Admiral's	Lost		
Comedy	Paul's	1602* & MS (frag.)	1885[121]	
Moral Interlude	Chapel	1602* F	1913 G (D)	
Foreign History	Oxford's	Lost		
Pseudo-history	Derby's	1605** F	1884†[100]	
Comedy	Chapel	1606*	1914[122]	**1602**
Comedy	Chapel	1611*	1914[122]	
Comedy	Chapel	1606 F	1914[122] (B)	
Tragedy	Admiral's	Lost		
Tragedy	Admiral's	1631* F	1950 (1951) G (T)	
Biblical History	Admiral's	Lost		
History	Worcester's	Lost (?)		

DATE	AUTHOR	TITLE	LIMITS
	Chettle; Dekker; Heywood; Webster	*Christmas Comes but Once a Year*	2–26 Nov. (P)
	Chettle; Hathway; Smith, Went.	*Too Good to Be True*	14 Nov. 1601– 7 Jan. 1602 (P)
	Chettle, H.; 'Mr. Robinson'	*Felmelanco*	9–15/27 Sept. (P)
	Chettle, H.; Smith, Went.	*Love Parts Friendship*	4 May (P)
	Davies, J. (& Cecil, R. ?)	*The Entertainment at Cecil House*	6 Dec.
	Davies, J. (& Lyly, J. ?)	*The Entertainment at Harefield*	31 July– 2 Aug.
	Day, John	*Bristow Tragedy* (Poss. same as *Baxter's Tragedy,* below.)	4–28 May (P)
	Day; Hathway; Smith, Went.	*As Merry as May Be*	9–17 Nov. (P)
	Dekker, Thomas	*A Medicine for a Curst Wife*	19 July– 22 Sept. (P)
	Dekker; Drayton; Middleton; Munday; Webster	*Caesar's Fall* (*Two Shapes*)	22–29 May (P)
	Dekker, T. (& others ?)	*II Lady Jane* (Not completed? Parts of *I & II Lady Jane* may be incorporated in *Sir Thomas Wyatt,* 1604.)	27 Oct.– 12 Nov.(?) (P)
	Dekker, T.; Munday, A.	*Jephthah*	5 May (P)
	Haughton, William	*William Cartwright* (Not completed ?)	8 Sept. (P)
	Heywood, T. ('additions' by)	*Cutting Dick*	1602 (revised)
	Heywood, T. (?) ('Joshua Cooke' now rejected)	*How a Man May Choose a Good Wife from a Bad*	c. 1601–1602
	Heywood, T.; Smith, Went.	*Albere Galles* (Same as *Nobody and Somebody,* 1605 ?)	4 Sept. (P)
	Heywood, T.; Smith, Went.	*Marshal Osric* (Same as following ?)	20–30 Sept. (P)
	Heywood, T. (& Smith, Went. ?)	*The Royal King and the Loyal Subject* (See play above.)	1602–1618
	Hobbes, Thomas	*Medea* (Trans. Euripides.)	1602
	Jonson, Ben	*Richard Crookback* (Not completed ?)	22 June (P)
	Lyly, John	*The Entertainment at Chiswick*	28–29 July
	Massey, Charles (?)	*Malcolm, King of Scots*	18 Apr. (P)
	Middleton, T. (& Dekker, T. ?)	*The Family of Love*	c. 1602–1607
	Middleton, Thomas	*Randall, Earl of Chester* (*Chester Tragedy*)	21 Oct.– 9 Nov. (P)
	Munday, Anthony	*The Set at Tennis* (Related to *The Fortewn Tenes,* 1600 ?)	2 Dec. (P)
	Percy, William	*The Aphrodisial, or Sea Feast*	1602

TYPE	AUSPICES	EARLIEST TEXTS	LAST ED.	DATE
Comedy (?)	Worcester's	Lost		
Comedy (?)	Admiral's	Lost		
Unknown	Admiral's	Lost		
Unknown	Admiral's	Lost		
Royal Entertainment	Host: Robert Cecil	1608/MSS (frags.)	1876[123]/ 1823[71]	
Royal Entertainment	Host: Thomas Egerton	MSS (frags.)	1902[79]	
Tragedy	Admiral's	Lost		
Comedy	Admiral's	Lost		
Comedy	Worcester's	Lost		
Tragedy	Admiral's	Lost		
History	Worcester's	Lost (?)		
Biblical History	Admiral's	Lost		
Unknown	Admiral's	Lost		
Topical Play	Worcester's	Lost		
Comedy	Worcester's	1602 F	1912 B (D)	
Pseudo-history (?)	Worcester's	Lost (?)		
Tragicomedy (?)	Worcester's	Lost (?)		
Tragicomedy	Worcester's (?) (Queen Henrietta's in 1637)	1637*	1906[124]	
Tragedy	Unacted	Lost		
History	Admiral's	Lost		
Royal Entertainment	Host: William Russell	MS	1953†[112]	
History	Admiral's	Lost		
Comedy	Admiral's (?) (King's Revels in 1607)	1608*	1885[121]	
History	Admiral's	Lost		
Unknown	Admiral's	Lost		
'Piscatory'	Essex House (?)	MSS		

DATE	AUTHOR	TITLE	LIMITS
	Percy, William	*A Country Tragedy in Vacunium, or Cupid's Sacrifice* (*A Forest Tragedy in Vacunium, or Love's Sacrifice*)	1602
	Rowley, Samuel	*Joshua*	27 Sept. (P)
	Shakespeare, William	*All's Well That Ends Well*	c. 1601–c. 1604
	Shakespeare, William	*Troilus and Cressida*	1601–1603
	Smith, W[entworth?]	*The Freeman's Honour*	c. 1600–1603
	Smith, Wentworth	*The Three* (or *Two*) *Brothers* (Poss. same as *Absalom*, below.)	1–15 Oct. (P)
	Vennar, Richard	*England's Joy*	1602
	'Antony (Wadeson? Munday?) the poet'	*The Widow's Charm* (Not completed?)	9 July– 11 Sept. (P)
	Anon.	*Absalom* (Character's name.) (Poss. same as *The Three Brothers*, above.)	3/11 Oct. (prop.)
	Anon.	*Baxter's Tragedy* (Poss. same as *Bristow Tragedy*, above.)	1602
	Anon.	*Biron* (*Berowne. Burone*)	25 Sept.– 2/3 Oct. (prop.)
	Anon.	*The Capture of Stuhlweissenburg*	13 Sept. (acted)
	Anon.	*De Humfredo Aulico Confessionem Repudiante* (See Supp. II, l.)	1602
	Anon.	*The Earl of Hertford* (Poss. not title but name of company that sold play.)	15/27 Sept. (prop.)
	Anon. (Heywood, T.?)	*The Fair Maid of the Exchange*	1594–1607
	Anon.	*II Fortune's Tennis* (See *The Fortewn Tenes*, 1600.)	1597–1603
	Anon. (poss. Dekker, T.)	*The Merry Devil of Edmonton* [Shakespeare Apocrypha]	1599–1604
	Anon.	*Philip of Spain* (An old play.)	8 Aug. (bought)
	Anon.	*A Royal Widow of England*	18 Sept. (acted)
	Anon.	*Samson*	29 July (bought)
	Anon.	*The Spanish Fig*	6 Jan. (bought)
	Anon. (poss. Rowley, S.)	*Wily Beguiled* (Revision of *Wylie Beguylie*, 1567?)	1596–1606
1603	Alexander, William	*Darius*	1603 (pub.)
	Chapman, George	*The Old Joiner of Aldgate*	Feb.
	Chettle, Henry	*II The London Florentine* (Not completed?)	12 Mar. (P)
	Chettle, H.; Day, J.	[*Jane*] *Shore* (Poss. based on *Edward IV*, 1599.)	9 May (P)
	Chettle, H.; Heywood, T.	*I The London Florentine*	18/21 Dec. 1602–7 Jan. 1603 (P)
	Day; Hathway; & another	*The Boss of Billingsgate*	1–12 Mar. (P)

TYPE	AUSPICES	EARLIEST TEXTS	LAST ED.	DATE
Tragedy	Privately acted (?)	MSS		
Biblical History	Admiral's	Lost		
Comedy	Chamberlain's	1623 F		
Tragedy	Chamberlain's	1609 F	1953 V	
Bourgeois Romance (?)	Chamberlain's	Lost		
Biblical History (?)	Worcester's	Lost		
Hoax Show	Unacted	1602* ('plot')	1931[81]	
Comedy	Admiral's	Lost		
Biblical History	Worcester's	Lost		
Tragedy	Chapel	Lost		
Unknown	Worcester's	Lost		
Foreign History	Unknown	Lost		
Latin Tragedy	St Omers	Lost		
History (?)	Admiral's	Lost		
Comedy	Unknown	1607	1962 (1963) G (T)	
Comedy (?)	Admiral's	MS ('plot' frag.) F	1931[81]	
Comedy	Chamberlain's	1608 F	1942[125] (DA)	
Foreign History	Admiral's	Lost		
History (?)	Chapel	Lost		
Biblical History	Admiral's	Lost		
Unknown	Admiral's	Lost		
Comedy	Paul's (?)	1606 F	1912 G (D)	
Tragedy	Closet	1603	1921[126]	**1603**
Comedy	Paul's	Lost		
Comedy (?)	Admiral's	Lost		
History	Worcester's	Lost		
Comedy (?)	Admiral's	Lost		
Unknown	Admiral's	Lost		

DATE	AUTHOR	TITLE	LIMITS
	Day; Hathway; Smith, Went.	*The Unfortunate General* (*The French History*)	7–19 Jan. (P)
	Day; Hathway; Smith, Went.; & 'the other poet'	*I & II The Black Dog of Newgate*	24 Nov. 1602–26 Feb. 1603 (P)
	Gwinne, Matthew	*Nero*	*c.* 1602–1603
	Hawkesworth, Walter	*Labyrinthus* (Adapt. Della Porta's *La Cintia.*)	1603–1606
	Heywood, Thomas	*The Blind Eats Many a Fly*	24 Nov. 1602–7 Jan. 1603 (P)
	Heywood, Thomas	*A Woman Killed with Kindness*	12 Feb.–6 Mar. (P)
	Jonson, Ben	*The Entertainment of the Queen and Prince at Althorp* (*The Satyr*)	25 June
	Jonson, Ben	*Sejanus His Fall*	1603
	Massey, Charles	*The Siege of Dunkirk, with Alleyn the Pirate* (Not completed?)	7 Mar. (P)
	Parkinson, —	*Speech to King James I at Berwick*	6 Apr.
	Percy, William	*The Fairy Pastoral, or Forest of Elves* (*The Fairy Chase, or A Forest of Elves*)	1603
	Savile, John (describer)	*The Entertainment at Theobalds*	3–7 May
	Shaw, Robert (?)	*The Four Sons of Aymon* (An old play?)	Feb. (?) (P)
	Singer, John	*Singer's Voluntary*	13 Jan. (P)
	Smith, Wentworth	*The Italian Tragedy*	7–12 Mar. (P)
	Anon.	*Narcissus, a Twelfth Night Merriment*	6 Jan.
	Anon. (Montgomery? Sempill?)	*Philotus*	1603 (pub.)
	Anon.	*Prince Henry's Welcome to Winchester*	20 Sept.–17 Oct.
	Anon. (Gwyn, O., in part?)	*II The Return from Parnassus, or The Scourge of Simony* (*The Progress to Parnassus*)	1601–1603
	Anon. ('T.M.', describer)	*The Welcome into England*	5 Apr.–11 May
1604	Alexander, William	*Croesus*	1604
	Bernard, Richard (?)	*The Birth of Hercules* (Adapt. Plautus's *Amphitryon.*)	1597–*c.* 1610
	Cary, Elizabeth	*Mariam, the Fair Queen of Jewry*	1602–1605
	Chapman, George	*All Fools* (See *All Fools but the Fool*, 1599.)	1599–1604
	Chapman, George	*Bussy D'Ambois* (Revised by Chapman, *c.* 1610?) (For *The Revenge of Bussy D'Ambois*, see 1610.)	1600–1604
	Chapman, George	*Monsieur D'Olive*	1604
	Daniel, Samuel	*Philotas* (Three acts written in 1600.)	1604
	Daniel, Samuel	*The Vision of the Twelve Goddesses* (*The Mask at Hampton Court*)	8 Jan.
	Day, J. (with Wilkins, G.?)	*Law Tricks, or Who Would Have Thought It*	1604–1607

TYPE	AUSPICES	EARLIEST TEXTS	LAST ED.	DATE
Foreign History	Worcester's	Lost		
Topical Play	Worcester's	Lost		
Latin Tragedy	St John's Col., Oxford	1603		
Latin Comedy	Trinity Col., Cambridge	1636* & MSS		
Comedy	Worcester's	Lost		
Tragedy	Worcester's	1607	1961[127] (MAT)	
Royal Entertainment	Host: Robert Spencer	1604	1941[109]	
Tragedy	King's	1605	1935 B (MA)	
History	Admiral's	Lost		
Royal Entertainment	Berwick, Northumberland	MS		
Pastoral	Syon House (?)	MS	1824†[120]	
Royal Entertainment	Theobalds and London	1603*	1903[35]	
Romance (?)	Admiral's (Prince's in 1624)	Lost		
Improvisation (?)	Admiral's	Lost		
Tragedy	Worcester's	Lost		
Farce	St John's Col., Oxford	MS	1893[128]	
Comedy	Closet (?)	1603	1933[129]	
Mask	Court	Lost		
Satirical Comedy	St John's Col., Cambridge	1606 F & MS	1949[117] (D)	
Royal Entertainment	Edinburgh to London	1603*	1903[35]	
Tragedy	Closet	1604	1921[126]	**1604**
Comedy	Christ's Col., Cambridge (?)	MS	1911 G	
Tragedy	Closet	1613**	1914 G†	
Comedy	Queen's Revels	1605*	1914[122] (M)	
Foreign History	Paul's	1607 or '08	1960[130] (MA)	
Comedy	Queen's Revels	1606*	1914[122]	
Tragedy	Queen's Revels	1605	1949[131]	
Mask	Court	1604	1897[56] (A)	
Comedy	King's Revels	1608*	1949 (1950) G	

DATE	AUTHOR	TITLE	LIMITS
	Dekker, T. (Zeal's speech by Middleton)	*The Magnificent Entertainment Given to King James* (Various descriptions of and verses from the entertainment appear in next item and below under Dugdale and Jonson.)	15 Mar.
	Dekker; Harrison; Webster	*Arches of Triumph*	15 Mar.
	Dekker, T., with Middleton, T.	*I The Honest Whore* (*I The Converted Courtesan*)	1604
	Dekker; Webster (& others ?)	*Sir Thomas Wyatt* (A version of *I & II Lady Jane*, 1602 ?)	1602–1607
	Dekker, T., with Webster, J.	*Westward Ho*	1604
	Dugdale, G. (describer)	*The Time Triumphant*	15 Mar.
	Heywood, Thomas	*How to Learn of a Woman to Woo* (Same as *The Wise Woman of Hogsdon*, below ?)	30 Dec. (acted)
	Heywood, Thomas	*I If You Know Not Me You Know Nobody, or The Troubles of Queen Elizabeth*	1603–1605
	Heywood, Thomas	*The Wise Woman of Hogsdon* (Same as *How to Learn of a Woman to Woo*, above ?)	c. 1604 (?)
	Jonson, Ben	*The Coronation Triumph* (Part by Jonson.)	15 Mar.
	Jonson, Ben	*The Entertainment at Highgate* (*The Penates*)	1 May
	Marston, John	*The Dutch Courtesan* (*Cockle de Moye*)	1603–1604
	Marston, J. (additions by Webster)	*The Malcontent*	1600–1604
	Middleton, Thomas	*The Phoenix*	1603–1604
	Rowley, Samuel	*When You See Me You Know Me* (*Henry VIII*)	1603–1605
	Shakespeare, William	*Measure for Measure*	c. 1603–1604
	Shakespeare, William	*Othello*	c. 1603–1604
	Verney, Francis	*Antipoe*	1603–1608
	Anon.	*Alice and Alexis*	a. 1603
	Anon.	*The Fair Maid of Bristow*	1603–1604
	Anon.	*Gowry*	Dec.
	Anon.	*Hippolytus*	13 Feb.
	Anon.	*I Jeronimo, with the Wars of Portugal*	1600–1605
	Anon.	*Lady Amity*	1600–c. 1604
	Anon. ('William Shakespeare'; Dekker ? Drayton ? or Marston ?)	*The London Prodigal* [Shakespeare Apocrypha]	1603–1605
	Anon.	*A Mask of the Knights of India and China*	1 Jan.
	Anon.	*A Mask of Scots*	6 Jan.
	Anon. (Quarles, W. ?)	*Pastor Fidus* (Trans. Guarini's *Il Pastor Fido*.)	1590–1605
	Anon. (Shakespeare, W. ?)	*Robin Goodfellow* (Revival of *A Midsummer-Night's Dream* ?)	1 Jan. (acted)
	Anon.	*The Wedding Mask for Sir Philip Herbert* (*Juno and Hymenaeus*)	27 Dec.
	Anon.	*The Wit of a Woman*	1604 (pub.)

TYPE	AUSPICES	EARLIEST TEXTS	LAST ED.	DATE
Coronation Entertainment	London	1604	1955[113]	
Coronation Entertainment	London	1604		
Comedy	Prince Henry's	1604	1955[113] (MA)	
History	Queen Anne's	1607 F	1953[113]	
Comedy	Paul's	1607* F	1955[113]	
Coronation Entertainment	Westminster	1604*	1903[35]	
Comedy	Queen Anne's	Lost (?)		
History	Queen Anne's	1605	1934 G	
Comedy	Queen Anne's	1638*	1888 M	
Coronation Entertainment	London	1604	1941[109]	
Royal Entertainment	Host: William Cornwallis	1616	1941[109]	
Comedy	Queen's Revels	1605	1938[115] (AT)	
Tragicomedy	Queen's Revels & King's	[1604]	1934[115] (A)	
Comedy	Paul's	1607	1885[121]	
History	Prince Henry's	1605 F	1952 G	
Comedy	King's	1623 F	V (in prog.)	
Tragedy	King's	1622 F	1886 V	
Tragedy	Trinity Col., Oxford (?)	MS		
Tragicomedy	Unknown	MS (frag.)		
Comedy	King's	1605* F	1902†[132]	
Tragedy	King's	Lost		
Latin (?) Tragedy	St John's Col., Oxford	Lost		
Pseudo-history	King's (?)	1605*	1901[94] (D)	
Unknown	Inner Temple	Lost		
Comedy	King's	1605 F	1908[119]	
Mask	Court	Lost		
Mask	Court	Lost		
Latin Pastoral	King's Col., Cambridge	MSS		
Comedy (?)	King's	Lost (?)		
Wedding Mask	Wedding: Herbert-Vere	Lost		
Comedy	Unacted (?)	1604* F	1913 G†	

DATE	AUTHOR	TITLE	LIMITS
1605	Burton, R.; & others	*Alba, or Vertumnus*	27 Aug.
	Chapman, George	*Caesar and Pompey (The Wars of Pompey and Caesar)*	1599–1607 (present II.i written 1610–1611)
	Chapman, George	*The Widow's Tears*	1603–1609
	Chapman; Jonson; Marston	*Eastward Ho*	1605
	Daniel, Samuel	*The Queen's Arcadia (Arcadia Reformed)*	30 Aug.
	Dekker, Thomas	*II The Honest Whore (II The Converted Courtesan)*	1604–c. 1605
	Dekker, T.; Webster, J.	*Northward Ho*	1605
	Gwinne, Matthew	*Tres Sibyllae*	29 Aug.
	Gwinne, Matthew	*Vertumnus sive Annus Recurrens*	29 Aug.
	Heywood, Thomas	*II If You Know Not Me You Know Nobody, with the Building of the Royal Exchange, and the Famous Victory of Queen Elizabeth* (Prob. same as *The Life and Death of Sir Thomas Gresham, with the Building of the Royal Exchange*, ment. in *The Knight of the Burning Pestle*, 1607.)	1605
	Jonson, Ben	*The Mask of Blackness (The Twelfth Night's Revels)*	6 Jan.
	Marston, John	*Parasitaster, or The Fawn*	1604–1606
	Marston, John	*The Wonder of Women, or Sophonisba*	1605–1606
	Middleton, Thomas	*A Trick to Catch the Old One*	1604–1607
	Middleton, Thomas	*Your Five Gallants (The Five Witty Gallants)*	1604–1607
	Munday, Anthony	*The Triumphs of Reunited Britannia*	29 Oct.
	Shakespeare, William	*King Lear*	1605–1606
	Anon.	*Ajax Flagellifer*	28 Aug.
	Anon.	*'Locus, Corpus, Motus'*, etc.	c. 1604–c. 1605
	Anon.	*Lucretia*	11 Feb.
	Anon.	*Nobody and Somebody* (A play of c. 1592 revised? *Albere Galles*, 1602, revised?)	1603–1606
	Anon.	*Richard Whittington*	1605 (S.R.)
	Anon.	*The Spanish Maze*	11 Feb. (acted)
1606	Beaumont, Francis (?)	*Madon, King of Britain* (S.R., 1660.)	c. 1605–1616
	Beaumont, F., with Fletcher, J.	*The Woman Hater (The Hungry Courtier)*	1606
	Burton, Robert	*Philosophaster* (Revised 1615, acted 16 Feb. 1618.)	1606
	Day, John	*The Isle of Gulls*	1606
	Dekker, Thomas	*The Whore of Babylon* (Revision of *Truth's Supplication to Candlelight*, 1600?)	c. 1606–1607

TYPE	AUSPICES	EARLIEST TEXTS	LAST ED.	DATE
Latin (?) Pastoral	Christ Church, Oxford	Lost		**1605**
Classical History	Unacted (?)	1631**	1910[101]	
Comedy	Queen's Revels (?)	1612*	1914[122]	
Comedy	Queen's Revels	1605 F	1939[115] (A)	
Pastoral	Christ Church, Oxford	1606	1885[133]	
Comedy	Prince Henry's	1630*	1955[113] (MA)	
Comedy	Paul's	1607* F	1955[113]	
Latin Royal Enter-tainment	St John's Col., Oxford	1607*		
Latin Play	St John's men at Christ Church, Oxford	1607*		
History	Queen Anne's	1606	1934 G	
Mask	Court	[c. 1608] & MS	1941[109]	
Comedy	Queen's Revels	1606	1938[115]	
Tragedy	Queen's Revels	1606	1938[115]	
Comedy	Paul's	1608	1915[134] (MA)	
Comedy	Paul's (?) (Queen's Revels in 1608)	[c. 1608]*	1885[121] (T)	
Civic Pageant	London	[1605]*	1931[135]	
Tragedy	King's	1608 F	1880 V	
Latin Tragedy	Magdalen men at Christ Church, Oxford	Lost		
Moral (English)	Trinity Col., Cambridge	MS (frag.)		
Latin (?) Tragedy	St John's Col., Oxford	Lost		
Pseudo-history	Queen's (Anne's ?)	[c. 1606]* F	1931[110]	
Pseudo-history	Prince Henry's	Lost		
Tragedy	King's	Lost		
Pseudo-history	Unknown	Lost		**1606**
Comedy	Paul's	1607	1910[136]	
Latin Comedy	Christ Church, Oxford	MSS	1931 (text & trans.)[137]	
Comedy	Queen's Revels	1606 F	1881†[138]	
Allegorical History	Prince Henry's	1607*	1955[113] (T)	

DATE	AUTHOR	TITLE	LIMITS
	Heywood, Thomas (?)	*The Bold Beauchamps*	*c.* 1600–1607
	Jonson, Ben	*The Entertainment of the Two Kings of Great Britain and Denmark* (*The Hours*)	24 July
	Jonson, Ben	*Hymenaei*	5 Jan.
	Jonson, Ben	*Volpone, or The Fox*	1605–1606
	Marston, John	*City Pageant*	31 July
	Middleton, Thomas	*A Mad World, My Masters*	1604–1607
	Middleton, Thomas	*Michaelmas Term*	1604–1606
	Middleton, Thomas	*The Viper and Her Brood*	1606
	Roberts, Henry (describer)	*England's Farewell to the King of Denmark*	16 July–11 Aug.
	Roberts, Henry (describer)	*The Honourable Entertainment of the King of Denmark*	16–31 July
	Shakespeare, William	*Macbeth*	1606–1611
	Sharpham, Edward	*The Fleer*	1606
	Wilkins, George	*The Miseries of Enforced Marriage*	1605–1606
	Anon.	*Abuses*	30 July (acted)
	Anon.	*The King of Denmark's Welcome*	18 July
	Anon. (by 'W.S.'; Middleton, T. ?)	*The Puritan, or The Widow of Watling Street* [Shakespeare Apocrypha]	1606
	Anon. (Tourneur? Middleton ?)	*The Revenger's Tragedy*	1606–1607
	Anon.	*Solomon and the Queen of Sheba*	24–28 July
	Anon. ('W. Shakespeare'; Wilkins ?)	*A Yorkshire Tragedy* (*All's One, or One of the Four Plays in One*) [Shakespeare Apocrypha]	1605–1608
	Anon. (Rollinson, F. ?)	*Zelotypus*	1606
1607	Alexander, William	*The Alexandraean Tragedy*	1605–1607
	Alexander, William	*Julius Caesar*	1607
	Barnes, Barnabe	*The Battle of Hexham*	*c.* 1607–1609
	Barnes, Barnabe	*The Devil's Charter, or Pope Alexander VI*	2 Feb.
	Beaumont, F. (with Fletcher, J. ?)	*The Knight of the Burning Pestle*	1607–*c.* 1610
	Campion, Thomas	*The Mask at Lord Hay's Marriage*	6 Jan.
	Day; Rowley, W.; Wilkins	*The Travels of the Three English Brothers*	1607
	Heywood, Thomas	*The Rape of Lucrece*	1606–1608
	Jonson, Ben	*The Entertainment at Merchant Taylors* (Songs, and speech by Angel of Gladness.)	16 July
	Jonson, Ben	*The Entertainment at Theobalds* (*The Genius*)	22 May
	Machin, Lewis (?)	*Every Woman in Her Humour*	1603–1608
	Marston, John	*The Entertainment at Ashby* (*Cynthia and Ariadne*)	Aug.
	Mason, John	*The Turk* (*Mulleasses the Turk*)	1607–1608

TYPE	AUSPICES	EARLIEST TEXTS	LAST ED.	DATE
History (?)	Unknown	Lost		
Royal Entertainment	Theobalds	1616	1941[109]	
Mask and Barriers	Court	1606	1941[109]	
Comedy	King's	1607	1962[138a] (MBA)	
Royal Entertainment	London	MS	1887†[139]	
Comedy	Paul's	1608	1885[121] (T)	
Comedy	Paul's	1607	1915[134] (AT)	
Tragedy	Queen's Revels	Lost		
Royal Entertainment	London	1606*	1828[140]	
Royal Entertainment	London	1606* & MS (?)	1828[140]	
Tragedy	King's	1623 F	1903 V	
Comedy	Queen's Revels	1607	1912 B†	
Domestic Drama	King's	1607 F	1874 D	
Comedy and Tragedy	Paul's	Lost		
Royal Entertainment	Theobalds and London	1606*	1828 (extracts)[140]	
Comedy	Paul's	1607 F	1908[119]	
Tragedy	King's	1607 or '08*	1958[141] (DMA)	
Show (for King of Denmark)	Theobalds	Lost		
Tragedy	King's	1608 F	1910[91] (A)	
Latin Comedy	St John's Col., Cambridge	MSS		

Tragedy	Closet	1607	1921[126]	**1607**
Tragedy	Closet	1607	1921[126]	
History	Unknown	MS (lost?)		
Tragedy	King's	1607** F	1904 B	
Burlesque Romance	Queen's Revels (?)	1613	1958[142] (MA)	
Wedding Mask	Court	1607*	1924[143]	
Topical Play	Queen Anne's	1607**	1881†[138]	
Tragedy	Queen Anne's	1608	1950[144] (M)	
Royal Entertainment	Merchant Taylors	Lost		
Royal Entertainment	Host: Salisbury	1616	1941[109]	
Comedy	King's Revels (?)	1609* F	1885†[100] (T)	
Mask and Speeches	At Lord Huntington's	MSS	1887[139]	
Tragedy	King's Revels	1610	1913 B†	

DATE	AUTHOR	TITLE	LIMITS
	Sansbury, J.; & others	*The Christmas Prince* (Included following; see also 1608.)	Xmas, 1607–1608
	Anon.	*Ara Fortunae*	30 Nov.
	Anon.	*Philomela, or Tereus and Progne*	29 Dec.
	Vertue, Owen (?)	*Saturnalia*	25 Dec.
	Shakespeare, William	*Antony and Cleopatra*	*c.* 1606–1608
	Shakespeare, William	*Timon of Athens*	*c.* 1606–*c.* 1608
	Sharpham, Edward	*Cupid's Whirligig*	1607
	Tomkis, Thomas	*Lingua, or The Combat of the Tongue and the Five Senses for Superiority*	1602–1607
	Anon.	*Aeneas and Dido* (An earlier play revived ?)	25 May (acted)
	Anon.	*Claudius Tiberius Nero*	1607 (pub.)
	Anon.	*The Jesuits' Comedy*	Oct.
1608	Armin, Robert	*The Two Maids of More-Clacke*	1607–1608
	Barry, Lording	*Ram Ally, or Merry Tricks*	1607–1608
	Chapman, George	*The Conspiracy and Tragedy of Charles Duke of Byron*	1608
	Day, John	*Humour out of Breath*	1607–1608
	Dekker, T.; Middleton, T.	*The Roaring Girl, or Moll Cutpurse*	1604–1610
	Fletcher, John	*The Faithful Shepherdess*	1608–1609
	Fletcher, J., with Beaumont, F.	*Cupid's Revenge*	*c.* 1607–1612
	Jonson, Ben	*The Mask at Lord Haddington's Marriage* (*The Hue and Cry after Cupid*)	9 Feb.
	Jonson, Ben	*The Mask of Beauty*	10 Jan.
	Markham, G.; Machin, L.	*The Dumb Knight*	1607–1608
	Rowley, William	*A Shoemaker a Gentleman*	1607–1609
	Rowley, W. (& another ?; 'William Shakespeare and William Rowley' on t.p.)	*The Birth of Merlin, or The Child Hath Found His Father* (Based on *Uther Pendragon*, 1597 ?) (Date *c.* 1620 also proposed.) [Shakespeare Apocrypha]	1597–1621
	Sansbury, J.; & others	*The Christmas Prince* (Included following; see also 1607.)	Xmas, 1607–1608
	Anon.	*The Creation of White Knights*	1608
	Anon.	*The Embassage from Lubber-Land*	1608
	Anon.	*Ira Fortunae*	9 Feb.
	Anon.	*Penelope's Wooers*	1608
	Sansbury, John	*Periander*	13 Feb.
	Anon.	*Philomathes*	15 Jan.
	Anon.	*The Seven Days of the Week*	10 Jan.
	Sansbury, J. (?); Alder, J. (?)	*Somnium Fundatoris*	10 Jan.
	Anon.	*Time's Complaint*	1 Jan.
	Sansbury, John (?)	*The Triumph of All the Founders in Oxford*	1608

TYPE	AUSPICES	EARLIEST TEXTS	LAST ED.	DATE
Dramatic Festival	St John's Col., Oxford	MS	1922 G†	
Latin Mock Coronation				
Latin Tragedy				
Latin Interlude				
Tragedy	King's	1623 F	1907 V	
Tragedy	Unacted (?)	1623 F		
Comedy	King's Revels	1607	1926†[145]	
Academic Moral	Trinity Col., Cambridge	1607 F	1874 D	
Tragedy	Earl of Arundel's Banquet	Lost (?)		
Tragedy	Closet (?)	1607* F	1914 G†	
Anti-Protestant Allegory	Jesuit Col., Lyons	Lost		
Comedy	King's Revels	1609* F	1880†[146]	**1608**
Comedy	King's Revels	1611 F	1952 B (D)	
Tragedy	Queen's Revels	1608	1910[101] (M)	
Comedy	King's Revels	1608*	1888 M	
Comedy	Prince Henry's	1611* F	1958[113] (M)	
Pastoral	Queen's Revels (?)	[c. 1609]	1908 V (MAT)	
Tragedy	Queen's Revels	1615	1906[136] (T)	
Wedding Mask	Court	[c. 1608]	1941[109] (A)	
Mask	Court	[c. 1608]	1941[109]	
Comedy	King's Revels	1608	1875 D	
Comedy	Queen Anne's (?)	1638*	1910†[147]	
Romance	Unknown	1662* F	1908[119]	
Dramatic Festival	St John's Col., Oxford	MS	1922 G†	
Show (intended)		(omitted)		
Show (intended)		(omitted)		
Latin Mock Dethrone- ment				
Mask (intended)		(omitted)		
Tragedy				
Latin Comedy				
Comedy				
Latin Allegory		(omitted)		
Moral				
Show (intended)		(omitted)		

H

DATE	AUTHOR	TITLE	LIMITS
	Anon.	*Yuletide*	21 Jan.
	Shakespeare, William	*Coriolanus*	1605–*c.* 1610
	Shakespeare, W. (reviser? collaborator? Wilkins, G., now rejected)	*Pericles*	1606–1608
	Anon. (Marston, J.?)	*The Silver Mine* (Subject; title assigned.)	Feb.-Mar.
	Anon.	*Torrismount*	*c.* 1607–1608
1609	Beaumont, F., with Fletcher, J.	*Philaster, or Love Lies a-Bleeding*	1608–1610
	Fletcher, with Beaumont (revised by Massinger or Rowley, W.?)	*The Coxcomb*	1608–1610
	Fletcher, J. (with Middleton? Rowley, W.?)	*Wit at Several Weapons* (Recently assigned almost entirely to Middleton and Rowley.)	*c.* 1609–1620
	Field, Nathan	*A Woman Is a Weathercock*	1609–1610
	Heywood, T.; Rowley, W.	*Fortune by Land and Sea*	*c.* 1607–1609
	Jonson, Ben	*Epicoene, or The Silent Woman*	1609
	Jonson, Ben	*The Mask of Queens*	2 Feb.
	Munday, Anthony	*Campbell, or The Ironmongers' Fair Field*	30 Oct.
	Shakespeare, William	*Cymbeline*	*c.* 1608–1611
	Tourneur, Cyril	*The Atheist's Tragedy, or The Honest Man's Revenge*	1607–1611
	Wren, Christopher, Sr	*Physiponomachia*	*c.* 1609–1611
	Anon.	*Bonos Nochios*	1609 (S.R.)
	Anon.	*St Christopher*	1609 (acted)
1610	Amerie, R.; Davies, R.	*Chester's Triumph*	23 Apr.
	Beaumont, F., with Fletcher, J.	*The Maid's Tragedy*	*c.* 1608–1611
	Chapman, George	*The Revenge of Bussy D'Ambois*	*c.* 1601–1612
	Daborne, Robert	*A Christian Turned Turk* (*The Two Famous Pirates*)	1609–1612
	Daniel, Samuel	*Tethys' Festival, or The Queen's Wake*	5 June
	Heywood, Thomas	*I The Fair Maid of the West, or A Girl Worth Gold*	1597–1610
	Heywood, Thomas	*The Golden Age, or The Lives of Jupiter and Saturn*	1609–1611
	Jonson, Ben	*The Alchemist*	1610
	Jonson, Ben	*Prince Henry's Barriers* (*The Lady of the Lake*)	6 Jan.
	Marston, J.; Barkstead, W.	*The Insatiate Countess*	*c.* 1610–1613
	Munday, Anthony	*London's Love to Prince Henry*	31 May
	Price, Daniel (describer)	*The Creation of Prince Henry*	4 June
	Shakespeare, William	*The Winter's Tale*	*c.* 1610–1611
	Anon.	*Belinus, Brennus* (One play or two?)	1610 (listed)

TYPE	AUSPICES	EARLIEST TEXTS	LAST ED.	DATE
Burlesque of *Christmas Prince*	Christ Church, Oxford	Lost		
Tragedy	King's	1623 F	1928 V	
Tragicomedy	King's	1609 F		
Comedy	Queen's Revels	Lost		
Tragedy (?)	King's Revels	Lost		
Tragicomedy	King's	1620	1905[136] (MVA)	**1609**
Comedy	Queen's Revels	1647	1910[136]	
Comedy	Unknown	1647	1910[136]	
Comedy	Queen's Revels	1612*	1950[148] (DM)	
Comedy	Queen Anne's	1655*	1874†[114] (T)	
Comedy	Queen's Revels	1616 (earliest extant)	1937[109] (MA)	
Mask	Court	1609 & MS	1941[109]	
Civic Pageant	London	[1609]* (frag.)		
Tragicomedy	King's	1623 F	1913 V	
Tragedy	King's (?)	1611 or '12*	[1929][149] (M)	
Latin Comedy	St John's Col., Oxford	MS		
'Interlude'	Unknown	Lost		
Neo-miracle (?)	Strollers in Yorkshire	Lost		
St George's Day Show	Chester	1610*	1844[150]	**1610**
Tragedy	King's	1619	1932[151] (MVA)	
Tragedy	Queen's Revels	1613*	1910[101] (MA)	
Tragedy	King's (?) Queen's Revels (?)	1612*	1898–99†[152]	
Mask	Court	1610*	1885[133]	
Comedy	Anne's (?) (Queen Henrietta's in 1631)	1631*	[1917][153] (M)	
Classical Legend	Queen Anne's	1611*	1874[114]	
Comedy	King's	1612 F	1950 B (MA)	
Speeches at Barriers	Court	1616	1941[109]	
Tragedy	Queen's Revels	1613	1939[115]	
Royal Entertainment	London	1610*	1828†[140]	
Tilt and Pageant	Court	1610*	1828[140]	
Tragicomedy	King's	1623 F	1898 V	
Legendary History	Unknown	Lost		

DATE	AUTHOR	TITLE	LIMITS
1611	Beaumont, F.; Fletcher, J.	*A King and No King*	1611
	Chapman, George (?)	*The Twelve Months*	1608–1612
	Cooke, John	*Greene's Tu Quoque, or The City Gallant*	1611
	Dekker, Thomas	*Match Me in London*	*c.* 1611–*c.* 1613
	Dekker, T. (with Daborne, R. ?)	*If It Be Not Good, the Devil Is in It* (*If This Be Not a Good Play, the Devil Is in It*)	1611–1612
	Field, Nathan	*Amends for Ladies*	*c.* 1610–1611
	Fletcher, John	*The Night Walker, or The Little Thief* (Revised by Shirley and lic. 11 May 1633.)	*c.* 1611 (?)
	Fletcher, John	*The Woman's Prize, or The Tamer Tamed*	1604–*c.* 1617
	Heywood, Thomas	*The Brazen Age* (Revision of *I Hercules*, 1595 ?)	1610–1613
	Heywood, Thomas	*The Silver Age* (Revision of *II Hercules*, 1595 ?)	1610–1612
	Jonson, Ben	*Catiline His Conspiracy*	1611
	Jonson, Ben	*Love Freed from Ignorance and Folly*	3 Feb.
	Jonson, Ben	*Oberon, the Fairy Prince*	1 Jan.
	Jordan, William (?)	*The Creation of the World, with Noah's Flood* (In Cornish; adapt. *Origo Mundi*, 14th cent.)	1611
	Middleton, Thomas	*A Chaste Maid in Cheapside*	1611–1613
	Munday, Anthony	*Chryso-Thriambos*	29 Oct.
	Shakespeare, William	*The Tempest*	*c.* 1609–1611
	Anon.	*The Almanac*	29 Dec. (acted)
	Anon.	*Richard II* (An older play revived ?)	30 Apr. (acted)
	Anon. (Middleton, T. ?)	*The Second Maiden's Tragedy*	lic. 31 Oct.
	Anon.	*The Ship* (Misprint for *The Slip* ?)	1611 (ment.)
1612	'R.A.' (Armin, R. ? Anton, R. ?)	*The Valiant Welshman* (*Caradoc the Great*)	1610–1615
	Dekker, Thomas	*Troia Nova Triumphans*	29 Oct.
	Fletcher, J. (with Beaumont, F. ?)	*The Captain*	1609–1612
	Fletcher, J. (with Beaumont ? or Field ?)	*Four Plays, or Moral Representations, in One* (Induction, by Beaumont or Field; *The Triumph of Honour*, by Beaumont or Field; *The Triumph of Love*, by Beaumont or Field; *The Triumph of Time* and *The Triumph of Death*, by Fletcher.)	*c.* 1608–1613
	Heywood, Thomas	*I The Iron Age*	1612–1613
	Heywood, Thomas	*II The Iron Age*	1612–1613
	Jonson, Ben	*Love Restored*	6 Jan.
	Niccolls, [Richard ?]	*The Twins' Tragedy*	1 Jan. (acted)
	Parsons, Philip	*Atalanta*	1612
	Rowley, William	*Hymen's Holiday, or Cupid's Vagaries* (Revised 1633; by J. Shirley ?)	24 Feb. (acted)

TYPE	AUSPICES	EARLIEST TEXTS	LAST ED.	DATE
Tragicomedy	King's	1619	1905[136] (MVA)	**1611**
Mask	Court (?)	MS (lost?)	1848†[154]	
Comedy	Queen Anne's	1614 F	1875 D	
Tragicomedy	Queen Anne's (?)	1631*	1958[113]	
Comedy	Queen Anne's	1612*	1958[113]	
Comedy	Queen's Revels (?)	1618	1950[148] (DM)	
Comedy	Lady Elizabeth's (?)	1640	1909[136]	
Comedy	Unknown (King's in 1633)	1647 & MS	1910[136] (T)	
Classical Legend	Queen's (and King's?)	1613*	1874†[114]	
Classical Legend	Queen's and King's	1613*	1874[114]	
Tragedy	King's	1611	1937[109]	
Mask	Court	1616	1941[109]	
Mask	Court	1616	1941[109] (A)	
Cornish Mystery	Cornwall	MSS	1863[155]	
Comedy	Lady Elizabeth's	1630*	1887[121] (MAT)	
Civic Pageant	London	1611	1844† (extracts)[156]	
Comedy	King's	1623 F	1892 V	
Comedy (?)	Prince Henry's	Lost		
History	King's	Lost		
Tragedy	King's	MS	1909 G (DT)	
Jig (?)	Prince Henry's	Lost		
History	Prince's Men	1615 F	1902†[157]	**1612**
Civic Pageant	London	1612*	1958[113]	
Comedy	King's	1647	1907[136]	
Moral	Unknown	1647	1912[136]	
Classical Legend	Queen's (and King's?)	1632**	1874†[114]	
Classical Legend	Queen's (and King's?)	1632*	1874†[114]	
Mask	Court	1616	1941[109]	
Tragedy	King's	Lost		
Latin Pastoral	St John's Col., Oxford	MS		
Comedy (?)	Prince's (later Queen Henrietta's)	Lost		

DATE	AUTHOR	TITLE	LIMITS
	Tourneur, Cyril	*The Nobleman* (Identified with following, S.R., 1653.)	23 Feb. (acted)
	Tourneur, Cyril (?)	*The Great Man* (See preceding; separately listed by Warburton.)	1612(?)
	Webster, John	*The White Devil* (*Vittoria Corombona*)	1609–1612
	Anon. (Ford, J. ?)	*A Bad Beginning Makes a Good Ending* (Prob. same as *An Ill Beginning Has a Good End*, assigned to Ford in S.R., 1660.)	1612–1613 (acted)
	Anon.	*Boot and Spur*	1611–1620(?)
	Anon.	*Cancer* (Adapt. Salviati's *Il Granchio*.)	1611–1613
	Anon.	*Captiva Religio*	1612–1613
	Anon.	'Garlic' (Prob. player rather than title.)	1612 (1st ment.)
	Anon.	*The Knot of Fools*	1612–1613 (acted)
	Anon.	'*Microcosmus*'	1612(?)
	Anon.	*The Proud Maid's Tragedy*	25 Feb. (acted)
	Anon.	*Roffensis* (With 'Intermedium' of Sensus, Fronto, Somnium, etc. [frag.].)	1612–1613
	Anon.	*Thomas Morus* (With 'Intermedium' of Mercurius.)	1612
1613	Beaumont, Francis	*The Mask of the Inner Temple and Gray's Inn*	20 Feb.
	Brooke, Samuel	*Adelphe* (Adapt. Terence.)	27 Feb.
	Brooke, Samuel	*Scyros* (Trans. Bonarelli's *Filli di Sciro*.)	3 Mar.
	Campion, Thomas	*The Entertainment at Cawsome*	27–28 Apr.
	Campion, Thomas	*The Lords' Mask*	14 Feb.
	Campion, Thomas	*The Mask at the Earl of Somerset's Marriage* (*The Mask of Squires*)	26 Dec.
	Chapman, George	*The Mask of the Middle Temple and Lincoln's Inn*	15 Feb.
	Chapman, George (?)	*A Yorkshire Gentlewoman and Her Son* (S.R., 1660, and Warburton.)	c. 1595–c. 1613
	Daborne, Robert	*Machiavel and the Devil*	1613
	Daborne, R.; Tourneur, C.	*The Arraignment of London* (Prob. same as *The Bellman of London*, listed by Henslowe.)	1613
	Ferebe, George	*The Shepherd's Song*	11 June
	Fletcher, John	*Bonduca*	1611–1614
	Fletcher, J., with Beaumont, F.	*The Scornful Lady*	1613–1616
	Fletcher (with Field ? Massinger ? Tourneur ?)	*The Honest Man's Fortune* (Re-lic. 8 Feb. 1624.)	1613
	Jonson, Ben	*A Challenge at Tilt*	27 Dec. 1613, 1 Jan. 1614
	Jonson, Ben	*The Irish Mask*	29 Dec.
	Jonson, Ben	*The May Lord* (Poss. non-dramatic.)	1613–1619
	Middleton, Thomas	*The New River Entertainment* (*The Running Stream Entertainment*)	29 Sept.

TYPE	AUSPICES	EARLIEST TEXTS	LAST ED.	DATE
'Tragicomedy'	King's	Lost		
'Tragedy'	King's (?)	Lost		
Tragedy	Queen Anne's	1612	1960[158] (MA)	
Comedy	King's	Lost		
Entertainment	Unknown	MS		
Latin Comedy	Trinity Col., Cambridge	1648* & MS		
Latin Tragicomedy	English Col., Rome	MSS		
Jig	Prince Henry's	Lost		
Comedy (?)	King's	Lost		
Latin Moral	Cambridge (?)	MS		
Tragedy	Lady Elizabeth's	Lost		
Latin Tragedy	English Col., Rome	MS		
Latin Tragedy	English Col., Rome	MS		
Mask	Court	[c. 1613]	1912[130]	**1613**
Latin Comedy	Trinity Col., Cambridge	MSS		
Latin Pastoral	Trinity Col., Cambridge	MSS		
Royal Entertainment	Host: Lord Knolles	1613* (descrip.)	1909[159]	
Wedding Mask	Court	1613*	1909[159]	
Wedding Mask	Court	1614* (descrip.)	1909[159]	
Mask	Court	[c. 1613]	1914[122]	
Tragedy	Unknown	Lost		
Tragedy	Lady Elizabeth's	Lost		
Comedy (?)	Lady Elizabeth's	Lost		
Royal Entertainment (Pastoral)	In Wiltshire	Lost		
Tragedy	King's	1647 & MS	1951 G (M)	
Comedy	Queen's Revels (?)	1616	1905[136] (V)	
Tragicomedy	Lady Elizabeth's	1647 & MS	1952[160]	
Tilt	Court	1616	1941[109]	
Mask	Court	1616	1941[109]	
Comic Pastoral	Unknown	Lost		
Civic Entertainment	London	1613*	1886[121]	

DATE	AUTHOR	TITLE	LIMITS
	Middleton, Thomas	*No Wit, No Help Like a Woman's* (Revised 1638; by J. Shirley?)	*c.* 1613–1627
	Middleton, Thomas	*The Triumphs of Truth*	29 Oct.
	Naile, Robert (describer?)	*The Entertainment at Bristol*	June
	Rowley, William	*The Fool without Book* (S.R., 1653. Related to *I* or *II Knaves*, below?)	*c.* 1607–1626
	Rowley, William	*A Knave in Print, or One for Another* (S.R., 1653. Related to *I* or *II Knaves*, below? Alternative title may be independent play.)	*c.* 1607–1626
	Shakespeare, W. (& Fletcher, J.?)	*Henry VIII* (*All Is True*)	June
	Shakespeare; Fletcher (& Beaumont?)	*The Two Noble Kinsmen* [Shakespeare Apocrypha]	1613–1616
	'Shakespeare, William'	*Duke Humphrey* (S.R., 1660, and Warburton.)	*c.* 1591–1616(?)
	'Shakespeare, William'	*Iphis and Iantha, or A Marriage without a Man* (S.R., 1660.)	*c.* 1591–1616(?)
	'Shakespeare, William'	*King Stephen* (S.R., 1660.)	*c.* 1591–1616(?)
	'Shakespeare; Fletcher'	*Cardenio* (or *Cardenno*, S.R., 1653. Poss. the basis of Theobald's *Double Falsehood, or The Distressed Lovers*, 1728.)	1612–1613 (acted)
	Stephens, John	*Cynthia's Revenge, or Maenander's Ecstasy*	1613 (pub.)
	Tailor, Robert	*The Hog Hath Lost His Pearl*	21 Feb.
	Taylor, John (describer)	*Heaven's Blessing and Earth's Joy*	11, 13 Feb.
	Anon.	*Gigantomachia, or Work for Jupiter*	*c.* 1600–1620(?)
	Anon.	*Heteroclitanomalonomia*	1613
	Anon.	*I The Knaves* (Related to *The Fool without Book* or *A Knave in Print*, above?)	2 Mar. (acted)
	Anon.	*II The Knaves* (Related to *The Fool without Book* or *A Knave in Print*, above?)	10 Mar. (acted)
	Anon. (describer)	*The Marriage of Frederick and Elizabeth*	11–15 Feb.
	Anon.	*Raymond, Duke of Lyons*	1 Mar. (acted)
	Anon.	*S. Thomas Cantuariis* (With 'Intermedium' of Minutum.)	1613
	Anon.	*The Sycophant*	1613
	Anon.	*The Triumph of the Cross*	1613
1614	Daborne, Robert	*The Owl*	1614
	Daborne, Robert	*The She Saint*	1614
	Daniel, Samuel	*Hymen's Triumph*	2 Feb.
	Fletcher, John	*Valentinian*	1610–1614
	Fletcher, J. (revised by another?)	*Wit without Money* (Prob. revised in 1620.)	1614–1620
	Jonson, Ben	*Bartholomew Fair*	31 Oct.
	Middleton, Thomas	*The Mask of Cupid*	4 Jan.
	Munday, Anthony	*Himatia-Poleos*	29 Oct.
	Smith, W[entworth?]	*The Hector of Germany, or The Palsgrave, Prime Elector*	*c.* 1614–1615
	Webster, John	*The Duchess of Malfi* (Revised 1617–1623?)	1612–1614

TYPE	AUSPICES	EARLIEST TEXTS	LAST ED.	DATE
Comedy	Lady Elizabeth's (?)	1657*	1885[121]	
Civic Pageant	London	1613**	1886[121]	
Royal Entertainment	Bristol	1613*	1828[140]	
Comedy (?)	Unknown	Lost		
Comedy (?)	Unknown	Lost		
History	King's	1623 F		
Tragicomedy	King's	1634	1910[136] (V in prog.) (AT)	
Tragedy	Unknown	Lost		
Comedy	Unknown	Lost		
History	Unknown	Lost		
Tragicomedy (?)	King's	Lost		
Tragedy	Closet	1613*		
Comedy	Apprentices at Whitefriars	1614*	1875 D	
Royal Entertainment	Westminster and London	1613	1828†[140]	
Academic Entertainment	Cambridge (?)	MS		
Academic Moral	Cambridge (?)	MS		
Comedy	Prince's Men	Lost		
Comedy	Prince's Men	Lost		
Pageants, etc.	Court	1613 & MS	1828[140]	
Foreign History	Lady Elizabeth's	Lost		
Latin Tragedy	English Col., Rome	MS		
Latin Comedy	Trinity Col., Cambridge	Lost		
Tragedy	St Omers	Lost		
Comedy	Lady Elizabeth's	Lost		**1614**
Unknown	Lady Elizabeth's	Lost		
Pastoral	Court (company unknown)	1615 & MS	1885†[133]	
Tragedy	King's	1647	1912 V (M)	
Comedy	Lady Elizabeth's (?)	1639	1906[136] (V)	
Comedy	Lady Elizabeth's	1631	1960[161] (MA)	
Mask	Merchant Taylors Hall	Lost		
Civic Pageant	London	1614*		
Pseudo-history	Tradesmen at Bull & Curtain	1615*	1906†[162]	
Tragedy	King's	1623	1959[163] (MA)	

DATE	AUTHOR	TITLE	LIMITS
	Anon.	*Cupid's Festival*	1614–1622
	Anon. ('Francis Beaumont and John Fletcher' in S.R.; Daborne? Massinger? Field?)	*The Faithful Friends*	1613–c. 1621
	Anon.	*Magister Bonus sive Arsenius*	14 Oct.
	Anon. (dedication signed 'I.G., W.D., T.B.')	*The Mask of Flowers*	6 Jan.
	Anon.	*The Noble Grandchild*	1614
1615	'Francis Beaumont and John Fletcher'	*A Right Woman* (S.R., 1660. Given as alternative title for *Women Beware Women*, S.R., 1653.)	c. 1608–1625
	Brooke, Samuel	*Melanthe*	10 Mar.
	Browne, William	*Ulysses and Circe (Circe and Ulysses)*	13 Jan.
	Cecil, T[homas?]	*Aemilia*	7 Mar.
	Fletcher, John	*Monsieur Thomas (Father's Own Son)*	1610–c. 1616
	Fletcher, Phineas	*Sicelides*	13 Mar.
	Jonson, Ben	*The Golden Age Restored*	6 Jan.
	Kynder, Philip	*Silvia*	1615–1616
	Middleton, Thomas	*More Dissemblers Besides Women* (Re-lic. 17 Oct. 1623.)	c. 1615(?)
	Middleton, Thomas	*The Witch*	c. 1609–c. 1616
	Munday, Anthony	*Metropolis Coronata*	30 Oct.
	Ruggle, George	*Ignoramus*	1615
	'S.S.'	*The Honest Lawyer*	c. 1614–1615
	Tomkis, Thomas	*Albumazar* (Adapt. Della Porta's *L'Astrologo*.)	9 Mar.
	Webster, John	*The Guise*	1614–1623
	Anon.	*Band, Cuff, and Ruff, or Exchange Ware at the Second Hand* (See also 1646.)	1615 (pub.)
	Anon.	*Romeus et Julietta*	1615
	Anon.	*Work for Cutlers (Sword, Rapier, and Dagger)*	1614–1615
1616	Chappell, John (?)	*Susenbrotus, or Fortunia*	12 Mar.
	Cruso, Aquila	*Euribates Pseudomagus*	1610–c. 1616
	Fletcher, J. (with Beaumont, F.?)	*Love's Pilgrimage* (Passages from Jonson's *New Inn*, 1629, incorporated in I. i.)	1616(?) (revised 1635)
	Fletcher (revised by Middleton or another?)	*The Nice Valour, or The Passionate Madman*	c. 1615–1625
	Jonson, Ben	*Christmas His Mask (Christmas His Show)*	Xmas
	Jonson, Ben	*The Devil Is an Ass*	Oct.-Nov.(?)
	Jonson, Ben	*Mercury Vindicated from the Alchemists at Court*	1 Jan.
	May, Thomas	*Julius Caesar*	c. 1613–c. 1630
	Middleton, Thomas	*Civitatis Amor*	4 Nov.
	Middleton (with 'Ben Jonson. John Fletcher'?)	*The Widow*	c. 1615–1617

TYPE	AUSPICES	EARLIEST TEXTS	LAST ED.	DATE
Comedy	Unknown	Lost		
Tragicomedy	Unknown	MS	1812†[164]	
Latin Tragedy	St Omers	MS		
Mask	Gray's Inn at Court	1614*	1897[56]	
Unknown	Unknown	Lost		
Comedy	Unknown	Lost (?)		**1615**
Latin Pastoral	Trinity Col., Cambridge	1615* & MS	1928†[165]	
Mask	Inner Temple	MSS	1954[166]	
Latin Comedy	St John's Col., Cambridge	Lost		
Comedy	Lady Elizabeth's (?)	1639	1912 V	
'Piscatory'	King's Col., Cambridge	1631* & MSS	1908[167]	
Mask	Court	1616	1941[109]	
Latin Pastoral	Pembroke Col., Camb. (acted?)	Lost		
Comedy	King's	1657*	1885[121]	
Tragicomedy	King's	MS	1948 (1950) G (MB)	
Civic Pageant	London	1615*	1828†[140]	
Latin Comedy	Clare Hall, Cambridge	1630 & MSS	1787[168]	
Comedy	Queen Anne's	1616* F		
Comedy	Trinity Col., Cambridge	1615	1944[169] (D)	
Tragedy (?)	Unknown	Lost		
Comic Dialogue	Trinity Col., Cambridge	1615 & MSS	1872[170]	
Latin Tragedy	Unacted	MS (frag.)		
Comic Dialogue	Trinity Col. (?), Cambridge	1615*	1904[171]	
Latin Comedy	Trinity Col., Cambridge	MSS		**1616**
Latin Play	Caius Col., Cambridge	MS		
Tragicomedy	King's	1647	1908[136]	
Comedy	Unknown	1647	1912[136]	
Christmas Show	Court	1641 & MSS	1941[109]	
Comedy	King's	1631	1938[109]	
Mask	Court	1616	1941[109]	
Latin Tragedy	Sidney Sussex Col., Camb. (?)	MS (lost)		
Civic Pageant	London	1616*	1886[121]	
Comedy	King's	1652*	1890 M	

DATE	AUTHOR	TITLE	LIMITS
	Munday, Anthony	*Chrysanaleia: The Golden Fishing, or Honour of Fishmongers*	29 Oct.
1617	Bernard, Samuel	*Julius et Gonzaga*	23 Jan.
	Brewer, Anthony	*The Lovesick King* (Revived 1680 as *The Perjured Nun.*)	1607–1617(?)
	Daborne, Robert	*The Poor Man's Comfort*	1610–1617
	Fletcher, John	*The Mad Lover*	5 Jan. (acted)
	Fletcher (& Massinger? Field?)	*The Queen of Corinth*	1616–c. 1618
	Fletcher; Field; Massinger	*The Jeweller of Amsterdam, or The Hague*	1616–1619
	Fletcher; Massinger (& Beaumont?)	*Thierry and Theodoret*	1607–1621
	Goffe, Thomas	*Orestes*	c. 1613–c. 1618
	Heylin, Peter	*Spurius*	8 Mar.
	Jonson, Ben	*Lovers Made Men* (*The Mask at Lord Hay's*) (Called *The Mask of Lethe* by Gifford.)	22 Feb.
	Jonson, Ben	*The Vision of Delight*	6 Jan.
	Middleton, Thomas	*The Triumphs of Honour and Industry*	29 Oct.
	Middleton, T.; Rowley, W.	*A Fair Quarrel*	c. 1615–1617
	Webster, John	*The Devil's Law Case* (*When Women Go to Law the Devil Is Full of Business*) (1610 recently urged.)	1610–1619
	White, Robert	*Cupid's Banishment*	4 May
	Anon.	*Marquis d'Ancre* [subject]	22 June (ordered suppressed)
	Anon.	*The Mask at the Middle Temple*	17 Jan.
	Anon.	*Pathomachia, or The Battle of Affections* (*Love's Loadstone*)	c. 1616–c. 1617(?)
	Anon.	*Stonyhurst Pageants*	1610–1625
	Anon.	*The Younger Brother*	3 Oct. (acted)
1618	Atkinson, Thomas	*Homo*	1615–1621
	Belchier, Daubridgcourt	*Hans Beer-Pot* (*See Me and See Me Not*)	1618 (pub.)
	Bernard, Samuel	*Andronicus Commenus* (*Alexius Imperator*)	26 Jan.
	Fletcher, John	*The Loyal Subject*	lic. 16 Nov. (revised 1633?)
	Fletcher; Field; Massinger	*The Knight of Malta*	1616–1619
	Goffe, Thomas	*The Courageous Turk, or Amurath I* (Same as *The Tragedy of Amurath*, MS dated 1618.)	21 Sept.
	Goffe, Thomas	*The Raging Turk, or Bajazet II*	c. 1613–c. 1618
	Heylin, Peter	*Theomachia*	1618
	Holiday, Barten	*Technogamia, or The Marriages of the Arts*	13 Feb.
	Jonson, Ben	*For the Honour of Wales* (Revision of *Pleasure Reconciled to Virtue*, below.)	17 Feb.

TYPE	AUSPICES	EARLIEST TEXTS	LAST ED.	DATE
Civic Pageant	London	1616*	1869[172]	
Latin Tragedy	Magdalen Col., Oxford	Lost		**1617**
Tragedy	Unknown (acted in Newcastle?)	1655* (1680 ed. a ghost?)	1907 B	
Pastoral Comedy	Queen Anne's	1655* & MS	1954 (1955) G (T)	
Tragicomedy	King's	1647	1908 V	
Tragicomedy	King's	1647	1908[136]	
Tragedy	King's	Lost		
Tragedy	King's	1621	1912[136] (M)	
Tragedy	Christ Church, Oxford	1633	(T)	
Latin Tragedy	Magdalen Col., Oxford	Lost		
Mask	House of Lord Hay	1617	1941[109]	
Mask	Court	1641	1941[109]	
Civic Pageant	London	1617*	1886[121]	
Tragicomedy	Prince's	1617	1915[134] (MA)	
Tragicomedy	Queen Anne's	1623*	1927[173]	
Mask	Ladies' Hall, Deptford	MS (lost?)	1828†[140]	
Topical Play	Unknown	Lost		
Mask	Middle Temple	Lost		
Moral	Trinity Col., Cambridge (acted?)	1630* & MSS	1942†[174]	
Old Testament Cycle	Closet (?)	MS	1920†[175]	
Comedy (?)	Prince's (?)	Lost		
Latin Tragedy	St John's Col., Oxford	MS		**1618**
Dialogue	Unacted (?)	1618*		
Latin Tragedy	Magdalen Col., Oxford	MS		
Tragicomedy	King's	1647	1908 V	
Tragicomedy	King's	1647	1909[136] (T)	
Tragedy	Christ Church, Oxford	1632 & MS		
Tragedy	Christ Church, Oxford	1631		
Latin Comedy	Unacted	Lost		
Moral	Christ Church, Oxford	1618 F	1942†[175a]	
Anti-mask	Court	1641	1941[109]	

DATE	AUTHOR	TITLE	LIMITS
	Jonson, Ben	*Pleasure Reconciled to Virtue* (See preceding.)	6 Jan.
	Middleton, T. (& Rowley, W.?)	*Hengist, King of Kent, or The Mayor of Queenborough* (See *Hengist*, 1599 add. Following fictitious [?] titles are mentioned in this play: *The Carwidgeon*; *The Cheater and the Clown*; *Gull upon Gull*; *The Whibble*; *The Whirligig*; *The Wild Goose Chase*; *Woodcock of Our Side*.)	1615–1620(?)
	Middleton; Rowley, W.; Massinger	*The Old Law, or A New Way to Please You* (Traditional date 1599 now rejected.)	*c.* 1615–1618
	Munday, Anthony	*Siderothriambos, or Steel and Iron Triumphing*	29 Oct.
	Shirley, H. (& Heywood, T.?)	*The Martyred Soldier*	b. 1627
	Anon.	*Antoninis Bassianus Caracalla*	1617–1619
	Anon.	*Christ's Passion*	1613–1622
	Anon.	*The Entertainment at Brougham Castle*	Aug.
	Anon. (Campion, T.?)	*The First Anti-Mask of Mountebanks* (*The Mask at Gray's Inn*)	2 and 19 Feb.
	Anon.	*The Marriage of a Farmer's Son* (Same as *Tom of Bedlam*, below?)	1617–1618
	Anon.	*The Mask of Amazons, or The Ladies' Mask*	1 Jan. (projected)
	Anon. (Jonson, B.?)	*A Mask Presented at Coleoverton*	2 Feb.(?)
	Anon.	*The Part of Poor* (Title assigned.)	1617–1619
	Anon.	*Stoicus Vapulans*	1618–1619
	Anon.	*Swetnam the Woman-Hater Arraigned by Women*	1615–1619
	Anon.	*Tom of Bedlam* (Same as *The Marriage of a Farmer's Son*, above?)	9 Jan.
1619	Bernard, Samuel	*Phocas*	27 Jan.
	'I.C.' (Cumber, John?)	*The Two Merry Milkmaids, or The Best Words Wear the Garland*	1619–1620
	Carleton, Thomas	*Fatum Vortigerni*	22 Aug.
	Drury, William	*Aluredus sive Alfredus*	1619
	Drury, William	*Mors Comoedia*	1619(?)
	Drury, William	*Reparatus sive Depositum*	1619(?)
	Field, N.; Massinger, P.	*The Fatal Dowry*	1616–1619
	Fletcher, John	*The Humorous Lieutenant* (*Generous Enemies. Demetrius and Enanthe. The Noble Enemy*)	1619(?)
	Fletcher (with Massinger?; Jonson?; & another?)	*The Bloody Brother* (*Rollo, Duke of Normandy*) (Revised, 1627–1630, by Massinger?)	1616–1624
	Fletcher, J.; Massinger, P.	*The Little French Lawyer*	1619–1623
	Fletcher, J.; Massinger, P.	*Sir John van Olden Barnavelt*	Aug.
	Goffe, Thomas	*Phoenissae* [subject]	*c.* 1613–1629

TYPE	AUSPICES	EARLIEST TEXTS	LAST ED.	DATE
Mask	Court	1641 & MS	1941[109]	
Tragedy	Unknown (King's in 1641)	1661** & MSS	1938[176] (M)	
Comedy	Unknown	1656*	1885[121]	
Civic Pageant	London	1618*		
Tragedy	Queen Anne's (?)	1638*	1882†[100]	
Latin Tragedy	Christ Church, Oxford	MSS		
Neo-miracle	Ely House	Lost		
Entertainment	Brougham Castle	Lost		
Christmas Entertainment	Gray's Inn	MSS	1887[139]	
Mask	Court	Lost		
Mask	Court	Lost		
Mask	Colcoverton	MS	1902[177]	
Moral	Christ Church, Oxford	MS (actor's part)		
Latin Moral	St John's Col., Cambridge	1648*		
Comedy	Queen Anne's	1620* F	1880†[178]	
Comic Show	Court	Lost		
Latin Tragedy	Magdalen Col., Oxford	Lost		**1619**
Comedy	Red Bull Company (Revels)	1620 F		
Latin Tragedy	English Col., Douai	MS		
Latin Tragicomedy	English Col., Douai	1620		
Latin Farce	English Col., Douai	1620		
Latin Tragicomedy	English Col., Douai	1628		
Tragedy	King's	1632*	1918[179] (M)	
Tragicomedy	King's	1647 & MS	1950 (1951) G (V)	
Tragedy	King's (?)	1639	1948[180]	
Comedy	King's	1647	1912 V	
Tragedy	King's	MS	1922[181]	
Tragedy	Christ Church, Oxford (?)	Lost		

DATE	AUTHOR	TITLE	LIMITS
	Goffe, Thomas (?)	*The Careless Shepherdess*	1618–1629 (revised *c.* 1638)
	Fletcher, J. (revised by another?)	*The Laws of Candy* (Recently assigned entirely to John Ford.)	1619–1623
	Middleton, Thomas	*The Inner-Temple Mask, or Mask of Heroes*	6 Jan.–2 Feb.
	Middleton, Thomas	*The Triumphs of Love and Antiquity*	29 Oct.
	Rowley, William	*All's Lost by Lust*	*c.* 1619–1620(?)
	Stub, Edmund	*Fraus Honesta* (*Callidamus et Callanthia*)	10 Feb.
	Anon.	*'A Christmas Messe'*	Xmas
	Anon.	*Fool's Fortune*	*c.* 1619–1622
	Anon.	*A Mask of Warriors*	21 Apr.
	Anon.	*Perkin Warbeck* [subject]	1619 (ment.)
	Anon.	*Two Wise Men and All the Rest Fools*	1619 (pub.)
		(Below are titles from fragments of Revels Office documents, prob. 1610–1622.)	
	Anon.	*The Bridegr[oom]* (Same as *The Bridegroom and the Madman* in King's list, 1641?)	*c.* 1610–1622
	Anon.	*The City*	*c.* 1610–1622
	Anon.	*The False Friend* (Same as *The False One,* 1620?)	*c.* 1610–1622
	Anon.	*Henry the Una . . .*	*c.* 1610–1622
	Anon.	*The House is Haunte[d]*	*c.* 1610–1622
	Anon.	*Look to the Lady* (Same as play by 'J. Shirley', with ident. title, in S.R., 1640?)	*c.* 1610–1622
	Anon.	*The Scholar Turned to School Again*	*c.* 1610–1622
	Anon.	*Titus and Vespasian* (Same as 1592 play?)	*c.* 1610–1622
	Anon.	*A Turk's Too Good for* [*Him?*]	*c.* 1610–1622
1620	Carleton, Thomas	*Emma Angliae Regina*	8 Sept.
	Davenport, R.; Drue, T.	*The Woman's Mistaken* (S.R., 1653.)	*c.* 1620–*c.* 1624
	Day, J.; Dekker, T.	*Guy of Warwick* (Revision of *Guy of Warwick,* 1593?)	1620 (S.R.)
	Dekker, T.; Massinger, P.	*The Virgin Martyr*	lic. 6 Oct.
	Fletcher, John	*Women Pleased* (An earlier play revised?)	1619–1623
	Fletcher, J.; Massinger, P.	*The Custom of the Country*	1619–1623
	Fletcher, J.; Massinger, P.	*The Double Marriage*	1619–1623
	Fletcher, J.; Massinger, P.	*The False One*	1619–1623
	Heylin, Peter	*Doublet, Breeches, and Shirt*	Jan.
	Jonson, Ben	*The Entertainment at Blackfriars* (*The Newcastle Entertainment*)	May(?)
	Jonson, Ben	*News from the New World Discovered in the Moon*	7 Jan.
	Jonson, Ben	*Pan's Anniversary, or The Shepherds' Holiday*	19 June(?)
	Massinger, Philip	*Antonio and Vallia* (S.R., 1660. Based on *Antony and Vallia,* 1599 add.?)	*c.* 1613–1640
	Massinger, Philip	*Philenzo and Hypollita* (Based on *Philipo and Hippolito,* 1594?)	*c.* 1613–1640

TYPE	AUSPICES	EARLIEST TEXTS	LAST ED.	DATE
Pastoral	Christ Church, Oxford (?) (Queen Henrietta's in c. 1638)	1656*		
Tragicomedy	King's	1647	1908 V	
Mask	Inner Temple	1619*	1886[121]	
Civic Pageant	London	1619*	1886[121]	
Tragedy	Prince's (later Lady Elizabeth's)	1633*	1910[147]	
Latin Comedy	Trinity Col., Cambridge	1632* & MSS		
Entertainment	Cambridge (?)	MS		
Jig	Amateurs of Shropshire	MS	1936†[119]	
Mask	Merchant Taylors Hall	Lost		
History	Unknown	Lost		
Dialogues	Privately acted (?)	1619* F	1889†[182]	
Unknown	King's (?)	Lost		
Unknown	Unknown Company at Court	Lost		
Unknown	Unknown Company at Court	Lost		
History (?)	Unknown Company at Court	Lost		
Unknown	Unknown Company at Court	Lost		
Comedy (?)	Unknown Company at Court	Lost		
Comedy (?)	King's (?)	Lost		
Classical or British History	Unknown Company at Court	Lost		
Tragedy	Unknown Company at Court	Lost		
Latin Tragedy	English Col., Douai	Lost		**1620**
Comedy (?)	Unknown	Lost		
Tragedy (?)	Unknown	Lost		
Tragedy	Red Bull Company (Revels)	1622	1958[113] (M)	
Tragicomedy	King's	1647	1909[136]	
Comedy	King's	1647	1905[136] (V)	
Tragedy	King's	1647	1908[136]	
Classical History	King's	1647	1912 V	
Christmas Show	Magdalen Col., Oxford	Lost		
Entertainment	Newcastle House, Blackfriars	MS	1941[109]	
Mask	Court	1641	1941[109]	
Mask	Court	1641	1941[109]	
Comedy	Unknown	Lost		
Tragicomedy	Red Bull Company (Revels) (?)	Lost		

I

DATE	AUTHOR	TITLE	LIMITS
	May, Thomas	*The Heir* (Orig. perf. at a college?)	1620 (acted)
	Middleton, T.; Row-ley, W.	*The World Tossed at Tennis*	1620 (pub.)
	Squire, John	*Tes Irenes Trophoea, or The Triumphs of Peace*	30 Oct.
	Anon.	*The Costly Whore*	*c.* 1619–1632
	Anon.	*Risus Anglicanus*	1614–1625
	Anon.	'Running' (or *Travelling*) *Mask* (Not a title but a type, also presented Xmas, 1627–1628.)	Feb.
	Anon.	*Sophomorus* (See Halliwell, *Dict.*, p. 233.)	1620(?)
1621	Dekker; Ford; Row-ley, W.	*The Witch of Edmonton*	1621
	Fletcher, John	*The Island Princess*	1619–1621
	Fletcher, John	*The Pilgrim*	1621(?)
	Fletcher, John	*The Wild Goose Chase*	1621(?)
	Garnett, Jasper	*The Tenants' Complaint against the Landlords* (Title assigned.)	1621
	Jonson, Ben	*The Gypsies Metamorphosed* (*The Metamorphosed Gypsies*)	3, 5 Aug.; Sept.
	Massinger, Philip	*The Duke of Milan*	1621–1623
	Massinger, Philip	*The Maid of Honour*	*c.* 1621–1632
	Massinger, Philip	*A New Way to Pay Old Debts*	1621–1625
	Massinger, Philip	*The Woman's Plot*	5 Nov. (acted)
	Middleton, T. (& Webster, J.?)	*Anything for a Quiet Life*	*c.* 1620–*c.* 1621
	Middleton, Thomas	*Honourable Entertainments* (A collection of ten brief entertainments: *The Entertainment at Bunhill on the Shooting Day* [*The Archer*], *The Entertainment at Sir Francis Jones's at Christmas* [*The Triumph of Temperance*], *The Entertainment at Sir Francis Jones's at Easter* [*The Seasons*], *The Entertainment at Sir Francis Jones's Welcome* [*Comus the Great Sir of Feasts*], *The Entertainment at Sir William Cokayne's in Easter Week* [*The Cock*], *The Entertainment at Sir William Cokayne's upon Simon and Jude's Day* [*The Year's Funeral*], *The Entertainment at the Conduit Head* [*The Water Nymph*], *The Entertainment for the General Training* [*Pallas*], *The Entertainment of the Lords of the Council by Sheriff Allen* [*Flora's Welcome*], *The Entertainment of the Lords of the Council by Sheriff Ducie* [*Flora's Servants*].)	1620–1621

TYPE	AUSPICES	EARLIEST TEXTS	LAST ED.	DATE
Comedy	Red Bull Company (Revels)	1622	1875 D	
Mask	Prince's Men	1620*	1886[121]	
Civic Pageant	London	1620*	1828†[140]	
Pseudo-history	Red Bull Company (Revels) (?) King's Revels (?)	1633*	1885†[100]	
Latin Anti-Catholic Comedy	Cambridge (?)	MS		
Mask	Court	Lost		
Latin Comedy	Cambridge (?)	Lost (?)		
Tragicomedy	Prince's Men	1658*	1958[113] (MAT)	**1621**
Tragicomedy	King's	1647	1910[136] (A)	
Comedy	King's	1647	1907[136]	
Comedy	King's	1652	1906[136] (MA)	
Topical Play	Kendal Castle, Westmorland	Lost		
Mask	Burley, Belvoir, and Windsor	1640 & MSS	1952[183]	
Tragedy	King's	1623	1918[184] (M)	
Tragicomedy	Red Bull Company (?) (later Queen Henrietta's)	1632**	1931[185] (MA)	
Comedy	Red Bull Company (?) (later Queen Henrietta's)	1633*	1949[186] (MA)	
Comedy	King's	Lost		
Comedy	King's	1662*	1927[173]	
Entertainments	London	1621*	1953 G†	

DATE	AUTHOR	TITLE	LIMITS
	Middleton, Thomas	*Women Beware Women* (*A Right Woman*, given as alternative title in S.R., 1653, prob. sep. piece; see 1615.)	*c.* 1620–1627
	Middleton, T. (& Munday, A. ?)	*The Sun in Aries*	29 Oct.
	Anon.	*Gramercy Wit*	30 Dec. (acted)
	Anon.	*The Man in the Moon Drinks Claret*	27 Dec. (acted)
	Anon.	*A Mask of the Middle Temple*	13 Feb.
	Anon.	*The Woman Is Too Hard for Him* (Same as *The Woman's Prize*, 1611, or *The Wild Goose Chase*, above ?)	26 Nov. (acted)
1622	Chapman, George	*Chabot, Admiral of France* (Revised by J. Shirley, 1635.)	1611–1622(?)
	Fletcher, J. (with Massinger, P. ?)	*Beggars' Bush* (Prob. same as *Beggars* of King's list, 1641.)	*c.* 1615–1622
	Fletcher, J.; Massinger, P.	*The Prophetess*	lic. 14 May
	Fletcher, J.; Massinger, P.	*The Sea Voyage*	lic. 22 June
	Fletcher, J.; Massinger, P.	*The Spanish Curate*	lic. 24 Oct.
	Jonson, Ben	*The Mask of Augurs*	6 Jan.
	Markham, G.; Sampson, W.	*Herod and Antipater*	*c.* 1619–1622
	Mease, Peter	*Adrastus Parentans sive Vindicta*	1619–1626
	Middleton, Thomas	*An Invention for the Service of Edward Barkham*	1622
	Middleton, Thomas	*The Triumphs of Honour and Virtue*	29 Oct.
	Middleton, T.; Rowley, W.	*The Changeling*	lic. 7 May
	Rowley, W. (& Middleton, T. ?)	*A Match at Midnight*	1621–1623
	Anon.	*Ambitio Infelix sive Absalom*	28 Nov.
	Anon.	*The Black Lady*	lic. 10 May
	Anon.	*The Dutch Painter, and the French Branke* (i.e. *Brawle? Branle?*)	lic. 10 June
	Anon. (Carlell, L. ?)	*Osmond, the Great Turk* (Same as *Osmond, the Great Turk*, 1637 ?)	lic. 6 Sept.
	Anon.	*The Two Noble Ladies and the Converted Conjurer*	1619–1623
	Anon.	*The Valiant Scholar*	lic. 3 June
	Anon.	*The Welsh Traveller*	lic. 10 May
1623	Bonen, William	*The Cra[fty ?] Merchant, or Come to My Country House*	lic. 12 Sept.
	Bonen, William	*Two Kings in a Cottage*	lic. 19 Nov.
	Brewer, Thomas	*A Knot of Fools*	1623 (S.R.)

TYPE	AUSPICES	EARLIEST TEXTS	LAST ED.	DATE
Tragedy	King's (?)	1657*	1890 M (AT)	
Civic Pageant	London	1621*	1886[121]	
Comedy (?)	Red Bull Company (Revels)	Lost		
Comedy	Prince's Men	Lost		
Mask	Court	Lost		
Comedy (?)	King's	Lost (?)		
Tragedy	Lady Elizabeth's (?)	1639*	1910[101]	**1622**
Comedy	King's	1647 & MS	1906[136] (VAT)	
Tragicomedy	King's	1647	1907[136]	
Comedy	King's	1647	1910[136]	
Comedy	King's	1647	1906[136] (MV)	
Mask	Court	[1622]	1941[109]	
Tragedy	Red Bull Company (Revels)	1622*		
Latin Tragedy	Jesus Col. (?), Cambridge	MS		
Dinner Entertainment	London	MS	1885†[121]	
Civic Pageant	London	1622*	1886[121]	
Tragedy	Lady Elizabeth's	1653**	1958[187] (MAT)	
Comedy	Red Bull Company (Revels) (?)	1633*	1875 D	
Latin Tragedy	St Omers	MS		
Comedy (?)	Lady Elizabeth's	Lost		
Unknown	Prince's	Lost		
Tragedy (?)	King's	Lost (?)		
Tragicomedy	Red Bull Company (Revels)	MS	1930 G†	
Comedy (?)	Lady Elizabeth's	Lost		
Unknown	Red Bull Company (Revels)	Lost		
Comedy	Lady Elizabeth's	Lost		**1623**
Tragedy	Palsgrave's Men	Lost		
Semi-dramatic Dialogue	Unknown	1624		

DATE	AUTHOR	TITLE	LIMITS
	Brome, R.; Jonson, 'Young'	*A Fault in Friendship*	lic. 2 Oct.
	Carleton, Thomas	*Henrico 8⁰*	10 Oct.
	Davenport, Robert	*The Fatal Brothers* (S.R., 1660.)	*c.* 1623–1636
	Davenport, Robert	*The Politic Queen, or Murder Will Out* (S.R., 1660.)	*c.* 1623–1636
	Day, J.; Dekker, T.	*The Bellman of Paris*	lic. 30 July
	Day, J. (& Dekker, T. ?)	*Come See a Wonder* (Same as *The Wonder of a Kingdom*, 1631 ?)	lic. 18 Sept.
	Dekker, T. (& Ford, J. ?)	*The Welsh Ambassador, or A Comedy in Disguises* (Reworking of *The Noble Spanish Soldier*, 1626 ? Related to *Connan, Prince of Cornwall*, 1598 ?)	*c.* 1623(?)
	Dering, Edward (?)	*Henry IV* (Adapt. Shakespeare's *Henry IV*, I & II.)	1613–*c.* 1624
	Fletcher, John	*The Devil of Dowgate, or Usury Put to Use*	lic. 17 Oct.
	Fletcher, J. (& Massinger, P. ?)	*The Wandering Lovers* (*The Lovers' Progress. Cleander*)	lic. 6 Dec. (revised, 1634, by Massinger)
	Fletcher, J.; Rowley, W.	*The Maid in the Mill*	lic. 29 Aug. (revised 1 Nov.)
	Gunnell, Richard	*The Hungarian Lion*	lic. 4 Dec.
	Hacket, John	*Loyola* (Revision, by E. Stub, of play written *c.* 1616 ?)	28 Feb. (acted)
	Jonson, Ben	*Time Vindicated to Himself and to His Honours*	19 Jan.
	Massinger, Philip	*The Bondman* (*The Noble Bondman*)	lic. 3 Dec.
	Maynard, John	*The Mask at York House* (Revived 5 Aug. 1624 ?)	18 Nov.
	Middleton, Thomas	*The Puritan Maid, Modest Wife, and Wanton Widow* (S.R., 1653, and Warburton.)	*c.* 1601–1627
	Middleton, Thomas	*The Triumphs of Integrity*	29 Oct.
	Middleton; Rowley, W. (Ford sometimes urged as part-author)	*The Spanish Gypsy*	lic. 9 July
	Rowley, Samuel	*Hard Shift for Husbands, or Bilboe's the Best Blade*	lic. 29 Oct.
	Rowley, Samuel	*Richard III, or The English Profit* [*Prophet* ?]	lic. 27 July
	Rowley, William	*The Four Honourable Loves* (S.R., 1660, and Warburton.)	*c.* 1607–1626
	Rowley, William	*The Nonesuch* (S.R., 1660, and Warburton.)	*c.* 1607–1626
	Shirley, Henry	*The Duke of Guise* (S.R., 1653.)	b. 1627
	Shirley, Henry	*The Dumb Bawd* (S.R., 1653. Prob. same as *The Dumb Bawd of Venice*, 1628.)	b. 1627
	Shirley, Henry	*Giraldo, the Constant Lover* (S.R., 1653.)	b. 1627
	'Henry Shirley' (Ford, J., also suggested)	*The Spanish Duke of Lerma* (S.R., 1653.)	b. 1627
	Simons, Joseph	*Vitus sive Christiana Fortitudo*	13 May

TYPE	AUSPICES	EARLIEST TEXTS	LAST ED.	DATE
Comedy	Prince's	Lost		
Latin Play	English Col., Douai	Lost		
Tragedy	King's (?)	Lost		
Tragedy	King's (?)	Lost (? see 1690)		
Tragedy	Prince's	Lost		
Comedy	'Strangers' at Red Bull	Lost (?)		
Pseudo-history	Lady Elizabeth's (?)	MS	1961[113] (G)	
History	Amateurs at Surrenden	MS	1845†[188]	
Comedy (?)	King's	Lost		
Tragicomedy	King's	1647	1907[136]	
Comedy	King's	1647	1909[136]	
Foreign History (?)	Palsgrave's	Lost		
Latin Comedy	Trinity Col., Cambridge	1648* & MSS		
Mask	Court	[1623] F	1941[109]	
Tragicomedy	Lady Elizabeth's	1624	1932[189]	
Mask	Court	Lost		
Comedy (?)	Unknown	Lost		
Civic Pageant	London	1623*	1886[121]	
Tragicomedy	Lady Elizabeth's	1653	1914[190] (MT)	
Comedy	Palsgrave's	Lost		
History	Palsgrave's	Lost		
Comedy	Unknown	Lost		
Comedy	Unknown	Lost		
Foreign History (?)	Unknown	Lost		
Comedy (?)	King's (acted at Court 15 Apr. 1628) (?)	Lost		
Unknown	Unknown	Lost		
Foreign History	King's (listed as theirs, 1641)	Lost (? see 1668)		
Latin Tragedy	St Omers	1656		

DATE	AUTHOR	TITLE	LIMITS
	Simons, Joseph (?)	*King Robert of Sicily* [subject]	19 June
	Smith, —	*The Fair Foul One, or The Baiting of the Jealous Knight*	lic. 28 Nov.
	'Will. Smithe'	*St George for England* (Warburton.)	b. 1642
	Ward, Robert (?)	*Fucus sive Histriomastix* (*Fucus Histriomastix*)	1622–1623
	Anon.	*The Buck Is a Thief*	28 Dec. (acted)
	Anon. ('P. Claretus')	*Innocentia Purpurata seu Rosa Candida et Rubicunda* (*Henry VI*)	26 Oct.(?)
	Anon.	*The Peaceable King, or The Lord Mendall* (An old play re-licensed.)	lic. 19 Aug.
	Anon.	*The Plantation of Virginia*	lic. Aug.
	Anon.	*S. Pelagius Martyr*	27 July
	Anon.	*A Vow and a Good One*	6 Jan. (acted)
1624	Barnes, —	*The Madcap*	lic. 3 May
	Davenport, Robert	*The City Nightcap, or Crede Quod Habes et Habes*	lic. 14 Oct.
	Davenport, R. ('Shakespeare, & Davenport', S.R., 1653, & Warburton)	*Henry I*	lic. 10 Apr.
	Davenport, R. ('Shakespeare, & Davenport', S.R., 1653)	*Henry II*	1624(?)
	Dekker, Thomas	*Joconda and Astols[f?]o* (S.R., 1660.)	b. 1632
	Dekker, T.; Ford, J.	*The Bristow Merchant* (Same as *The London Merchant*, below?)	lic. 22 Oct.
	Dekker, T.; Ford, J.	*The Fairy Knight*	lic. 11 June
	Dekker, T.; Ford, J.	*The Sun's Darling*	lic. 3 Mar. (revised 1638–1639)
	Dekker; Ford; Rowley, W.; Webster	*The Late Murder in White Chapel, or Keep the Widow Waking* (*The Late Murder of the Son upon the Mother*)	lic. Sept.
	Drue, Thomas	*The Duchess of Suffolk*	lic. 2 Jan.
	Fletcher, John	*Rule a Wife and Have a Wife*	lic. 19 Oct.
	Fletcher, John	*A Wife for a Month*	lic. 27 May
	Ford, J. (& Dekker, T.?)	*The London Merchant* (S.R., 1660, and Warburton. Same as *The Bristow Merchant*, above?)	1624(?)
	Gunnell, Richard	*The Way to Content All Women, or How a Man May Please His Wife*	lic. 17 Apr.
	Heywood, Thomas	*The Captives, or The Lost Recovered*	lic. 3 Sept.
	Jonson, Ben	*The Mask of Owls*	19 Aug.
	Jonson, Ben	*Neptune's Triumph for the Return of Albion*	6 Jan. (projected)
	Massinger, Philip	*The Renegado, or The Gentleman of Venice*	lic. 17 Apr.
	Massinger, P. (& Rowley, W.?)	*The Parliament of Love*	lic. 3 Nov.

TYPE	AUSPICES	EARLIEST TEXTS	LAST ED.	DATE
Latin Tragedy	St Omers	Lost		
Comedy (?)	'Strangers' at Red Bull	Lost		
Heroical Romance (?)	Unknown	Lost		
Latin Comedy	Queen's Col., Cambridge	MSS	1909†[191]	
Comedy (?)	King's	Lost		
Latin Tragedy	St Omers	MS		
Unknown	Prince's	Lost		
Tragedy	Unknown	Lost		
Latin Tragedy	St Omers	MS		
Unknown	Prince's	Lost		
Comedy (?)	Prince's	Lost		**1624**
Comedy	Lady Elizabeth's	1661*	1890[192] (D)	
History	King's	Lost		
History	King's (?)	Lost (? see 1692)		
Comedy	Unknown	Lost		
Comedy (?)	Palsgrave's	Lost		
Mask (?)	Prince's (?)	Lost		
Moral Mask	Lady Elizabeth's	1656**	1961[113]	
Comedy and Tragedy	Prince's (?)	Lost		
History	Palsgrave's	1631*		
Comedy	King's	1640	1914[190] (VA)	
Tragicomedy	King's	1647	1907[136]	
Comedy	Palsgrave's (?)	Lost		
Comedy	Palsgrave's	Lost		
Tragicomedy	Lady Elizabeth's	MS	1953 G	
Entertainment	Court	1641	1941[109]	
Mask	Court	[1624]	1941[109]	
Tragicomedy	Lady Elizabeth's	1630*	1871[193] (T)	
Comedy	Lady Elizabeth's	MS (frag.)	1928 G	

DATE	AUTHOR	TITLE	LIMITS
	Maynard, John	*The Mask at Burley* (Revival of *The Mask at York House*, 1623 ?)	5 Aug.
	Middleton, Thomas	*A Game at Chess*	lic. 12 June
	Rowley, Samuel (?) (or William ?)	*A Match or No Match*	lic. 6 Apr.
	Shank, John	*Shank's Ordinary*	lic. 16 Mar.
	Simons, Joseph	*Mercia seu Pietas Coronata*	7 Feb.
	Simons, Joseph	*Theoctistus sive Constans in Aula Virtus*	8 Aug.
	Webster, John	*Monuments of Honour*	29 Oct.
	Webster, J. (& Heywood, T. ?)	*Appius and Virginia*	c. 1608–1634(?)
	Anon.	*The Angel King*	lic. 15 Oct.
	Anon.	*The Fair Star of Antwerp*	lic. 15 Sept.
	Anon.	*Honour in the End*	lic. 21 May
	Anon. (Gunnell, R. ?)	*The Mask* (Same as 'Govell's' *Mask* ?; see Supp. II, g.)	lic. 3 Nov.
	Anon.	*Nero* (Date ? Text quoted in *The Little French Lawyer*, 1619.)	1624 (pub.)
	Anon.	*The Parricide*	lic. 27 May
	Anon.	*The Spanish Contract*	1624 (acted)
	Anon.	*The Spanish Viceroy*	c. Dec. (acted)
	Anon.	*The Whore in Grain*	lic. 26 Jan.
1625	Beaumont, John	*The Theatre of Apollo*	1625
	Davenport, Robert	*A New Trick to Cheat the Devil*	c. 1624–1639
	Fisher, Jasper	*Fuimus Troes* (*The True Trojans*)	c. 1611–1633
	Fletcher, John	*The Chances*	1613–1625
	Fletcher, J. (revised by Massinger ?)	*The Elder Brother*	1625(?)
	Heywood, Thomas	*The English Traveller*	1621–1633
	Jonson, Ben	*The Fortunate Isles and Their Union* (Revision of *Neptune's Triumph*, 1624. Same as *Virtue and Beauty Reconciled* [Hazlitt, *Manual*, p. 247] ?)	9 Jan.
	Massinger (revising Beaumont & Fletcher ?)	*Love's Cure, or The Martial Maid*	1625(?)
	Rowley, William	*A New Wonder, a Woman Never Vexed* (Based on *The Wonder of a Woman*, 1595 ?)	1624–1626
	Sampson, William	*The Vow Breaker, or The Fair Maid of Clifton*	1625(?)–1636
	Sampson, William	*The Widow's Prize, or The Woman Captain*	lic. 25 Jan.
	Shirley, James	*St Albans* (S.R., 1640.)	c. 1625–1640
	Shirley, James	*The School of Compliment* (*Love Tricks*)	lic. 11 Feb.
	Webster; Rowley, W. (& Heywood ?)	*A Cure for a Cuckold*	1624–c. 1625
	Anon. (Ainsworth, William, 'scriptor')	*Clytophon*	c. 1620–c. 1630
	Anon. (Davenport, R. ?)	*A Fool and Her Maidenhead Soon Parted*	c. 1624(?)–1639
	Anon.	*The Partial Law*	c. 1615–1630(?)

TYPE	AUSPICES	EARLIEST TEXTS	LAST ED.	DATE
Mask	Burley-on-the-Hill	Lost		
Political Satire	King's	[1625?] & MSS	1929[194]	
Comedy	Palsgrave's	Lost		
Jig (?) Variety (?)	King's	Lost		
Latin Tragedy	St Omers	1648		
Latin Tragedy	St Omers	1653		
Civic Pageant	London	1624* F	1927[173]	
Tragedy	Unknown (Beeston's Boys in 1639)	1654**	1927[173]	
Unknown	Palsgrave's	Lost		
Tragedy	Palsgrave's	Lost		
Comedy	Palsgrave's	Lost		
Unknown	Palsgrave's	Lost		
Tragedy	Unknown	1624 & MSS	1888 M	
Tragedy	Prince's	Lost		
Comedy	Lady Elizabeth's at Norwich	Lost		
Unknown	King's	Lost		
Tragedy	Palsgrave's	Lost		
Entertainment	Intended for Court	MS	1926[195]	**1625**
Comedy	Queen Henrietta's (?)	1639**	1890†[192]	
History	Magdalen Col., Oxford	1633*	1875 D†	
Comedy	King's	1647	1906[136] (V)	
Comedy	King's	1637 & MS	1912 V	
Tragicomedy	Queen Henrietta's	1633*	1888 M	
Mask	Court	[1625]	1941[109]	
Comedy	King's (?)	1647	1909[136]	
Comedy	Unknown	1632*	1875 D†	
Tragedy and History	Unknown	1636*	1914 B†	
Comedy	Prince's	Lost		
Tragedy	Unknown	Lost		
Comedy	Lady Elizabeth's	1631	1833†[196] (T)	
Comedy	Unknown	1661**	1927[173]	
Latin Comedy	Emmanuel Col., Cambridge (?)	MS		
Unknown	Queen Henrietta's (?)	Lost		
Tragicomedy	Closet (?)	MS	1908†[197]	

DATE	AUTHOR	TITLE	LIMITS
	Anon.	*Wine, Beer, and Ale Together by the Ears* (Augmented in 1630 ed. as *Wine, Beer, Ale, and Tobacco Contending for Superiority.*)	1624–1626(?)
1626	Bellamy, Henry	*Iphis*	1621–1633
	Beuil, Honorat de, Seigneur de Racan	*L'Artenice (Les Bergeries. The Queen's Pastoral)* (Written by a foreigner, but often attrib. to Henrietta Maria.)	21 Feb. (acted)
	Davenport, Robert	*The Pirate*	*c.* 1623–1640
	Dekker, T. ('S.R.' [Samuel Rowley?] on t.p.)	*The Noble Spanish Soldier (The Noble Soldier, or A Contract Broken Justly Revenged)* (Revision of earlier play? Rewritten as *The Welsh Ambassador*, 1623?)	1622(?)–1631 (revised?)
	Fletcher (poss. completed or revised by another)	*The Noble Gentleman* (Poss. an early play revised.)	lic. 3 Feb.
	Fletcher (with Massinger? Rowley, W.? & Ford?)	*The Fair Maid of the Inn*	lic. 22 Jan.
	Hemming, William	*The Jews' Tragedy*	*c.* 1622–1642
	Jonson, Ben	*The Staple of News*	Feb.
	Massinger, Philip	*The Painter* (S.R., 1653.)	*c.* 1613–1640
	Massinger, Philip	*The Roman Actor*	lic. 11 Oct.
	Massinger, Philip	*The Unnatural Combat*	1621–*c.* 1626
	May, Thomas	*Cleopatra, Queen of Egypt*	1626
	Mewe, William	*Pseudomagia*	1618–*c.* 1627
	Middleton, Thomas	*The Conqueror's Custom, or The Fair Prisoner* (Ment. by Hill; see Supp. II, m.)	*c.* 1601–1627
	Middleton, Thomas	*The Triumphs of Health and Prosperity*	30 Oct.
	Randolph, Thomas	*Aristippus, or The Jovial Philosopher*	1625–1626
	Shirley, James	*The Brothers*	lic. 4 Nov.
	Shirley, James	*The Maid's Revenge*	lic. 9 Feb.
	Shirley, James	*The Wedding*	1626–1629
	Simons, Joseph (?)	*S. Damianus*	13 Feb.
	Anon. (Heywood? Davenport?)	*Dick of Devonshire*	1626
	Anon.	*Parthenia* (Trans. Groto's *Il Pentimento amoroso*.)	*c.* 1625–*c.* 1630 (?)
	Anon.	*Queen Henrietta's Mask*	16 Nov.
1627	Crowther, Joseph	*Cephalus et Procris*	1626–1628
	Davenant, William	*The Cruel Brother*	lic. 12 Jan.
	Hawkins, William	*Apollo Shroving*	6 Feb.
	Heywood, Thomas	*Calisto, or The Escapes of Jupiter* (Episodes from *The Golden Age* and *The Silver Age*, 1610 and 1611.)	*c.* 1620–1641
	Massinger, Philip	*The Great Duke of Florence (The Great Duke)*	lic. 5 July
	Massinger, Philip	*The Judge*	lic. 6 June
	May, Thomas	*Antigone, the Theban Princess*	1627–1631

TYPE	AUSPICES	EARLIEST TEXTS	LAST ED.	DATE
Academic Entertainment	Cambridge (?)	1629 & MS	1915[198]	
Latin Comedy	St John's Col., Oxford	MS		**1626**
French Pastoral	Henrietta's Maids	1625	1857[199]	
Unknown	Unknown	Lost		
Foreign Pseudo-history	Admiral's (?)	1634* F	1961[113]	
Comedy	King's	1647	1910[136]	
Comedy	King's	1647	1927[173]	
Tragedy	Unknown	1662*	1913 B†	
Comedy	King's	1631	1938[109]	
Unknown	Unknown	Lost		
Tragedy	King's	1629*	1929[200] (MA)	
Tragedy	King's	1639*	1932[201]	
Tragedy	Unknown	1639** & MS	(T)	
Latin Comedy	Emmanuel Col., Cambridge	MSS		
Tragicomedy (?)	Unknown	Lost		
Civic Pageant	London	1626*	1886[121]	
Comic Show	Trinity Col., Cambridge	1630 & MS	1875[202]	
Unknown	Queen Henrietta's (?)	Lost		
Tragedy	Queen Henrietta's	1639*	1833[196] (T)	
Comedy	Queen Henrietta's	1629	1833†[196] (A)	
Latin Play	St Omers	MSS		
Tragicomedy	Unknown	MS	1955 G	
Latin Pastoral	Cambridge (?)	MS		
Mask	Court	Lost		
Latin Comedy	St John's Col., Oxford (?)	MS		**1627**
Tragedy	King's	1630	1872[203]	
Comedy	Hadleigh School, Suffolk	[c. 1627]*	1936†[204]	
Classical Legend	Unknown	MS		
Tragicomedy	Queen Henrietta's	1636*	1933[205] (M)	
Comedy (?)	King's	Lost		
Tragedy	Unacted	1631*		

DATE	AUTHOR	TITLE	LIMITS
	Newman, Thomas	*The Andrian Woman* (*Andria*) (Trans. Terence.)	1627
	Newman, Thomas	*The Eunuch* (Trans. Terence's *Eunuchus*.)	1627
	Randolph, Thomas	*The Conceited Pedlar* (*The University Pedlar*) (Prob. same as *The Pedlar*, assigned to Davenport in S.R., 1630.)	1 Nov.
	Randolph, T. (revised by 'F.J.')	*Plutophthalmia Plutogamia* (*Hey for Honesty, Down with Knavery*) (Adapt. Aristophanes' *Plutus*.)	c. 1626–c. 1628 (revised 1648–c. 1649)
	Randolph, Thomas	*Thomas Randolph's Salting*	1627
	Simons, Joseph	*Leo Armenus* (*Ultio Divina*)	1624–1629(?)
	Anon.	*The Duke of Buckingham's Mask*	15 May
	Anon.	*Queen Henrietta's Mask*	14 or 15 Jan.
1628	Davenant, William	*Albovine, King of the Lombards*	1626–1629
	Dekker, Thomas	*Britannia's Honour*	29 Oct.
	Ford, John	*The Lover's Melancholy*	lic. 24 Nov.
	Ford, John (?)	*The Queen, or The Excellency of Her Sex*	c. 1621–1642
	Gomersall, Robert	*Lodovick Sforza*	1628 (pub.)
	Massinger, Philip	*The Honour of Women* (Title coupled in S.R., 1653, with *The Spanish Viceroy*, 1624.)	lic. 6 May
	Massinger, Philip	*The Tyrant* (Identification with *The King and the Subject*, 1638, prob. incorrect.)	c. 1613–1640
	May, Thomas	*Julia Agrippina, Empress of Rome*	1628
	Reynolds, Henry	*Aminta* (Trans. Tasso.)	1628
	Shirley, James	*The Witty Fair One*	lic. 3 Oct.
	Vincent, Thomas	*Paria*	3 Mar.
	Anon. (Shirley, H.?)	*The Dumb Bawd of Venice* (Prob. same as H. Shirley's *The Dumb Bawd*, 1623.)	15 Apr. (acted)
	Anon.	*Philander, King of Thrace*	a. 1627
1629	Brome, Richard	*The Lovesick Maid, or The Honour of Young Ladies*	lic. 9 Feb.
	Brome, Richard	*The Northern Lass*	lic. 29 July(?)
	Carlell, Lodowick	*The Deserving Favourite*	c. 1622–1629
	Clavell, J. (?) ('Shakerly Marmion' in S.R., 1653)	*The Soddered Citizen*	c. 1629–1631
	Davenant, William	*The Just Italian*	lic. 2 Oct.
	Davenant, William	*The Siege* (Prob. same as *The Colonel*, lic. 22 July.)	1629 (?)
	Dekker, Thomas	*Believe It Is So and 'Tis So* (Ment. by Hill.)	c. 1594–c. 1629
	Dekker, Thomas	*London's Tempe, or The Field of Happiness*	29 Oct.
	Dekker, Thomas	*The White Moor* (Ment. by Hill; see Supp. II, m.)	c. 1594–c. 1629
	Ford, John	*The Broken Heart*	c. 1625–1633
	Jonson, Ben	*The New Inn, or The Light Heart*	lic. 19 Jan.

TYPE	AUSPICES	EARLIEST TEXTS	LAST ED.	DATE
Comedy	For acting in schools	1627*		
Comedy	For acting in schools	1627*		
Monologue	Trinity Col., Cambridge	1630 & MSS	1875[202]	
Comedy	Trinity Col., Cambridge (?)	1651*	1875†[202]	
Monologue	Trinity Col., Cambridge	MS		
Latin Tragedy	St Omers	1656 & MSS		
Mask	Court	Lost		
Mask	Court	Lost		
Tragedy	Unacted	1629	1872[203]	**1628**
Civic Pageant	London	1628*	1961[113]	
Tragicomedy	King's	1629*	1908 B (M)	
Tragicomedy	Unknown	1653*	1906 B†	
Tragedy	Unacted (?)	1628	1933 B†	
Comedy	Unknown	Lost		
Tragedy	Unknown	Lost		
Tragedy	Unknown	1639**	1914 B†	
Pastoral	Closet	1628*		
Comedy	Queen Henrietta's	1633*	1888 M (T)	
Latin Comedy	Trinity Col., Cambridge	1648* & MSS		
Comedy (?)	King's	Lost		
Tragicomedy	Unknown	MS ('author-plot') (frag.)	1945†[206]	
Comedy (?)	King's	Lost		**1629**
Comedy	King's	1632	1873†[207] (T)	
Tragicomedy	King's	1629	1905†[208]	
Comedy	King's	MS	1936 G†	
Comedy	King's	1630	1872†[203]	
Tragicomedy	King's (?)	1673*	1873†[203]	
Unknown	Unknown	Lost		
Civic Pageant	London	[1629]*	1961[113]	
Tragicomedy (?)	Unknown	Lost		
Tragedy	King's	1633*	1954[208a] (MBA)	
Comedy	King's	1631	1938[109]	

DATE	AUTHOR	TITLE	LIMITS
	Massinger, Philip	*Minerva's Sacrifice* (*The Forced Lady*, alternative title, added in S.R. 1653, an independent Massinger play; see 1633.)	lic. 3 Nov.
	Massinger, Philip	*The Picture*	lic. 8 June
	Randolph, Thomas	*Praeludium*	Nov.(?)
	Randolph, Thomas	*The Prodigal Scholar* (S.R., 1660. May be same as following.)	*c.* 1623–1635
	Randolph, Thomas (?)	*The Drinking Academy, or The Cheaters' Holiday* (May be same as preceding.)	1626–1631
	Shirley, James	*The Grateful Servant* (*The Faithful Servant*)	lic. 3 Nov.
	Anon. ('Reverardus')	*Hierarchomachia, or The Anti-Bishop*	1629(?)
1630	Brome, Richard	*The City Wit, or The Woman Wears the Breeches*	1629–1637
	Ford, John	*Beauty in a Trance* (S.R., 1653.)	28 Nov. (acted)
	Randolph, Thomas	*Amyntas, or The Impossible Dowry*	lic. 26 Nov.
	Randolph, Thomas	*The Muses' Looking Glass* (*The Entertainment*)	lic. 25 Nov.
	Sidnam, Jonathan	*Filli di Sciro, or Phillis of Scyros* (Trans. Bonarelli.)	*c.* 1630–*c.* 1631
	Sidnam, Jonathan	*Il Pastor Fido* (Trans. Guarini.)	1630
	Wilson, Arthur	*The Inconstant Lady, or Better Late Than Never*	*c.* 1629–1630
	Anon.	*An Induction for the House*	Nov.
	Anon.	*The Wasp*	*c.* 1630–1638(?)
1631	Brome, Richard	*The Queen's Exchange* (*The Royal Exchange*, 1661.)	1629–1632(?)
	Davenport, Robert	*King John and Matilda*	*c.* 1628–1634
	Dekker, Thomas	*Gustavus, King of Sweden* (S.R., 1660.)	1630(?)–1632
	Dekker, T. (& Day, J.?)	*The Wonder of a Kingdom* (Same as *Come See a Wonder*, 1623?)	1623–1631
	Hausted, Peter	*Senile Odium*	*c.* 1627–1631
	Heywood, Thomas	*II The Fair Maid of the West, or A Girl Worth Gold*	*c.* 1630–1631
	Heywood, Thomas	*London's Jus Honorarium*	29 Oct.
	Jonson, Ben	*Chloridia: Rites to Chloris and Her Nymphs*	22 Feb.
	Jonson, Ben	*Love's Triumph through Callipolis*	9 Jan.
	Knevet, Ralph	*Rhodon and Iris*	3 May
	Mabbe, James	*The Spanish Bawd* (*Calisto and Meliboea*) (Trans. Rojas's *Celestina*.)	1631
	Marmion, Shackerly	*Holland's Leaguer*	Dec. (acted)
	Massinger, Philip	*Believe as You List* (See *Sebastian, King of Portugal*, 1601.)	lic. 6 May
	Massinger, Philip	*The Emperor of the East*	lic. 11 Mar.
	Massinger, Philip	*Fast and Welcome* (S.R., 1660.)	*c.* 1613–1640
	Massinger, Philip	*The Unfortunate Piety*	lic. 13 June

TYPE	AUSPICES	EARLIEST TEXTS	LAST ED.	DATE
Tragedy (?)	King's	Lost		
Tragicomedy	King's	1630*	1871[193]	
Dialogue	King's Revels (?)	MS	1917[209]	
Comedy	Trinity Col., Cambridge (?)	Lost (?)		
Comedy	Westminster School (?)	MS	1930[210]	
Tragicomedy	Queen Henrietta's	1630	1833†[196]	
'Comic Satire'	Unknown	MS		
Comedy	King's Revels (?) (Revived by Queen Henrietta's, 1637–39 ?)	1653*	1873†[207]	**1630**
Unknown	King's	Lost		
Pastoral	King's Revels	1638	1917[209]	
Comedy	King's Revels	1638	1875[202]	
Pastoral	Closet	1655**		
Pastoral	Closet	MS		
Comedy	King's	MSS	1814†[211]	
Curtain-raiser (?)	King's	Lost		
'Comical History'	King's Revels	MS		
Tragicomedy	King's (?)	1657**	1873†[207]	**1631**
History	Queen Henrietta's	1655	1890†[192]	
Foreign History	Unknown	Lost		
Comedy	Queen Henrietta's	1636*	1958[113]	
Latin Comedy	Queen's Col., Cambridge	1633* & MS	1949† (text & trans.)[212]	
Comedy	Queen Henrietta's	1631*	1888 M	
Civic Pageant	London	1631*	1874†[114]	
Mask	Court	[1631]	1941[109]	
Mask	Court	1630[31]	1941[109]	
Pastoral	Florists' Feast, Norwich	1631**		
Romance	Closet	1631** & MS	[1908][213]	
Comedy	Prince Charles's	1632*	1875†[214]	
Tragedy	King's	MS F	1928 G (M)	
Tragicomedy	King's	1632*	1871[193] (T)	
Comedy	Unknown	Lost		
Tragedy (?)	King's	Lost		

K

DATE	AUTHOR	TITLE	LIMITS
	Shirley, James	*The Contention for Honour and Riches* (See *Honoria and Mammon*, 1658.)	*c.* 1625–1632
	Shirley, James	*The Humorous Courtier* (*The Duke*)	lic. 17 May
	Shirley, James	*Love's Cruelty*	lic. 14 Nov.
	Shirley, James	*The Traitor*	lic. 4 May
	Simons, Joseph	*Zeno sive Ambitio Infelix* (*Fratrum Concordia Saeva*)	7 Aug.
	Wilson, Arthur	*The Swisser*	1631
	Wright, Abraham	*The Reformation*	1629–1633
	Zouche, Richard	*The Sophister* (*Fallacy, or The Troubles of Great Hermenia*)	1610–1631
1632	'T.B.' (Brewer, Anth. or Th.?)	*The Country Girl*	1632–*c.* 1633
	Brome, Richard	*The Novella*	1632–1633
	Brome, Richard	*The Weeding of the Covent Garden, or The Middlesex Justice of Peace* (*The Covent Garden Weeded*)	1632
	Ford, John	*Love's Sacrifice*	1632(?)
	Ford, John	*'Tis Pity She's a Whore*	1629(?)–1633
	Hausted, Peter	*The Rival Friends*	19 Mar.
	Heywood, Thomas	*Londini Artium et Scientiarum Scaturigo, or London's Fountain of Arts and Sciences*	29 Oct.
	Jonson, Ben	*The Magnetic Lady, or Humours Reconciled*	lic. 12 Oct.
	Massinger, Philip	*The City Madam*	lic. 25 May
	Percy, William	*Necromantes, or The Two Supposed Heads*	1632
	Pestell, Jr (?), Thomas	*Versipellis*	1631–1632
	Randolph, Thomas	*The Jealous Lovers*	20 Mar.
	Shirley, James	*The Ball* (Chapman's name associated with Shirley's prob. through error.)	lic. 16 Nov.
	Shirley, James	*Changes, or Love in a Maze*	lic. 10 Jan.
	Shirley, James	*Hyde Park*	lic. 20 Apr.
	Tatham, John	*Love Crowns the End*	1632
	Townshend, Aurelian	*Albion's Triumph*	8 Jan.
	Townshend, Aurelian	*Tempe Restored*	14 Feb.
	Anon.	*The Invisible Knight* (Ment. in *The Bird in a Cage*, 1633. Ghost?)	*c.* 1632–1633
	Anon.	*The Ring* (Also ment. in above. Ghost?)	*c.* 1632–1633
1633	Blencowe, John	*Mercurius sive Literarum Lucta*	1629–1638(?)
	Brome, R.; Chapman, G.	*Christianetta, or Marriage and Hanging Go by Destiny* (Ment. by Hill; see Supp. II, m.)	*c.* 1623–1634
	Cokain, Aston	*Trappolin Creduto Principe, or Trappolin Supposed a Prince*	1633
	Cowley, Abraham	*Love's Riddle*	*c.* 1630–1636
	Drummond, William (?)	*The Entertainment at Edinburgh*	15 June
	Ford, J. (& Dekker, T.?)	*Perkin Warbeck*	*c.* 1629–1634
	Hemming, William	*The Coursing of a Hare, or The Madcap*	Mar.

TYPE	AUSPICES	EARLIEST TEXTS	LAST ED.	DATE
Moral	Privately acted (?)	1633*	1833†[196]	
Comedy	Queen Henrietta's	1640*	1833†[196] (T)	
Tragedy	Queen Henrietta's	1640*	1833†[196] (T)	
Tragedy	Queen Henrietta's	1635	1888 M (AT)	
Latin Tragedy	St Omers	1648 & MSS		
Tragicomedy	King's	MS	1904†[215]	
Comedy	St John's Col., Oxford	Lost		
Moral	Oxford	1639* & MS		
Comedy	King's (?)	1647*		**1632**
Comedy	King's	1653*	1873†[207]	
Comedy	King's (?)	1659*	1873†[207]	
Tragedy	Queen Henrietta's	1633*	1908 B (M)	
Tragedy	Queen Henrietta's	1633**	1927 B (MA)	
Tragicomedy	Queens' Col., Cambridge	1632*	1951†[216]	
Civic Pageant	London	1632*	1953†[217]	
Comedy	King's	1641	1938[109]	
Comedy	King's	1658 or 1659*	1934[218] (M)	
Comedy	Closet (?)	MSS		
Latin Comedy	Queens' Col., Cambridge	Lost		
Comedy	Trinity Col., Cambridge	1632	1875†[202]	
Comedy	Queen Henrietta's	1639*	1914[122]	
Comedy	'King's Revels' (Prince Charles's ?)	1632*	1833†[196] (T)	
Comedy	Queen Henrietta's	1637*	1888 M (T)	
Pastoral	Bingham School, Notts.	1640**	1879†[219]	
Mask	Court	1631[32]*	1912†[220]	
Mask	Court	1631[32]*	1912†[220]	
Unknown	Unknown	Lost		
Unknown	Unknown	Lost		
Latin Comedy	St John's Col., Oxford (?)	MS		**1633**
Comedy (?)	Unknown	Lost		
Comedy	Unknown	1658**	1874†[221]	
Pastoral	Unacted	1638	1906[222]	
Royal Entertainment	Edinburgh	1633*	1913[223]	
History	Queen Henrietta's	1634* & MS	1927 B (MA)	
Comedy	King's Revels	Lost		

DATE	AUTHOR	TITLE	LIMITS
	Heywood, Thomas	*Londini Emporia, or London's Mercatura*	29 Oct.
	Heywood, Thomas	*A Maidenhead Well Lost*	*c.* 1625–1634
	Jonson, Ben	*The King's Entertainment at Welbeck* (*Love's Welcome at Welbeck*)	21 May
	Jonson, Ben	*A Tale of a Tub* (Revised version?)	lic. 7 May
	Marmion, Shackerly	*A Fine Companion*	1632–1633
	Massinger, Philip	*The City Honest Man* (S.R., 1653; see *The Guardian*, below.)	*c.* 1615–1641
	Massinger, Philip	*The Forced Lady* (King's list, 1641; see *Minerva's Sacrifice*, 1629.)	*c.* 1615–1641
	Massinger, Philip	*The Guardian* (Title coupled in S.R., 1653, with *The City Honest Man*, above.)	lic. 31 Oct.
	Milton, John	*Arcades* (Fragment.)	1630–1634
	Montague, Walter	*The Shepherd's Paradise*	9 Jan.
	Mountfort, Walter	*The Launching of the Mary, or The Seaman's Honest Wife*	lic. 27 June
	Nabbes, Thomas	*Covent Garden*	1633
	Rickets, John	*Byrsa Basilica sive Regale Excambium*	1633(?)
	Shirley, James	*The Bird in a Cage* (*The Beauties*)	lic. 21 Jan.
	Shirley, James	*The Gamester*	lic. 11 Nov.
	Shirley, James	*The Young Admiral*	lic. 3 July
	Wilson, Arthur	*The Corporal*	lic. 14 Jan.(?)
	Anon.	*II The City Shuffler* (First part unknown.)	1633(?)
1634	Brome, R.; Heywood, T.	*The Late Lancashire Witches*	1634
	Brome, R.(?) & Heywood, T.(?)	*The Apprentice's Prize* (S.R., 1654.)	*c.* 1633–1641
	Brome, R.; Heywood, T.	*Sir Martin Skink* (S.R., 1654.)	*c.* 1633–1641
	Carew, Thomas	*Coelum Britannicum*	18 Feb.
	Carlell, Lodowick	*The Spartan Ladies* (*The Spartan Lady*)	1 May (acted)
	Davenant, William	*Love and Honour* (*The Courage of Love. The Nonpareilles, or The Matchless Maids*)	lic. 20 Nov.
	Davenant, William	*The Wits*	lic. 19 Jan.
	Glapthorne, Henry	*Albertus Wallenstein*	1634–1639
	Heywood, Thomas	*Love's Mistress, or The Queen's Mask* (*Cupid and Psyche, or Cupid's Mistress*)	1634
	Jonson, Ben	*Love's Welcome at Bolsover*	30 July
	Le Grys, Robert	*Nothing Impossible to Love* (S.R., 1660.)	b. 1635
	Lovelace, Richard	*The Scholars*	1634–1635(?)
	Massinger, Philip (reviser)	*Cleander* (*Lisander and Calista*) (Revision of *The Wandering Lovers*, 1623.)	lic. 7 May
	Massinger, Philip (reviser)	*A Very Woman, or The Prince of Tarent* (Poss. reworking of Fletcher and Massinger play of *c.* 1619–1622.)	lic. 6 June
	Milton, John	*Comus* (*The Mask at Ludlow Castle*)	29 Sept.

TYPE	AUSPICES	EARLIEST TEXTS	LAST ED.	DATE
Civic Pageant	London	1633*	1953†[217]	
Comedy	Queen Henrietta's	1634*	1874[114]	
Royal Entertainment	Host: William Cavendish	1641 & MS	1941[109]	
Comedy	Queen Henrietta's	1640	1927[109]	
Comedy	Prince Charles's	1633*	1875†[214]	
Unknown	Unknown	Lost		
Tragedy	King's	Lost		
Comedy	King's	1655*	1889 M	
Entertainment	Harefield	1645 F & MS F	1958[224]	
Pastoral Romance	Court	1629 [1659] or 1659* & MSS		
Comedy	Unknown	MS	1933 G†	
Comedy	Queen Henrietta's	1638**	1887†[225]	
Latin Comedy	Jesus Col., Cambridge (?)	MS	1939 B†	
Comedy	Queen Henrietta's	1633*	1833[196] (T)	
Comedy	Queen Henrietta's	1637*	1833[196] (T)	
Tragicomedy	Queen Henrietta's	1637*	1833†[196]	
Comedy	King's	MSS (frags.)		
Comedy (?)	King's Revels	Lost		
Topical Play	King's	1634*	1874[114] (T)	**1634**
Comedy (?)	King's (?)	Lost		
History	King's (?)	Lost		
Mask	Court	1634	1949[226]	
Tragicomedy (?)	King's	Lost		
Tragicomedy	King's	1649	1909[227] (A)	
Comedy	King's	1636	1872[203] (AT)	
Foreign History	King's	1639 or 1640*	1874[228]	
Classical Legend	Queen Henrietta's	1636	1886[229]	
Royal Entertainment	Host: William Cavendish	1641 & MS	1941[109]	
Tragicomedy (?)	Unknown	Lost		
Comedy	Gloucester Hall, Oxford (?), & Queen Henrietta's in 1637–42 (?)	Lost		
Tragicomedy	King's	1647	1907[136]	
Tragicomedy	King's	1655*	1871[193]	
Moral Mask	Ludlow Castle	1637 F & MSS F	1958[224] (A)	

DATE	AUTHOR	TITLE	LIMITS
	Nabbes, Thomas	*Tottenham Court*	1633–1634
	Peaps, [William ?] (?)	*Love in Its Ecstasy, or The Large Prerogative*	c. 1634–1642
	Rutter, Joseph	*The Shepherds' Holiday*	1633–1635
	Shirley, James	*The Example*	lic. 24 June
	Shirley, James	*The Opportunity*	lic. 29 Nov.
	Shirley, James	*The Triumph of Peace*	3 Feb.
	Sparrow, Thomas	*Confessor*	c. 1630–1640(?)
	Taylor, John	*The Triumphs of Fame and Honour*	29 Oct.
	Anon.	*Doctor Lamb and the Witches* (An earlier play revived, with additions.)	lic. 16 Aug. (as old)
	Anon.	*The Entertainment at Chirke Castle* (*The Mask of the Four Seasons*)	1634(?)
	Anon.	*Love's Aftergame, or The Proxy*	lic. 24 Nov.
1635	Bristowe, Francis	*King Free-Will* (Trans. Bassano's *Tragedia del libero arbitrio*.) (See *Biog. Dram.*, I, 68.)	1635
	Brome, Richard	*The New Academy, or The New Exchange*	1623–1640
	Brome, Richard	*The Queen and Concubine*	1635–1639
	Brome, Richard	*The Sparagus Garden* (*Tom Hoydon o' Tanton Deane*)	1635
	Cartwright, William	*The Ordinary, or The City Cozener*	1634–1635
	Davenant, William	*News from Plymouth*	lic. 1 Aug.
	Davenant, William	*The Platonic Lovers*	lic. 16 Nov.
	Davenant, William	*The Temple of Love*	10 Feb.
	Davenport, Robert	*A Dialogue between Policy and Piety*	c. 1635
	Digby, Kenelm	*Amyntas* (Trans. Tasso's *Aminta*.)	c. 1630–1638
	Digby, Kenelm	*Il Pastor Fido* (Trans. Guarini.)	c. 1630–1638
	Ford, John	*The Fancies Chaste and Noble* (1631 play revised ?)	1635–1636
	Glapthorne, Henry	*The Lady Mother*	lic. 15 Oct.
	Glapthorne, Henry	*The Noble Husbands*	c. 1633–1642
	Glapthorne, Henry	*The Noble Trial* (S.R., 1653.)	c. 1633–1642
	Henrietta Maria (?)	*Florimene*	21 Dec.
	Heywood, Thomas	*A Challenge for Beauty*	1634–1636
	Heywood, Thomas	*Londini Sinus Salutis, or London's Harbour of Health and Happiness*	29 Oct.
	Heywood, Thomas	*Pleasant Dialogues and Dramas* (A miscellany, including playlets, some of which may have been parts of lost dramas: *Amphrisa, or The Forsaken Shepherdess* [*Pelopaea and Alope*], *Apollo and Daphne* [from Ovid], *Jupiter and Io*.)	1635 (S.R.)
	Jones, John	*Adrasta, or The Woman's Spleen and Love's Conquest*	1635 (pub.)
	Jordan, Thomas	*Money Is an Ass* (*Wealth Outwitted*)	c. 1635(?)
	Killigrew, Henry	*The Conspiracy* (*Pallantus and Eudora*)	8 Jan.(?)
	Killigrew, Thomas	*The Prisoners*	1632–1636
	Kirke, John	*The Seven Champions of Christendom*	c. 1600–1638
	Marmion, Shackerly	*The Antiquary*	1634–1636

TYPE	AUSPICES	EARLIEST TEXTS	LAST ED.	DATE
Comedy	Prince's Men, or King's Revels	1638**	1887†[225]	
Pastoral Tragicomedy	Unacted	1649*		
Pastoral	Queen Henrietta's	1635*	1875 D	
Comedy	Queen Henrietta's	1637*	1833†[196]	
Comedy	Queen Henrietta's	1640*	1833†[196]	
Mask	Inns of Court at Court	1633[34]	1897[56] (M)	
Latin Comedy	St John's Col., Camb. (?)	MS		
Civic Pageant	London	1634*		
Topical Play	King's Revels	Lost		
Entertainment	Thomas Middleton's	MS	1848†[230]	
Comedy (?)	King's Revels	Lost		
Anti-Catholic Moral	Closet (?)	1635* or MS (lost)		**1635**
Comedy	King's Revels (?)	1659*	1873†[207]	
Tragicomedy	King's Revels	1659*	1873†[207]	
Comedy	King's Revels	1640*	1873†[207]	
Comedy	Christ Church, Oxford (?)	1651*	1951[231] (D)	
Comedy	King's	1673*	1873†[203]	
Comedy	King's	1636	1872[203] (T)	
Mask	Court	1634[35]	1872†[203] (T)	
Moral Dialogue	Closet	MSS		
Pastoral	Closet	Lost		
Pastoral	Closet	MS (frag.)	1877†[232]	
Comedy	Queen Henrietta's	1638*	1927 B	
Tragicomedy	King's Revels	MS	1958 G	
Unknown	Unknown	Lost		
'Tragicomedy'	Unknown	Lost		
French Pastoral	Queen's Maids at Court	1635* (design)		
Tragicomedy	King's	1636*	1874[114] (T)	
Civic Pageant	London	1635*	1874†[114]	
Dialogues	Unacted (?)	1637*	1903 B	
Tragicomedy	Unacted	1635*		
Comedy	King's Revels (?)	1668**		
Tragicomedy	York House (?) & King's	1638		
Tragicomedy	Queen Henrietta's	1641		
Heroical Romance	Prince Charles's (?)	1638*	1929†[233]	
Comedy	Queen Henrietta's	1641*	1875[214] (D)	

DATE	AUTHOR	TITLE	LIMITS
	Massinger, Philip	*The Orator* (*The Noble Choice, or The Orator,* S.R., 1653. *The Noble Choice* may be an independent Massinger play.)	lic. 10 Jan.
	Nabbes, Thomas	*Hannibal and Scipio*	1635
	Richards, Nathaniel	*Messalina, the Roman Empress*	1634–1636
	Rider, William	*The Twins*	1629–1655
	Shirley, James	*The Coronation*	lic. 6 Feb.
	Shirley, James	*The Lady of Pleasure*	lic. 15 Oct.
	Speed, John	*Stonehenge* (Same as *The Converted Robber,* 1637?)	1635
	Wilde, George	*Eumorphus sive Cupido Adultus*	5 Feb.
	Anon.	*Icon Ecclesiastici*	1635
	Anon.	*Love's Changelings' Change*	c. 1630–c. 1640(?)
	Anon.	*Truth's Triumphs* (Poss. sub-title of known play.)	Feb. (acted)
	Anon.	*Wit's Triumvirate, or The Philosopher*	1635 (MS date)
1636	Carlell, Lodowick	*I & II Arviragus and Philicia*	1635–1636
	Cartwright, William	*The Royal Slave*	30 Aug.
	Davenant, William	*The Triumphs of the Prince d'Amour*	23 or 24 Feb.
	Glapthorne, Henry	*The Hollander*	lic. 12 Mar.
	Killigrew, Thomas	*Claracilla* (*Claricilla. Clarasilla*)	1635–1636
	Killigrew, Thomas	*The Princess, or Love at First Sight*	1635–1637(?)
	Kynaston, Francis (?)	*Corona Minervae*	27 Feb.
	Massinger, Philip	*The Bashful Lover*	lic. 9 May
	May, Thomas	*The Old Couple*	lic. 1636
	Rawlins, Thomas	*The Rebellion*	1629–1639
	Sackville, E.(?); & others	*The Entertainment at Richmond*	12 Sept.
	Shirley, James	*The Duke's Mistress*	lic. 18 Jan.
	Strode, William	*The Floating Island* (*Passions Calmed. Prudentius*)	29 Aug.
	Townshend, Aurelian	*A Pastoral Mask* [*with Anti-Mask of Man of Canada, Egyptians, Pantaloons, and Spaniards*]	c. 1632–1640
	Wilde, George	*Love's Hospital* (*Lovers' Hospital*)	30 Aug.
	Anon.	*Moore's Mask* (*The Moor's Mask*) (See *Biog. Chron.*, II, 358.)	1636(?)
	Anon.	*The Presentment of Bushell's Rock*	23 Aug.
	Anon.	*A Projector Lately Dead* (Ghost title?)	1636 (ment.)
	Anon. (Hausted, P., now rejected)	*Senilis Amor*	1635–1636
	Anon.	*A Spanish Tragedy* [*of Petrus Crudelis*]	1626–1648(?)
1637	Berkeley, William	*The Lost Lady*	1637–1638
	Brome, Richard	*The English Moor, or The Mock Marriage*	1637
	Brome, Richard	*Wit in a Madness* (S.R., 1640.)	c. 1635–1640

TYPE	AUSPICES	EARLIEST TEXTS	LAST ED.	DATE
Unknown	King's	Lost		
Tragedy	Queen Henrietta's	1637*	1887†[225]	
Tragedy	King's Revels	1640*	1910 B†	
Tragicomedy	King's Revels (?)	1655*		
Comedy	Queen Henrietta's	1640	1910[136]	
Comedy	Queen Henrietta's	1637*	1888 M (A)	
Pastoral	St John's Col., Oxford	Lost (?)		
Latin Comedy	St John's Col., Oxford	MS		
Latin Comedy	Unknown	MS		
Pastoral	Closet (?)	MS		
Unknown	Queen Henrietta's (?)	Lost (?)		
Comedy	Unknown	MS		
Tragicomedy	King's	1639* & MSS	(T)	**1636**
Tragicomedy	Christ Church, Oxford	1639 & MSS	1951†[231]	
Mask	Middle Temple	1635[36]	1872†[203]	
Comedy	Queen Henrietta's	1640*	1874†[228]	
Tragicomedy	Queen Henrietta's	1641 & MS	(T)	
Tragicomedy	King's (?)	1664*		
Academic Entertainment	Museum Minervae	1635[36]**		
Tragicomedy	King's	1655*	1871[193]	
Comedy	Unknown	1658*	1875 D (T)	
Tragedy	King's Revels	1640**	1875 D	
Comic Show	Courtiers at Richmond	1636*	1903 B†	
Tragicomedy	Queen Henrietta's	1638*	1833†[106]	
Moral Allegory	Christ Church, Oxford	1655*	1907†[234]	
Mask	Court	[c. 1636?]* (frag.)		
Comedy	St John's Col., Oxford	MSS		
Mask	'near Eastgate', Oxford	MS (?)		
Royal Entertainment	Host: Thomas Bushell	1636*		
Comedy	Unknown	Lost		
Latin Comedy	Trinity Col. (?), Cambridge	MS	1952† (text & trans.)[235]	
Tragedy	Oxford	Lost		
Tragicomedy	King's	1638 & MS	1875 D	**1637**
Comedy	Queen's	1659* & MS	1873†[207]	
Comedy (?)	Queen's (?)	Lost		

DATE	AUTHOR	TITLE	LIMITS
	Carlell, Lodowick	*The Fool Would Be a Favourite, or The Discreet Lover*	*c.* 1632–*c.* 1638
	Carlell, Lodowick	*Osmond the Great Turk, or The Noble Servant* (Same as *Osmond the Great Turk*, 1622?)	1622–*c.* 1638
	Cartwright, William	*The Lady Errant*	1628–1643
	Formido, Cornelius (?)	*The Governor* (Same as *The Governor*, 1656?)	16 or 17 Feb. (acted)
	Glapthorne, Henry	*The Ladies' Privilege* (*The Lady's Privilege*)	1637–1640
	Heywood, Thomas	*Londini Speculum, or London's Mirror*	30 Oct.
	Jonson, Ben	*Mortimer His Fall* (Left incomplete.)	1595–1637
	Jonson, Ben	*The Sad Shepherd, or A Tale of Robin Hood* (Left incomplete.)	*c.* 1612–1637
	Mayne, Jasper	*The City Match*	1637–1638 (?)
	Nabbes, Thomas	*Microcosmus*	1637
	Nabbes, Thomas	*The Spring's Glory*	*c.* 1625–1638
	Neale, Thomas	*The Ward*	1637
	Rutter, J. (with Sackville, E. & R. ?)	*I The Cid* (*The Valiant Cid*) (Trans. Corneille.)	1637–1638
	Shirley, James	*The Royal Master*	1637 (lic. 23 Apr. 1638, for Queen's)
	Speed, J. (?) (Wilde, G., now rejected)	*The Converted Robber* (Same as *Stonehenge*, 1635?)	1637 (MS date)
	Suckling, John	*Aglaura*	1637
	Suckling, John	*The Sad One* (Left incomplete.)	*c.* 1637–1641
	'J.W.'	*The Valiant Scot*	1637 (pub.)
1638	Baylie, Simon	*The Wizard*	*c.* 1620–*c.* 1640
	Brome, Alexander (?)	*The Cunning Lovers*	1632–1639
	Brome, Richard	*The Antipodes*	1638
	Brome, Richard	*The Damoiselle, or The New Ordinary*	1637–1638(?)
	Carlell, Lodowick	*I & II The Passionate Lovers*	1629–1638
	Cartwright, William	*The Siege, or Love's Convert*	1628–1643
	Cowley, Abraham	*Naufragium Joculare*	2 Feb.
	Davenant, William	*Britannia Triumphans*	lic. 8 Jan.
	Davenant, William	*The Fair Favourite*	lic. 17 Nov.
	Davenant, William	*Luminalia, or The Festival of Light*	6 Feb.
	Davenant, William	*The Unfortunate Lovers*	lic. 16 Apr.
	Ford, John	*The Lady's Trial*	lic. 3 May
	Ford, John (?)	*The Royal Combat* (S.R., 1660.)	*c.* 1621–1642
	Glapthorne, Henry	*Argalus and Parthenia*	*c.* 1632–1638
	Glapthorne, Henry	*Wit in a Constable*	1636–1638 (revised 1639)
	Heywood, Thomas	*Porta Pietatis, or The Port or Harbour of Piety*	29 Oct.
	Johnson, William	*Valetudinarium*	6 Feb.
	Massinger, Philip	*The King and the Subject*	lic. 5 June
	Mayne, Jasper	*The Amorous War*	*c.* 1628–1648

TYPE	AUSPICES	EARLIEST TEXTS	LAST ED.	DATE
Tragicomedy	Queen's (?)	1657*	1926†[236]	
Tragicomedy	Queen's (?)	1657*	1926†[237]	
Tragicomedy	Privately acted	1651*	1951†[231]	
Unknown	King's	Lost (?)		
Tragicomedy	Beeston's Boys	1640*	1874[228]	
Civic Pageant	London	1637*	1874†[114]	
History	Unacted	1641	1941[109]	
Comic Pastoral	Unacted	1641	1941[109] (BA)	
Comedy	King's	1639	1875 D	
Moral Mask	Queen's	1637*	1887[225]	
Mask	Unacted (?)	1638**	1887†[225]	
Tragicomedy	Unacted	MS	1937†[238]	
Tragicomedy	Beeston's Boys	1637[38]		
Comedy	I Ogilby's Men & Queen's	1638* & MS (lost)	1914[190]	
Pastoral	St John's Col., Oxford	MS		
Tragedy	King's	1638 & MSS	1910[239] (T)	
Tragicomedy (?)	Unacted	1659	1910[239]	
Tragedy	Acted at Fortune in 1639 (?) (by King's Provincial Company ?)	1637*		
Comedy	Unknown	MSS	1930 B†	**1638**
Comedy	Beeston's Boys	1654*		
Comedy	Queen's	1640*	1914[190] (A)	
Comedy	Beeston's Boys (?)	1653*	1873†[207]	
Tragicomedy	King's	1655**		
Tragicomedy	Unacted (?)	1651*	1951†[231]	
Latin Comedy	Trinity Col., Cambridge	1638*	1881[240]	
Mask	Court	1637[38]*	1872†[203]	
Tragicomedy	King's	1673*	1873†[203]	
Mask	Court	1637[38]*	1872†[241]	
Tragedy	King's	1643	1873†[203]	
Comedy	Beeston's Boys	1639*	1927 B	
'Comedy'	Unknown	Lost		
Tragicomedy	Beeston's Boys	1639*	1874†[228]	
Comedy	Beeston's Boys	1640*	1874†[228]	
Civic Pageant	London	1638*	1874[114]	
Latin Comedy	Queens' Col., Cambridge	MSS		
Unknown	King's	Lost		
Comedy	Unknown	1648		

DATE	AUTHOR	TITLE	LIMITS
	Mead, Robert	*The Combat of Love and Friendship*	1634–1642
	Nabbes, Thomas	*The Bride*	Summer
	Nabbes, Thomas	*A Presentation for the Prince* (*Time and the Almanac-Makers*)	29 May (projected)
	Oldisworth, Gyles	*The Pattern of Piety*	1638
	'T.R.' (Randolph, T., completed by Brathwait, R. ?)	*Cornelianum Dolium*	1638 (pub.)
	Rutter, J. (with Sackville, E. & R. ?)	*II The Cid* (Trans. Desfontaines' *La Vraie suite du Cid.*)	1637–1639
	Shirley, James	*The Constant Maid, or Love Will Find out the Way*	1636(?)–1640
	Shirley, James	*The Doubtful Heir* (*Rosania, or Love's Victory*)	c. 1638 (lic. 1 June 1640, for King's)
	Suckling, John	*Aglaura* (Second version.)	1638
	Suckling, John	*The Goblins*	c. 1637–1641
	Anon.	*The Fairy Knight, or Oberon the Second* (Based on Westminster School play by T. Randolph, 1623–1624 ?)	1637(?)– 1658(?)
	Anon. (Boyle, R. ?)	*The General* (Poss. earlier version of Boyle's play, 1662.)	c. 1637–1640
	Anon.	*Hocus-Pocus*	1638 (acted)
	Anon.	*The Irish Gentleman*	1636–1640
	Anon.	*The Toy*	1636–1640
1639	Brome, Richard	*The Lovesick Court, or The Ambitious Politic*	c. 1639–1640
	Brome, Richard	*A Mad Couple Well Matched*	1637(?)–1639
	Cokain, Aston	*The Obstinate Lady*	c. 1630–1642
	'J.D.' (author or reviser ?)	*The Knave in Grain, New Vamped* (Revision of play originally written c. 1625 ?) (See Supp. II, m.)	c. 1639
	'T.D.' (Drue, Thomas ?)	*The Bloody Banquet*	1639 (pub.)
	Davenant, William	*The Spanish Lovers* (*The Distresses*)	lic. 30 Nov.
	Freeman, Ralph	*Imperiale*	1639 (pub.)
	Glapthorne, Henry	*The Duchess of Fernandina* (S.R., 1660.)	c. 1633–1642
	Glapthorne, Henry	*The Vestal* (S.R., 1660.)	c. 1633–1642
	Hemming, William	*The Fatal Contract* (*The Eunuch* in 1687 ed.)	c. 1638–1639(?)
	Heywood, Thomas	*Londini Status Pacatus, or London's Peaceable Estate*	29 Oct.
	Lower, William	*The Phoenix in Her Flames*	1639 (pub.)
	Massinger, Philip	*Alexius, or The Chaste Lover* (or *Gallant*)	lic. 25 Sept.
	Nabbes, Thomas	*The Unfortunate Mother*	1639(?)
	Sharpe, Lewis	*The Noble Stranger*	1638–1640
	Shirley, James	*The Gentleman of Venice*	lic. 30 Oct. (for Queen's)
	Shirley, James	*The Politician*	c. 1639(?)

TYPE	AUSPICES	EARLIEST TEXTS	LAST ED.	DATE
Tragicomedy	Christ Church, Oxford	1654*		
Comedy	Beeston's Boys	1640*	1887†[225]	
Mask	Court	1638**	1887†[225]	
Interlude	Westminster	MS		
Latin Comedy	Unknown	1638*		
Tragicomedy	Unacted (?)	1640*		
Comedy	I Ogilby's Men, Dublin (?)	1640	1833[196]	
Tragicomedy	I Ogilby's Men, Dublin, & King's	1653*	1833†[196]	
Tragicomedy	King's	1638	1910[239] (T)	
Comedy	King's	1646	1910[239]	
Comedy	Unknown	MS	1942†[242]	
Unknown	I Ogilby's Men, Dublin	Lost (?)		
Comedy	Red Bull Company at Coventry	Lost		
Unknown	I Ogilby's Men, Dublin	Lost		
Comedy (?)	I Ogilby's Men, Dublin	Lost		
Tragicomedy	Prince Charles's (?)	1659^	1873†[207]	**1639**
Comedy	Beeston's Boys (?)	1653*	1873[207] (A)	
Comedy	Unknown	1657	1874†[221]	
Comedy	Red Bull Company at Fortune	1640*	1960 (1961) G†	
Tragedy	Beeston's Boys (in 1639)	1639* F	1961 (1962) G†	
Comedy	King's	1673*	1873†[203]	
Tragedy	Closet (?)	1639 & MS		
Tragedy	Unknown	Lost		
Tragedy	Unknown	Lost		
Tragedy	Queen Henrietta's	1653		
Civic Pageant	London	1639*	1874†[114]	
Tragedy	Unacted (?)	1639*		
Comedy (?)	King's	Lost		
Tragedy	Unacted	1640*	1887†[225]	
Tragicomedy	Queen's	1640*		
Tragicomedy	I Ogilby's Men, Dublin (?), & Queen's	1655**	1833†[196]	
Tragedy	I Ogilby's Men, Dublin (?), & Queen's	1655**	1833†[196] (T)	

DATE	AUTHOR	TITLE	LIMITS
	Shirley, James	*I St Patrick for Ireland* (Second part unknown.)	*c.* 1637–1640
	Suckling, John	*Brennoralt, or The Discontented Colonel*	1639–1641
	Anon.	*The Cardinal's Conspiracy* (An old play revived.)	1639 (acted)
	Anon.	*The Conceited Duke*	1639 (Cockpit list)
	Anon. (Dekker, T. ?)	*The Telltale*	1605–*c.* 1640
	Anon.	*The Whore New Vamped*	29 Sept. (ordered suppressed)
	Anon. (Middleton and Rowley ?)	*The World* (Same as *The World Tossed at Tennis*, 1620 ?)	1639 (Cockpit list)
1640	Brome, Richard	*The Court Beggar*	1639–1640
	Brome, Richard	*The Jewish Gentleman*	1640 (S.R.)
	Burnell, Henry	*Landgartha*	1639–1640
	Cavendish, W.; Shirley, J.	*The Country Captain* (*Captain Underwit*)	*c.* 1639–*c.* 1640
	Chamberlain, Robert	*The Swaggering Damsel*	1640 (pub.)
	Cokain, Aston	*A Mask at Bretbie*	6 Jan.
	Davenant, William	*Salmacida Spolia*	21 Jan.
	Day, John	*The Parliament of Bees*	*c.* 1634–1640
	Fane, Mildmay	*Raguaillo D'Oceano*	1640
	Glapthorne (?) ('George Chapman' on t.p., 'Henry Glapthorne' in S.R. Glapthorne prob. author rather than reviser.)	*Revenge for Honour* (*The Parricide, or Revenge for Honour*, S.R., 1653.)	1637–1641
	Gough, John	*The Strange Discovery*	1640 (pub.)
	Habington, William	*The Queen of Aragon* (*Cleodora*)	9 Apr.
	Harding, Samuel	*Sicily and Naples, or The Fatal Union*	1640 (pub.)
	Heywood, Thomas	*Love's Masterpiece*	1640 (S.R.)
	Holles, William	*The Country Court*	1635–1643
	Jordan, Thomas	*Love Hath Found His Eyes, or Distractions* ‡	*c.* 1640–1649
	Massinger, Philip	*The Fair Anchoress of Pausilippo* (See following.)	lic. 26 Jan.
	Massinger, Philip	*The Prisoner[s]* (Identified with above in S.R., 1653, but separately listed as a tragicomedy in S.R., 1660.)	*c.* 1613–1640(?)
	Sadler, John	*Masquerade du Ciel*	1640
	Sandys, George	*Christ's Passion* (Trans. Grotius's *Christus Patiens*.)	1640
	Shirley, James	*The Imposture* (*The Impostor*)	lic. 10 Nov.
	Shirley, James (?)	*The Arcadia* (An older play falsely ascribed ?)	1640 (pub.)
	Snelling, Thomas	*Thibaldus sive Vindictae Ingenium* (*Pharamus sive Libido Vindex*, in 1650 issue.)	1634–1640

‡ (Prol. and Epil. extant.)

TYPE	AUSPICES	EARLIEST TEXTS	LAST ED.	DATE
Neo-miracle	I Ogilby's Men, Dublin	1640*	1833[196]	
Tragedy	King's	[1642?]	1910†[239]	
Unknown	Red Bull Company at Fortune	Lost		
Comedy (?)	Beeston's Boys	Lost		
Tragicomedy	Unknown	MS (IV incomplete)	1959 (1960) G†	
Topical Comedy	Prince Charles's	Lost		
Mask (?)	Beeston's Boys	Lost (?)		
Comedy	Beeston's Boys	1653*	1873†[207]	**1640**
Comedy (?)	Unknown	Lost		
Tragicomedy	I Ogilby's Men, Dublin	1641*		
Comedy	King's	1649** & MS	1883†[100]	
Comedy	Beeston's Boys (?)	1640**		
Mask	Earl of Chesterfield's	1658 or 1659**	1874†[221]	
Mask	Court	1639[40][A]	1897[50]	
Dialogue	Closet	1641* & MS	1888 M	
Mask	At Apthorpe	MS	1938 B†	
Tragedy	Unknown	1654**	1910[101]	
Tragicomedy	Closet (?)	1640*		
Tragicomedy	Amateurs at Court, & King's	1640**	1875 D	
Tragedy	Unacted (?)	1640*		
Comedy	Unknown	Lost		
Comedy	Pembroke Col., Cambridge (?)	Lost		
Comedy	Unknown	Lost		
Unknown	King's	Lost		
Tragicomedy	Unknown	Lost		
'Mask'	Closet	1640*		
Neo-miracle	Closet	1640	1872†[244]	
Tragicomedy	King's	1653*	1833†[196]	
Pastoral Tragicomedy	'Queen Henrietta's'	1640*	1833[196]	
Latin Tragedy	St John's Col., Oxford	1640**		

DATE	AUTHOR	TITLE	LIMITS
	Suckling, John	*A Mask at Witten*	*c.* 1637(?)–1641
	Anon.	*The Cyprian Conqueror, or The Faithless Relict*	b. 1642
	Anon.	*The Ghost, or The Woman Wears the Breeches*	1640(?)
	Anon. (Dekker and Middleton?)	*The Roaring Girl, or The Catchpole* (Revision of *The Roaring Girl*, 1608?)	*c.* 1640(?)
1641	Brathwait, Richard	*Mercurius Britannicus, or The English Intelligencer* (*The Censure of the Judges, or The Court Cure*)	1641
	Brome, Richard	*A Jovial Crew, or The Merry Beggars*	1641
	Cavendish, W. (& Shirley, J.?)	*The Variety*	1639–1642
	Denham, John	*The Sophy*	1641(?)
	Fane, Mildmay	*Candy Restored* (*Candia Restaurata*)	12 Feb.
	Jordan, Thomas	*The Walks of Islington and Hogsdon* (*Tricks of Youth*)	lic. 2 Aug.
	Killigrew, Thomas	*The Parson's Wedding* (Revised after closing of theatres.)	1640–1641
	Lovelace, Richard	*The Soldier*	1640–1642
	Quarles, Francis	*The Virgin Widow*	*c.* 1640–1642
	Salusbury, Thomas	*A Mask at Knowsley*	6 Jan.
	Shipman, R.(?) & Taylor, W.(?)	*Grobiana's Nuptials*	1636(?)–1641(?)
	Shirley, James	*The Brothers* (*The Politic Father*)	lic. 26 May
	Shirley, James	*The Cardinal*	lic. 25 Nov.
	Tatham, John	*The Distracted State*	1641–1650
	Tatham, John (?)	*The Whisperer, or What You Please*	*c.* 1640–1650
	Taylor, John (describer)	*England's Comfort and London's Joy*	25 Nov.
	Wild, Robert	*The Benefice*	1641(?)
	Anon.	*Canterbury His Change of Diet*	1641
	Anon.	*Charles, Duke of Bourbon* (Poss. same as *Burben*, 1599 add.)	1641 (S.R.)
	Anon.	*The Doge and the Dragon*	lic. 23 June
	Anon.	*England's First Happiness, or The Life of St Austin*	1641 (S.R.)
	Anon.	*Five Most Noble Speeches*	1641
	Anon.	*King Charles His Entertainment, and London's Loyalty*	1641
	Anon.	*The Parroiall* (i.e. *Pareil? Parol?*) *of Princes*	1641 (S.R.)
	Anon.	*Read and Wonder*	1641
1642	Cowley, Abraham	*The Guardian* (See *Cutter of Coleman Street*, 1661.)	12 Mar.
	Fane, Mildmay	*The Change*	Dec. (written)
	Fane, Mildmay	*Time's Trick upon the Cards*	22 Feb.
	Jaques, Francis	*The Queen of Corsica*	1642
	'J.S.'	*Andromana, or The Merchant's Wife*	1642–1660

TYPE	AUSPICES	EARLIEST TEXTS	LAST ED.	DATE
Mask	House of Lionel Cranfield (?)	Lost		
Comedy	Closet (?)	MS		
Comedy	Unknown	1653*		
Comedy	Red Bull Company (?)	Lost (?)		
{ Latin Political Comedy	Closet	[1641]**	1811[245]	**1641**
{ English Translation	......	1641		
Comedy	Beeston's Boys	1652	1873[207] (AT)	
Comedy	King's	1649*		
Tragedy	King's	1642	1928[246]	
Political Allegory	At Apthorpe	MSS	1938 B†	
Comedy	Red Bull Company (?)	1657**		
Comedy	King's	1664*	1921[247] (DA)	
Tragedy	Unacted	Lost		
Tragicomedy	Privately acted (by 1649)	1649	1880†[248]	
Mask	Lord Strange's House	MS	1926|[249]	
Comedy	St John's Col., Oxford (?)	MS	1904†[250]	
Comedy	King's	1653*	1870[251]	
Tragedy	King's	1653*	1888 M (A)	
Tragedy	Unacted (?)	1651*	1879†[219]	
Comedy (?)	Red Bull Company (?)	Lost		
Royal Entertainment	London	1641*		
Comedy	Cambridge (?)	1689* & MSS		
Political Dialogue	Closet	1641* F		
Tragedy	Unknown	Lost		
Romance (?)	Prince Charles's	Lost		
Neo-miracle (?)	Unknown	Lost		
Royal Entertainment	York to London	1641*		
Royal Entertainment	London	1641*		
Unknown	Unknown	Lost		
Political Dialogue	Closet	1641*		
Comedy	Trinity Col., Cambridge	1650**	1906[222]	**1642**
Political Allegory	Unacted (?)	MS		
Moral	At Apthorpe (?)	MS		
Tragedy	Unacted (?)	MS		
Tragedy	Unacted (?)	1660*	1875 D	

L

DATE	AUTHOR	TITLE	LIMITS
	Shirley, James	*The Court Secret*	1642
	Shirley, James	*The Sisters*	lic. 26 Apr.
	Anon. (often assumed to be Kirke, J.)	*The Irish Rebellion*	lic. 8 June
1643	Fuller, T. (?) (Wilson, J., now rejected)	*Andronicus: Impiety's Long Success, or Heaven's Late Revenge*	c. 1642–1643
	Anon.	*Bel and the Dragon*	1643 (acted)
	Anon.	*The Cruel War*	1643
	Anon.	*Fraus Pia*	c. 1643–1660(?)
	Anon. (Fane, M. ?)	*Time's Triumph (Sight and Search. Juno in Arcadia)*	1643
	Anon.	*Tyrannical Government Anatomized, or A Discourse Concerning Evil Counsellors (Trans. Buchanan's Baptistes sive Calumnia.)*	1643
1644	Fane, Mildmay	*Virtue's Triumph*	1644
	Anon.	*Titus, or The Palm of Christian Courage*	1644
1645	Burkhead, Henry	*Cola's Fury, or Lirenda's Misery*	1645
	Cavendish, J.; Brackley, E.	*The Concealed Fancies*	1644–1646
	Cavendish, J.; Brackley, E.	*A Pastoral*	1644–1646
	Fane, Mildmay	*Don Phoebo's Triumph*	1645(?)
1646	Burroughs, —	*The Fatal Friendship*	1646 (S.R.)
	Killigrew, Thomas	*The Pilgrim*	1646(?)
	Shirley, James	*The Triumph of Beauty*	1646 (pub.)
	Anon.	*Ruff, Cuff, and Band (Same as Band, Cuff, and Ruff, 1615?)*	1646 (acted?)
1647	Baron, Robert	*Deorum Dona*	1647
	Baron, Robert	*Gripsius and Hegio, or The Passionate Lovers*	1647
	Fanshawe, Richard	*Il Pastor Fido (The Faithful Shepherd) (Trans. Guarini.)*	1647
	Mason, John	*School Moderator, or The Combat of Caps (Princeps Rhetoricus)*	21 Dec.
	Nedham, Marchmont	*The Levellers Levelled, or The Independents' Conspiracy to Root out Monarchy*	1647
	Sheppard, Samuel	*I The Committee-Man Curried*	1647
	Sheppard, Samuel	*II The Committee-Man Curried*	1647
	Anon.	*News out of the West, or The Character of a Mountebank*	1647
	Anon.	*The Scottish Politic Presbyter Slain by an English Independent, or The Independents' Victory over the Presbyterian Party*	1647
1648	Sherburne, Edward	*Medea (Trans. Seneca.)*	1648
	Anon.	*I Crafty Cromwell, or Oliver Ordering Our New State*	1648

TYPE	AUSPICES	EARLIEST TEXTS	LAST ED.	DATE
Tragicomedy	Unacted	1653* & MS	1833†[196]	
Comedy	King's	1653*	1833†[196]	
Topical Play	Prince Charles's (?)	Lost		
Tragedy	Oxford (?)	1661*		**1643**
Puppet Show	Holborn Bridge	Lost		
Political Dialogue	Closet	1643*		
Latin Comedy	Unknown	MS		
Pastoral–Allegorical Entertainment	Closet (?)	MS	(T)	
Political Allegory	Closet	1642[43]*	1907[41]	
Moral	Closet (?)	MS		**1644**
Biblical Moral	Jesuit Col., Kilkenny	1644*		
Political Tragicomedy	Closet	1646*		**1645**
Comedy	Closet	MS	1931†[252]	
Pastoral Dialogues	Closet	MS		
Moral Mask	At Apthorpe	MS		
Tragedy	King's (?)	Lost		**1646**
Tragedy	English players at Paris (?)	1664*		
Mask	Privately acted	1646*	1833†[196]	
Comic Dialogue (?)	Oxford (?)	MS (1646)		
Mask	Closet	1647**		**1647**
Pastoral	Closet	1647**		
Pastoral	Closet	1647		
Academic Allegory	Mason's School, Surrey	1648* (extracts)		
Political Dialogue	Closet	1647*		
Political Dialogue	Closet	1647*		
Political Dialogue	Closet	1647*		
Comic Interlude	Unknown	1647*		
Political Dialogue	Closet	1647*	1811†[253]	
Tragedy	Closet	1648*		**1648**
Political Dialogue	Closet	1648*		

DATE	AUTHOR	TITLE	LIMITS
	Anon.	*II Crafty Cromwell, or Oliver in His Glory as King*	1648
	Anon.	*The Cuckow's Nest at Westminster, or The Parliament between the Two Lady-Birds, Queen Fairfax and Lady Cromwell*	1648
	Anon.	*The Devil and the Parliament, or The Parliament and the Devil*	1648
	Anon.	*Ding-Dong, or Sir Pitiful Parliament on His Death-bed*	1648
	Anon.	*The Kentish Fair, or The Parliament Sold to Their Best Worth*	1648
	Anon.	*A Key to the Cabinet of the Parliament*	1648
	Anon.	*Marcus et Marcellianus*	1648
	Anon.	*Mercurius Honestus, or News from Westminster*	1648
	Anon.	*Mistress Parliament Brought to Bed*	1648
	Anon.	*Mistress Parliament, Her Gossiping*	1648
	Anon.	*Mistress Parliament, Her Invitation of Mistress London*	1648
	Anon.	*Mistress Parliament Presented in Her Bed*	1648
1649	'T.B.'	*The Rebellion of Naples, or The Tragedy of Massenello*	1649
	Wase, Christopher	*Electra* (Trans. Sophocles.)	1649–1650 (pub.)
	Anon.	*A Bartholomew Fairing*	1649
	Anon.	*Charles I*	1649
	Anon.	*The Disease of the House, or The State Mountebank Administering Physic to a Sick Parliament*	1649
	Anon.	*A New Bull-Baiting, or A Match Played at the Town Bull of Ely by Twelve Mongrels*	1649
	Anon.	*I Newmarket Fair, or A Parliament Outcry of State Commodities, Set to Sale*	1649
	Anon.	*II Newmarket Fair, or Mistress Parliament's New Figaries*	1649
	Anon.	*Women Will Have Their Will, or Give Christmas His Due*	1649
1650	Cartwright, George	*The Heroic Lover, or The Infanta of Spain*	c. 1645–c. 1655
	Fane, Mildmay	*De Pugna Animi*	1650
	Flecknoe, Richard	*Love in Its Infancy* (Earlier version of *Love's Dominion*, 1654.)	1650
	Flecknoe, Richard	*Love Stripped from Suspicion of Harm* (Projected. Became the above?)	1650
	Garfield, Benjamin	*The Unfortunate Fortunate*	b. 1650
	Killigrew, Thomas	*I & II Cicilia and Clorinda, or Love in Arms*	1649–1650
	Anon.	*Love's Victory*	c. 1630–c. 1650

TYPE	AUSPICES	EARLIEST TEXTS	LAST ED.	DATE
Political Dialogue	Closet	1648*		
Political Dialogue	Closet	1648*	1810[253]	
Political Dialogue	Closet	1648*		
Political Dialogue	Closet	1648*		
Political Dialogue	Closet	1648*		
Political Dialogue	Closet	1648*		
Latin Tragedy	St Omers	MS		
Political Dialogue	Closet	1648*		
Political Dialogue	Closet	1648*	1808†[25]	
Political Dialogue	Closet	1648*		
Political Dialogue	Closet	1648*		
Political Dialogue	Closet	1648*		
Contemporary Foreign History	Closet	1649*		**1649**
Tragedy	Closet	1649[/50?]*		
Political Dialogue	Closet	1649*		
Topical Tragedy	Closet	1649		
Political Dialogue	Closet	1649*		
Political Dialogue	Closet	1649*		
Political Dialogue	Closet	1649		
Political Dialogue	Closet	1649		
Political Dialogue	Closet	1649*		
Rimed Tragicomedy	Closet	1661*		**1650**
Moral	Unacted (?)	MS		
Pastoral Tragicomedy	Berseel: Duchess of Lorraine	Lost		
Pastoral Tragicomedy	Berseel	......		
Tragicomedy	Closet	Lost		
Tragicomedy	Closet	1664* & MS		
Pastoral	Closet (?)	MS	1853† (ex-tracts)[254] (T)	

DATE	AUTHOR	TITLE	LIMITS
	Anon.	*The White Ethiopian*	*c.* 1640(?)– *c.* 1650(?)
1651	Denny, William	*The Shepherd's Holiday*	1651
	Johnson, Nathaniel	*Pyrander* (Trans. from French. Of Bois- robert's *Pyrandre et Lisimène*?)	1633(?)–1663
	Prestwich, Edmund	*Hippolytus* (Trans. Seneca.)	1651
	'J.S.'	*The Prince of Prigs' Revels*	3 Sept.– 11 Nov.
	Sheppard, Samuel	*The Jovial Crew, or The Devil Turned Ranter*	1651
	Willan, Leonard	*Astraea, or True Love's Mirror*	1651
	Anon.	*Felix Concordia Fratrum sive Joannes et Paulus*	1651
	Anon.	*Fortunae Ludibrium sive Belisarius*	17 Aug.
	Anon.	*Marcus Tullius Cicero*	1651 (pub.)
1652	Goldsmith, Francis	*Sophompaneas, or Joseph* (Trans. Grotius.)	1652
	Killigrew, Thomas	*I & II Bellamira Her Dream, or The Love of Shadows*	1650–1652
	Manuche, Cosmo	*The Just General*	1652 (pub.)
	Manuche, Cosmo	*The Loyal Lovers*	1652 (pub.)
	Tatham, John	*The Scots Figgaries, or A Knot of Knaves*	1652
	Anon. (prob. not Manuche, C.)	*The Bastard*	1652 (pub.)
	Anon.	*Simo* (Ment. in Hazlitt's *Manual*. Ghost title?)	1652 (pub.) (?)
1653	Cox, Robert (author or adapter)	*Actaeon and Diana*	*c.* 1650–1655
	Cox, Robert (author or adapter)	*John Swabber*	9 June
	Cox, Robert (author or adapter)	*Rural Sports, or The Birthday of the Nymph Oenone*	*c.* 1650–1655
	Cox, Robert (author or adapter)	*Simpleton the Smith*	*c.* 1650–1655
	Cox, Robert (adapter?)	*The Black Man* (A traditional piece.)	*c.* 1600–1673
	Cox, Robert (?)	*Diphilo and Granida*	*c.* 1650–1673
	Cox, Robert (?)	*King Ahasuerus and Queen Esther*	*c.* 1650–1673
	Cox, Robert (?)	*King Solomon's Wisdom*	*c.* 1650–1673
	Cox, Robert (?)	*Philetis and Constantia*	*c.* 1650–1673
	Cox, Robert (?)	*Venus and Adonis, or The Maid's Philosophy*	*c.* 1650–1673
	Pepys, Samuel	*Love a Cheat*	1650–1653
	Shirley, James	*Cupid and Death*	26 Mar.
	Stapylton, Robert	*The Royal Choice* (Same as the 'Pastor Stapilton' in Rogers and Ley's list, 1656?)	1653 (S.R.)
	Anon.	*S. Edoardus Confessor sive Mites Terram Possidebunt*	16 Aug.

TYPE	AUSPICES	EARLIEST TEXTS	LAST ED.	DATE
Tragicomedy	Closet (?)	MS	(T)	
Pastoral	Closet	MS	1870†[255]	**1651**
Tragicomedy	Unknown	Lost		
Tragedy	Closet	1651*		
Comic Interlude	Unknown	1651*		
Political Dialogue	Closet	1651*		
Rimed Tragicomedy	Closet	1651*		
Latin Tragedy	St Omers	MS		
Latin Tragedy	St Omers	MS		
Tragedy	Closet (?)	1651*		
Biblical Play	Closet	1652*		**1652**
Tragicomedy	Closet	1664*		
Tragicomedy	Closet (?)	1652*		
Tragicomedy	Closet (?)	1652*		
Political Comedy	Closet	1652	1879†[219]	
Tragedy	Unknown	1652*		
Latin Comedy	Unknown	1652* (?)		
Pastoral	At Red Bull (?)	[1655?]**	1932†[102]	**1653**
Droll	By Cox at Red Bull	[1655?]	1932†[102]	
Pastoral	At Red Bull (?)	[1655?]	1932†[102]	
Droll	At Red Bull (?)	1656	1932†[102]	
Jig	Unknown	1673	1932[102]	
Pastoral	Unknown	1673	1932†[102]	
Dialogue	Unknown	1673	1932†[102]	
Dialogue	Unknown	1673	1932†[102]	
Droll	Unknown	1673	1932†[102]	
Droll	Unknown	1673	1932†[102]	
Comedy (?)	Closet (?)	Lost		
Mask	'Gentlemen' for Portuguese Ambassador	1653 & MS	1833†[196]	
Pastoral (?)	Closet (?)	Lost		
Latin Tragedy	St Omers	MS		

DATE	AUTHOR	TITLE	LIMITS
1654	Fanshawe, Richard	*To Love Only for Love's Sake* (Trans. Mendoza's *Querer por solo querer.*)	1654
	Flecknoe, Richard	*Ariadne*	1654 (pub.)
	Flecknoe, Richard	*Love's Dominion* (See *Love's Kingdom*, 1664.)	1654
	Howell, James	*The Nuptials of Peleus and Thetis* (*The Great Royal Ball*)	1654
	Jordan, Thomas	*Cupid His Coronation* (See *Fancy's Festivals*, 1657.)	1654
	Killigrew, Thomas	*I & II Thomaso, or The Wanderer*	1654
	'T.R.'	*The Extravagant Shepherd* (Trans. T. Corneille's *Le Berger extravagant.*)	1654
	Anon.	*The New Brawl, or Turnmill Street against Rosemary Lane*	1654
	Anon.	*The True Tragicomedy* [of Robert Carr and Francis Howard]	*c.* 1654
1655	Baron, Robert	*Mirza*	1655
	Gayton, Edmund (describer)	*Charity Triumphant, or The Virgin Show*	29 Oct.
	Lower, William	*Polyeuctes, or The Martyr* (Trans. Corneille's *Polyeucte.*)	1655
	Lower, William	*Scaevoli*	*c.* 1655–1656
	Stanley, Thomas	*The Clouds* (Trans. Aristophanes.)	1655
	Anon.	*The Gossips' Brawl, or The Women Wear the Breeches*	1655 (pub.)
	Anon. ('P. Claretus')	*Homo Duplex sive Funestum Corporis et Animae Duellum*	July
1656	'I.B.' (Bulteel, John?)	*London's Triumph*	29 Oct.
	Davenant, William	*The Athenians' Reception of Phocion*	1656–1657
	Davenant, William	*The First Day's Entertainment at Rutland House*	23 May
	Davenant, William	*Satirical Declamations* (Same as above?)	1656–1657
	Davenant, William	*I The Siege of Rhodes*	Sept.
	Holland, Samuel	*Cupid and Psyche*	1656
	Holland, Samuel	*The Enchanted Grove*	1656 (?)
	Holland, Samuel	*Venus and Adonis*	1656
	Lower, William	*Horatius* (Trans. Corneille's *Horace.*)	1656
	Anon.	*Crux Vindicata*	8 Aug.
	Anon. (Formido, C.?)	*The Governor* (Same as *The Governor*, 1637?)	1656 (MS date)
	Anon. (wrongly assigned to Prestwich, E.)	*The Hectors, or The False Challenge*	1656
1657	D'Ouvilley, George Gerbier	*The False Favourite Disgraced, and The Reward of Loyalty*	1657
	Jordan, Thomas	*Fancy's Festivals* (Incorporates *Cupid His Coronation*, 1654.)	1654–1657

TYPE	AUSPICES	EARLIEST TEXTS	LAST ED.	DATE
Romance	Closet	1670 & MS		**1654**
Pastoral with Recitative	Unknown	1654*		
Tragicomedy	Closet	1654**		
Translation of French Royal Entertainment	Closet	1654*		
Mask	Girls' School, Spittle	MS		
Comedy	Closet	1664*		
Pastoral	Closet	1654*		
'Mock Comedy' (Dialogue)	Closet	1654*		
Thesis Play	Closet	MS		
Tragedy	Closet	[1655]*		**1655**
Civic Pageant	London	1655*		
Tragedy	Closet	1655*		
Unknown	Closet (?)	Lost		
Comedy	Closet	1655		
Comic Interlude	Unknown	1655*		
Latin Moral	St Omers	MSS		
Civic Pageant	London	1656*		**1656**
Entertainment	Rutland House 'Opera'	Lost		
Disputation	Rutland House 'Opera'	1657	1873†[203]	
Disputations	Rutland House 'Opera'	Lost (?)		
Tragicomedy	Rutland House 'Opera'	1656	1909[227] (A)	
Burlesque Mask	Closet	Lost		
Mask	Unknown	MS (lost?)		
Burlesque Mask	Closet	1656**		
Tragedy	Closet	1656*		
Latin Tragedy	St Omers	MS		
Tragicomedy	King's (?)	MS		
Comedy	Closet	1656*		
Tragicomedy	Closet	1657**		**1657**
Medley	Private entertainment	1657**		

DATE	AUTHOR	TITLE	LIMITS
	Lower, William	*Don Japhet of Armenia* (Trans. Scarron's *Don Japhet d'Arménie.*)	1657
	Lower, William	*The Three Dorothies, or Jodelet Boxed* (Trans. Scarron's *Les Trois Dorotées, ou le Jodelet souffleté.*)	c. 1655–1660
	Talbot, Gilbert	*Filli di Sciro* (Trans. Bonarelli.)	1657
	Tatham, John	*London's Triumphs*	29 Oct.
	Anon. (Davenant, W. ?)	*The Countryman* (Prob. same as *The Countryman,* S.R., 1653; see Supp. II, a.)	5 Nov.(?) (acted)
1658	Cavendish, Margaret	*Plays* (Published in folio, in 1662, were the anomalous dramas of the Marchioness of Newcastle, mostly sketches of morals and comedies. The titles of these, most of which were probably written during the Interregnum, are as follows: *The Apocryphal Ladies*; *Bell in Campo*; *The Comical Hash*; *The Female Academy*; *The Lady Contemplation*; *Love's Adventures*; *The Matrimonial Trouble*; *Nature's Three Daughters – Beauty, Love, and Wit*; *The Public Wooing*; *The Religious*; *Several Wits*; *The Unnatural Tragedy*; *The Wits' Cabal*; *Youth's Glory and Death's Banquet*. For Lady Margaret's second flowering, see 1665.)	1653–1662
	Cavendish, William	*A Pleasant and Merry Humour of a Rogue* (See *The Triumphant Widow,* 1674.)	c. 1655–1660 (?)
	Chamberlaine, William	*Love's Victory*	1658
	Davenant, William	*The Cruelty of the Spaniards in Peru* (Same as *II Sir Francis Drake*?) (Included as Act IV of *The Playhouse to Be Let,* 1663.)	1658
	Davenant, William	*I Sir Francis Drake* (Included as Act III of *The Playhouse to Be Let,* 1663.)	1658–1659
	Fane, Mildmay	*Ladrones, or The Robber's Island*	c. 1656–c. 1660
	Fanshawe, Richard	*La Fida Pastora* (Trans. Fletcher's *The Faithful Shepherdess.*)	1658
	Lower, William	*The Enchanted Lovers*	1658 (pub.)
	Meriton, Thomas	*The Chaste Virgin*	c. 1658
	Meriton, Thomas	*Love and War*	1658
	Meriton, Thomas	*The Several Affairs*	c. 1658
	Meriton, Thomas	*The Wandering Lover*	1658
	Shirley, James	*The Contention of Ajax and Ulysses for the Armour of Achilles*	c. 1645–1658
	Shirley, James	*Honoria and Mammon* (Adapt. *The Contention for Honour and Riches,* 1631.)	1658 (pub.)
	Swinhoe, Gilbert	*The Unhappy Fair Irene*	1658 (pub.)
	Tatham, John	*London's Triumph, Presented by Industry and Honour*	29 Oct.

TYPE	AUSPICES	EARLIEST TEXTS	LAST ED.	DATE
Comedy	Closet	MS		
Comedy	Closet	MS		
Pastoral	Closet	MSS		
Civic Pageant	London	[1657]*		
Unknown	At Inner Temple	Lost		
Dialogues	Closet	1662*		**1658**

Comic Interlude	See 1674	MS	1933†[256]	
Tragicomedy	Closet	1658*	1914[257]	
Operatic Show	Cockpit 'Opera'	1658	1873†[203]	
Pseudo-history	Cockpit 'Opera'	1659	1873†[203]	
'Opera'	Unknown	MS (lost?)		
Latin Pastoral	Closet	1658**		
Pastoral Tragicomedy	Unacted (?)	1658** & MS	1932†[258]	
'Romance'	Closet	Lost		
Tragedy	Unacted	1658*		
Comedy	Closet	Lost		
Tragicomedy	Privately acted	1658*		
Entertainment	Shirley's school (?)	[1658]**	1833†[196]	
Moral	Unacted (?)	[1658]	1833†[196]	
Tragedy	Unacted (?)	1658*		
Civic Pageant	London	1658*		

DATE	AUTHOR	TITLE	LIMITS
	Willan, Leonard	*Orgula, or The Fatal Error*	1658
1659	'H.B.' (Burkhead, H.? or Birkhead, H.? or Burnell, H.?)	*The Female Rebellion*	*c.* 1657–*c.* 1659
	'H.H.B.'	*The World's Idol, Plutus* (Trans. Aristophanes.)	1659
	Davenant, William	*II The Siege of Rhodes*	1657–*c.* 1659
	Flecknoe, Richard	*The Marriage of Oceanus and Britannia*	1659 (pub.)
	Kirkham, R. (?)	*Alfred, or Right Re-enthroned*	1659
	Jordan, Thomas	*An Eclogue, or Representation in Four Parts*	18 Dec.
	Lower, William	*The Noble Ingratitude* (Trans. Quinault's *La Généreuse ingratitude*.)	1659
	Neville, Henry	*Shuffling, Cutting, and Dealing in a Game of Picquet*	1659
	Reymes, William	*Self-Interest, or The Belly Wager* (Trans. Secchi's *L'Interesse*.)	*c.* 1650–1660
	Tatham, John	*London's Triumph*	29 Oct.
	Anon. (Jordan, T.?)	*The Florentine Ladies*	*c.* 1659–1660
	Anon.	*Lady Alimony, or The Alimony Lady* (Revis. of Caroline play?)	1659 (revised?)
	Anon.	*The London Chanticleers*	1659 (pub.)
1660	Dancer, John	*Aminta* (Trans. Tasso.)	1660
	Forde, Thomas	*Love's Labyrinth, or The Royal Shepherdess*	1660
	Howard, Robert	*The Blind Lady*	1660
	Jordan, Thomas	*Bacchus' Festival, or A New Medley*	12 Apr.
	Jordan, Thomas	*The Cheaters Cheated* (In *Rosary of Rarities Planted in the Garden of Poetry*.)	*c.* 1660 (pub.)
	Lower, William	*The Amorous Fantasm* (Trans. Quinault's *Le Fantôme amoureux*.)	1660 (pub.)
	Manuche, Cosmo	*The Banished Shepherdess*	1659–1660
	Pordage, Samuel	*Troades* (Trans. Seneca.)	1660
	Richards, William (preserver?)	*The Christmas Ordinary*	1633–1660
	Sadler, Anthony	*The Subject's Joy for the King's Restoration*	1660
	Tatham, John	*London's Glory Represented by Time, Truth, and Fame*	5 July
	Tatham, John	*The Royal Oak*	29 Oct.
	Tatham, John	*The Rump, or The Mirror of the Late Times*	June
	T[homson?], T[homas?]	*The English Rogue*	1660–1668
	Anon.	*Le Ballet de la paix*	1660 (pub.)
	Anon.	*Cromwell's Conspiracy*	8 Aug. (MS date)
	Anon.	*England's Joy* (Descrip. of welcome of Charles II.)	1660
	Anon.	*The Life and Death of Mrs Rump*	1660
	Anon.	*Love's Mystery* (Alternative title for older play, or error for Heywood's *Love's Mistress*?)	12 Nov. (?)

TYPE	AUSPICES	EARLIEST TEXTS	LAST ED.	DATE
Tragedy	Unacted (?)	1658*		
Tragicomedy	Closet	MSS	1872†[259]	**1659**
Comedy	Closet	1659*		
Tragicomedy	Cockpit 'Opera' (?)	1663	1909[227]	
Mask	Unknown	1659*		
Pseudo-history	Closet	MS		
Entertainment	London	1659**	1866[260]	
Pastoral Tragicomedy	Closet (?)	1659**		
Political Dialogue	Closet	1659*	1810†[253]	
Comedy	Unacted (?)	MS	1953†[261]	
Civic Pageant	London	1659*		
Comedy	'at night by Gentlemen'	Lost		
Comedy	Rhodes's Company at Cockpit (?)	1659*	1875 D	
Comic Interlude	Acted out of London	1659*	1875 D	
Pastoral	Closet	1660*		**1660**
Pastoral Tragicomedy	Closet	1660		
Tragicomedy	Closet	1660**		
Entertainment	Vintners' Hall	1660*		
Jig	Unknown	[c. 1660]	1929[03]	
Tragicomedy	'Acted at Court' (?)	1660**		
Political Allegory	Unknown	MS		
Tragedy	Closet	1660*		
Christmas Play	Trinity Col., Oxford (?)	1682* & MS (frag.)		
Biblical Allegory	Closet	1660*		
Royal Entertainment	London	1660**	1879†[219]	
Civic Pageant	London	1660*	1931†[135]	
Topical Comedy	Salisbury Court Company	1660	1879†[219]	
Comedy	Privately acted (?)	1668*		
Ballet	Court	1660*		
History	Unknown	1660*		
Triumph	Dover to Westminster	1660		
Political Dialogue	Closet	1660*		
Unknown	King's	Lost (?)		

DATE	AUTHOR	TITLE	LIMITS
	Anon.	*A Phanatique Play*	1660
	Anon.	*The Tragical Actors, or The Martyrdom of the Late King Charles*	1660
1661	Carpenter, Richard	*The Pragmatical Jesuit New Leavened*	*c.* 1660–1670
	Cowley, Abraham	*Cutter of Coleman Street* (Adapt. *The Guardian,* 1642.)	16 Dec. (Pepys)
	Davenant, William (?)	*Hamlet* (Adapt. Shakespeare.)	1661 (?)
	Flecknoe, Richard	*Erminia, or The Fair and Virtuous Lady*	1661 (pub.)
	Fountain, John	*The Rewards of Virtue* (See *The Royal Shepherdess,* 1669.)	1661
	Howard, Henry	*The United Kingdoms*	1660–*c.* 1664
	Jordan, Thomas	*The New Medley* (In *Merry Drollerie.*)	1661 (pub.)
	Kirkman, Francis (?)	*Bottom the Weaver* (From *A Midsummer-Night's Dream.*)	Apr. (?)
	Kirkman, Francis (?)	*The Presbyterian Lash, or Noctroff's Maid Whipped*	1661
	Ogilby, John (describer)	*The Coronation Entertainment for Charles II*	22 Apr.
	Tatham, John	*London's Triumphs*	29 Oct.
	Tatham, John	*Neptune's Address* [*to King Charles*]	22 Apr.
	Anon.	*The Fall of Sodom and Gomorrah*	Aug.
	Anon.	*Hell's Higher Court of Justice, or The Trial of the Three Politic Ghosts*	1661
	Anon.	*Hewson Reduced, or The Shoemaker Returned to His Trade*	1661
	Anon.	*The Liar* (Same as *The Mistaken Beauty,* 1684?) (Adapt. P. Corneille's *Le Menteur?*)	1661–1664
	Anon.	*Lot Debauched*	Aug.
	Anon.	*Love's Quarrel* (Alternative title for earlier play revived?)	6 Apr. (Pepys)
	Anon.	*Robin Hood and His Crew of Soldiers*	23 Apr.
1662	Bartley (Berkeley?), William	*Cornelia*	1662–1663
	Bayley, George	*Noah's Flood*	1662
	Boyle, Roger	*The General* (Altered, and pub. as *Altemira,* 1702.) (Related to *The General,* 1638?)	18 Oct.
	Clerke, William	*Marciano, or The Discovery*	27 Dec.
	Codrington, Robert	*Ignoramus* (Trans. Ruggle. Related to Parkhurst's trans.?)	1662 (pub.)
	Cokain, Aston	*Ovid*	1662 (pub.)
	Davenant, William	*The Law against Lovers* (Adapt. Shakespeare's *Measure for Measure* and *Much Ado about Nothing.*)	10 Feb.
	Howard, Robert	*The Committee*	27 Nov. (at Court)
	Howard, Robert	*The Surprisal*	23 Apr.
	Killigrew, William	*Selindra*	3 Mar.

TYPE	AUSPICES	EARLIEST TEXTS	LAST ED.	DATE
Political Dialogue	Closet	1660**		
Political Dialogue	Closet	[1660]*		
Satirical Comedy	Unacted	[1661 ?]*		**1661**
Comedy	Duke's	1663	1936[190]	
Tragedy	Duke's (?)	1676*		
Tragicomedy	Unacted (?)	1661		
Tragicomedy	Unacted	1661*		
Tragedy (?)	Duke's (?)	Lost		
Jig	Acted 1671 in Civic Pageant	1661	1929[93]	
Droll	King's (?)	1661	1932[102]	
Topical Comedy	Unacted	1661*		
Coronation Entertainment	London	1661		
Civic Pageant	London	1661*		
Entertainment	London	1661*		
Puppet Show	Bartholomew Fair	Current		
Political Dialogue	Closet	1661*		
Political Dialogue	Closet	1661*		
Comedy (?)	King's	1661* (lost ?)		
Puppet Show	Bartholomew Fair	Current		
Tragicomedy (?)	Duke's	Lost		
Dialogue	At Nottingham	1661*		
Tragicomedy (?)	King's	Lost		**1662**
Musical Show	By Bayley in London	Lost		
Tragicomedy	II Ogilby's Men, Dublin; King's in 1664	MSS	1937[262]	
Tragicomedy	Holyrood House, Edinburgh	1663*	1871†[263]	
Comedy	Unacted (?)	1662*		
Tragedy	Unacted (?)	1662	1874†[221]	
Comedy	Duke's	1673*	1874†[203]	
Comedy	King's	1665	1921†[264]	
Comedy	King's	1665		
Tragicomedy	King's	1665		

DATE	AUTHOR	TITLE	LIMITS
	Kirkman, Francis (?)	*I The Wits, or Sport upon Sport:* A collection of drolls fashioned from comic scenes in older plays: *The Bouncing Knight, or The Robbers Robbed* (from *I Henry IV*); *The Bubble* (from *Greene's Tu Quoque*); *The Club-Men* (from *Philaster*); *The Doctors of Dull-Head College* (from *Monsieur Thomas*); *The Encounter* (from *The Knight of the Burning Pestle*); *An Equal Match* (from *Rule a Wife and Have a Wife*); *The False Heir and Formal Curate* (from *The Scornful Lady*); *Forced Valour* (from *The Humorous Lieutenant*); *The Grave-Makers* (from *Hamlet*); *The Humour of Bumpkin* (from Cox's *Actaeon and Diana*); *The Humour of Hobbinol* (from Cox's *Rural Sports*); *The Humour of John Swabber* (from Cox's *Actaeon and Diana*); *The Humour of Simpleton* (from Cox's *Simpleton the Smith*); *The Humours of Monsieur Galliard* (from *The Variety*); *The Humours of Simpkin* (from Cox's *Actaeon and Diana*); *The Imperick* (from *The Alchemist*); *Invisible Smirk, or The Pen Combatants* (from *Two Merry Milkmaids*); *Jenkin's Love-Course and Perambulation* (from *Love Tricks*); *The Lame Commonwealth* (from *Beggars' Bush*); *The Landlady* (from *The Maid's Tragedy*); *The Loyal Citizens* (from *Cupid's Revenge*); *A Prince in Conceit* (from *The Opportunity*); *The Sexton, or The Mock Testator* (from *The Spanish Curate*); *The Stallion* (from *The Custom of the Country*); *The Surprise* (from *The Maid in the Mill*); *The Testy Lord* (from *The Maid's Tragedy*); *The Three Merry Boys* (from *The Bloody Brother*). For *II The Wits*, see 1673.	1662 (pub.)
	Neville, Robert	*The Poor Scholar*	1662 (pub.)
	Ogilby, John	*The Merchant of Dublin* (Poss. pre-Restoration.)	1662(?)–1663 (?)
	Parkhurst, Ferdinando	*Ignoramus, or The Academical Lawyer* (Three versions in MS.) (Trans. Ruggle.)	1 Nov. (at Court)
	Porter, Thomas	*The Villain*	18 Oct. (Pepys)
	Tatham, John	*Aqua Triumphalis*	23 Aug.
	Tatham, John	*London's Triumph*	29 Oct.
	Anon.	*The Faithful Virgins*	1661–1663
	Anon.	*The New-Made Nobleman* (An old play revived?)	22 Jan. (acted)
	Anon.	*The Renegado* (Adapt. or revival of Massinger.)	6 June (acted)

TYPE	AUSPICES	EARLIEST TEXTS	LAST ED.	DATE
Drolls	Offered for acting	1662	1932†[102]	

Comedy	Unacted (?)	1662*	
Unknown	II Ogilby's Men, Dublin (?)	Lost	
Comedy	Duke's	MSS	
Tragedy	Duke's	1663	
Royal Entertainment	London	1662	
Civic Pageant	London	1662*	
Tragedy	Duke's	MS	
Comedy	At Red Bull	Lost (?)	
Tragicomedy	King's	MS (?)	

M

DATE	AUTHOR	TITLE	LIMITS
1663	Cary, Henry	*The Marriage Night*	*c.* Sept.
	Davenant, William	*The Playhouse to Be Let* (One act from Molière's *Sganarelle*. See *The Cruelty of the Spaniards in Peru* and *I Sir Francis Drake*, 1658.)	*c.* Aug.
	Digby, George	*Elvira, or The Worst Not Always True* (Adapt. Calderón's *No siempre lo peor es cierto*.)	1663–1664
	Dryden, John	*The Wild Gallant* (Revised for a revival before publication.) (Adapt. Brome?)	5 Feb.
	Evelyn, John	*Thyrsander*	1663
	Filmer; Godolphin; Sackville, C.; Sedley; Waller	*Pompey the Great* (Trans. Corneille's *Pompée*.)	*c.* Dec.
	Green, Alexander	*The Politician Cheated*	1663
	Head, Richard	*Hic et Ubique, or The Humours of Dublin*	1663 (pub.)
	Hoole, Charles	*Comoedia Sex Anglo-Latinae* (Trans. Terence's *Adelphi, Andria, Eunuchus, Heautontimorumenos, Hecyra, Phormio*.)	1663
	Howard, James	*The English Monsieur*	30 July (acted)
	Killigrew, William	*Pandora, or The Converts*	1662–1663
	Philips, Katherine	*Pompey* (Trans. Corneille's *Pompée*.)	10 Feb.
	Porter, Thomas	*The Carnival*	1663–1664
	P[orter?], T[homas?]	*A Witty Combat, or The Female Victor*	June
	Rhodes, Richard	*Flora's Vagaries* (First produced at Christ Church, Oxford, 8 Jan. 1663.)	3 Nov.
	S[outhland?], T[homas?]	*Love à la Mode*	1662–1663
	Stanley, Thomas	*Aeschyli Tragoediae Septem* (The seven plays edited and translated.)	1663
	Stapylton, Robert	*The Slighted Maid*	23 Feb. (Pepys)
	Stapylton, Robert	*The Stepmother*	*c.* Nov.
	Tatham, John	*Londinium Triumphans*	29 Oct.
	Tuke, Samuel	*The Adventures of Five Hours* (Adapt. Coello's *Los Empeños de seis horas*.)	8 Jan. (Pepys)
	Wilson, John	*The Cheats*	lic. 6 Mar.
	Anon.	*Encyclochoria, or Universal Motion*	3 Jan.
	Anon.	*The Exposure*	*c.* Nov.
	Anon.	*School-Play*	1663
	Anon.	*The Unfortunate Usurper*	1663
	Anon.	*The Wandering Whores' Complaint*	1663 (pub.)
1664	Banister, William	*Andronichus sive Aulae Byzantinae Vota*	1664
	Banister, William	*Jephte sive Christi Naturam Humanam Immolantis Expressa Figura*	1664
	Banister, William	*Perseus et Demetrius sive Discordia Omnis Pessima Imperii Lues*	7 Aug. (acted)
	Boyle, Roger	*Henry V*	Aug.
	Bulteel, John	*Amorous Orontus, or The Love in Fashion* (*The Amorous Gallant*, 1675) (Adapt. T. Corneille's *L'Amour à la mode*.) (Poss. same as *Love in and Love out of Fashion*, 1689.)	1664

TYPE	AUSPICES	EARLIEST TEXTS	LAST ED.	DATE
Tragicomedy	Duke's	1664*	1876 D†	**1663**
Comic Medley	Duke's	1673*	1873†[203]	
Comedy	Duke's	1667 & MS	1876 D	
Comedy	King's	1669	1962[265a]	
Tragicomedy	Unacted	Lost		
Tragedy	Duke's	1664**		
Comedy	Unacted	1663*		
Comedy	Acted privately	1663*		
Comedies	Closet	1663		
Comedy	King's	1674		
Comedy altered from Tragedy	Duke's	1664		
Tragedy	II Ogilby's Men, Dublin	1663		
Comedy	King's	1664*		
Comedy	Privately acted (?)	1663*		
Comedy	King's	1670		
Comedy	Middlesex House	1663**		
Latin Tragedies	Closet	1663		
Tragicomedy	Duke's	1663		
Tragicomedy	Duke's	1664**		
Civic Pageant	London	1663*		
Tragicomedy	Duke's	1663	[1928][266] (D)	
Comedy	King's	1664 & MS	1935[267]	
Royal Entertainment	Lincoln's Inn	1662[63]*		
Pastoral	King's	Lost		
Academic Moral	A Middlesex school	1664*		
Tragedy	Unacted	1663*		
Comedy	Unacted (?)	1663*		
Latin Tragedy	St Omers	MS		**1664**
Latin Tragedy	St Omers	MS		
Latin Tragedy	St Omers	MS		
Tragicomedy	Duke's	1668 & MSS	1937†[262]	
Comedy	King's	1665		

DATE	AUTHOR	TITLE	LIMITS
	Carlell, Lodowick	*Heraclius, Emperor of the East* (Trans. Corneille.)	9 Mar. (imprim.)
	Davenant, William	*Macbeth* (Adapt. Shakespeare.)	5 Nov. (Pepys)
	Davenant, William	*The Rivals* (Adapt. Shakespeare & Fletcher's *The Two Noble Kinsmen.*)	1664
	Digby, George	*'Tis Better Than It Was* (Adapt. Calderón's *Mejor está que estaba.*)	1662–1666
	Digby, George	*Worse and Worse* (Adapt. Calderón's *Peor está que estaba.*)	20 July (Pepys)
	Dryden, John	*The Rival Ladies*	*c.* May
	Etherege, George	*The Comical Revenge, or Love in a Tub*	Mar.
	Flecknoe, Richard	*Love's Kingdom* (Adapt. *Love's Dominion*, 1654.)	1663–1664
	Holden, John (?)	*The German Princess*	15 Apr. (Pepys)
	Howard, Edward	*The Usurper*	2 Jan. (Pepys)
	Howard, James	*Romeo and Juliet* (Adapt. Shakespeare; with happy ending.)	1664 (?)
	Howard, Robert	*The Vestal Virgin, or The Roman Ladies* (With alternative endings.)	1664–1665
	Howard, R.; Dryden, J.	*The Indian Queen*	25 Jan.
	Killigrew, William	*Ormasdes, or Love and Friendship*	23 Aug. (imprim.)
	Lacy, John	*The Old Troop, or Monsieur Raggou*	1662–1665
	Southland, Thomas (?)	*The Ungrateful Favourite*	11 May. (imprim.)
	Tatham, John	*London's Triumphs*	29 Oct.
	Waller, Edmund	*The Maid's Tragedy* (Adapt. Beaumont & Fletcher; with happy ending.)	*c.* 1664
	Wilson, John	*Andronicus Commenius*	1664
	Wilson, John	*The Projectors*	13 Jan. (imprim.)
	Anon.	*Heraclius* (Trans. Corneille.)	8 Mar. (Pepys)
	Anon.	*Irena*	1664
	Anon.	*Judith and Holofernes*	1664 (acted)
	Anon.	*Knavery in All Trades, or The Coffee-House*	'Christmas Holidays'
	Anon.	*The Labyrinth*	2 May (Pepys)
1665	Boyle, Roger	*Mustapha, Son of Solyman the Magnificent*	3 Apr. (Pepys)
	Boyle, Roger (?)	*The Widow* (Poss. Middleton's play revived.)	4 May
	Brathwait, Richard	*Regicidium*	1665
	Cavendish, Margaret	*Plays* (Composed between 1662–1668; see above under 1658. Present volume contains *The Bridals*; *The Convent of Pleasure*; *The Presence*; *The Sociable Companions, or The Female Wits*; and fragments.)	1662–1668
	Cotton, Charles	*Horace* (Trans. Corneille.)	1665 (?)
	Dryden, John	*The Indian Emperor, or The Conquest of Mexico by the Spaniards*	*c.* Apr.

TYPE	AUSPICES	EARLIEST TEXTS	LAST ED.	DATE
Tragedy	Unacted	1664*		
Dramatic Opera	Duke's	1674 & MS	1961†[268]	
Comedy	Duke's	1668**	1874†[203]	
Comedy	Duke's (?)	Lost		
Comedy	Duke's	Lost		
Tragicomedy	King's	1664	1962[265a]	
Comedy	Duke's	1664	1927[269]	
Tragicomedy	Duke's	1664**		
Comedy (?)	Duke's	Lost		
Tragedy	King's	1668*		
Tragicomedy	Duke's	Lost		
Tragedy and Tragicomedy	King's	1665		
Tragicomedy	King's	1665	1962[265a] (A)	
Tragicomedy	Unacted (?)	1665		
Comedy	King's	1672	1875[270]	
Tragedy	Unacted	1664*		
Civic Pageant	London	1664*		
Tragicomedy	Unacted (?)	1690		
Tragedy	Unacted	1664*	1874†[271]	
Comedy	Unacted (?)	1665*	1874†[271]	
Tragedy	Duke's	Lost		
Tragicomedy	Unacted	1664*		
Droll	Bartholomew Fair	Lost		
Comedy	'By Several Apprentices'	1664*		
Comedy (?)	King's	Lost		
Tragedy	Duke's	1668 & MSS	1937†[262] (A)	**1665**
Comedy	Unknown	Lost		
Latin Topical Play	Closet	1665*		
Dramatic Sketches	Closet	1668*		
Tragedy	Closet	1671*		
Tragedy	King's	1667 & MSS	1931[265]	

DATE	AUTHOR	TITLE	LIMITS
	Holden, John	*The Ghosts*	17 Apr. (Pepys)
	Killigrew, William	*The Siege of Urbin*	1665–1666
	Manuche, Cosmo	*The Feast* (Other MS plays by Manuche, as yet undated, are *Agamemnon* [Tragedy, frag.]; *The Captives* [Comedy, frag.; trans. Plautus ?]; *Lenotius, King of Cyprus* [Tragedy]; *The Mandrake* [Comedy]; *Mariamne* [Tragedy]; a titleless comedy and titleless tragedy.)	1664–*c.* 1665
	Stroude, —	*All Plot, or The Disguises*	1662–1671
1666	Hoadley, S. (?)	*The War of Grammar* (*Basileia seu Bellum Grammaticale*)	1666
	Medbourne, Matthew (?)	*St Cecily, or The Converted Twins* ('E.M.' on t.p., but dedication signed by Medbourne.)	11 June (imprim.)
	Anon.	*Punchinello* (*Polichinello. Punch and Judy*)	1666 (lic.)
1667	Bailey, Abraham	*The Spiteful Sister*	10 Apr. (imprim.)
	Boyle, Roger	*The Black Prince*	19 Oct. (Pepys)
	Caryl, John	*The English Princess, or The Death of Richard III*	7 Mar. (Pepys)
	Cavendish, W. (& Dryden ? Shirley ? or Shadwell ?)	*The Humorous Lovers*	28 Mar.
	Davenant, William	*Greene's Tu Quoque* (Adapt. Cooke.)	12 Sept. (Pepys)
	Davenant, W.; Dryden, J.	*The Tempest, or The Enchanted Island* (Adapt. Shakespeare.)	7 Nov. (Pepys)
	Dover, John	*The Roman Generals, or The Distressed Ladies*	7 Nov. (imprim.)
	Dryden, John	*Secret Love, or The Maiden Queen*	2 Mar. (Pepys)
	Dryden, J. (adapting trans. by Cavendish, W.?)	*Sir Martin Mar-all, or The Feigned Innocence* (Adapt. Quinault's *L'Amant indiscret* and Molière's *L'Étourdi*.)	15 Aug. (Pepys)
	Flecknoe, Richard	*The Damoiselles à la Mode* (Adapt. Molière's *Les Précieuses ridicules*, etc.)	15 May (imprim.)
	Flecknoe, Richard	*The Physician against His Will* (Adapt. Molière's *Le Médecin malgré lui*.)	*c.* 1667
	Howard, Edward	*The Change of Crowns*	15 Apr. (Pepys)
	Howard, Edward	*The London Gentleman*	1667 (S.R.)
	Howard, James	*All Mistaken, or The Mad Couple*	20 Sept. (Pepys)
	Lacy, John	*Sauny the Scot, or The Taming of the Shrew* (Adapt. Shakespeare.)	9 Apr. (Pepys)
	St Serfe, Thomas	*Tarugo's Wiles, or The Coffee-House* (Adapt. Moreto's *No puede ser guarda una mujer*.)	5 Oct. (Pepys)
	Villiers, George	*The Chances* (Adapt. Fletcher.)	Feb. (Pepys)

TYPE	AUSPICES	EARLIEST TEXTS	LAST ED.	DATE
Comedy (?)	Duke's	Lost		
Tragicomedy	Unacted (?)	1666* & MS F	(T)	
Comedy	Unknown	MS		
Comedy	Duke's	Lost		
Academic Allegory	Cranebrook School	MS		**1666**
Tragedy	Unacted (?)	1666**		
Puppet Show	Bartholomew Fair	Current		
Comedy	Unacted	1667**		**1667**
Tragicomedy	King's	1669	1937†[262]	
Tragedy	Duke's	1667		
Comedy	Duke's	1677* & MS		
Comedy	Duke's	Lost		
Comedy	Duke's	1670	1931[265]	
Tragedy	Unacted	1667*		
Tragicomedy	King's	1668	1931[265]	
Comedy	Duke's	1668	1931[265]	
Comedy	Unacted (?) (see 1668)	1667*		
Comedy	Unacted (?)	Lost		
Tragicomedy	King's	MS	1949†[273]	
Comedy	King's (?)	Lost		
Tragicomedy	King's	1672	1876 D	
Comedy	King's	1698	1875†[271]	
Comedy	Duke's	1667*		
Comedy	King's	1682		

DATE	AUTHOR	TITLE	LIMITS
	Weston, John	*The Amazon Queen, or The Amours of Thalestris to Alexander the Great*	11 Feb. (imprim.)
	Anon.	*The Northern Castle* (Brome's *The Northern Lass*?)	14 Sept. (Pepys)
	Anon.	*Patient Grizill*	30 Aug. (Pepys)
	Anon.	*The Poetess*	7 Oct.
1668	Boyle, Roger	*Tryphon*	8 Dec. (Pepys)
	Davenant, William	*The Man's the Master* (Trans. Scarron's *Jodelet, ou le maître valet.*)	26 Mar. (Pepys)
	Denham, J. (completing Philips, K.)	*Horace* (Trans. Corneille. K. Philips's trans. ends at Act IV, Sc. 6.)	4 Feb.
	Dryden, John	*An Evening's Love, or The Mock Astrologer*	12 June
	'Dryden' (Flecknoe, R. ?)	*The Ladies à la Mode* (Same as *The Damoiselles à la Mode*, pub. by Flecknoe, 1667?)	14 Sept. (Pepys)
	Etherege, George	*She Would if She Could*	6 Feb. (Pepys)
	Howard, Robert	*The Great Favourite, or The Duke of Lerma* (*The Spanish Duke of Lerma*, 1623, revised?)	20 Feb. (Pepys)
	Sedley, Charles	*The Mulberry Garden* (*The Wandering Ladies*)	18 May (Pepys)
	Shadwell, Thomas	*The Sullen Lovers, or The Impertinents*	2 May (Pepys)
	Anon.	*Dick Whittington*	21 Sept. (Pepys)
	Anon.	*The Feigned Astrologer* (Adapt. T. Corneille's *Le Feint astrologue.*)	1668 (pub.)
	Anon.	*Merry Andrew*	29 Aug. (Pepys)
1669	Betterton, Thomas (?)	*Appius and Virginia* (*The Roman Virgin, or Unjust Judge*) (Adapt. Webster.)	12 May (Pepys)
	Boothby, Mrs Frances	*Marcelia, or The Treacherous Friend*	*c.* July
	Boyle, Roger	*Guzman*	15 Apr.
	Boyle, Roger	*Mr Anthony*	14 Dec.
	Carr, William	*Pluto Furens et Vinctus, or The Raging Devil Bound*	1669 (pub.)
	Dancer, John	*Agrippa, King of Alba, or The False Tiberinus* (Adapt. Quinault's *Agrippa roy d'Albe.*)	1666–1669
	Dryden, John	*Tyrannic Love, or The Royal Martyr*	June
	Howard, R.; Villiers, G.	*The Country Gentleman*	27 Feb. (projected)
	Killigrew, William (?)	*The Imperial Tragedy* (Adapt. Simons's *Zeno.*)	1669 (pub.)
	Lacy, John	*The Dumb Lady, or The Farrier Made Physician* (Adapt. Molière's *L'Amour médecin* and *Le Médecin malgré lui.*)	*c.* 1669
	Shadwell, Thomas	*The Hypocrite* (Adapt. Molière's *Tartuffe*? ‡)	14 June
	Shadwell, Thomas	*The Royal Shepherdess* (Adapt. Fountain's *The Rewards of Virtue*, 1661.)	25 Feb. (Pepys)
	Stapylton, Robert	*Hero and Leander*	1669

‡ Or Scarron's *Les Hypocrites?*

TYPE	AUSPICES	EARLIEST TEXTS	LAST ED.	DATE
Tragicomedy	Unacted	1667*		
Unknown	King's	Lost (?)		
Puppet Show	Bartholomew Fair	Lost		
Unknown	Duke's	Lost		
Tragedy	Duke's	1669 & MS	1937†[262]	**1668**
Comedy	Duke's	1669	1874†[203]	
Tragedy	Amateurs at Court (King's in 1669)	1669 (1st 4 acts, 1667) & MS		
Comedy	King's	1671	1931[265]	
Comedy	King's	1667 (?)		
Comedy	Duke's	1668	1927[269]	
Tragicomedy	King's	1668	1929†[274]	
Comedy	King's	1668	1928†[275]	
Comedy	Duke's	1668 & MS	1927[276] (M)	
Puppet Show	Southwark Fair	Lost		
Comedy	Unacted (?)	1668*		
Droll	Bartholomew Fair	Lost		
Tragedy	Duke's	Lost		**1669**
Tragicomedy	King's	1670*		
Comedy	Duke's	1693	1937†[262]	
Comedy	Duke's	1690**	1937†[262]	
Satirical Dialogue	Unacted (?)	1669*		
Tragicomedy	II Ogilby's Men, Dublin	1675*		
Tragedy	King's	1670	1931[265]	
Comedy	'Forbidden' (intended for King's)	Lost		
Tragedy	Nursery Company (?)	1669*		
Comedy	King's	1672*	1875†[270]	
Comedy	Duke's	Lost		
Tragicomedy	Duke's	1669	1927†[276]	
Tragedy	Unacted	1669*		

DATE	AUTHOR	TITLE	LIMITS
	Taylor, Silas	*The Serenade, or The Disappointment*	1669
	Anon. (Cavendish, W. ?)	*The Heiress* (Same as *The Triumphant Widow*, 1674?)	29 Jan. (Pepys)
	Anon.	*The Island Princess, or The Generous Portugal* (Adapt. Fletcher.)	7 Jan.
1670	Behn, Aphra	*The Forced Marriage, or The Jealous Bridegroom*	20 Sept.
	Betterton, Thomas	*The Amorous Widow, or The Wanton Wife* (In part from Molière's *Georges Dandin*.)	15 Nov.– 9 Dec.
	Betterton, Thomas	*The Woman Made a Justice*	19 Feb.
	Caryl, John	*Sir Salomon, or The Cautious Coxcomb* (Adapt. Molière's *L'École des femmes*, etc.)	9 May
	Dancer, John	*Nicomede* (Trans. Corneille.)	*c.* 1670
	Dryden, John	*I The Conquest of Granada*	Dec.
	Howard, Edward	*The Women's Conquest*	*c.* Nov.
	Howard, R.; Wilmot, J.	*The Conquest of China by the Tartars* (Only a frag. by Wilmot extant.)	*c.* 1670–*c.* 1680
	Joyner, William	*The Roman Empress*	*c.* Aug.
	Medbourne, Matthew	*Tartuffe, or The French Puritan* (Adapt. Molière.)	*c.* May
	Shadwell, Thomas	*The Humorists*	10 Dec.
	T[homson?], T[homas?]	*The Life of Mother Shipton*	1668–1671 (pub.)
	Anon.	*She's Jealous of Herself* (Alternative title of known play?)	20 Oct.
1671	Aubrey, John	*The Country Revel, or The Revel of Aldford*	1669–1671
	Behn, Aphra	*The Amorous Prince, or The Curious Husband*	24 Feb.
	Corye, John	*The Generous Enemies, or The Ridiculous Lovers*	*c.* July
	Crowne, John	*Charles VIII of France, or The Invasion of Naples by the French*	*c.* Nov.
	Crowne, John	*Juliana, or The Princess of Poland*	*c.* Aug.
	Dryden, John	*II The Conquest of Granada* (*Almanzor and Almahide*)	3 or 10 Jan.
	Dryden, John	*Marriage à la Mode*	1671–1672
	Howard, Edward	*The Six Days' Adventure, or The New Utopia*	6 Mar.
	Jordan, Thomas	*London's Resurrection to Joy and Triumph*	30 Oct.
	Milton, John	*Samson Agonistes*	1671
	Polwhele, Elizabeth	*The Frolic, or The Lawyer Cheated*	1671
	Revet, Edward	*The Town Shifts, or The Suburb Justice*	15 Mar.
	Settle, Elkanah	*Cambyses, King of Persia*	10 Jan.
	S[herman?], T[homas?]	*Youth's Tragedy*	1671
	Villiers; with Clifford, M.; Sprat (& Butler? Waller? Cowley?)	*The Rehearsal* (First drafted in *c.* 1663.)	7 Dec.
	Wycherley, William	*Love in a Wood, or St James's Park*	*c.* Mar.
	Anon.	*The Religious Rebel, or The Pilgrim Prince*	1671

TYPE	AUSPICES	EARLIEST TEXTS	LAST ED.	DATE
Comedy (?)	Unacted (?)	Lost		
Comedy	King's	Lost		
Tragicomedy	King's	1669*		
Tragicomedy	Duke's	1671	1915†[277]	**1670**
Comedy	Duke's	1706		
Comedy	Duke's	Lost		
Comedy	Duke's	1671**		
Tragicomedy	II Ogilby's Men, Dublin	1671*		
Tragicomedy	King's	1672	1932[265] (MA)	
Tragicomedy	Duke's	1671*		
Tragedy (?)	Unacted	MS (frag.)	1926†[278]	
Tragedy	King's	1671* & MS		
Comedy	King's	1670		
Comedy	Duke's	1671 & MS	1927†[276]	
Comedy	Unknown	[1668–71]*		
Comedy	Duke's	Lost (?)		
Comedy	Unacted	MS (frag.)	1898†[270]	**1671**
Comedy	Duke's	1671	1915†[277]	
Comedy	King's	1672*		
Tragedy	Duke's	1672	1873†[280]	
Tragedy	Duke's	1671*	1873†[280]	
Tragicomedy	King's	1672	1932[265] (MA)	
Comedy	King's	1673	1935[281] (M)	
Comedy	Duke's	1671*		
Civic Pageant	London	1671	1844†[156]	
Tragedy	Closet	1671 F	1958[224]	
Comedy	Unacted	Lost		
Comedy	Duke's	1671*		
Tragedy	Duke's	1671		
Moral	Closet	1671		
Burlesque	King's	1672	1921[282] (A)	
Comedy	King's	1672	1924[283] (M)	
Political Dialogue	Unacted	1671*		

DATE	AUTHOR	TITLE	LIMITS
1672	Boyle, Roger	*Herod the Great*	*c.* 1672
	Dryden, John	*Amboyna, or The Cruelties of the Dutch to the English Merchants*	1672–1673
	Dryden, John	*The Assignation, or Love in a Nunnery*	*c.* Nov.
	Jordan, Thomas	*London Triumphant, or The City in Jollity and Splendour*	29 Oct.
	Payne, Nevil	*The Fatal Jealousy*	3 Aug.
	Payne, Nevil	*The Morning Ramble, or The Town Humours*	4 Nov.
	Ravenscroft, Edward	*The Citizen Turned Gentleman* (*Mamamouchi*)	4 July
	Shadwell, Thomas	*Epsom Wells*	2 Dec.
	Shadwell, Thomas	*The Miser* (Adapt. Molière's *L'Avare*.)	Jan.
	Shipman, Thomas	*Henry III of France, Stabbed by a Friar, with the Fall of the Guise*	1672–*c.* July 1678
	Tuke, Richard	*The Soul's Warfare* (*The Divine Comedian, or The Right Use of Plays*)	1672
	Wycherley, William	*The Gentleman Dancing-Master*	6 Feb.
	Anon.	*The Dutch Cruelties at Amboyna, with the Humours of the Valiant Welshman*	11 Nov.
	Anon.	*Emilia*	1672
	Anon.	*The Illustrious Slaves*	Nov.
	Anon.	*The Romantic Lady*	13 Mar.
	Anon.	*Wit à la Mode* (Alternative title of known play?)	28 Feb.
1673	Arrowsmith, Joseph	*The Reformation*	*c.* Sept.
	Behn, Aphra	*The Dutch Lover*	6 Feb.
	Duffett, Thomas	*The Empress of Morocco*	*c.* Dec.
	Duffett, Thomas	*The Spanish Rogue*	*c.* May
	Jordan, Thomas	*London in Its Splendour*	29 Oct.
	Kirkman, Francis (compiler)	*II The Wits, or Sport upon Sport*: A collection of drolls, etc., fashioned from comic scenes in older plays: *Bottom the Weaver* (from *A Midsummer-Night's Dream*; see 1661), *The Cheater Cheated* (from *The Dutch Courtesan*), *Oenone* (expansion of Cox's *Rural Sports*), *Wiltshire Tom* (from *The King and Queen's Entertainment at Richmond*), and six other pieces attributed to Robert Cox (?); see 1653. For *I The Wits*, see 1662.	1673 (pub.)
	Pordage, Samuel	*Herod and Mariamne* (Written 1661–1662 according to Prol. First performance in 1671 recently urged.)	28 Oct. (revived?)
	Ravenscroft, Edward	*The Careless Lovers*	12 Mar.
	Settle, Elkanah	*The Empress of Morocco*	3 July
	Anon.	*The Recovery* (Listed mistakenly by Summers and Nicoll as *The Rectory*.)	27 Sept.
1674	Carleton, R.	*The Concealed Royalty, or The May Queen*	1674

TYPE	AUSPICES	EARLIEST TEXTS	LAST ED.	DATE
Tragedy	Unacted	1694	1937†[262]	**1672**
Tragedy	King's	1673	1932[265]	
Comedy	King's	1673	1932[265]	
Civic Pageant	London	1672		
Tragedy	Duke's	1673** F		
Comedy	Duke's	1673**		
Comedy	Duke's	1672		
Comedy	Duke's	1673	1930[284]	
Comedy	King's	1672	1927†[276]	
Tragedy	King's	1678**		
Moral	Unacted	1672**		
Comedy	Duke's	1673	1924[283] (M)	
Droll	Booth at Charing Cross	Lost		
Tragicomedy	Unacted	1672*		
Tragedy	Unknown	MS		
Unknown	King's	Lost		
Comedy	Duke's	Lost (?)		
Comedy	Duke's	1673**		**1673**
Comedy	Duke's	1673	1915†[277]	
Burlesque	King's	1674*	(A)	
Comedy	King's	1674*		
Civic Pageant	London	1673*		
Drolls	Offered for acting	1673** (reprint of 1662 ed. with new material incorporated.)	1932†[102]	
Tragedy	Duke's	1673		
Comedy	Duke's	1673*		
Tragedy	Duke's	1673		
Unknown	Duke's	Lost		
Pastoral	Acted privately (by Lord Bruce and his family)	MS		**1674**

DATE	AUTHOR	TITLE	LIMITS
	Cavendish, W.; Shadwell, T.	*The Triumphant Widow, or The Medley of Humours* (An elaboration of *A Pleasant and Merry Humour of a Rogue,* 1658.)	26 Nov.
	Crowne, John (reviser)	*Andromache* (Trans. Racine.)	*c.* Aug.
	'J.D.' (Dover, John?)	*The Mall, or The Modish Lovers*	*c.* Jan.
	Duffett, Thomas	*The Mock Tempest, or The Enchanted Castle* ‡	19 Nov.
	Jordan, Thomas	*The Goldsmiths' Jubilee, or London's Triumphs*	29 Oct.
	Lee, Nathaniel	*Nero, Emperor of Rome*	16 May
	Payne, Nevil	*The Siege of Constantinople*	2 Nov.
	Perrin, Pierre	*Ariadne, or The Marriage of Bacchus* (*Ariane, ou le mariage de Bacchus*)	30 Mar.
	Rant, Humphrey	*Phormio* (Trans. Terence.)	1674
	Settle, Elkanah	*Love and Revenge* (Adapt. Hemming's *The Fatal Contract.*)	9 Nov.
	Shadwell, T. (?) (& Betterton, T.?)	*The Tempest, or The Enchanted Island* (Adapt. Shakespeare.) ‡	30 Apr.
	Wright, John	*Thyestes* (trans. Seneca) and *Mock Thyestes*	1674
	Anon. (Duffett, T.?)	*The Amorous Old Woman, or 'Tis Well if It Take* (*The Fond Lady*)	*c.* Mar.
	Anon. (one scene by Dryden, J.)	*The Mistaken Husband* (Adapt. lost Brome comedy?)	*c.* Mar.
	Anon.	*Mock Pompey*	1674 (ment.)
	Anon.	*The Sea Captains*	18 Mar.
1675	Barnes, Joshua	*The Academy, or The Cambridge Dons*	28 June
	Belon, Peter (?)	*The Mock Duellist, or The French Valet*	*c.* May
	Carleton, R.	*The Martial Queen*	*c.* 1675
	Crowne, John	*Calisto, or The Chaste Nymph*	15 Feb. (performed)
	Dryden, John	*Aureng-Zebe*	17 Nov.
	Duffett, Thomas	*Psyche Debauched*	*c.* Aug.
	Fane, Francis	*Love in the Dark, or The Man of Business*	10 May
	Jordan, Thomas	*The Triumphs of London*	29 Oct.
	Lee, Nathaniel	*Sophonisba, or Hannibal's Overthrow*	30 Apr.
	Lesley, George	*Abraham's Faith*	1675
	Lesley, George	*Dives' Doom, or The Rich Man's Misery*	1675
	Lesley, George	*Fire and Brimstone, or The Destruction of Sodom* (*Sodom's Flames*)	1675
	Otway, Thomas	*Alcibiades*	22 Sept. (?)
	Settle, Elkanah	*The Conquest of China by the Tartars*	28 May (?)
	Shadwell, Thomas	*The Libertine*	12 June
	Shadwell, Thomas	*Psyche*	27 Feb.
	Wycherley, William	*The Country Wife*	12 Jan.
	Anon. (Crowne, J.?)	*The Country Knight* (Same as *The Country Wit,* 1676?)	19 Mar.
	Anon.	*The Cure of Pride, or Everyone in Their Way* (Adapt. Massinger's *The City Madam.*)	*c.* 1675 (?)

‡ (Songs and mask pub. sep. [1674?].)

TYPE	AUSPICES	EARLIEST TEXTS	LAST ED.	DATE
Comedy	Duke's	1677		
Tragedy	Duke's	1675		
Comedy	King's	1674*	1882†[285]	
Burlesque	King's	1675*	1922†[286]	
Civic Pageant	London	1674*	1844[156]	
Tragedy	King's	1675	1954[287]	
Tragedy	Duke's	1675*		
Opera (French and English)	King's	1674		
Comedy	Unacted	MS		
Tragedy	Duke's	1675** & MS		
Dramatic Opera	Duke's	1674	1927[276]	
Tragedy and Burlesque	Closet	1674*		
Comedy	King's	1674**		
Comedy	King's	1675*	1931[265]	
Droll (?)	At fairs (?)	Lost		
Unknown	Duke's	Lost		
Comedy	Emmanuel Col., Cambridge	MSS		**1675**
Comedy	King's	1675*		
Tragedy	Acted privately (by Lord Bruce and his family)	MSS		
Mask	Court	1675*	1873†[280]	
Tragedy	King's	1676	1952[287a] (MA)	
Burlesque	King's	1678*		
Comedy	King's	1675**		
Civic Pageant	London	1675*		
Tragedy	King's	1676	1954[287] (A)	
Religious Dialogue	Closet	1678		
Moral	Closet	1678		
Biblical Tragedy	Closet	1678		
Tragedy	Duke's	1675	1932[288]	
Tragedy	Duke's	1676*		
Comedy	Duke's	1676	1927†[276]	
Dramatic Opera	Duke's	1675	1927†[276]	
Comedy	King's	1675	1931[289] (MA)	
Comedy	Duke's	Lost (?)		
Tragicomedy	Unknown	MS		

DATE	AUTHOR	TITLE	LIMITS
	Anon.	*Paradise*	1675
	Anon.	*Piso's Conspiracy* (Adapt. *Nero,* 1624.)	*c.* Aug.
	Anon.	*The Woman Turned Bully*	24 Mar.
1676	Behn, Aphra	*Abdelazer, or The Moor's Revenge* (Adapt. *Lust's Dominion,* 1600.)	*c.* Apr.
	Behn, Aphra	*The Town Fop, or Sir Timothy Tawdrey*	*c.* Sept.
	Boyle, Roger	*King Saul*	*c.* 1676–1679
	Boyle, Roger	*Zoroastres*	1675–*c.* 1676
	Crowne, John	*The Country Wit* (Same as *The Country Knight,* 1675 ?)	10 Jan.
	Duffett, Thomas	*Beauty's Triumph*	1675–1676
	D'Urfey, Thomas	*The Fool Turned Critic*	18 Nov.
	D'Urfey, Thomas	*Madam Fickle, or The Witty False One*	4 Nov.
	D'Urfey, Thomas	*The Siege of Memphis, or The Ambitious Queen*	*c.* Sept.
	Etherege, George	*The Man of Mode, or Sir Fopling Flutter*	11 Mar.
	Jordan, Thomas	*London's Triumphs*	30 Oct.
	Lee, Nathaniel	*Gloriana, or The Court of Augustus Caesar*	29 Jan.
	Otway, Thomas	*Don Carlos, Prince of Spain*	8 June
	Ravenscroft, Edward	*The Wrangling Lovers, or The Invisible Mistress*	25 July
	Rawlins, —	*Tom Essence, or The Modish Wife*	*c.* Aug.
	Settle, Elkanah	*Ibrahim, the Illustrious Bassa*	*c.* Mar.
	Settle, Elkanah	*Pastor Fido, or The Faithful Shepherd* (Adapt. Guarini.)	*c.* Dec.
	Shadwell, Thomas	*The Virtuoso*	25 May
	Wycherley, William	*The Plain Dealer*	11 Dec.
	Anon.	*The Armenian Queen* (Prol. and Epil. by T. Duffett extant.)	*c.* 1673–1676
	Anon.	*I Music, or A Parley of Instruments*	30 Oct. (imprim.)
	Anon.	*No Fool Like the Old Fool*	13 June
1677	Banks, John	*The Rival Kings, or The Loves of Oroondates and Statira*	*c.* June
	Behn, Aphra	*I The Rover, or The Banished Cavaliers* (Adapt. T. Killigrew's *Thomaso.*)	24 Mar.
	Behn, Aphra (?)	*The Debauchee, or The Credulous Cuckold* (Adapt. Brome's *A Mad Couple Well Matched.*)	*c.* Feb.
	Crowne, John	*I & II The Destruction of Jerusalem by Titus Vespasian*	Pt I: 12 Jan. Pt II: 18 Jan.
	Davenant, Charles	*Circe*	12 May
	Dryden, John	*All for Love, or The World Well Lost*	12 Dec.
	Dryden, John	*The State of Innocence, and Fall of Man* (*The Fall of Angels, and Man in Innocence*)	1677
	D'Urfey, Thomas	*A Fond Husband, or The Plotting Sisters*	31 May
	Jordan, Thomas	*London's Triumphs*	29 Oct.

TYPE	AUSPICES	EARLIEST TEXTS	LAST ED.	DATE
Scenic Display (?)	Hatton House, Holborn	Lost		
Tragedy	Duke's	1676*		
Comedy	Duke's	1675*		
Tragedy	Duke's	1677	1915†[277]	**1676**
Comedy	Duke's	1677	1915†[277]	
Tragedy	Unacted	1703*	1937†[262]	
Tragedy	Unacted	MS	1937†[262]	
Comedy	Duke's	1675[76]	1874†[280]	
Mask	School at Chelsea	1676*		
Comedy	King's	1678*		
Comedy	Duke's	1677		
Tragedy	King's	1676*		
Comedy	Duke's	1676	1927[269] (A)	
Civic Pageant	London	1676*		
Tragedy	King's	1676	1954†[287]	
Tragedy	Duke's	1676	1932[288] (M)	
Comedy	Duke's	1677**		
Comedy	Duke's	1677*		
Tragedy	Duke's	1677		
Pastoral	Duke's	1677 & MS		
Comedy	Duke's	1676	1927†[276]	
Comedy	King's	1677	1936[190] (MA)	
Unknown	King's (?)	Lost		
Dialogues with Music	A music school	1676*		
Comedy	King's	Lost		
Tragedy	King's	1677**		**1677**
Comedy	Duke's	1677	1915†[277]	
Comedy	Duke's	1677	1915†[277]	
Tragedy	King's	1677	1874†[280] (Pt II:A)	
Dramatic Opera	Duke's	1677		
Tragedy	King's	1678 F	1952[287a] (MA)	
Dramatic Opera	Unacted	1677 & MSS	1932[265] (T)	
Comedy	Duke's	1677		
Civic Pageant	London	1677*		

N

DATE	AUTHOR	TITLE	LIMITS
	Leanerd, John	The Country Innocence, or The Chambermaid Turned Quaker (Adapt. 'T.B.''s The Country Girl.)	c. Mar.
	Lee, Nathaniel	The Rival Queens, or The Death of Alexander the Great	17 Mar.
	Otway, Thomas	Titus and Berenice, with The Cheats of Scapin (Adapt. Racine's Bérénice and Molière's Les Fourberies de Scapin.)	c. Jan.
	Pordage, Samuel	The Siege of Babylon	c. Sept.
	P[orter ?], T[homas ?]	The French Conjurer	c. Mar.
	Ravenscroft, Edward	The English Lawyer (Adapt. Ruggle's Ignoramus.)	c. Dec.
	Ravenscroft, Edward	King Edgar and Alfreda ‡	c. Oct.
	Ravenscroft, Edward	Scaramouch a Philosopher, Harlequin a Schoolboy, Bravo, Merchant, and Magician	5 May
	Roche-Guilhen, Mlle de la	Rare en tout	29 May
	Rymer, Thomas	Edgar, or The English Monarch	13 Sept. (imprim.)
	Sedley, Charles	Antony and Cleopatra (Remodelled as Beauty the Conqueror, or The Death of Marc Antony, pub. 1702.)	12 Feb.
	Smith, John	Cytherea, or The Enamouring Girdle	30 May (imprim.)
	Wilson, John	Belphegor, or The Marriage of the Devil	1677–1678
	Anon.	The Captain, or Town Miss (Adapt. Fletcher ?)	2 Apr.
	Anon.	The Constant Nymph, or The Rambling Shepherd	c. July
	Anon. (Behn ? Betterton ?)	The Counterfeit Bridegroom, or The Defeated Widow (Adapt. Middleton's No Wit, No Help Like a Woman's.)	c. Sept.
	Anon. (Behn, A. ?)	Midnight's Intrigues (Same as The Feigned Courtesans, 1679 ?)	1677
	Anon.	The Politician, or Sir Popular Wisdom	17 Nov.
	Anon. (Chamberlaine, W. ?)	Wits Led by the Nose, or A Poet's Revenge (Adapt. Chamberlaine's Love's Victory.)	16 or 18 June
1678	Banks, John	The Destruction of Troy	c. Nov.
	Behn, Aphra	Sir Patient Fancy	17 Jan.
	Cooke, Edward	Love's Triumph, or The Royal Union	1678
	Dryden, John	The Kind Keeper, or Mr Limberham	11 Mar.
	Dryden, J.; Lee, N.	Oedipus	c. Sept.
	D'Urfey, Thomas	Squire Oldsapp, or The Night Adventurers	c. June
	D'Urfey, Thomas	Trick for Trick, or The Debauched Hypocrite (Adapt. Fletcher's Monsieur Thomas.)	c. Mar.
	Howard, Edward	The Man of Newmarket	c. Mar.
	Johns, William (?)	The Traitor to Himself, or Man's Heart His Greatest Enemy	1678 (pub.)

‡ (Revision of play written c. 1667.)

TYPE	AUSPICES	EARLIEST TEXTS	LAST ED.	DATE
Comedy	King's	1677*		
Tragedy	King's	1677	1954[287] (A)	
Tragedy and Farce	Duke's	1677**	1932[288]	
Tragedy	Duke's	1678*		
Comedy	Duke's	1678*		
Comedy	King's	1678**		
Tragicomedy	King's	1677*		
Imitation Commedia dell'Arte	King's	1677*		
French Comedy with Music and Dance	Court	1677*		
Tragedy	Duke's (?)	1678**		
Tragedy	Duke's	1677	1928†[275]	
Comedy	Unacted	1677*		
Tragicomedy	Smock Alley, Dublin (United in 1690)	1691** & MS	1874†[271]	
Comedy	King's	Lost		
Pastoral	Duke's	1678*		
Comedy	Duke's	1677*		
Comedy	Duke's (?)	Lost		
Comedy	Duke's	Lost		
Tragicomedy	King's	1678**		
Tragedy	Duke's	1679*		**1678**
Comedy	Duke's	1678	1915†[277]	
Tragedy	Unacted	1678*		
Comedy	Duke's	1680	1932[265]	
Tragedy	Duke's	1679	1954[287]	
Comedy	Duke's	1679*		
Comedy	King's	1678*		
Comedy	King's	1678*		
Moral	School at Evesham	1678*		

DATE	AUTHOR	TITLE	LIMITS
	Jordan, Thomas	*The Triumphs of London*	29 Oct.
	Leanerd, John	*The Counterfeits*	28 May
	Leanerd, John	*The Rambling Justice, or The Jealous Husbands* (Adapt. Middleton's *More Dissemblers Besides Women*.)	*c.* Mar.
	Lee, Nathaniel	*Mithridates, King of Pontus*	Feb.
	Otway, Thomas	*Friendship in Fashion*	5 Apr.
	Philips, Joan	*Pair Royal of Coxcombs* (Prol., 2 songs, and Epil. printed in *Female Poems on Several Occasions*, 1679.)	*c.* 1678
	Rawlins, —	*Tunbridge Wells, or A Day's Courtship*	*c.* Mar.
	Shadwell, Thomas	*Timon of Athens, the Man-Hater* (Adapt. Shakespeare.)	*c.* Jan.
	Shadwell, Thomas	*A True Widow*	21 Mar. (?)
	Shaw, Samuel	*Words Made Visible, or Grammar and Rhetoric Accommodated to the Lives and Manners of Men* (*Minerva's Triumphs, or Grammar and Rhetoric*) (In two parts.)	1678
	Shipman, Thomas	*Henry IV* [of France]	1672–1680
	Tate, Nahum	*Brutus of Alba, or The Enchanted Lovers*	*c.* July
	Wilmot, John	*Lucina's Rape, or Valentinian* (Adapt. Fletcher.) (See also 1684.)	1678–1679
	Wilmot, J. (?) or Fishbourne, C. (?)	*Sodom, or The Quintessence of Debauchery*	*c.* 1678–1680
	Anon. ('W.M.')	*The Huntingdon Divertisement*	20 June
	Anon.	*The Rival Mother* (Ghost? No extant copy known.)	1678
1679	Bancroft, John	*Sertorius*	*c.* Mar.
	Bedloe, W. (?) or Walter, T. (?)	*The Excommunicated Prince, or The False Relique*	1679
	Behn, Aphra	*The Feigned Courtesans, or A Night's Intrigue* (Same as *Midnight's Intrigues*, 1677?)	*c.* Mar.
	Behn, Aphra	*The Young King, or The Mistake*	*c.* Sept.
	Crowne, John	*The Ambitious Statesman, or The Loyal Favourite*	*c.* Mar.
	Dryden, John	*Troilus and Cressida, or Truth Found Too Late* (Adapt. Shakespeare.)	*c.* Apr.
	D'Urfey, Thomas	*The Virtuous Wife, or Good Luck at Last*	*c.* Sept.
	Ecclestone, Edward	*Noah's Flood, or The Destruction of the World* (*The Cataclysm, or General Deluge of the World. The Deluge, or The Destruction of the World*)	1679
	Jordan, Thomas	*London in Lustre*	29 Oct.
	Lee, Nathaniel	*Caesar Borgia, Son of Pope Alexander VI*	1679
	Otway, Thomas	*Caius Marius* (Adapt. Shakespeare's *Romeo and Juliet*.)	*c.* Sept.
	Ravenscroft, Edward	*Titus Andronicus, or The Rape of Lavinia* (Adapt. Shakespeare.)	1679–1686

TYPE	AUSPICES	EARLIEST TEXTS	LAST ED.	DATE
Civic Pageant	London	1678*	1844†[156]	
Comedy	Duke's	1679*		
Comedy	King's	1678		
Tragedy	King's	1678 & MS	1954†[287]	
Comedy	Duke's	1678	1932[288]	
Comedy	'Acted at a Dancing-School'	Lost		
Comedy	Duke's	1678*		
Tragedy	Duke's	1678	1927†[276]	
Comedy	Duke's	1679	1927[276] (M)	
Academic Allegory	School at Ashby-de-la-Zouch	1678–79		
Tragedy	King's (?)	Lost		
Tragedy	Duke's	1678*		
Tragedy	King's	MSS		
Comedy	Unacted	1684 (?) & MSS	1904[289a]	
Entertainment	Merchant Taylors Hall	1678*		
Comedy	Unacted	1678* (?)		
Tragedy	King's	1679*		**1679**
Political Dialogue	Unacted	1679*		
Comedy	Duke's	1679	1915†[277]	
Tragicomedy	Duke's	1683	1915†[277]	
Tragedy	King's	1679**	1874†[280]	
Tragicomedy	Duke's	1679	1932[265]	
Comedy	Duke's	1680*		
Dramatic Opera	Unacted (?)	1679**		
Civic Pageant	London	1679*		
Tragedy	Duke's	1680	1955†[287]	
Tragedy	Duke's	1680	1932[288] (T)	
Tragedy	King's	1687		

DATE	AUTHOR	TITLE	LIMITS
	Shadwell, Thomas	*The Woman Captain*	*c.* Sept.
	Sherburne, Edward	*Troades, or The Royal Captives* (Trans. Seneca.)	1679
	Tate, Nahum	*The Loyal General*	*c.* Dec.
1680	Barnes, Joshua	*Englebert*	*c.* 1680
	Behn, A. (?) (prob. hers rather than Betterton's)	*The Revenge, or A Match in Newgate* (*The Vintner Tricked*) (Adapt. Marston's *The Dutch Courtesan*.)	*c.* June
	Butler, Samuel	*Nero* (Left incomplete.)	b. 1680
	Crowne, John	*The Misery of Civil War* (*II Henry VI. The Miseries of Civil War*) (Adapt. Shakespeare's *III Henry VI*.)	*c.* Feb.
	Crowne, John	*Thyestes*	*c.* Mar.
	Dryden, John	*The Spanish Friar, or The Double Discovery*	*c.* Oct.
	Jordan, Thomas	*London's Glory*	29 Oct.
	Lee, Nathaniel	*Lucius Junius Brutus, Father of His Country*	8 Dec. (?)
	Lee, Nathaniel	*Theodosius, or The Force of Love*	*c.* Sept.
	Maidwell, Lewis	*The Loving Enemies*	*c.* Jan.
	Otway, Thomas	*The Orphan, or The Unhappy Marriage*	Feb.
	Otway, Thomas	*The Soldier's Fortune*	*c.* June
	Settle, Elkanah	*Fatal Love, or The Forced Inconstancy*	*c.* Sept.
	Settle, Elkanah	*The Female Prelate, Being the History of the Life and Death of Pope Joan*	31 May
	Tate, Nahum	*Richard II* (*The Sicilian Usurper*) (Adapt. Shakespeare.)	11 Dec.
	Whitaker, William	*The Conspiracy, or The Change of Government*	*c.* Mar.
	Anon.	*Anna Bullen* (Date *c.* 1680 suggested, but may be an 18th-cent. play.)	*c.* 1680 (?)
	Anon.	*The Coronation of Queen Elizabeth with the Restoration of the Protestant Religion, or The Downfall of the Pope*	Aug.
	Anon.	*Fools Have Fortune, or Luck's All* (MS Prol. and Epil. extant.)	*c.* 1680
	Anon.	*Love Lost in the Dark, or The Drunken Couple* (From Massinger's *The Guardian*.)	1680
	Anon.	*Marriage Revived, or The Mistress Returned*	*c.* 1680 (?)
	Anon.	*The Merry Milkmaid of Islington, or The Rambling Gallants Defeated* (From Nabbes's *Tottenham Court*.)	*c.* 1680
	Anon.	*The Politic Whore, or The Conceited Cuckold* (From Davenport's *The City Nightcap*.)	*c.* 1680
1681	Banks, John	*The Unhappy Favourite, or The Earl of Essex*	*c.* May
	Behn, Aphra	*The False Count, or A New Way to Play an Old Game*	*c.* Nov.
	Behn, Aphra	*The Roundheads, or The Good Old Cause* (Adapt. Tatham's *The Rump*.)	*c.* Dec.

TYPE	AUSPICES	EARLIEST TEXTS	LAST ED.	DATE
Comedy	Duke's	1680	1927†[276]	
Tragedy	Closet	1679		
Tragedy	Duke's	1680*		
Opera and Tragedy	Emmanuel Col., Cambridge (?)	MS		**1680**
Comedy	Duke's	1680*		
Tragedy	Unacted	Lost		
Tragedy	Duke's	1680**		
Tragedy	King's	1681*	1874†[280]	
Comedy	Duke's	1681 & MS	1952[287a] (MA)	
Civic Pageant	London	1680*	1931†[135]	
Tragedy	Duke's	1681	1955†[287]	
Tragedy	Duke's	1680	1955[287]	
Comedy	Duke's	1680*		
Tragedy	Duke's	1680	1932[288] (M)	
Comedy	Duke's	1681	1932[288] (M)	
Tragedy	King's	1680*		
Tragedy	King's	1680		
Tragedy	King's	1681**		
Tragedy	Duke's	1680*		
Tragedy	Unknown	MS		
Popular Chronicle	Bartholomew and Southwark Fairs	1680*		
Comedy	Duke's	Lost		
Droll	Court at Newmarket (Robert Parker's Strollers ?)	1680*		
Comedy	Oxford (?) Privately acted (?)	MS		
Droll	Court at Newmarket (Robert Parker's Strollers ?)	1680*		
Droll	Court at Newmarket (Robert Parker's Strollers ?)	1680*		
Tragedy	King's	1682	1939†[290]	**1681**
Comedy	Duke's	1682	1915†[277]	
Comedy	Duke's	1682	1915†[277]	

DATE	AUTHOR	TITLE	LIMITS
	Behn, Aphra	*II The Rover* (Adapt. T. Killigrew's *Thomaso.*)	1680–1681
	Crowne, John	*Henry VI, the First Part, with the Murder of Humphrey Duke of Gloucester* (Adapt. Shakespeare's *II Henry VI.*)	*c.* Apr.
	D'Urfey, Thomas	*Sir Barnaby Whigg, or No Wit Like a Woman's*	*c.* Oct.
	Jordan, Thomas	*London's Joy*	29 Oct.
	Lee, Nathaniel	*The Princess of Cleve*	1680–1681
	'N.N.'	*Rome's Follies, or The Amorous Friars*	1681–1682
	Ravenscroft, Edward	*The London Cuckolds*	22 Nov.
	Saunders, Charles	*Tamerlane the Great*	*c.* Mar.
	Shadwell, Thomas	*The Lancashire Witches, and Tegue O'Divelly the Irish Priest*	*c.* Sept.
	Tate, Nahum	*The Ingratitude of a Commonwealth, or The Fall of Caius Martius Coriolanus* (Adapt. Shakespeare.)	*c.* Dec.
	Tate, Nahum	*King Lear* (Adapt. Shakespeare.)	*c.* Mar.
1682	Banks, John	*Virtue Betrayed, or Anna Bullen*	*c.* Mar.
	Behn, Aphra	*The City Heiress, or Sir Timothy Treat-all*	*c.* Apr.
	Behn, Aphra	*Like Father Like Son, or The Mistaken Brothers* (Adapt. Randolph's *The Jealous Lovers.*) (Prol. and Epil. extant.)	*c.* Mar.
	Blow, John	*Venus and Adonis*	1680–1682
	Dryden, J.; Lee, N.	*The Duke of Guise* (Prepared for July, but banned.)	28 Nov.
	D'Urfey, Thomas	*The Injured Princess, or The Fatal Wager* (Adapt. Shakespeare's *Cymbeline.*)	*c.* Mar.
	D'Urfey, Thomas	*The Royalist*	23 Jan. (?)
	Jordan, Thomas	*The Lord Mayor's Show*	30 Oct. (intended)
	Lacy, John	*Sir Hercules Buffoon, or The Poetical Squire* (Poss. first acted *c.* June 1684.)	*c.* May (?)
	Luttrell, N. (?) (owner rather than author?)	*Love's Metamorphosis, or The Disguised Lovers*	1682 (?)
	Otway, Thomas	*Venice Preserved, or A Plot Discovered*	9 Feb.
	Settle, Elkanah	*The Heir of Morocco, with the Death of Gayland*	11 Mar.
	Southerne, Thomas	*The Loyal Brother, or The Persian Prince*	4 Feb. (?)
	Anon.	*The Irish Evidence, The Humours of Teague, or The Mercenary Whore*	Aug.
	Anon.	*Mr Turbulent, or The Melancholics* (*The Factious Citizen, or The Melancholy Visioner*)	27 Jan. (?)
	Anon.	*The Prince's Ball, or The Conquest of Queen Judith* (Listed by Summers.)	Aug.
	Anon.	*Romulus and Hersilia, or The Sabine War*	10 Aug.

TYPE	AUSPICES	EARLIEST TEXTS	LAST ED.	DATE
Comedy	Duke's	1681	1915†[277]	
Tragedy	Duke's	1681*		
Comedy	King's	1681*		
Civic Pageant	London	1681*		
Tragedy	Duke's	1689	1955†[287]	
Political Dialogue	Privately acted (?)	1681*		
Comedy	Duke's	1682	1921†[247]	
Tragedy	King's	1681*		
Comedy	Duke's	1682	1927[276]	
Tragedy	King's	1682*		
Tragedy	Duke's	1681	1922[286]	
Tragedy	Duke's	1682		**1682**
Comedy	Duke's	1682	1915†[277]	
Comedy	Duke's	Lost		
Opera	Oxford (?)	MSS	1949[291]	
Tragedy	United	1683	1955[287]	
Tragicomedy	King's	1682*		
Comedy	Duke's	1682*		
Civic Pageant	London (not performed)	1682*	1931†[135]	
Comedy	United	1684*	1875†[270]	
Comedy	Unacted (?)	MS		
Tragedy	Duke's	1682	1932[288] (MA)	
Tragedy	King's	1682		
Tragedy	King's	1682**		
Droll	Bartholomew Fair	Lost		
Comedy	Duke's	1682**		
Droll	Bartholomew Fair	Lost		
Tragedy	Duke's	1683*		

DATE	AUTHOR	TITLE	LIMITS
1683	Barnes, Joshua	Landgartha, or The Amazon Queen of Denmark (Sigward the Famous King of Norway)	1682–1683
	Crowne, John	City Politiques	19 Jan.
	Jordan, Thomas	The Triumphs of London	29 Oct.
	Lee, Nathaniel	Constantine the Great	12 Nov. (?)
	Otway, Thomas	The Atheist, or The Second Part of the Soldier's Fortune	c. July
	Ravenscroft, Edward	Dame Dobson, or The Cunning Woman	31 May (?)
	Anon.	Mr Doolittle	1682–1683 (?)
1684	Banks, John	The Island Queens, or The Death of Mary Queen of Scotland (The Albion Queens)	1684
	Behn, Aphra	The Wavering Nymph, or Mad Amyntas (Adapt. Randolph's Amyntas.) (Two songs extant.)	c. 1683–1684
	Fane, Francis	A Mask (Frightful Dream to Lucina) (Written to be inserted into Valentinian; see Anon., below.)	Feb. (?)
	Horne, John	Fortune's Task, or The Fickle Fair One	1684
	Jordan, Thomas	London's Royal Triumph	29 Oct.
	Southerne, Thomas	The Disappointment, or The Mother in Fashion	5 Apr. (?)
	Tate, Nahum	A Duke and No Duke (Adapt. Cokain's Trappolin Creduto Principe.)	18 Aug. (?)
	Anon.	The Indian Empress	c. 1684
	Anon.	The Mistaken Beauty, or The Liar (Revival of The Liar, 1661 ?) (Adapt. P. Corneille's Le Menteur.)	1661–c. Sept. 1684
	Anon.	Valentinian (Adapt. Wilmot's Lucina's Rape.)	11 Feb.
1685	Crowne, John	Sir Courtly Nice, or It Cannot Be	9 May (?)
	Dryden, John	Albion and Albanius	3 June
	D'Urfey, Thomas	A Commonwealth of Women (Adapt. Fletcher's The Sea Voyage.)	20 Aug. (?)
	Tate, Nahum	Cuckolds Haven, or An Alderman No Conjurer (Adapt. Jonson, et al., Eastward Ho.)	c. June
	Taubman, Matthew	London's Annual Triumph	29 Oct.
	Tutchin, John	The Unfortunate Shepherd	1685
	Wharton, Anne (née Lee)	Love's Martyr, or Wit above Crowns	c. 1685 (S.R.)
	Anon.	The Rampant Alderman, or News from the Exchange (Adapt. Marmion's A Fine Companion.)	1685 (pub.)
	Anon.	The Whore of Babylon, the Devil, and the Pope	Aug.
1686	Behn, Aphra	The Lucky Chance, or An Alderman's Bargain (The Disappointed Marriage, or The Generous Mistress)	c. Apr.
	D'Urfey, Thomas	The Banditti, or A Lady's Distress	c. Feb.
	Fane, Francis	The Sacrifice	1686

TYPE	AUSPICES	EARLIEST TEXTS	LAST ED.	DATE
Tragedy	Emmanuel Col. (?), Cambridge	MSS		**1683**
Comedy	United	1683	1874†[280]	
Civic Pageant	London	1683*		
Tragedy	United	1684	1955[287]	
Comedy	United	1684	1932[288]	
Comedy	United	1684*		
Comedy	Unknown	MS & MS (frag.)		
Tragedy	Unacted until 1704	1684	(T)	**1684**
Pastoral	Unknown	Lost		
Operatic Interlude	United (?)	1685*		
Pastoral	Oxford (?)	MS		
Civic Pageant	London	1684*		
Comedy	United	1684		
Farce	United	1685	1948†[292]	
Unknown	Acted privately	Lost		
Comedy	United	1685*		
Tragedy	United	1685 (i.e. '84)	1926†[278]	
Comedy	United	1685	1921[247] (T)	**1685**
Dramatic Opera	United	1685	1932[205] (M)	
Comedy	United	1686	1886†[229]	
Farce	United	1685*		
Civic Pageant	London	1685*		
Pastoral	Unacted	1685*		
Tragedy	Unacted	MS		
Farce	Unacted (?)	1685*		
Droll	Bartholomew Fair	Lost		
Comedy	United	1687	1915†[277]	**1686**
Comedy	United	1686*		
Tragedy	Unacted	1686		

DATE	AUTHOR	TITLE	LIMITS
	Jevon, Thomas	*The Devil of a Wife, or A Comical Transformation*	4 Mar.
	Mountfort, William	*Doctor Faustus, with the Humours of Harlequin and Scaramouche* (Adapt. Marlowe.)	Oct.–Nov.
	Talbot, John	*Troas* (Trans. Seneca.)	1686
	Taubman, Matthew	*London's Yearly Jubilee*	29 Oct.
	Villiers, George (?)	*The Restoration, or Right Will Take Place* (Adapt. Beaumont and Fletcher's *Philaster*.) (Doubtful plays printed in Villiers's *Works: The Militant Couple, or The Husband May Thank Himself*, 1704; *The Belgic Hero Unmasked, or The Deliverer Set Forth in His Proper Colours*, 1704; *The Battle, or The Rehearsal at Whitehall* [*Sedgemoor Fight*], 1704.)	c. 1685–1686 (?)
	Anon.	*St George and the Dragon*	Aug.
	Anon.	*Vienna Besieged*	Aug.
1687	Behn, Aphra	*The Emperor of the Moon*	c. Mar.
	Sedley, C. (& Shadwell, T.?)	*Bellamira, or The Mistress* (Adapt. Terence's *Eunuchus*.)	12 May
	Tate, Nahum	*The Island Princess* (Adapt. Fletcher.)	25 Apr.
	Taubman, Matthew	*London's Triumph, or The Goldsmiths' Jubilee*	29 Oct.
	Anon.	*Augustus Caesar*	c. 1687
	Anon.	*The Critics* (Poss. Villiers's *The Rehearsal*.)	1687
	Anon.	*Woman Rules*	1687
1688	Crowne, John	*Darius, King of Persia*	Apr.
	D'Urfey, Thomas	*A Fool's Preferment, or The Three Dukes of Dunstable* (Adapt. Fletcher's *The Noble Gentleman*.)	c. Apr.
	Finch, Anne	*The Triumphs of Love and Innocence*	c. 1685–1690
	Mountfort, William	*The Injured Lovers, or The Ambitious Father*	6 Feb.
	Shadwell, Thomas	*The Squire of Alsatia*	4 May (?)
	Taubman, Matthew	*London's Anniversary Festival*	29 Oct.
1689	Behn, Aphra	*The Widow Ranter, or The History of Bacon in Virginia*	c. Nov.
	Carlisle, James	*The Fortune Hunters, or Two Fools Well Met*	c. Mar.
	Dryden, John	*Don Sebastian, King of Portugal*	c. Nov.
	Lee, Nathaniel	*The Massacre of Paris* (Prob. written c. 1679.)	7 Nov.
	Mountfort, William	*The Successful Strangers*	c. Dec.
	Shadwell, Thomas	*Bury Fair*	c. Apr.
	Singleton, Thomas	*Talpae sive Conjuratis Papistica* (Transcribed 1689.)	c. 1642–1689
	Tate, Nahum	*Dido and Aeneas*	c. Dec.
	Taubman, Matthew	*London's Great Jubilee*	29 Oct.

TYPE	AUSPICES	EARLIEST TEXTS	LAST ED.	DATE
Comedy	United	1686		
Farce	United	1697		
Tragedy	Closet	1686*		
Civic Pageant	London	1686*		
Tragicomedy	Unacted (?)	1714		
Droll	Bartholomew Fair	Lost		
Droll	Bartholomew Fair	Lost		
Farce	United	1687	1948[292]	**1687**
Comedy	United	1687	1928†[275]	
Tragicomedy	United	1687*		
Civic Pageant	London	1687*		
Tragedy (?)	Unknown	Lost		
Comedy	Acted privately at Norwich	Lost (?)		
Comedy (?)	Unknown	Lost		
Tragedy	United	1688**	1874†[280]	**1688**
Comedy	United	1688*	1917†[293]	
Tragicomedy	Closet	MS	1903†[294]	
Tragedy	United	1688		
Comedy	United	1688	1927[276] (MA)	
Civic Pageant	London	1688*		
Tragicomedy	United	1690	1915†[277]	**1689**
Comedy	United	1689*		
Tragedy	United	1690	1952[287a] (M)	
Tragedy	United	1690	1955†[287]	
Tragicomedy	United	1690		
Comedy	United	1689	1927[276] (MA)	
Latin Tragicomedy	Hoxton Wells (1689)	MS		
Dramatic Opera	J. Priest's Boarding School, Chelsea	MS	1926[295]	
Civic Pageant	London	1689*		

DATE	AUTHOR	TITLE	LIMITS
	Anon. (Bulteel, J.?)	*Love in and Love out of Fashion* (See *Amorous Orontus*, 1665.)	1689 (?)
1690	Betterton, Thomas	*The Prophetess, or The History of Diocletian* (Adapt. Fletcher and Massinger.)	*c.* May
	'W.C.'	*The Rape Revenged, or The Spanish Revolution* (Adapt. W. Rowley's *All's Lost by Lust*.)	*c.* 1690
	Crowne, John	*The English Friar, or The Town Sparks* (Prol. and Epil., imprim., 17 Mar. 1689[90].)	*c.* Mar.
	Dryden, John	*Amphitryon, or The Two Socias*	*c.* Oct.
	Finch, Anne	*Aristomenes, or The Royal Shepherd* (Title altered from *The Queen of Cypress, or Love above Ambition*.)	1688–1691
	Harris, J. (one scene by Mountfort, W.)	*The Mistakes, or The False Report*	*c.* Dec.
	Mountfort, W. (?)(adapter?) (often attributed to Bancroft, J.)	*Edward III, with the Fall of Mortimer* (Adapt. Davenport's *The Politic Queen*?)	*c.* Nov.
	Pitcairne, Archibald	*The Assembly, or Scotch Reformation*	*c.* 1690
	Powell, George	*Alphonso, King of Naples*	*c.* Dec.
	Powell, George	*The Treacherous Brothers*	*c.* Jan.
	Settle, E. (one scene by Mountfort, W.)	*Distressed Innocence, or The Princess of Persia*	*c.* Oct.
	Shadwell, Thomas	*The Amorous Bigot, with the Second Part of Tegue O'Divelly*	*c.* Mar.
	Shadwell, Thomas	*The Scowrers*	*c.* Dec.
	Southerne, Thomas	*Sir Anthony Love, or The Rambling Lady*	*c.* Dec.
	Anon.	*The Abdicated Prince, or The Adventures of Four Years*	1690
	Anon.	*The Banished Duke, or The Tragedy of Infortunatus*	1690
	Anon.	*The Bloody Duke, or The Adventures for a Crown*	1690
	Anon.	*The Folly of Priest-Craft* (*The Converts*)	1690
	Anon.	*The Gordian Knot Untied*	*c.* Nov.
	Anon.	*The Late Revolution, or The Happy Change*	1690
	Anon.	*The Royal Flight, or The Conquest of Ireland*	1690
	Anon.	*The Royal Voyage, or The Irish Expedition*	1690
1691	Dryden, John	*King Arthur, or The British Worthy*	*c.* May
	D'Urfey, Thomas	*Bussy D'Ambois, or The Husband's Revenge* (Adapt. Chapman.)	*c.* Mar.
	D'Urfey, Thomas	*Love for Money, or The Boarding School*	*c.* Jan.
	Mountfort, William	*Greenwich Park*	*c.* Apr.
	Popple, William	*The Cid* (Trans. Corneille.)	1691
	Settle, Elkanah	*The Triumphs of London*	29 Oct.
	Shaw, Samuel	*Poikilo-Phronesis, or The Different Humours of Men*	15 Dec.

TYPE	AUSPICES	EARLIEST TEXTS	LAST ED.	DATE
Comedy	United	Lost (?)		
Dramatic Opera	United	1690		**1690**
Tragedy	Unknown	MS (extant?)		
Comedy	United	1690	1874†[280]	
Comedy	United	1690	1932[265]	
Tragedy	Closet	1713 & MS	1903†[294]	
Tragicomedy	United	1691*		
Tragedy	United	1691	1949†[294a]	
Political Comedy	Closet	1722* & MS		
Tragedy	United	1691*		
Tragedy	United	1690		
Tragedy	United	1691*		
Comedy	United	1690	1927†[276]	
Comedy	United	1691	1927†[276]	
Comedy	United	1691		
Political Dialogue	Closet	1690		
Political Dialogue	Unacted	1690*		
Political Dialogue	Closet	1690*		
Political Dialogue	Closet	1690**		
Comedy	United	Lost		
Political Dialogue	Closet	1690*		
Political Dialogue	Closet	1690*		
Political Dialogue	Closet	1690*		
Dramatic Opera	United	1691	1932[265]	**1691**
Tragedy	United	1691*		
Comedy	United	1691	(T)	
Comedy	United	1691		
Tragedy	Unacted	MS		
Civic Pageant	London	1691*		
Academic Allegory	School at Ashby-de-la-Zouch	1692*		

DATE	AUTHOR	TITLE	LIMITS
	Smythe, J. (?) or Underhill, C. (?)	*Win Her and Take Her, or Old Fools Will Be Meddling*	1691
	Southerne, Thomas	*The Wives' Excuse, or Cuckolds Make Themselves*	Dec.
	Anon.	*The Braggadocio, or The Bawd Turned Puritan*	1691
	Anon.	*The Siege and Surrender of Mons*	1691
	Anon.	*Wit for Money, or Poet Stutter*	1691
1692	Bourne, Reuben	*The Contented Cuckold, or The Woman's Advocate*	1692
	Brady, Nicholas	*The Rape, or The Innocent Impostors*	Feb.
	Crowne, John	*Regulus*	June
	Dryden, J. (& Southerne, T. ?)	*Cleomenes, the Spartan Hero*	Apr.
	D'Urfey, Thomas	*The Marriage Hater Matched*	*c.* Jan.
	Haynes, Joe	*A Fatal Mistake, or The Plot Spoiled*	1692
	Mountfort, W. (?) (adapter ?) (often attributed to Bancroft, J.)	*Henry II, King of England, with the Death of Rosamond* (Adapt. Davenport's *Henry II* ?)	8 Nov.
	Mountfort, William (?)	*Zelmane, or The Corinthian Queen*	*b.* 1692 (?)
	Popple, William	*Tamerlane the Beneficent*	1692
	'Mr Rivers'	*The Traitor* (Adapt. Shirley; not by the Jesuit Anthony Rivers, as often supposed.)	Mar.
	Settle, Elkanah	*The Triumphs of London*	29 Oct.
	Settle, Elkanah (?)	*The Fairy Queen* (Adapt. Shakespeare's *A Midsummer-Night's Dream*.)	2 May
	Shadwell, Thomas	*The Volunteers, or The Stock Jobbers*	*c.* Nov.
	Anon.	*Piety and Valour, or Derry Defended* (Same as *The Siege of Derry*, below ?)	1692
	Anon.	*The Rehearsal of Kings*	1692
	Anon.	*The Siege of Derry* (Same as *Piety and Valour, or Derry Defended*, above ?)	1692
1693	Barnes, Joshua	*Plautus His Trinummi Imitated*	1693
	Congreve, William	*The Double Dealer*	Oct.–Nov.
	Congreve, William	*The Old Bachelor* (Written originally in 1689.)	Mar.
	D'Urfey, Thomas	*The Richmond Heiress, or A Woman Once in the Right*	*c.* Apr.
	Higden, Henry	*The Wary Widow, or Sir Noisy Parrot*	*c.* Mar.
	Keigwyn, John	*The Creation of the World, with Noah's Flood* (Trans. Jordan; see 1611.)	1693
	Powell, George	*A Very Good Wife*	*c.* Apr.
	Settle, Elkanah	*The New Athenian Comedy*	1693
	Settle, Elkanah	*The Triumphs of London*	30 Oct.
	Southerne, Thomas	*The Maid's Last Prayer, or Any Rather Than Fail*	*c.* Feb.

TYPE	AUSPICES	EARLIEST TEXTS	LAST ED.	DATE
Comedy	United	1691*		
Comedy	United	1692		
Comedy	Unacted	1691*		
Political Dialogue	Closet	1691*		
Critical Dialogue	Closet	1691*		
Comedy	Unacted	1692*		**1692**
Tragedy	United	1692**		
Tragedy	United	1694*		
Tragedy	United	1692	1932[265] (T)	
Comedy	United	1692		
Burlesque	Unacted (?)	1692		
Tragedy	United	1693		
Tragedy	Unacted until 1704	1705		
Tragicomedy	Unacted	MS		
Tragedy	United	1692		
Civic Pageant	London	1692*		
Opera	United	1692		
Comedy	United	1693	1930[284]	
'Tragicomedy' (Political Dialogue?)	Closet (?)	1692* (extant?)		
Farce	United (?)	Lost		
'Tragicomedy' (Political Dialogue?)	Closet (?)	1692* (extant?)		
Comedy	Emmanuel Col., Cambridge (?)	MS		**1693**
Comedy	United	1694	1948[296] (M)	
Comedy	United	1693	1948[296] (M)	
Comedy	United	1693	(T)	
Comedy	United	1693*		
Cornish Mystery	Closet	MSS	1827†[297]	
Comedy	United	1693		
Comedy (Satire)	Closet	1693*		
Civic Pageant	London	1693*	1931†[135]	
Comedy	United	1693		

o

DATE	AUTHOR	TITLE	LIMITS
	Wright, Thomas	*The Female Virtuosos* (Adapt. Molière's *Les Femmes savantes*.)	*c.* May
	Anon.	*The Royal Cuckold, or Great Bastard*	1693
1694	Banks, John	*The Innocent Usurper, or The Death of the Lady Jane Grey*	1694 (pub.)
	Crowne, John	*The Married Beau, or The Curious Impertinent*	*c.* May
	Dryden, John	*Love Triumphant, or Nature Will Prevail*	*c.* Jan.
	D'Urfey, Thomas	*I & II The Comical History of Don Quixote*	*c.* May
	Echard, Lawrence	*Plautus's Comedies: Amphitryon, Epidicus, and Rudens Made English*	1694
	Echard, Lawrence	*Terence's Comedies Made English* (The six plays translated.)	1694
	Ravenscroft, Edward	*The Canterbury Guests, or A Bargain Broken*	*c.* Sept.
	Settle, Elkanah	*The Ambitious Slave, or A Generous Revenge* (Written originally in 1681–1682.)	21 Mar.
	Settle, Elkanah	*The Triumphs of London*	29 Oct.
	Southerne, Thomas	*The Fatal Marriage, or The Innocent Adultery*	Feb.
	Williams, Joseph	*Have at All, or The Midnight Adventures* (Same as *Midnight's Intrigues,* 1677 ?)	*c.* Apr.
	Anon.	*The Rape of Europa by Jupiter*	1694
	Anon.	*The Unhappy Marriage*	5 Sept.
1695	Banks, John	*Cyrus the Great, or The Tragedy of Love*	Dec.
	Congreve, William	*Love for Love*	30 Apr.
	Dilke, Thomas	*The Lover's Luck*	*c.* Dec.
	D'Oyley, E.	*Britannicus, or The Man of Honour*	1695
	D'Urfey, Thomas	*III The Comical History of Don Quixote, with the Marriage of Mary the Buxom*	*c.* Nov.
	Gould, Robert	*Innocence Distressed, or The Royal Penitents*	*c.* 1695–1708
	Gould, Robert	*The Rival Sisters, or The Violence of Love*	*c.* Oct.
	Granville, George	*The She Gallants (Once a Lover Always a Lover)*	*c.* Dec.
	Hopkins, Charles	*Pyrrhus, King of Epirus*	*c.* Aug.
	Keigwyn, John	*Origo Mundi,* etc. (Trans.; see 14th cent.)	1695
	Motteux, Peter	*The Taking of Namur, and His Majesty's Safe Return*	1695
	Scott, Thomas	*The Mock Marriage*	*c.* Sept.
	Settle, Elkanah	*Philaster, or Love Lies a-Bleeding* (Adapt. Beaumont and Fletcher.)	*c.* Dec.
	Settle, Elkanah	*The Triumphs of London*	29 Oct.
	Southerne, Thomas	*Oroonoko*	*c.* Nov.
	Trotter, Catherine	*Agnes de Castro*	*c.* Dec.
	Anon. (not Powell, G.)	*Bonduca, or The British Heroine* (Adapt. Fletcher.)	*c.* Sept.
	Anon.	*The Indian Queen* (Adapt. Dryden and Howard.)	1695

TYPE	AUSPICES	EARLIEST TEXTS	LAST ED.	DATE
Comedy	United	1693		
Political Dialogue	Closet	1693*		
Tragedy	Unacted (banned)	1694*		**1694**
Comedy	United	1694*	1874†[280]	
Tragicomedy	United	1694	1932[265]	
Comedy	United	I: 1694 II: 1694**		
Comedies	Closet	1694*		
Comedies	Closet	1694		
Comedy	United	1695*		
Tragedy	United	1694*		
Civic Pageant	London	1694*		
Tragicomedy	United	1694		
Comedy	United	Lost		
'Mask'	United	1694*		
Droll	Bartholomew Fair	Lost		
Tragedy	Betterton's	1696		**1695**
Comedy	Betterton's	1695	1948[290] (MA)	
Comedy	Betterton's	1696**		
Comedy	Closet	MS		
Comedy	Patent	1696		
Tragedy	Unacted	1737*		
Tragedy	Patent	1696*		
Comedy	Betterton's	1696		
Tragedy	Betterton's	1695*		
Cornish Mystery	Closet	MSS		
'Musical Entertainment'	Betterton's	[1695?]*		
Comedy	Patent	1696*		
Tragicomedy	Patent	1695*		
Civic Pageant	London	1695*		
Tragedy	Patent	1696	(A)	
Tragedy	Patent	1696*		
Tragedy	Patent	1696*		
Dramatic Opera	Patent	MS		

DATE	AUTHOR	TITLE	LIMITS
	Anon.	*The Marshal of Luxemburgh upon His Death-bed* (Adapt. from French.) (See Hazlitt, *Manual*, 151.)	1695 (?)
	Anon. ('Ariadne')	*She Ventures and He Wins*	Sept.
1696	Behn, Aphra	*The Younger Brother, or The Amorous Jilt*	c. Feb.
	Cibber, Colley	*Love's Last Shift, or The Fool in Fashion*	Jan.
	Cibber, Colley	*Woman's Wit, or The Lady in Fashion*	c. Dec.
	Doggett, Thomas	*The Country Wake (Hob)*	c. Apr.
	Doggett, Thomas	*Mad Tom of Bedlam, or The Distressed Lovers, with the Comical Humours of Squire Numskull*	c. 1696 (?)
	Dryden, John, Jr	*The Husband His Own Cuckold*	c. Feb.
	D'Urfey, Thomas	*Cinthia and Endimion, or The Loves of the Deities*	c. Dec.
	D'Urfey, Thomas	*A Wife for Any Man*	1695–1697
	Gildon, Charles	*The Roman Bride's Revenge*	c. Nov.
	Harris, Joseph	*The City Bride, or The Merry Cuckold* (Adapt. Webster's *A Cure for a Cuckold*.)	c. Mar.
	Hopkins, C. (?) (Pref. signed by Horden, H.)	*Neglected Virtue, or The Unhappy Conqueror*	1695–1696
	Hughes, John	*Amalasont, Queen of the Goths, or Vice Destroys Itself*	1696
	Manley, Mary	*The Lost Lover, or The Jealous Husband*	c. Mar.
	Manley, Mary	*The Royal Mischief*	c. May
	Motteux, Peter	*Love's a Jest*	c. June
	Motteux, Peter	*The Loves of Mars and Venus* (Performed with *The Anatomist*, below.)	14 Nov.
	Norton, [Richard?]	*Pausanious, the Betrayer of His Country*	c. Apr.
	Pix, Mary	*Ibrahim, the Thirteenth Emperor of the Turks*	c. June
	Pix, Mary	*The Spanish Wives*	c. Sept.
	Powell, G.; Verbruggen, J.	*Brutus of Alba, or Augusta's Triumph* (Adapt. Tate.)	c. Oct.
	Powell, George (?)	*The Cornish Comedy*	c. June
	Ravenscroft, Edward	*The Anatomist, or The Sham Doctor*	14 Nov.
	Vanbrugh, John	*I Aesop*	c. Dec.
	Vanbrugh, John	*The Relapse, or Virtue in Danger*	21 Nov.
1697	Browne, Thomas	*Physic Lies a-Bleeding, or The Apothecary Turned Doctor*	1697
	Congreve, William	*The Mourning Bride*	20 Feb. (?)
	Dennis, John	*A Plot and No Plot*	8 May
	Dilke, Thomas	*The City Lady, or Folly Reclaimed*	Jan.
	Drake, James	*The Sham Lawyer, or The Lucky Extravagant*	31 May
	D'Urfey, Thomas	*The Intrigues at Versailles, or A Jilt in All Humours*	c. Feb.
	Filmer, Edward	*The Unnatural Brother* (See *The Novelty*, below.)	c. Jan.
	Granville, George	*Heroic Love*	c. Dec.

TYPE	AUSPICES	EARLIEST TEXTS	LAST ED.	DATE
Tragicomedy	Closet (?)	1695 (?)		
Comedy	Betterton's	1696*		
Comedy	Patent	1696 & MS	1915†[277]	**1696**
Comedy	Patent	1696	(A)	
Comedy	Patent	1697		
Comedy	Betterton's	1696		
Droll	Bartholomew Fair	Lost		
Comedy	Betterton's	1696*		
Dramatic Opera	Patent	1697		
Comedy	Patent (?)	Lost		
Tragedy	Patent	1697*		
Comedy	Betterton's	1696* F		
Play	Patent	1696*		
Tragedy	Unacted	MS (lost?)		
Comedy	Patent	1696*		
Tragedy	Betterton's	1696*		
Comedy	Betterton's	1696*		
Dramatic Opera	Betterton's	1697*		
Tragedy	Patent	1696*		
Tragedy	Patent	1696*		
Comedy	Patent	1696*		
Dramatic Opera	Patent	1697**		
Comedy	Patent	1696*		
Farce	Betterton's	1697**	1948[292]	
Comedy	Patent	1697	1927[298]	
Comedy	Patent	1697	1927[298] (MA)	
Comedy	Closet	1697		**1697**
Tragedy	Betterton's	1697	1923[299] (M)	
Comedy	Patent	[1697]*		
Comedy	Betterton's	1697*		
Comedy	Patent	1697*		
Comedy	Betterton's	1697		
Tragedy	Betterton's	1697*		
Tragedy	Betterton's	1698		

DATE	AUTHOR	TITLE	LIMITS
	Hopkins, Charles	*Boadicea, Queen of Britain*	*c.* Nov.
	Motteux, Peter	*Europe's Revels for the Peace, and His Majesty's Happy Return*	Nov.
	Motteux; Oldmixon; Filmer	*The Novelty: Every Act a Play:* Consists of *Thyrsis* (Pastoral), by Oldmixon; *All without Money* (Comedy), by Motteux; *Hercules* ('Mask'), by Motteux; *The Unfortunate Couple* (Tragedy; alteration of *The Unnatural Brother,* above), by Filmer; *Natural Magic* (Farce), by Motteux.	*c.* June
	Pix, Mary	*The Deceiver Deceived* (*The French Beau*) (Includes dialogues by D'Urfey [Act IV] and Motteux [Act V].)	*c.* Dec.
	Pix, Mary	*The Innocent Mistress*	*c.* June
	Powell, George	*The Imposture Defeated, or A Trick to Cheat the Devil* (Songs and Mask, *Endymion, the Man in the Moon,* in Act V, printed separately as *The Mask of Cynthia and Endimion,* 1697.)	*c.* Sept. (poss. first acted in summer, 1695)
	Ravenscroft, Edward	*The Italian Husband*	*c.* Nov.
	Scott, Thomas	*The Unhappy Kindness, or A Fruitless Revenge* (*The Unfortunate Kindness*) (Adapt. Fletcher's *A Wife for a Month.*)	*c.* July
	Settle, Elkanah	*The World in the Moon*	June
	Vanbrugh, John	*II Aesop*	*c.* Mar.
	Vanbrugh, John	*The Provoked Wife*	*c.* May
	Anon. ('W.M.')	*The Female Wits, or The Triumvirate of Poets at Rehearsal*	*c.* 1697
	Anon. (Southby?)	*Timoleon, or The Revolution*	1697
	Anon.	*The Triumphs of Virtue*	*c.* Jan.
	Anon. ('Ariadne'?)	*The Unnatural Mother* (*Love's Reward*)	*c.* Aug.
1698	Crowne, John	*Caligula*	*c.* Mar.
	Dennis, John	*Rinaldo and Armida*	*c.* Nov.
	Dilke, Thomas	*The Pretenders, or The Town Unmasked*	*c.* Mar.
	D'Urfey, Thomas	*The Campaigners, or The Pleasant Adventures at Brussels*	*c.* June
	Farquhar, George	*Love and a Bottle*	*c.* Dec.
	Gildon, Charles	*Phaeton, or The Fatal Divorce* (Adapt. Quinault.)	*c.* Mar.
	Motteux, Peter	*Beauty in Distress*	*c.* Apr.
	Oldmixon, John	*Amintas* (Trans. Tasso.)	1698
	Phillips, William	*The Revengeful Queen*	*c.* June
	Phillips, William (?)	*Alcamenes and Menalippa*	*c.* 1698 (?)
	Pix, Mary	*Queen Catherine, or The Ruins of Love*	*c.* June
	Settle, Elkanah	*Glory's Resurrection, Being the Triumphs of London Revived*	29 Oct.
	Trotter, Catherine	*Fatal Friendship*	*c.* May

TYPE	AUSPICES	EARLIEST TEXTS	LAST ED.	DATE
Tragedy	Betterton's	1697*		
Entertainment	Betterton's	1697*		
Comedy, etc.	Betterton's	1697*		
Comedy	Betterton's	1698**		
Comedy	Betterton's	1697**		
Comedy	Patent	1698*		
Tragedy	Betterton's	1698		
Tragedy	Patent	1697*		
Dramatic Opera	Patent	1697		
Comedy	Patent	1697	1927[298]	
Comedy	Betterton's	1697	1936[190] (MA)	
Burlesque	Patent	1697		
Tragicomedy	Unacted (?)	1697*		
Tragicomedy	Patent	1697*		
Tragedy	Betterton's	1698*		
Tragedy	Patent	1698*	1874†[280]	**1698**
Dramatic Opera	Betterton's	1699*		
Comedy	Betterton's	1698*		
Comedy	Patent	1698*		
Comedy	Patent	1699	1930[300]	
Tragedy	Patent	1698*		
Tragedy	Betterton's	1698*		
Pastoral	Patent	1698*		
Tragedy	Patent	1698*		
Tragedy	Patent (?)	Lost		
Tragedy	Betterton's	1698*		
Civic Pageant	London	1698*		
Tragedy	Betterton's	1698*		

DATE	AUTHOR	TITLE	LIMITS
	Vanbrugh, John	*The Country House* (Trans. Dancourt's *La Maison rustique.*)	18 Jan. (première ?)
	Walker, William	*Victorious Love*	*c.* June
	Anon. (Powell, G. ?)	*The Fatal Discovery, or Love in Ruins*	*c.* Mar.
	Anon.	*The Fool's Expectation, or The Wheel of Fortune* (Prol. and Epil. only.)	18 Oct.
	Anon.	*Jephtha's Rash Vow, or The Virgin Sacrifice*	23 Aug. (acted)
	Anon.	*The Mad Wooing, or A Way to Win and Tame a Shrew* (From Shakespeare's *The Taming of the Shrew.*)	1698 (pub.)
	Anon.	*Puritanical Justice, or The Beggars Turned Thieves*	1698
	Anon.	*The Siege of Namur*	23 Aug. (acted)
	Anon.	*The Strollers*	b. 1698 (?)
1699	Boyer, Abel	*Achilles, or Iphigenia in Aulis* (*The Victim, or Achilles and Iphigenia in Aulis*)	*c.* Dec.
	Cibber, Colley	*Richard III* (Adapt. Shakespeare.)	*c.* Dec.
	Cibber, Colley	*Xerxes*	*c.* Feb.
	Corye, John	*A Cure for Jealousy*	*c.* Dec.
	Dennis, John	*Iphigenia*	*c.* Dec. (première ?)
	D'Urfey, Thomas	*I & II Massaniello, or A Fisherman a Prince*	*c.* May
	Farquhar, George	*The Constant Couple, or A Trip to the Jubilee*	28 Nov.
	Harris, Joseph	*Love's a Lottery and a Woman the Prize, with Love and Riches Reconciled*	*c.* Mar.
	Hopkins, Charles	*Friendship Improved, or The Female Warrior*	7 Nov.
	Maittaire, Michael (?)	'Comoedia, Adoptivus'	*c.* 1699 (?)
	Maittaire, Michael (?)	*Dido* (Adapted from Virgil.)	*c.* 1699 (?)
	Maittaire, Michael (?)	*Excidium Trojae* (Adapted from Virgil.)	*c.* 1699 (?)
	Maittaire, Michael (?)	*Inferno Navigatio* (Adapted from Virgil.)	*c.* 1699 (?)
	Motteux, Peter	*The Four Seasons, or Love in Every Age* (Included in following.)	*c.* Jan.
	Motteux, Peter	*The Island Princess, or The Generous Portuguese* (Adapt. Fletcher.)	*c.* Jan.
	Penkethman, William (?)	*Love without Interest, or The Man Too Hard for the Master*	*c.* June
	Pix, Mary	*The False Friend, or The Fate of Disobedience*	*c.* May
	Settle, Elkanah	*The Triumphs of London*	30 Oct.
	Smith, Henry	*The Princess of Parma*	*c.* Apr.
	Anon.	*The Devil of a Wife*	23 Aug.
	Anon.	*Feigned Friendship, or The Mad Reformer*	*c.* May
	Anon. (Doggett, T. ?)	*Friar Bacon, or The Country Justice* (Performance listed for 1691 prob. error for 1699.)	23 Aug.
1700	Betterton, Thomas	*Henry IV, with the Humours of Sir John Falstaff* (Adapt. Shakespeare.)	9 Jan.
	Burnaby, William	*The Reformed Wife*	*c.* Mar.

TYPE	AUSPICES	EARLIEST TEXTS	LAST ED.	DATE
Farcical Comedy	Patent	1715	1927[298]	
Tragedy	Patent	1698*		
Tragedy	Patent	1698*		
Lottery Show	Patent	1698*	1940†[300a]	
Droll	Bartholomew Fair	Lost		
Droll	Unknown	1698*		
'Farce' (Political Dialogue ?)	Closet	1698*		
Droll	Bartholomew Fair	Lost		
Comedy	Patent (?)	Lost		
Tragedy	Patent	1700		**1699**
Tragedy	Patent	[1700]	1818[300]	
Tragedy	Betterton's	1699		
Comedy	Betterton's	1701*		
Tragedy	Betterton's	1700*		
Tragedy	Patent	1700*		
Comedy	Patent	1699	1930[301] (M)	
Comedy and Mask	Betterton's	1699*		
Tragedy	Betterton's	1700*		
Latin Comedy	Closet (?)	MS		
Latin Tragedy	Closet (?)	MS		
Latin Tragedy	Closet (?)	MS		
Latin Tragedy	Closet (?)	MS		
Musical Interlude	Patent	1699		
Opera	Patent	1699 & MS		
Comedy	Patent	1699*		
Tragedy	Betterton's	1699		
Civic Pageant	London	1699*		
Tragedy	Betterton's	1699*		
Droll	Bartholomew Fair	Lost		
Comedy	Betterton's	[1699]*		
Droll	Bartholomew Fair	Lost		
Tragicomedy	Betterton's	1700*		**1700**
Comedy	Patent	1700	1931†[302]	

DATE	AUTHOR	TITLE	LIMITS
	Centlivre, Susannah	*The Perjured Husband, or The Adventures of Venice*	*c.* Oct.
	Cibber, Colley	*Love Makes a Man, or The Fop's Fortune*	9 Dec.
	Congreve, William	*The Way of the World*	5 Mar. (?)
	Crauford, David	*Courtship à la Mode*	9 July
	Crowne, John	*Justice Busy, or The Gentleman Quack* (Song extant.)	1699–1700
	Dryden, John	*The Secular Mask* (Incorporated in Vanbrugh's *The Pilgrim*.)	29 Apr.
	Gildon, Charles	*Measure for Measure, or Beauty the Best Advocate* (Adapt. Shakespeare.)	*c.* Feb.
	Lister, Martin	*Eunuchus* (Trans. Terence.)	b. 1700 (?)
	Manning, Francis	*The Generous Choice*	*c.* Feb.
	Oldmixon, John	*The Grove, or Love's Paradise*	19 Feb. (première ?)
	Phillips, William	*St Stephen's Green, or The Generous Lovers*	1699–1700
	Pix, Mary	*The Beau Defeated, or The Lucky Younger Brother* (Based on Dancourt's *Le Chevalier à la mode*.)	*c.* Mar.
	Rowe, Nicholas	*The Ambitious Stepmother*	*c.* Dec.
	Settle, Elkanah	*The Triumphs of London*	29 Oct.
	Sherburne, Edward	*Hippolytus* (Trans. Seneca.)	*c.* 1700 (?)
	Southerne, Thomas	*The Fate of Capua*	*c.* Apr.
	Trotter, Catherine	*Love at a Loss, or The Most Votes Carry It*	Nov.
	Vanbrugh, John	*The Pilgrim* (Adapt. Fletcher.)	29 Apr.
	Waterhouse, David	*Cleophilus*	1700 (pub.)
	Wright, James	*La Mallad* (Trans. Molière's *Le Malade imaginaire*.)	b. 1700 (?)
	Anon.	*Hengist, the Saxon King of Kent*	3 June
	Anon.	*The Tempest, or The Distressed Lovers*	*c.* 1700

TYPE	AUSPICES	EARLIEST TEXTS	LAST ED.	DATE
Tragedy	Patent	1700	1872[303]	
Comedy	Patent	1701		
Comedy	Betterton's	1700	1948[296] (MA)	
Comedy	Patent	1700★		
Comedy	Betterton's	Lost		
Mask	Patent	1700	1932[265]	
Comedy	Betterton's	1700★		
Comedy	Closet	MS		
Comedy	Betterton's	1700★		
Opera	Patent	1700★		
Comedy	Smock Alley, Dublin	1700		
Comedy	Betterton's	[1700]★		
Tragedy	Betterton's	1701		
Civic Pageant	London	1700★		
Tragedy	Closet	1701★		
Tragedy	Betterton's	1700		
Comedy	Patent	1701★		
Comedy	Patent	1700	1927[298]	
Latin Comedy	Closet (?)	1700★		
Comedy	Closet (?)	MS		
Tragedy	Patent	Lost		
Droll	Bartholomew Fair	Lost		

SUPPLEMENTARY LIST I

(The following are extant plays omitted from the foregoing Chronology because of their uncertain date and identity. Most are in manuscript copies, the location of which may be found in the Appendix. Such facts as are given often derive from library catalogues, but other sources have been consulted, and in a number of cases the manuscripts themselves have been examined.)

Buchanan, George; Schonaeus, Cornelius; Plautus. Bodleian MS. Rawlinson 1388–91 consists of anon. translations, of uncertain date, of the following plays: *Jephthes, The Baptist, Medea, Alcestis* (all from the Lat. plays of Buchanan); *Naamen, Tobit, Nehemiah, Saul, Joseph, Judith* (all from *Terentius Christianus*, 1592, of Schonaeus); *Bacchides, Mostellaria, Menaechmi, Pseudolus, Miles Gloriosus, Mercator* (all from Plautus).

Alice and Alexis. Anon. 17th-cent. tragicomedy. MS (frag.).

Ananias, Azarias, Mesael. Anon. Lat. St Omers play, 17th cent. MS.

Antipolargesis. Anon. Lat. St Omers play, 17th cent. MS.

Antonio of Ragusa. A prose comedy, prob. late 17th cent., beginning 'Antonio, All this is most true', and featuring the characters Octavio and Allesandra, daughter of a Turk. The title has been assigned to it. MS.

Artaxerxes. Anon. Lat. St Omers play, 17th cent. MS.

Ascanius. Anon. Lat. religious play, prob. 17th cent., poss. Continental. MS.

Basilindus. Anon. Lat. St Omers play, 17th cent. MS.

The Battle of the Vices against the Virtues. Moral, '*tempe* Charles I'. Ment. by Fleay (*Biog. Chron.*, II, 337) as extant in MS. Poss. Fane's *De Pugna Animi.*

Britanniae Primitiae sive S. Albanus Protomartyr. Anon. Lat. St Omers play, 17th cent. MSS.

Cinna. Anon. trans. Corneille. MS.

The Country Gentleman. Anon. comedy, *c.* 1700? MS.

Diana's Grove, or The Faithful Genius. Anon tragi-comedy, 'never acted'. Prob. 17th cent. MSS.

The Disloyal Favourite, or The Tragedy of Mettellus. Anon. tragedy of 17th cent. MS.

Don Pedro, the Cruel King of Castile. Anon. Lat. play, 'early 17th cent.'. MS.

The Fatal Marriage, or A Second Lucretia. Anon. tragedy, 'early 17th cent.'. The name of its leading male character suggests a relation of the play with Henslowe's *Galiaso*, 1594. MS (ed. 1958 [1959] G†).

Gallomyomachia. A play in Greek. MS.

Gemitus Columbae. Anon. Lat. St Omers play, 17th cent. MS.

Ghismonda (Tancred and Ghismonda). Anon. tragedy, 17th cent. (after 1623). MS (ed. H. G. Wright, 1944†).

Glausamond and Fidelia. Anon. tragedy, prob. of Stuart period. MS.

Gown, Hood, and Cap. Anon. dialogue or entertainment, early 17th cent. MS.

The Great Cham. Anon. tragedy, 17th cent. MS (frag.).

Hannibal. Anon. Lat. play, later 16th cent. MS frag. (ed. C. Moore, *The Dramatic Works of Thomas Nabbes*, 1918†).

Hercules Furens. Anon. trans. Seneca, prob. later 17th cent. MS.

The Hypochondriac, or The Turmoils of Love. Apparently 'notes for a play and odd speeches, rather than fragments of a once complete play' (Bentley, *J. & C. S.*, V, 1353). Mid-17th cent.? Adapt. *Le Malade imaginaire*? MS (frag.).

Jovis et Junonis Nuptiae. Anon. Lat. play, prob. 17th cent. MS.

Jugurtha, or The Faithless Cousin German. Anon. tragedy, prob. late 17th cent. Poss. related to *Jugurth*, 1600. MS.

The Lover's Stratagem, or Virtue Rewarded. Anon. comedy, prob. late 17th cent. MS.

Lusiuncula. Lat. play with same story as *Macbeth* (Hazlitt, *Manual*, p. 145). MS.

The Marriage Broker, or The Pander. Comedy published as by 'M.W.' in *Gratiae Theatrales*,

1662*. 'At least in part post-Restoration' (Greg, *Bibl.*, II, 922), and prob. a redaction of an older play, as appear to be the other two plays in the collection: *Thorney Abbey* (see below) and *Grim the Collier of Croydon* (see *The Devil and His Dame*, 1600).

Medea. Anon. trans. Seneca. Early 17th cent. ? MS.

Mercurius Rusticans. Anon. Lat. comedy. 'Scena Hyneksey vel Hincksie.' According to Madan, 'written in 1663' (*Summary Cat.*, vol. II, pt. ii, 1183). MS.

The Merry Loungers. Anon. 'A farce as it was acted by a private company in Cambridge.' Before 1700? MS.

Montezuma sive Mexici Imperii Occasus. Anon. Lat. St Omers play, 17th cent. MS.

Morus. Anon. Lat. St Omers play, 17th cent. MS.

The New Moon. Anon. play in three acts. MS.

Nottola. Anon. Lat. comedy. Earlier 17th cent.? MS.

Oedipus. Anon. tragedy, 'between 1583 and 1603', intended for performance at a school, poss. in Newcastle or Berwick. MS.

Oedipus. Anon. trans. Seneca, later 17th cent. MS.

Pelopidarum Secunda. Anon. Eng. tragedy associated with Winchester School. Written during Elizabeth's reign? MS.

Perfidus Hetruscus. Anon. Lat. tragedy, 17th cent.? MS.

Preist the Barber. Anon. early 17th cent. (Cambridge?) dialogue or entertainment. MS.

Psyche et Filii ejus. Anon. Lat. Valladolid play, 17th cent., poss. acted at St Omers in 1643. MS.

Publius Cornelius Scipio sui Victor. Anon. Lat. play, prob. 17th cent. MS.

Pygmalion. Anon. Lat. playlet. Mid-17th cent.? MS (ed. R. H. Bowers, *Mod. Phil.*, XLVII [1949–50], 73–81†).

The Review. Anon. comedy, 'probably though not certainly after 1700'. MS.

Rodogune. Anon. 'English verse translation of the tragedy [by Corneille], *c.* 1700?' MS.

Romanus. Two scenes and synopsis of anon. Eng. tragedy. MS (frag.).

S. Franciscus Xaverius. Anon. Lat. St Omers play, 17th cent. MS.

Sanguis Sanguinem sive Constans Fratricida. Anon. Lat. tragedy, prob. St Omers. 'About A.D. 1600.' MS. Prob. not *Sanguis Sanguinem* acted at St Omers 14 Apr. 1640, but may be same as *Furor*

Impius sive Constans Fratricida in Stonyhurst MS.

The Siege of Croya. Anon. tragedy, *c.* 1700? MS.

Sisigambis, Queen of Syracuse. Anon. tragedy, poss. Restoration. MS (frag.).

Thorney Abbey, or The London Maid. History play published as by 'T.W.' in *Gratiae Theatrales*, 1662*. Prob. a redaction of a 16th-cent. play. Some parts appear to be Elizabethan; 'others are considerably later, but not necessarily after the closing of the theatres' (Greg, *Bibl.*, II, 922).

Tragoedia Miserrima Pyrami et Thisbes fata enuncians. By 'N.R.'. One-act Eng. tragedy, transcribed *c.* 1624–31 (?). MS (ed. G. Bullough, *Nar. and Dram. Sources of Shakespeare*, I, 1957†).

Troilus and Cressida. Anon. Welsh closet tragedy, before 1613. MS.

Try before You Trust. Anon. comedy. Before 1700? MS.

The Whimsies of Señor Hidalgo, or The Masculine Bride. Anon. comedy, once apparently bound with *Sir Thomas More.* Dated 1649–65 (?) by Bentley (*J. & C. S.*, V, 1436–37). MS.

TITLELESS PLAYS AND FRAGMENTS

'Masque', *c.* 1625. Huntington Lib. MS. HM 22 (frag.).

'A pastoral' in five acts, with scene 'the Isle of Scyros', and characters Xamolxis, Perindo, Rascipolis, Cotys, Cleta, etc. Prob. late 17th cent., and poss. adapt. Sidnam's trans. (1655) of *Filli di Sciro.* Brit. Mus. Add. MS 29496.

'Fragment of a play.' Chief characters are Ethel-[bert?], the Duch[ess] his wife, Os[wald] their son, Orina, Sir Ingram, Mousetrap, etc.; contains a Collier forgery. Brit. Mus. MS. Egerton 2623, ff. 37–38.

Prol., 15th cent., to a moral play of a rich knight who loses his fortune; in northern dialect. Durham Dean and Chapter MS. Archia. Dunelm. 60 (ed. J. Cooling, *Rev. Eng. Stud.*, N.S., X [1959], 172–3†).

'A Dramatic Fragment from a Caesar Augustus Play', *c.* 1500 (speech by a 'Secundus Miles'). Bodl. MS. Ashmolean 750 (ed. R. H. Robbins, *Anglia*, LXXII [1954], 31–34†).

'A Sixteenth Century English Mystery Fragment' (Epil. only). Bodl. MS. Tanner 407 (ed. R. H. Robbins, *Eng. Studies*, XXX [1949], 134–6).

'A Christmas Entertainment' in five acts, with characters Leonides, Ingenio, Roscius, Sapientia, Obligia, Charita, Justitia, etc. Bodl. MS. Rawlinson D. 1361, ff. 306–28.

'A comedy without a title', by 'R.M.'. The characters are Wardho, Leyman, two English Cavaliers; Bubble, a Frenchman; Grim; etc. Bodl. MS. Rawlinson C. 923.

'An unfinished indecent comedy.' The characters are a Quaker, Woodfall a lawyer, Sir Tho. Trueman, Capt. Mackforrest, Sally Salisbury, the Gaolkeeper at Newgate. The last three named suggest that this is an 18th-cent. play related to *The Beggar's Opera*. Bodl. MS. Rawlinson D. 1413.

'Dramatic fragment in verse, c. 1620.' *Dramatis personae* include Pilades and Horestes. Folger Shakespeare Lib. MS. X. d. 391, 1 f.

'Dramatic fragment in verse, c. 1630', with characters Eusebius, Timotheus, Theopilus. Folger Shakespeare Lib. MS. X. d. 390, 2 ff.

'Fragment of a religious play in verse, c. 1550.' Folger Shakespeare Lib. MS. L. b. 554, 2 ff.

'Play in blank verse, the scene Samos and Thrace.' Anon. pastoral comedy, with principal characters shepherds Ellaenus, Syringus, Ormillus, Melarchus, Armissus, and Nanthus, and nymphs Chloris, Charia, Spinella, and Lyncida. Prob. mid-17th cent. Folger Shakespeare Lib. MS. V. b. 222, f. 63.

'An English Mystery Play Fragment Ante 1300.' Camb. Univ. Lib. MS. Mm. 1. 18, f. 58a (ed. R. H. Robbins, *Mod. Lang. Notes*, XLV [1950], 30–35†).

'A play of the 17th cent., written by John Pallin, Chancellor of the Church of Lincoln.' MS cited in *Hist. MSS. Comm.*, I, 61 (MSS formerly at Helmingham Hall, Suffolk; now at Peckforton Castle, Tarporley, Cheshire [lib. of Lord Tollemache]).

Titleless Lat. play, based on life of early Christians in Rome at time of Julian the Apostate. 17th cent., frag. English Col., Rome, Archives MS. C. 17 (v).

Titleless English play in three acts, with characters Quadro, Rectangulum, Compasse, Line, Circulus, etc. 17th cent. English Col., Rome, Archives MS. Z. 141.

Fragment of a play in the Journal of Benjamin Greene, factor on the *Darling*, 1610–13. See William Foster, *Notes and Queries*, 23 July 1900, pp. 41–42.

SUPPLEMENTARY LIST II

(The following are non-extant plays omitted from the Chronology because of their uncertain date and identity. Some of them may be extant under alternative titles.)

(a) On 9 Sept. 1653, Humphrey Moseley entered in the Stationers' Register a number of plays dating between 1600 and 1642. The following unidentified anonymous plays appear in the list: *The Countryman*; *The King's Mistress*; *The Politic Bankrupt, or Which Is the Best Girl?* (alternative title may be an independent play). Also listed is *The Jew of Venice*, 'by Tho: Decker'.

(b) On 29 Nov. [Dec.?] 1653, Richard Marriott entered a number of anonymous plays in the Stationers' Register; the titles of most of them suggest composition during the decade before 1642, but the list is otherwise a miscellaneous one. The titles of the unidentified plays are as follows: *The Black Wedding*; *The Bondwoman*; *Castara, or Cruelty without Hate*; *The Conceits*; *The Divorce*; *The Eunuch* ('a Tragedy'); *The Florentine Friend*; *The Law Case*; *The Noble Ravishers*; *Pity the Maid*; *Salisbury Plain* ('a comedy'; Speed's *The Converted Robber?*); *Supposed Inconstancy*; *The Woman's Law*; *The Woman's Masterpiece*.

(c) The following titles appear in Rogers and Ley's play-list of 1656: *Bays*; *Cleopatra* (possibly Daniel's or May's play); *Play of the Netherlands*; *Robin Conscience* (possibly *The Book in Meter of Robin Conscience*, 1550, non-dramatic dialogue).

(d) The following additional titles appear in Edward Archer's play-list of 1656, which is derived from that of Rogers and Ley; the majority of them probably do not represent lost plays: *Baggs Seneca* (Trag.); *Battle of Affliction* ('Trag.'; probably a misprint for *Battle of Affections*, alternative title of *Pathomachia*, 1617); *English Arcadia* ('Com.'; probably not a play, but Markham's romance); *Impatient Grissel* (Com.); *Mother Rumming* (Com.); *Ortenus* (Com.) or *Ortenas* (Trag.) [probably one play rather than two]; *The Owl* (Com.); *Virgil's Eclogues* (Trag.).

(e) The following plays were advertised as 'Books in the Press, and ready for Printing' in E. Phillips's *New World of English Words*, 1658, and in other such lists, 1658–62: *The Chaste Woman against Her Will* (Com.); *The Fair Spanish Captive* (Tragicom.); *The Fool Transformed* (Com.); *The History of Don Quixote, or The Knight of the Ill-Favoured Face* (Com.); *The History of Louis XI, King of France* (Tragicom.); *The Tooth-Drawer* (Com.). In *The Wits*, Part I, 1662, a comedy entitled *The French Schoolmaster* is advertised for sale.

(f) The following titles are mentioned by Malone (*Plays and Poems of Shakespeare* [1821], II, 438–9) as anonymous plays not known to have been printed: *Love Yields to Honour*; *The Noble Friend*; *The Tragedy of Heildebrand*.

(g) The following titles appear in the list of plays which were claimed by John Warburton to have been burned by his cook: *A Mask*, by R. Govell (*The Mask*, 1624, by R. Gunnell?); *The Flying Voice*, by Ra. Wood; *An Interlude*, by Ra. Wood; *Fairy Queen*; *The Lovers of Ludgate*; *Orpheus* (Com.); *The Spanish Purchase* (Com.). In the Warburton sale of 1759 appeared the title, not previously listed, *Demetrius and Marina* (or *Marsina*), or *The Imperial Impostor and Unhappy Heroine* (Trag.).

(h) Listed as extant in MS in Hazlitt's *Manual* are the following: *Otho*, translated from Corneille by Corbet Owen; *The Death of the Black Prince* (Trag.); *The Yorkshire Gentleman* (Trag.). The present whereabouts of these MSS is unknown. *Catilina Triumphans* (Latin Com.), also listed by Hazlitt, is probably an erroneous entry.

(i) The following are titles from books of masking airs. A few may indicate lost masks, but the majority probably derive from known masks or from independent dancing airs: From Brit.

Mus. Add. MS. 10444: *Adson's Mask*; *The Amazonians' Mask*; *Are Mask*; *Bateman's Mask*; *Blackfriars Mask*; *Brox(burn)bury Mask*; *The Bull Mask*; *The Cuckolds' Mask*; *Durance Mask*; *Essex Antic Mask*; *The Fairy Mask*; *The Fools' Mask*; *The Goats' Mask*; *Gray's Inn Antic Mask*; *The Gypsies' Mask*; *Hampton Court Mask*; *The Haymakers' Mask*; *The Lady Lucy's Mask*; *Lincoln's Inn Mask*; *Mary Magdalene Mask*; *A Mask in Flowers*; *The Old Antic Mask*; *The Pages' Mask*; *Pearce His Mask*; *The Prince's Mask*; *The Queen's Mask*; *The Sailors' Mask*; *The Satyrs' Mask*; *The Shepherds' Mask* (MS date 1635); *Sir Jerome Poole's Mask*; *The Standing Mask*; *The Temple Antic Mask*; *York House Mask*. From Playford's *Musick's Handmaid*, 1678: *The Queen's Mask*. From Brit. Mus. Add. MS. 10338: *The Mask of Vices* (possibly part of Randolph's *Muses' Looking Glass*, 1630). Mentioned in Halliwell[-Phillipps]'s *Dictionary*: *Death of Dido*, by 'R. C.', 1621; *The Furies' Mask*, c. 1624.

(j) The following are lost plays mentioned in various works: *Comoediae aliquot Sacrae* (attributed by Bishop Bale to Gawain Douglas, Bishop of Dunkeld); *Comoediae* (attributed by Bishop Bale to John Scogan, time of Edward IV); *Priscianus Vapulans* (Latin Com., mentioned by Peacham, *The Complete Gentleman*, 1622); *The Greeks and Trojans* [possibly Heywood's *Iron Age*] and *The Guelphs and Ghibellines* (mentioned by E. Gayton, *Pleasant Notes upon Don Quixote*, 1654); *The Famous History of Petronius Maximus* (Trag., by 'W. S.', 1619, described in Constable's *Edinburgh Magazine*, IX [July 1821], 3–8); *Kynes Redux* (attributed to W. Gager by M. L. Lee, ed., *Narcissus* [1893], p. xiv); *Pharaoh's Daughter* (mentioned by K. L. Bates, *The English Religious Drama* [1893], p. 251); *The Revenge* (appearing among the titles of his plays in the engraving of Thomas Killigrew, frontispiece of his *Comedies and Tragedies*, 1664); *Saturnalia* (Com. attributed to John Edwards by M. J. Simmonds, *Merchant Taylor Fellows* [1930], p.18); *The Secrets* (attributed to Davenant and Ellis by Summers, *Playhouse of Pepys*, p. 153); *The Guiltless Adulteress, or Judge in His Own Cause* (adaptation of *The Fatal Dowry*, supposedly by Davenant; MS in existence *c.* 1750; see J. F. Kermode, 'A Note on the History of Massinger's *The Fatal Dowry* in the Eighteenth Century', *Notes and Queries*, CXCII [1947], 186–7); *The Creation of the World, The Conspiracy of Gunpowder Treason under the Parliament House, The Destruction of Sodom and Gomorrha, The Story of Dives and Lazarus* ('strange sights', i.e. Motions, licensed by Sir George Buc to William Jones, William Selby, and Thomas Wrench on 16 July 1619; see B. M. Wagner, *Notes and Queries*, CLXIX [1935], 97–98); *The Chaos of the World, The Creation of the World* (Motions licensed by Herbert; see Adams, ed., *Dramatic Records of Sir Henry Herbert*, p. 47).

(*k*) A number of plays of English origin are known through records of performances by English actors on the Continent, or through publication there of German versions of certain plays in the visitors' repertories. The principal English actors who headed Continental troupes were Robert Browne, active at intervals between 1590 and 1620, and his co-adjutor John Green, who made a last expedition in 1626. The activities of these two were usually associated with ruling houses of Hesse-Cassel and Brunswick. A third actor-manager of Continental troupes was John Spencer, patronized by the houses of Brandenburg and Saxony, and active abroad at intervals from 1603 to 1623. Those plays in the Continental repertories certainly of German origin are not included in the following list; a few of those which are included may not be of English origin. In Aug. 1593 Browne performed *Abraham and Lot* and *The Destruction of Sodom and Gomorrha* at Frankfort. In Sept. 1603 *Susanna* (probably a Continental play) was performed by English actors at Stuttgart. In 1604 a company, probably English, performed at Rothenburg: *An Ancient Roman, Botzarius* (probably not English); *Celinde and Sedea* (also acted by Spencer at Nuremberg in 1613); *Lewis, King of Spain; Melone, King of Dalmatia.* In Jan. 1604 Eichelin, a German actor heading what seems to have been an English company, performed at Nördlingen: *Annabella, a Duke's Daughter of Ferrara* (usually identified as Marston's *Parasitaster* and probably the same play as *The Duke of Ferrara*

acted by Green at Dresden in 1626); *Charles, Duke of Burgundy; Daniel in the Lions' Den; The Merchant's Disobedient Son* (*The London Prodigal,* 1604?); *Pyramus and Thisbe* (possibly from *Midsummer-Night's Dream,* since the repertory included also *Romeo and Juliet*). In 1607 the Browne-Green troupe performed at Cassel: *The King of England and the King of Scotland* (also performed by Green at Dresden in 1626); at Passau: *The Prodigal Son* (common in Continental records); at Gräz: *The King of England and the Goldsmith's Wife* (*Edward IV,* 1599?); at Passau: *The Jew* (variously identified as *The Jew of Malta, The Merchant of Venice,* and Dekker's *Jew of Venice,* and perhaps the same play as *Joseph the Jew of Venice* performed by Green at Dresden in 1626). In Feb. 1608 the Browne-Green troupe at Gräz performed: *Dives and Lazarus* (probably same as *The Rich Man* acted by Green at Dresden in 1626); *A Duke of Florence and a Nobleman's Daughter* (also acted by Green at Dresden in 1626); *King Louis and King Frederick of Hungary; A King of Cyprus and a Duke of Venice; A Proud Woman of Antwerp* (probably Day and Haughton's *Friar Rush*). In June 1613 Spencer at Nuremberg performed: *The Destruction of Constantinople; The Destruction of Troy* (Heywood's *Iron Age?*); *Philole and Mariana* (Machin's *Dumb Knight?*); *The Turk* (Mason's *The Turk?*). In May–July 1614 at Strassburg, Spencer repeated *The Destruction of Constantinople,* and performed also a play of *Government.* Between 31 May and 4 Dec. 1626 Green at Dresden performed: *Amphitruo* (Heywood's *Silver Age?* or an adaptation of Plautus?); *Christabella; The Clever Thief* (*The Winter's Tale?*); *The Count of Angiers; Crysella* (Dekker, Chettle, and Haughton's *Patient Grissil?*); *The Duke of Mantua and the Duke of Verona; The Godfather; Haman and Esther; The King of Aragon* (*Mucedorus?* or Greene's *Alphonsus, King of Aragon?*); *The King of Denmark and the King of Sweden* (*Clyomon and Clamydes,* 1570? or Dekker's *Gustavus, King of Sweden?*); *The Martyr Dorothea* (*The Virgin Martyr?*). Additional plays, chiefly based on those of Shakespeare and Marlowe, were in Green's repertory: *Doctor Faustus; Fortunatus*

(Dekker); *Hamlet*; *Hieronymo* (Kyd's *Spanish Tragedy*?); *The Jew of Malta*; *Julius Caesar*; *King Lear*; *Nobody and Somebody*; *Orlando Furioso* (Greene?); *Romeo and Juliet*. A few of the plays listed above survive in seventeenth-century German versions, the dates of which, however, are not necessarily the dates of performance indicated above. German scholars have printed from MSS: *The Duke of Ferrara* (based on Marston's *Parasitaster*); *Hamlet*; *The Merchant of Venice*; *Nobody and Somebody*; *Romeo and Juliet*. In *Engelische Comedien und Tragedien*, 1620, appeared, besides two farces and five jigs, *Esther and Haman*; *Fortunatus* (related to Dekker's *Old Fortunatus*); *Julio and Hyppolita* (related to *Two Gentlemen of Verona*); *A King's Son of England and a King's Daughter of Scotland* (same as *A King of England and a King of Scotland*, above?); *Nobody and Somebody*; *The Prodigal Son*; *Titus Andronicus* (related to Shakespeare's play); and an additional play of known German origin. In *Liebeskampff oder Ander Theil der Englischen Comödien und Tragödien*, 1630, appear two additional jigs and six additional plays. The plays of Shakespearean interest have been edited by A. Cohn, *Shakespeare in Germany*, 1865. For the jigs (edited by J. Bolte, 1893), see the reprints and discussion in C. R. Baskervill, *The Elizabethan Jig*, 1929.

(*l*) The following are lost anonymous plays written at the English Jesuit College of St Omers. The dates of these are known, and here indicated, but the plays have been omitted from their regular place in the Chronology because they were seldom more than academic exercises. See W. H. McCabe, 'The Play-List of the English College of St Omers (1592–1762)', *Revue de littérature comparée*, XVII (1937), 355–75: *Guido Varvicensis*, 9 Feb. 1623; *Trebellius Bulgarorum Rex*, 2 May 1624; *Paulus Japonensis*, 11 June 1624; *Ovo Frisius*, 11 July 1624; *Astraea*, 9 Oct. 1625; *Syrgiannes*, 16 Aug. 1630; *Geminus Alcides*, 7 Feb. 1640; *Fratrum Discordia Felix sive Stanislaus Fuga Victor*, May 1640; *Gonsalvus Sylveira*, 1640; *Aloysius sive Saeculi Fuga*, Apr. 1640; *Sanguis Sanguinem* (probably not same as *Sanguis Sanguinem*, Supp. I), 14 Apr. 1640; *Haeresis Triumphata sive B.*

Ignatius Societatis Jesu Fundator, Aug. (?) 1640; *Odoardus Varvici Comes*, 27 Feb. 1642; *Alexander et Aristobulus*, 24 July 1642; *Mors Valentiniani Imperatoris*, 16 Dec. 1642; *Nicephorus*, Autumn 1646; *Sigibertus*, 1647; *Joseph*, 1649; *Barlaam et Josaphat*, Aug. 1650; *Ferdinandus Rex Castellae*, 17 Feb. 1652; *S. Augustinus Angliae Apostolus*, 2 Oct. 1653; *S. Sigismundus*, 22 Jan. 1659; *Leontius, Hypatius, et Theodulus*, Aug. (?) 1659; *Leo Sapiens*, 10 Nov. 1659; *Rex Oswius*, 26 Jan. 1660; *S. Kenelmus Rex*, 1661; *Phoenix* (?), 1661; *Geaner et Hamarte*, Nov. 1661; *SS. Petrus et Paulus*, 1662; *Vincentius et Anastasius* (?), 22 Jan. 1663; *Constantinus*, 1665; *Catilina*, 1666; *S. Justus et S. Pastor*, 1666; *Valentinianus*, 31 Aug. 1667; *Abenner, Josaphat, et Barachias*, 1668; *Julianus et Celsus*, 1668; *Judicium Ultimum*, 8 Aug. 1669; *Crux Vindicata*, 1670 (revival? see Chronology, 1656); *Bellum Grammaticale*, 1676.

(*m*) The following are titles of plays once existing in a MS collection catalogued by Abraham Hill, probably at some time between 1677 and 1703. The collection also contained plays by known dramatists, and the titles of these have been incorporated in the foregoing chronological list. Most of the plays below probably were written before 1642, and in a greater number of instances than here indicated may be identical with works known under alternative titles. For a scholarly annotation of Hill's list, see J. Q. Adams, 'Hill's List of Early Plays in Manuscript', *Library*, N.S., XX (1939), 71–99: *Aleumista* (in Latin); *All Is Not Gold that Glisters* (Chettle's play?); *The Ambitious Brother* (by 'G. Buc'); *A Christmas Tale, or The Knight and the Cobbler* (by Philip Lane); *The Cloudy Queen and Singing Moor*; *A Court Purge*; *The False Friend* (the play of *c.* 1619?); *The Fatal Banquet*; *A Gentleman No Gentleman, a Metamorphosed Courtier* (Actors: Eustace, Frampole, Friswood, etc.); *Look on Me and Love Me, or Marriage in the Dark*; *Love's Infancy* (possibly same as Flecknoe's *Love in Its Infancy*, earlier version of *Love's Dominion*, 1654); *The Lover's Holiday*; *The Lover's Holiday, or The Bear* (another copy of the preceding?); *The Marriage Night* (Cary's play?); *A Match without Money, or The Wives' Prize*; *More Than Nine Days Wonder*,

P

Two Constant Women; *Mull Sack, or The Looking Glass, the Bachelor, or the Hawk* (possibly the original of the Jack Cottington play, which was altered and published in 1640 as *The Knave in Grain New Vamped*); *Mustapha* (Greville's play? Boyle's play?); *Osman the Turk, or The Ottoman Custom* (possibly Carlell's *Osmond the Great Turk*); *The Painted Lady*; *Pandorae Pyxis* (in Latin); *Philip of Macedon*; *Roxolana, or The Ambitious Step-Dame* (possibly same as Boyle's *Mustapha*); *Spanish Preferment*; *Tereus with a Pastoral* (by 'M. A.'; actors: Agnostus, Eupathus, etc., Mufti, Nassuf, etc.; one play or two?); *Tradeway's Tragedy*; *The Tragedy of Tomerania*; *The Triumph of Innocence*; *The Two Spanish Gentlemen*; *The Unfaithful Wife*; *Valentinian, or Rape's Revenge* (probably Fletcher's *Valentinian*, or Rochester's adaptation of it); *The Wandering Jew*; *A Way to Make a Knave Honest*; *The White Witch of Westminster, or Love in a Lunacy*; *The Widow Captain*; *The Wronged Widow's Tragedy*; *The Younger Brother, or Male Courtesan* (possibly same as *The Younger Brother*, 1617).

2 · LIST OF EDITIONS

(The sequence of the editions here listed is that of the superior figures following entries in the seventh column [Last Ed.] of the Chronology. For editions of several volumes published at intervals over a period of years, the inclusive dates of publication for the entire edition are provided in square brackets; in such instances the publication date given in the Chronology is that of the particular volume in which the entry appeared.)

1. D. T. Symons, ed. and trans., *Regularis Concordia*.
2. K. Young, *The Drama of the Medieval Church*.
3. P. Studer, ed., *Le Mystère d'Adam* (Manchester Mod. Lang. Texts).
4. E. N. Stone, trans., *Adam* (Univ. of Washington Pubs. in Lang. and Lit.).
5. A. W. Pollard, ed., *English Miracle Plays, Moralities, and Interludes*.
6. J. G. Wright, ed., *La Résurrection du Sauveur* (Les Classiques français du moyen âge).
7. M. K. Pope and J. G. Wright, *La Seinte resureccion* (Anglo-Norman Text Soc., No. 4).
8. W. Heuser, ed., 'Dux Moraud', *Anglia*, XXX, 180–208.
9. C. Brown, 'Caiphas as a Palm-Sunday Prophet', *Kittredge Anniversary Papers*, ed. F. N. Robinson *et al.*
10. B. Dickins and R. M. Wilson, eds., *Early Middle English Texts*.
11. E. Norris, ed., *The Ancient Cornish Drama*.
12. F. E. Halliday, ed. and trans., *The Legend of the Rood, with the Three Maries, and the Death of Pilate*.
13. J. P. Gilson, 'A Fourteenth Century Fragment', *T.L.S.*, XX, 340–1.
14. L. T. Smith, ed., *York Plays*.
15. J. S. Purvis, ed. and trans., *The York Cycle of Mystery Plays*.
15a. M. Hussey, trans., *The Chester Mystery Plays* (The Drama Lib.).
15b. T. Wright, ed., *De Concordia inter Ric. II et Civitatem London* (Camden Soc., No. 3).
16. G. W. Wickham, *Early English Stages* [1953–].
16a. A. C. Cawley, ed., *The Wakefield Pageants in the Towneley Cycle* (Old and Middle Eng. Texts Ser., No. 1).
17. M. Rose, ed. and trans., *The Wakefield Mystery Plays*.

18. P. Dustoor, ed., 'The Newcastle "Noah's Ark"', *Allahabad Univ. Stud.*, VIII, Pt. i, No. 8, pp. 1–30.
19. J. S. Farmer, ed., *Recently Recovered 'Lost' Tudor Plays*.
20. J. Leland, comp., *De Rebus Britannicis Collectanea*.
21. A. H. Smith, 'A York Pageant, 1486', *London Mediaeval Studies*, ed. R. W. Chambers *et al.* (vol. I).
22. A. C. Cawley, ed., *Everyman* (Old and Middle Eng. Texts Ser., No. 3).
23. F. S. Boas and A. W. Reed, eds., *Fulgens and Lucres*.
24. J. Somers, comp., *A Collection of Rare Tracts* [1807–9].
25. F. Grose, comp., *The Antiquarian Repertory* [1807–9].
26. W. M. Mackenzie, ed., *The Poems of William Dunbar*.
27. W. Stokes, ed. and trans., *The Life of St Meriasek*.
28. W. C. Hazlitt, ed., *Remains of the Early Popular Poetry of England* [1864–66].
29. J. S. Farmer, ed., *Six Anonymous Plays* (1st Ser.).
30. R. de la Bere, *John Heywood, Entertainer*.
31. A. Gowans, trans., *The Interlude of Youth*.
32. R. Withington, *English Pageantry* [1918–20].
33. J. S. Farmer, ed., *Six Anonymous Plays* (2nd Ser.).
34. J. S. Farmer, ed., *The Dramatic Writings of John Heywood*.
35. E. Arber, ed., *An English Garner*.
36. K. W. Cameron, ed., *The Play of Love*.
37. J. S. Farmer, ed., *The Dramatic Writings of John Bale*.
38. L. R. Merrill, ed., *The Life and Poems of Nicholas Grimald* (Yale Stud. in Eng., No. 69).

39. D. Hamer, ed., *The Works of Sir David Lindsay* [1931–36].
40. J. Kinsley, ed., *Ane Satyre of the Thrie Estaits.*
41. J. T. T. Brown, 'An English Translation of Buchanan's *Baptistes* Attributed to John Milton', *George Buchanan: Glasgow Quatercentenary Studies.*
42. A. Brown, trans., *The Sacred Dramas of George Buchanan.*
43. F. H. Fobes, ed. and trans., *Jephthah.*
44. Entry cancelled.
45. J. S. Farmer, ed., *The Dramatic Writings of Richard Wever and Thomas Ingelend.*
46. H. F. B. Brett-Smith, ed., *Gammer Gvrtons Nedle* (Percy Reprints, No. 2).
47. F. Holthausen, ed., *An Enterlude of Welth and Helth* (Englische Textbibliothek, XVII).
48. G. Becker, 'Lady Lumley's Übersetzung von Euripides' Iphigenie in Aulis', *Jahrbuch der deutschen Shakespeare Gesellschaft*, XLVI, 28–59.
49. F. I. Carpenter, ed., *The Life and Repentaunce of Marie Magdalene* (Univ. of Chicago Decennial Pubs., 2nd Ser., vol. 1).
50. *Seneca His Tenne Tragedies Translated into English* (Tudor Trans., 2nd Ser.).
51. A. Brandl, ed., 'The Longer Thou Livest, the More Fool Thou Art', *Jahrbuch der deutschen Shakespeare Gesellschaft*, XXXVI, 1–64.
52. H. Walpole, *A Catalogue of the Royal and Noble Authors of England, Scotland, and Ireland*, ed. T. Park (vol. I).
53. J. M. Manley, ed., *Specimens of the Pre-Shaksperean Drama* [1897–98].
54. A. J. Mill, *Mediaeval Plays in Scotland* (Univ. of St Andrews Pubs., No. XXVI).
55. J. W. Cunliffe, ed., *Early English Classical Tragedies.*
56. H. A. Evans, ed., *English Masques.*
57. R. Keith, *History of the Affairs of Church and State in Scotland* (Spottiswoode Soc. [1844–50]).
58. R. W. Bond, ed., *Early Plays from the Italian.*
59. J. S. Farmer, ed., *Anonymous Plays* (3rd Ser.).
60. G. Bullough, ed., *Narrative and Dramatic Sources of Shakespeare* [1957–].
61. E. Brydges, ed., *The British Bibliographer*, II, 612–7.
62. E. R. Payne, ed. and trans., *Sapientia Solomonis* (Yale Stud. in Eng., No. 89).
63. J. S. Farmer, ed., *The Dramatic Writings of Ulpian Fulwell.*
64. J. W. Cunliffe, ed., *The Complete Works of George Gascoigne* [1907–10].
65. J. P. Collier, ed., 'Churchyard's Chippes', *Illustrations of Early English Poetry*, II [1866–70].
66. A. W. Pollard, ed., *The Queen's Majesty's Entertainment at Woodstock 1575.*
67. M. W. Wallace, ed., *A Tragedie of Abrahams Sacrifice* (Univ. of Toronto Philol. Ser.).
68. E. Rühl, ed., 'The Tide Taryeth No Man', *Jahrbuch der deutschen Shakespeare Gesellschaft*, XLIII, 1–52.
69. C. F. T. Brooke, ed., *Common Conditions* (Yale Elizabethan Club Reprints).
70. E. Vogel, ed., 'All for Money', *Jahrbuch der deutschen Shakespeare Gesellschaft*, XL, 129–86.
71. J. Nichols, ed., *The Progresses and Public Processions of Queen Elizabeth.*
72. A. Feuillerat, ed., *The Works of Sir Philip Sidney* [1921–26].
73. G. C. Moore Smith, ed., *Hymenaeus.*
74. J. S. Farmer, ed., *Five Anonymous Plays* (4th Ser.).
75. W. C. Hazlitt, ed., *Shakespeare's Library.*
76. J. Bolte, *Andrea Guarnas, Bellum Grammaticale und Seine Nachahmungen.*
77. A. Dyce, ed., *The Works of Christopher Marlowe.*
78. R. H. Bowers, 'William Gager's *Oedipus*', *Stud. in Philol.*, XLVI, 141–53.
79. R. W. Bond, ed., *The Complete Works of John Lyly.*
80. C. T. Prouty, gen. ed., *The Life and Works of George Peele* [1952–].
81. W. W. Greg, ed., *Dramatic Documents from the Elizabethan Playhouses.*
82. P. Edwards, ed., *The Spanish Tragedy* (Revels Plays).
83. R. H. Case, gen. ed., *The Life and Works of Christopher Marlowe* [1930–33].
84. F. O. Mann, ed., *The Works of Thomas Deloney.*
85. J. Craigie, ed., *The Poems of James VI of Scotland* (Scottish Text Soc. Pubs., 3rd Ser., Nos. 22, 26 [1955–58]).
86. J. P. Brawner, ed., *The Wars of Cyrus* (Univ. of Illinois Stud. in Lang. and Lit., vol. XXVIII, nos. 3–4).

87. B. Cellini, ed., *Friar Bacon and Friar Bungay. John of Bordeaux* ...
88. P. V. Rubow, ed., *Tvold kan taemmes, The Taming of a Shrew.*
89. A. Luce, ed., *The Countess of Pembroke's Antonie.*
90. F. R. Cady, ed., *The Old Wives Tale.*
91. C. F. T. Brooke, ed., *The Shakespeare Apocrypha.*
92. R. Fischer, *Quellen zu König Lear.*
93. G. R. Baskervill, *The Elizabethan Jig.*
94. F. S. Boas, ed., *The Works of Thomas Kyd.*
94a. F. Carrière, ed., *Arden de Faversham* (Collection bilingue).
95. H. E. Rollins, ed., *A Poetical Rhapsody, 1602–21.*
96. J. D. Jump, ed., *Doctor Faustus* (Revels Plays).
97. R. B. McKerrow, ed., *The Works of Thomas Nashe* [1904–10, rev. F. P. Wilson, 1958].
98. A. P. Rossiter, ed., *Woodstock.*
99. B. Brown, *Law Sports at Gray's Inn (1594).*
100. A. H. Bullen, ed., *Old English Plays* [1882–85].
101. T. M. Parrott, ed., *The Tragedies of George Chapman.*
102. J. Elson, ed., *The Wits, or Sport upon Sport.*
103. C. J. Sisson, ed., William Shakespeare, *Complete Works.*
104. W. Mühlfeld, ed., 'The Tragedie of Caesar and Pompey, or Caesars Reuenge', *Jahrbuch der deutschen Shakespeare Gesellschaft*, XLVII, 132–55 and XLVIII, 37–80.
105. A. G. Jones, 'A Play of Judith', *Mod. Lang. Notes*, XXXII, 1–6.
106. G. C. Moore Smith, ed., *Laelia.*
107. J. Spedding, R. L. Ellis, and D. D. Heath, eds., *The Works of Francis Bacon* [1857–74].
108. G. Bullough, ed., *The Poems and Dramas of Fulke Greville.*
109. C. H. Herford and P. and E. Simpson, eds., *Ben Jonson* [1925–53].
110. R. Simpson, ed., *The School of Shakespeare.*
111. A. C. Baugh, ed., *William Haughton's Englishmen for My Money; or, A Woman Will Have Her Will.*
111a. A. B. Kernan, ed., *Volpone* (The Yale Ben Jonson).
112. L. Hotson, ed., *Queen Elizabeth's Entertainment at Mitcham.*
113. F. Bowers, ed., *The Dramatic Works of Thomas Dekker* [1953–61].
113a. J. Loiseau, ed., *Le Jour de fête des cordonniers* ... (Collection bilingue).
114. R. H. Shepherd, ed., *The Dramatic Works of Thomas Heywood* (Pearson Reprints).
115. H. H. Wood, ed., *The Plays of John Marston* [1934–39].
116. G. C. Moore Smith, ed., *Club Law.*
117. J. B. Leishman, ed., *The Three Parnassus Plays.*
118. W. C. Hazlitt, ed., *The Plays of John Webster* (Lib. of Old Authors).
119. C. J. Sisson, *Lost Plays of Shakespeare's Age.*
120. J. Haslewood, introd., *The Cuck-Queanes and Cuckolds Errants ... The Faery Pastorall ... By W. P. Esq.* (Roxburghe Club).
121. A. H. Bullen, ed., *The Works of Thomas Middleton* [1885–86].
122. T. M. Parrott, ed., *The Comedies of George Chapman.*
123. A. B. Grosart, ed., *The Poems of John Davies* (Early Eng. Poets).
124. K. W. Tibbals, ed., *The Royal King and the Loyal Subject (1637)* (Univ. of Pennsylvania Pubs. in Philol., Lit., and Archaeol.).
125. W. A. Abrams, ed., *The Merry Devil of Edmonton.*
126. L. Kastner and H. B. Charlton, eds., *The Dramatic Works of William Alexander.*
127. R. W. Van Fossen, ed., *A Woman Killed with Kindness* (Revels Plays).
128. M. L. Lee, ed., *Narcissus, a Twelfth Night Merriment.*
129. A. J. Mill, ed., 'Philotus', *Miscellany Volume* (Scottish Text Soc.).
130. J. Jacquot, ed., *Bussy D'Amboise* (Collection bilingue).
131. L. Michel, ed., *Philotas* (Yale Stud. in Eng., No. 110).
132. A. H. Quinn, ed., *The Faire Maide of Bristow* (Univ. of Pennsylvania Pubs. in Philol., Lit., and Archaeol.).
133. A. B. Grosart, ed., *The Complete Works in Verse and Prose of Samuel Daniel* [1885–96].
134. M. W. Sampson, ed., *Thomas Middleton.*
135. R. T. D. Sayle, ed., *Lord Mayor's Pageants of the Merchant Taylors' Company in the XVth, XVIth, and XVIIth Centuries.*
136. A. Glover and A. R. Waller, eds., *The Works of Beaumont and Fletcher* [1905–12].
137. P. Jordan-Smith, ed. and trans., *Robert Burton's Philosophaster.*

138. A. H. Bullen, ed., *The Works of John Day.*
139. A. H. Bullen, ed., *The Works of John Marston.*
140. J. Nichols, ed., *The Progresses, Processions, and Magnificent Festivities, of King James the First. . .*
141. H. Fluchère, ed., *La Tragédie du vengeur* (Collection bilingue).
142. M. T. Jones-Davies, ed., *Le Chevalier de l'ardent pilon* (Collection bilingue).
143. K. Talbot, ed., *The Maske by Thomas Campion.*
144. A. Holaday, ed., *The Rape of Lucrece* (Univ. of Illinois Stud. in Lang. and Lit., vol. 34, no. 3).
145. A. Nicoll, ed., *Cupids Whirligig (1607)* (The Berkshire Ser., I).
146. A. B. Grosart, ed., *Choice Rarities of English Poetry.*
147. C. W. Stork, ed., *William Rowley, His All's Lost by Lust, and A Shoemaker, a Gentleman* (Univ. of Pennsylvania Pubs. in Lit. and Philol., vol. 13).
148. W. Peery, ed., *The Plays of Nathan Field.*
149. A. Nicoll, ed., *The Works of Cyril Tourneur.*
150. T. Corser(?), ed., *Chester's Triumph in Honor of Her Prince . . .* (Chetham Soc. Pubs., III).
151. C. Morley, ed., *The Maid's Tragedy.*
152. A. E. H. Swaen, 'Robert Daborne's Plays', *Anglia*, XX, 153–256, and XXI, 373–440.
153. K. L. Bates, ed., *'A Woman Killed with Kindness' and 'The Fair Maid of the West'* (Belles-Lettres Ser.).
154. J. P. Collier, ed., *Five Court Masques.*
155. W. Stokes, ed., *Gwreans an Bys. The Creation of the World* (Trans. of the Philol. Soc., 1864).
156. F. W. Fairholt, ed., *The Lord Mayor's Pageants.*
157. V. Kreb, ed., *The Valiant Welshman, by R. A., Gent.*
158. J. R. Brown, ed., *The White Devil* (Revels Plays).
159. P. Vivian, ed., *The Works of Thomas Campion.*
160. J. Gerritsen, ed., *The Honest Mans Fortune.*
161. A. E. Horsman, ed., *Bartholomew Fair* (Revels Plays).
162. L. W. Payne, Jr., ed., *The Hector of Germanie; or, The Palsgrave Prime Elector, Written by Wentworth Smith* (Univ. of Pennsylvania Pubs. in Philol. and Lit., vol. XI).
163. F. L. Lucas, ed., *The Duchess of Malfi.*
164. H. W. Weber, ed., *The Works of Beaumont and Fletcher.*

165. J. S. G. Bolton, ed., *Melanthe* (Yale Stud. in Eng., No. 79).
166. G. Jones, ed., *Ulysses and Circe.*
167. F. S. Boas, ed., *The Poetical Works of Giles and Phineas Fletcher* [1908–9].
168. J. S. Hawkins, ed., *Ignoramus.*
169. H. G. Dick, ed., *Alhumazar: A Comedy* (Univ. of California Pubs. in Eng., XIII).
170. C. Hindley, ed., *The Old Book Collector's Miscellany* [1871–73].
171. A. F. Sieveking, ed., *Worke for Cvtlers.*
172. *The Fishmongers' Pageant on Lord Mayor's Day 1616.*
173. F. L. Lucas, ed., *The Complete Works of John Webster.*
174. P. E. Smith, ed., *Pathomachia.*
175. C. Brown, ed., *The Stonyhurst Pageants, Hesperia.*
176. R. C. Bald, ed., *Hengist, King of Kent; or The Mayor of Queenborough.*
177. R. Brotanek, *Die Englischen Maskenspiele.*
178. A. B. Grosart, ed., *Swetnam the Woman-Hater Arraigned by Women.*
179. C. L. Lockert, Jr., ed., *The Fatal Dowry.*
180. J. D. Jump, ed., *Rollo Duke of Normandy or The Bloody Brother.*
181. W. P. Frijlinck, ed., *The Tragedy of Sir John Van Olden Barnavelt.*
182. R. H. Shepherd, ed., *The Works of George Chapman* [1875–92].
183. W. W. Greg, ed., *The Gypsies Metamorphosed.*
184. T. W. Baldwin, ed., *The Duke of Milan.*
185. E. A. W. Byrne, ed., *The Maid of Honour.*
186. M. S. C. Byrne, ed., *A New Way to Pay Old Debts.*
187. N. W. Bawcutt, ed., *The Changeling* (Revels Plays).
188. J. O. Halliwell[-Phillipps], ed., *Shakespeare's Play of King Henry IV Printed from a Contemporary Manuscript.*
189. B. T. Spencer, ed., *The Bondman: An Antient Storie.*
190. C. M. Gayley, gen. ed., *Representative English Comedies* [1903–36].
191. G. C. Moore Smith, ed., *Fucus Histriomastix.*
192. A. H. Bullen, ed., *The Works of Robert Davenport* (Old Eng. Plays, N.S., III).
193. F. Cunningham, ed., *The Plays of Philip Massinger.*
194. R. C. Bald, ed., *A Game at Chesse.*

195. W. W. Greg, ed., *The Theatre of Apollo*.
196. W. Gifford and A. Dyce, eds., *The Dramatic Works of James Shirley*.
197. B. Dobell, ed., *The Partial Law*.
198. J. H. Hanford, '"Wine, Beer, Ale, and Tobacco"', *Stud. in Philol.*, XII, 1–54.
199. J. B. T. de Latour, ed., *Œuvres complètes de Racan*.
200. W. L. Sandidge, ed., *The Roman Actor*.
201. R. S. Telfer, ed., *The Unnatural Combat*.
202. W. C. Hazlitt, ed., *The Dramatic Works of Thomas Randolph*.
203. J. Maidment and W. H. Logan, eds., *The Dramatic Works of Sir William D'Avenant*.
204. H. G. Rhoads, ed., *Wm. Hawkins' Apollo Shroving*.
205. J. M. Stochholm, ed., *The Great Duke of Florence*.
206. J. Q. Adams, 'The Author-Plot of an Early Seventeenth Century Play', *Library*, 4th Ser., XXVI, 17–27.
207. *The Dramatic Works of Richard Brome* (Pearson Reprints).
208. C. H. Gray, ed., *Lodowick Carliell . . . and 'The Deserving Favourite'*.
208a. R. Davril, ed., *Le Cœur brisé* (Collection bilingue).
209. J. J. Parry, ed., *The Poems and Amyntas of Thomas Randolph*.
210. S. A. Tannenbaum and H. E. Rollins, eds., *The Drinking Academy*.
211. P. Bliss, ed., *The Inconstant Lady, A Play*.
212. L. J. Mills, ed. and trans., *Peter Hausted's Senile Odium* (Indiana Univ. Pubs., Humanities Ser., XIX).
213. H. W. Allen, ed., *Celestina; or, The Tragicomedy of Calisto and Melibea*.
214. J. Maidment and W. H. Logan, eds., *The Dramatic Works of Shackerley Marmion*.
215. A. Feuillerat, ed., *Arthur Wilson. The Swisser*.
216. L. J. Mills, ed., *Peter Hausted's The Rival Friends* (Indiana Univ. Pubs., Humanities Ser., XXIII).
217. A. M. Clark, ed., 'Two Pageants by Heywood', *Theatre Miscellany* (Luttrell Soc. Reprints, No. 14).
218. R. Kirk, ed., *The City Madam* (Princeton Stud. in Eng.).
219. J. Maidment and W. H. Logan, eds., *The Dramatic Works of John Tatham*.
220. E. K. Chambers, ed., *Aurelian Townshend's Poems and Masks*.
221. J. Maidment and W. H. Logan, eds., *The Dramatic Works of Sir Aston Cokain*.
222. A. Waller, ed., *The English Works of Abraham Cowley* [1905–6].
223. L. E. Kastner, ed., *The Poetical Works of Drummond of Hawthornden*.
224. G. and M. Bullough, eds., John Milton, *Dramatic Poems*.
225. A. H. Bullen, ed., *The Dramatic Works of Thomas Nabbes* (Old Eng. Plays, N.S.).
226. R. Dunlap, ed., *The Poems of Thomas Carew*.
227. J. W. Tupper, ed., *'Love and Honour' and 'The Siege of Rhodes'* (Belles-Lettres Ser.).
228. R. H. Shepherd, ed., *The Plays and Poems of Henry Glapthorne* (Pearson Reprints).
229. E. Goldsmid, ed., *Bibliotheca Curiosa*.
230. P. Cunningham and J. P. Collier, *Inigo Jones, a Life; and Five Court Masques*.
231. G. B. Evans, ed., *The Plays and Poems of William Cartwright*.
232. *Poems from Sir Kenelm Digby's Papers, in the Possession of Henry A. Bright*.
233. G. Dawson, ed., *The Seven Champions of Christendom by John Kirke* (Western Reserve Univ. Bull., N.S., XXXII, 16).
234. B. Dobell, ed., *The Poetical Works of William Strode*.
235. L. J. Mills, ed. and trans., *Senilis Amor* (Indiana Univ. Pubs., *Humanities Ser.*, XXVII).
236. *The Fool Would Be a Favourit: or The Discreet Lover (1657) By Lodowick Carlell*.
237. A. Nicoll, ed., *The Tragedy of Osmond the Great Turk, or The Noble Servant (1657)*.
238. J. A. Mitchell, ed., *The Warde by Thomas Neale*.
239. A. H. Thompson, ed., *The Works of Sir John Suckling*.
240. A. B. Grosart, ed., *The Complete Works in Verses and Prose of Abraham Cowley* (The Chertsey Worthies' Lib.).
241. A. B. Grosart, ed., *Miscellanies of the Fuller Worthies' Library* [1872–76].
242. F. Bowers, ed., *The Fary Knight, or Oberon the Second*.
243. Entry cancelled.
244. R. Hooper, ed., *The Poetical Works of George Sandys*.

245. W. Scott, ed., *A Collection of Scarce and Valuable Tracts (Somers Tracts)* [1809–15].

246. T. H. Banks, ed., *The Poetical Works of Sir John Denham.*

247. M. Summers, ed., *Restoration Comedies.*

248. A. B. Grosart, ed., *The Complete Works of Francis Quarles* [1880–1].

249. R. J. Broadbent, ed., 'A Masque at Knowsley', *Trans. of the Historic Soc. of Lancashire and Cheshire*, N.S., XLI, 1–17.

250. E. Rühl, *Grobianus in England, Palaestra*, XXXVIII, 164–91.

251. J. S. Keltie, ed., *The Works of the British Dramatists.*

252. N. C. Starr, '*The Concealed Fansyes:* A Play by Lady Jane Cavendish and Lady Elizabeth Brackley', *PMLA*, XLVI, 802–38.

253. W. Oldys and T. Park, *The Harleian Miscellany* [1808–13].

254. J. O. Halliwell-Phillipps, *A Brief Description of Ancient and Modern Manuscripts Preserved in the Public Library of Plymouth.*

255. W. C. Hazlitt, ed., *Inedited Poetical Miscellanies, 1584–1700.*

256. F. Needham, ed., 'A Pleasante & Merrye Humor off a Roge', *Welbeck Miscellany*, No. 1.

257. C. K. Meschter, ed., *Love's Victory.*

258. W. B. Gales, ed., *The Dramatic Works and Translations of Sir William Lower.*

259. A. S. (i.e. Alexander Smith), ed., *The Female Rebellion.*

260. J. P. Collier, ed., *A Royal Arbor of Loyal Poesie* (Illus. of Old Eng. Lit., vol. 3, No. 7).

261. H. A. Kaufman, ed., Niccolò Secchi, *Self-Interest; Translated by William Reymes.*

262. W. S. Clark, II, ed., *The Dramatic Works of Roger Boyle.*

263. W. H. Logan, ed., *Marciano; or, The Discovery. A Tragi-comedy, by William Clark, Advocate.*

264. C. N. Thurber, ed., *Sir Robert Howard's Comedy, 'The Committee'.*

265. M. Summers, ed., *The Dramatic Works of John Dryden* [1931–32].

265a. H. T. Swedenberg, Jr., gen. ed., *The Works of John Dryden* [1956–].

266. B. Van Thal, ed., *The Adventures of Five Hours.*

267. M. C. Nahm, ed., *John Wilson's The Cheats.*

268. C. Spencer, ed., *Davenant's Macbeth from the Yale Manuscript* (Yale Stud. in Eng., No. 146).

269. H. F. B. Brett-Smith, ed., *The Dramatic Works of Sir George Etherege* (Percy Reprints, No. 6).

270. J. Maidment and W. H. Logan, eds., *The Dramatic Works of John Lacy.*

271. J. Maidment and W. H. Logan, eds., *The Dramatic Works of John Wilson.*

272. Entry cancelled.

273. F. S. Boas, ed., *The Change of Crowns.*

274. D. D. Arundell, ed., *Dryden and Howard, 1664–1668; the Text of 'An Essay of Dramatic Poesy' . . . and 'The Duke of Lerma'.*

275. V. de Sola Pinto, ed., *The Poetical and Dramatic Works of Sir Charles Sedley.*

276. M. Summers, ed., *The Complete Works of Thomas Shadwell.*

277. M. Summers, ed., *The Works of Aphra Behn.*

278. J. Hayward, ed., *Collected Works of John Wilmot, Earl of Rochester.*

279. A. Clark, ed., John Aubrey, *Brief Lives.*

280. J. Maidment and W. H. Logan, eds., *The Dramatic Works of John Crowne* [1873–74].

281. J. R. Sutherland, ed., *Marriage a la Mode* (Temple Dramatists).

282. A. G. Barnes, ed., *The Rehearsal.*

283. M. Summers, ed., *The Complete Works of William Wycherley.*

284. D. M. Walmsley, ed., *Epsom Wells, and The Volunteers, or The Stock-Jobbers.*

285. G. Saintsbury, ed., *The Works of John Dryden* [1882–93].

286. M. Summers, ed., *Shakespeare Adaptations.*

287. T. B. Stroup and A. L. Cooke, eds., *The Works of Nathaniel Lee* [1954–55].

288. J. C. Ghosh, ed., *The Works of Thomas Otway.*

289. U. Todd-Naylor, ed., *The Country Wife by William Wycherley* (Smith Coll. Stud. in Mod. Lang., vol. XII).

289a. L. S. A. M. von Römer, *Rochester's Sodom.*

290. T. M. H. Blair, ed., *The Unhappy Favourite; or, The Earl of Essex, by John Banks.*

291. A. Lewis, ed., *Venus and Adonis* (Editions de l'oiseau lyre).

292. L. Hughes and A. H. Scouten, eds., *Ten English Farces.*

293. R. S. Forsythe, *A Study of the Plays of Thomas Durfey . . . and The Fool's Preferment* (Western Reserve Stud., vol. I).

294. M. Reynolds, ed., *The Poems of Anne, Countess of Winchilsea* (Univ. of Chicago Decennial Pubs., 2nd Ser., vol. 5).

295. *Dido and Aeneas.*

296. N. Marshall, ed., *The Comedies of William Congreve.*

297. D. Gilbert, ed., *The Creation of the World, with Noah's Flood.*

298. B. Dobree, ed., *The Works of Sir John Vanbrugh* [1927–28].

299. M. Summers, ed., *The Complete Works of William Congreve.*

300. C. Stonehill, ed., *The Complete Works of George Farquhar.*

301. F. E. Budd, ed., *The Dramatic Works of William Burnaby.*

302. *The Dramatic Works of the Celebrated Mrs Centlivre.*

3 · LIST OF DISSERTATIONS

(The following are typescript editions of plays submitted as theses for the Ph.D. degree. Theses subsequently published have been excluded [e.g. R. W. Van Fossen's edition of *A Woman Killed with Kindness*, a Harvard University dissertation revised for publication in the Revels Plays series]. Titles follow the form of the Chronology – except that alternative titles are omitted – and are not necessarily identical with the titles of the theses. There should be no difficulty, however, in locating any of the editions with the aid of this list.)

Absalom, ed. and trans. J. H. Smith (Univ. of Illinois, 1958).

Aglaura, ed. L. A. Beaurline (Univ. of Chicago, 1959–60).

Alphonsus, King of Aragon, ed. N. J. Sanders (Univ. of Birmingham, 1957–58).

The Arraignment of Paris, ed. R. M. Benlow (Yale Univ., 1950–1).

I & II Arviragus and Philicia, ed. J. E. Ruoff (Univ. of Pennsylvania, 1954).

The Bird in a Cage, ed. Frances F. Senescu (Univ. of Chicago, 1948).

Caius Marius, ed. J. E. Spring (Univ. of Denver, 1952–53).

The Cardinal, ed. C. Forker (Harvard Univ., 1957).

A Challenge for Beauty, ed. W. W. Powell (Duke Univ., 1958).

The Changeling, ed. R. G. Lawrence (Univ. of Wisconsin, 1956).

Changes, ed. Henrietta Louise Herod (Univ. of Chicago, 1942).

A Chaste Maid in Cheapside, ed. R. J. Wall (Univ. of Michigan, 1958).

Claracilla, ed. W. T. Reich (Univ. of Pennsylvania, 1953).

Cleomenes, the Spartan Hero, ed. S. W. Brossman (Univ. of Southern California, 1954–55).

Cleopatra (Daniel), ed. D. N. Dennett (Cornell Univ., 1951).

Cleopatra, Queen of Egypt (May), ed. Sister Mary R. Burke, S.C.N. (Fordham Univ., 1943).

The Cobbler's Prophecy, ed. Sarah T. Sisson (Univ. of Illinois, 1942).

Cupid's Revenge, ed. J. E. Savage (Univ. of Chicago, 1942).

Damon and Pithias, ed. J. L. Jackson (Univ. of Illinois, 1949).

The Death of Robert, Earl of Huntingdon, ed. J. C. Meagher (King's Col., London, 1961).

The Downfall of Robert, Earl of Huntingdon, ed. J. C. Meagher (King's Col., London, 1961).

The Dutch Courtesan, ed. M. L. Wine (Harvard Univ., 1959–60).

Edmond Ironside, ed. E. B. Everitt (Univ. of Pennsylvania, 1955).

I & II Edward II, ed. Yu-cheng Lo (Univ. of Wisconsin, 1954).

Edward III, ed. J. Cadwalader (Univ. of Pennsylvania, 1949).

Every Woman in Her Humour, ed. A. M. Tyson (Univ. of Pennsylvania, 1952).

Fair Em, the Miller's Daughter, ed. R. W. Barzak (Univ. of Illinois, 1959); ed. S. Henning (Harvard Univ., 1959–60).

The Fair Maid of the Exchange, ed. K. E. Snyder (Northwestern Univ., 1949).

The Faithful Shepherdess, ed. Florence A. Kirk (Northwestern Univ., 1944).

The Famous Victories of Henry V, ed. W. S. Wells (Stanford Univ., 1935).

Fedele and Fortunio, ed. R. H. Hosley (Yale Univ., 1949–50).

Fortune by Land and Sea, ed. H. H. Doh, Jr. (Univ. of Pennsylvania, 1962).

Friar Bacon and Friar Bungay, ed. D. Seltzer (Harvard Univ., 1959).

The Gamester, ed. S. H. Ronay (Univ. of Chicago, 1948).

Hoffman, ed. E. J. Schlochauer (Princeton Univ., 1948).

The Humorous Courtier, ed. M. M. Morillo (Univ. of Michigan, 1958).

Hyde Park, ed. T. K. Miles (Univ. of Chicago, 1940).

The Island Queens, ed. J. J. Devlin (Univ. of Pennsylvania, 1957–58).

John a Kent and John a Cumber, ed. A. E. Pennell (Univ. of Illinois, 1959).

A Jovial Crew, ed. G. R. Floyd (Univ. of Iowa, 1942).

A Knack to Know a Knave, ed. P. E. Bennett (Univ. of Pennsylvania, 1952).

The Knight of Malta, ed. Marianne Brock (Bryn Mawr Col., 1944).

The Late Lancashire Witches, ed. L. H. Barber, Jr. (Univ. of Michigan, 1962).

Love for Money, ed. D. W. Sanville (Univ. of Pennsylvania, 1949–50).

The Love of King David and Fair Bethsabe, ed. E. Blistein (Brown Univ., 1953).

Love's Cruelty, ed. J. F. Nims (Univ. of Chicago, 1945).

Love's Victory, ed. Helena Maxwell (Stanford Univ., 1933).

A Mad World, My Masters, ed. G. J. Eberle (Univ. of Wisconsin, 1945); ed. R. H. Lane (George Washington Univ., 1946).

The Maid's Revenge, ed. A. H. Carter (Univ. of Chicago, 1940).

Michaelmas Term, ed. G. R. Price (Univ. of Wisconsin, 1941).

The Miseries of Enforced Marriage, ed. G. B. Dickson (New York Univ., 1934).

The Northern Lass, ed. H. Fried (New York Univ., 1959).

The Old Couple, ed. Sister M. Simplicia Fitzgibbons (Catholic Univ. of America, 1940).

The Old Wives Tale, ed. R. L. Blair (Univ. of Illinois, 1935–36).

Orestes, ed. N. F. O'Donnell (Univ. of Ohio, 1950).

Patient and Meek Grissil, ed. C. W. Roberts (Univ. of Illinois, 1938).

The Platonic Lovers, ed. A. S. Johnston, Jr. (Univ. of Florida, 1951).

The Politician, ed. E. Huberman (Duke Univ., 1934.)

The Poor Man's Comfort, ed. Sister Marie E. McIlvaine (Univ. of Pennsylvania, 1934).

The Rare Triumphs of Love and Fortune, ed. J. I. Owen (Univ. of Illinois, 1952).

The Renegado, ed. Alice Senob (Univ. of Chicago, 1939).

Richardus Tertius, ed. and trans. R. J. Lordi (Univ. of Illinois, 1957–58).

The Richmond Heiress, ed. R. A. Biswanger, Jr. (Univ. of Pennsylvania, 1950–51).

The School of Compliment, ed. Nixon Mumper (Univ. of Pennsylvania, 1959).

The Second Maiden's Tragedy, ed. H. L. Stenger, Jr. (Univ. of Pennsylvania, 1954).

The Siege of Urbin, ed. I. E. Taylor (Univ. of Pennsylvania, 1941–42).

Sir Courtly Nice, ed. Charlotte Bradford Hughes (Brown Univ., 1959–60).

Sir Thomas More, ed. B. W. Black (Univ. of Michigan, 1953).

Soliman and Perseda, ed. J. J. Murray (New York Univ., 1959).

The Spanish Gypsy, ed. Kate P. Smith (Northwestern Univ., 1944).

The State of Innocence, and Fall of Man, ed. M. H. Hamilton (Univ. of Virginia, 1951–52).

The Temple of Love, ed. D. J. Steible (Univ. of Cincinatti, 1939).

The Three Ladies of London, ed. H. S. D. Mithal (Univ. of Birmingham, 1958–59).

The Three Lords and Three Ladies of London, ed. H. S. D. Mithal (Univ. of Birmingham, 1958–59).

Time's Triumph, ed. R. C. Elsely (Univ. of Birmingham, 1950).

The Traitor, ed. J. S. Carter (Univ. of Chicago, 1941).

The Two Noble Kinsmen, ed. F. O. Waller (Univ. of Chicago, 1957).

Ulysses Redux, ed. and trans. E. F. Henley (Florida State Univ., 1962).

A Warning for Fair Women, ed. Dorothy Cohen (Radcliffe Col., 1957).

The White Ethiopian, ed. A. D. Matthews (Univ. of Florida, 1951).

The Whore of Babylon, ed. Marrianne G. Riely (Univ. of Pennsylvania, 1953).

The Witch of Edmonton, ed. Etta Soiref (Brown Univ., 1953).

The Wits, ed. A. S. Johnston, Jr. (Univ. of Florida, 1951).

The Witty Fair One, ed. Esther M. Power (Univ. of Chicago, 1942).

Women Beware Women, ed. Elizabeth R. Jacobs (Univ. of Wisconsin, 1941).

Your Five Gallants, ed. C. L. Colegrove (Univ. of Michigan, 1961).

4 · INDEX OF ENGLISH PLAYWRIGHTS

(Of the six hundred-odd writers here listed, about two-thirds are noticed in the *Dictionary of National Biography*. Many of the others are noticed in *Biographia Dramatica*, and in *Alumni Oxonienses* and *Alumni Cantabrigienses*. When the dates given below differ from those in these four reference works, as happens in a number of instances, the reason is that recent research has yielded new biographical facts; in such instances the source of my information is that indicated in the prefatory essay. Initials of anonymous authors are listed, but not in cases where the authors have been satisfactorily identified. In library catalogues it should be noted: (*a*) translated or adapted plays are sometimes listed under the name of the original author and not of the translator or adaptor, and (*b*) plays may be listed under the author's name alternatively spelled: thus, Broke for Brooke, Bellon for Belon, Corey for Corye, Crawford for Crauford, Stapleton for Stapylton, Sydserff for St Serfe, etc. When an author is cited in the Chronology more than once in any given year the number of listings is indicated below in round brackets following the date. References to Nicoll are to *Early Eighteenth Century Drama*, 3rd ed. [*A History of English Drama 1660–1900*, Vol. II], 1952.)

A., M., Supp. II, m.

A., R., 1612.

Adamson, William (Scottish Poet), 1558.

Aethelwold, Bishop of Winchester (908?–984), 10th cent.

Ainsworth, William (*c.* 1607–1671: Clergyman), 1625.

Al., G., 1566.

Alabaster, William (1567–1640: Clergyman), 1592.

Alder, John (*c.* 1588–1609: Student), 1608.

Alexander, Sir William, Earl of Stirling (*c.* 1568–1640: Courtier), 1603, 1604, 1607(2).

Alley, William, Bishop of Exeter (*c.* 1510–1570), 1560.

Amerie, Robert (d. 1613: Chester Ironmonger), 1610.

Anton, Robert (Satirist), 1612.

'Ariadne', 1695, 1697.

Armin, Robert (*c.* 1565?–1615: Actor), 1608, 1612.

Arrowsmith, Joseph (*c.* 1647–*c.* 1708: Clergyman), 1673.

Artour, or Arthur, Thomas (*c.* 1495?–1532: Cambridge Fellow), 1525(2).

Ascham, Roger (1515–1568: Tutor), 1543.

Ashton, Thomas (*c.* 1540–1578: Schoolmaster), 1561, 1566.

Aske, James (same as James Askew, Stationer, *fl.* 1588–1593?), 1588.

Atchelow, Thomas (Unknown), may have written plays, *c.* 1589; see Chambers, *E. S.*, III, 211.

Atkinson, Thomas (1599–1639: Oxford Proctor), 1618.

Attowell, George (*fl.* 1590–1595: Actor), 1593.

Aubrey, John (1626–1697: Antiquary), 1671.

Authinleck, Patrick (Schoolmaster), 1574.

B., H., 1659.

B., H. H., 1659.

B., I., 1656.

B., R., 1564.

B., T., 1614.

B., T., 1632; adapt., 1677.

B., T., 1649.

Bacon, Francis (1561–1626: Jurist), 1588, 1594, 1595.

Badger, John (*fl.* 1555–1577: Oxford Univ. Beadle), 1575.

Bailey, Abraham (*fl.* 1667–1670: Lincoln's Inn Lawyer), 1667.

Baldwin, William (*fl.* 1547–1571: Proof Reader, etc.), 1556.

Bale, John, Bishop of Ossory (1495–1563), 1536(3), 1537(5), 1538(8), 1545.

Bancroft, John (d. 1696: Surgeon), 1679, 1690, 1692.

Banister, William, *vere* Selby, William (1636–1666: Master of St Omers), 1664(3).

Banks, John (*c.* 1650?–1706: Playwright), 1677, 1678, 1681, 1682, 1684, 1694, 1695.

Barjona, Laurentius, *see* Johnson, Laurence.

C., I., 1619; adapt., 1662.

C., R., 15th cent.

C., W., 1690.

Calfhill, James (c. 1530–1570: Cambridge Professor of Divinity), 1566.

Campion, Edmund (1540–1581: Jesuit), 1577, 1578.

Campion, Thomas (1567–1620: Musician), 1594, 1607, 1613(3), 1618.

Carew, Thomas (1594 or 1595–1640: Courtier), 1634.

Carlell, Lodowick (1601 or 1602–1675: Courtier), 1622, 1629, 1634, 1635, 1636, 1637(2), 1638, 1664.

Carleton, R. (Unknown), 1674, 1675.

Carleton, Thomas, alias Medcalf (1593?–1666: Jesuit), 1619, 1620, 1623.

Carlisle, or Carlile, James (d. 1691: Actor), 1689.

Carpenter, Richard (1606–1670: Clergyman), 1661.

Carr, William (fl. 1667–1669: Paymaster), 1669.

Cartwright, George (Unknown), 1650.

Cartwright, William (1611–1643: Oxford Proctor), 1635, 1636, 1637, 1638.

Cary, Elizabeth, Viscountess Falkland (1586–1639), 1604.

Cary, Henry, 4th Viscount Falkland (d. 1663), 1663.

Caryl, John (1625–1711: Diplomatist), 1667, 1670.

Cavendish, Lady Jane (1621–1669), 1645(2).

Cavendish, née Lucas, Margaret, Duchess of Newcastle (1623–1673), 1658, 1665.

Cavendish, William, Duke of Newcastle (1593–1676), 1640, 1641, 1658, 1667(2), 1669, 1674; adapt., 1662.

Cayworth, John (c. 1595–a.1637: Clergyman), author of Enchiridion Christiados, 1636, sometimes mistakenly regarded as a mask or entertainment.

Cecil, Sir Robert, Earl of Salisbury (1563–1612), 1594, 1602.

Cecil, T(homas? c. 1580?–1628: Clergyman), 1615.

Centlivre, Mrs Susannah (c. 1670–1723: Actress), 1700; for later plays, see Nicoll, pp. 303–6, 433.

Chaloner, Sir Thomas (1521–1565: Diplomatist), 1552.

Chamberlain, Robert (1607–a.1640: Clerk), 1640.

Chamberlaine, William (c. 1619–1689: Physician), 1658; adapt., 1677.

Chamberleyn, Thomas (Unknown), 15th cent.

Chapman, George (c. 1560–1634: Playwright), 1594, 1596, 1597, 1598, 1599(4), 1600, 1602(3), 1603, 1604(3), 1605(3), 1608, 1610, 1613(2), 1622, 1632, 1633, 1640; adapt., 1685, 1691.

Chappell, John (c. 1590–a.1632: Clergyman), 1616.

Cheke, Henry (same as Henry Cheke, c. 1548–1586, Politician?), 1568.

Chettle, Henry (c. 1560–1607: Printer and Playwright), 1592, 1595, 1598(15), 1599(8), 1600(6), 1601(6), 1602(8), 1603(3), Supp. II, k.

Christopherson, John, Bishop of Chichester (c. 1520?–1558), 1544.

Churchyard, Thomas (1520?–1604: Poet), 1574, 1578, 1579, 1587.

Cibber, Colley (1671–1757: Actor), 1696(2), 1699(2), 1700; for later plays, see Nicoll, pp. 306–13, 433–4.

'Claretus, Pater' (fl. 1623–1655: Jesuit of St Omers), 1623, 1655.

Clavell, John (1601–1643: ex-Highwayman), 1629.

Clerke, or Clark, William (d. b. 1699: Lawyer), 1662.

Clifford, George, 3rd Earl of Cumberland (1558–1605), author of tilting speeches as Knight of the Crown; see Chambers, E.S., III, 268.

Clifford, Martin (c. 1625?–1677: Courtier), 1671.

Codrington, Robert (1601–1665: Translator), 1662.

Cokain, or Cokayne, Sir Aston (1608–1684: Literary Amateur), 1633, 1639, 1640, 1662; adapt., 1684.

Compton, Thomas, see Carleton, Thomas.

Congreve, William (c. 1670–1729: Playwright), 1693(2), 1695, 1697, 1700; for later compositions, see Nicoll, pp. 315, 434.

Cooke, Edward (Unknown), 1678.

Cooke, Jo[shua?] (Unknown), 1602, 1611; adapt., 1662, 1667.

Cornish, William (d. 1523: Master of Chapel), 1494, 1501, 1514, 1517, 1522.

Corye, John (d. a. 1731?: Actor?), 1671, 1699; for later plays, see Nicoll, p. 316.

Cotton, Charles (1630–1687: Poet), 1665.

Cowley, Abraham (1618–1667: Poet), 1633, 1638, 1642, 1661, 1671.

Cox, Robert (1604?–1655?: Strolling Actor), 1653(10); adapt., 1662(5), 1673.

Crauford, David (1665–1726: Historiographer for Scotland), 1700; for later plays, see Nicoll, pp. 316, 434.

Ecclestone, Edward (Unknown), 1679.

Echard, or Eachard, Lawrence (*c.* 1670–1730: Historian), 1694(2).

Edes, Richard (1555–1604: Clergyman), 1582, 1592.

Edward VI, King (1537–1553), 1548.

Edwards, John (1600–a.1648: Oxford Proctor), Supp. II, j.

Edwards, Richard (*c.* 1523–1566: Master of Chapel), 1565, 1566.

Elizabeth I, Queen (1533–1603), 1561.

Essex, Earl of, *see* Devereux, Robert.

Etherege, Sir George (*c.* 1634–1691: Courtier), 1664, 1668, 1676.

Evelyn, John (1620–1706: Virtuoso), 1663.

Falkland, Viscount, *see* Cary, Henry.

Falkland, Viscountess, *see* Cary, Elizabeth.

Fane, Sir Francis (d. 1691: Courtier), 1675, 1684, 1686.

Fane, Mildmay, 2nd Earl of Westmorland (1602–1666), 1640, 1641, 1642(2), 1643, 1644, 1645, 1650, 1658.

Fanshawe, Sir Richard (1608–1666: Diplomatist), 1647, 1654, 1658.

Farquhar, George (1678–1707: Army Officer), 1698, 1699; for later plays, *see* Nicoll, pp. 321–3, 435–6.

Farrant, Richard (d. 1580: Master of Children of Windsor), 1588.

Ferebe, George (*c.* 1573–a.1613: Composer), 1613.

Ferrers, George (*c.* 1500–1579: Politician), 1553, 1575.

Field, Nathan (1587–1619 or 1620: Actor), 1609, 1611, 1612, 1613, 1614, 1617(2), 1618, 1619.

Filmer, Sir Edward (*c.* 1619–1669: Courtier), 1663.

Filmer, Edward (1652–a.1707: Lawyer), 1697(2).

Finch, Anne, Countess of Winchilsea (1661–1720), 1688, 1690.

Fishbourne, Christopher (*fl.* 1678–1685), 1678.

Fisher, Jasper (1591–1643: Clergyman), 1625.

Flecknoe, Richard (d. 1678?: Lay Brother), 1650(2), 1654(2), 1659, 1661, 1664, 1667(2), 1668.

Fletcher, John (1579–1625: Playwright), 1606, 1607, 1608(2), 1609(3), 1610, 1611(3), 1612(2), 1613(6), 1614(3), 1615(2), 1616(3), 1617(4), 1618(2), 1619(5), 1620(4), 1621(3), 1622(4), 1623(3), 1624(2), 1625(3), 1626(2), 1634; adapt., 1658, 1662(14), 1664(2), 1667, 1669, 1677, 1678, 1685, 1686, 1687, 1688, 1690, 1695(2), 1697, 1699, 1700.

Fletcher, Phineas (1582–1650: Clergyman), 1615.

Flower, Francis (Lawyer?), 1588.

Ford, John (1586–a. 1639: Playwright), 1612, 1621, 1623(3), 1624(5), 1626, 1628(2), 1629, 1630, 1632(2), 1633, 1635, 1638(2). [Also 1619.]

Forde, Thomas (*fl.* 1647–1661: Bookseller's Assistant), 1660.

Formido, Sir Cornelius (Unknown), 1637, 1656.

Forsett, Edward (*c.* 1553–*c.* 1630: Political Writer), 1581.

Fountain, John (d. *c.* 1667?), 1661; adapt., 1669.

Fowler, William (*fl.* 1581–1609: Scottish Poet), 1594.

Fox, or Foxe, Richard, Bishop of Winchester, Lord Privy Seal (1448?–1528), 1502.

Foxe, John (1516–1587: Martyrologist), 1556.

Francis, Sir Henry (Monk of St Werburgh), formerly mentioned as possible author of *Chester Plays*, 14th cent.

Fraunce, Abraham (*c.* 1558–a.1633: Poet), 1579, 1582, 1591.

Freeman, Sir Ralph (*c.* 1590–1667: Master of the Mint), 1639.

Fulbeck, William (1560–1603?: Historian), 1588.

Fuller, Thomas (1608–1661: Clergyman), 1643.

Fulwell, Ulpian (*c.* 1546–a.1578: Clergyman), 1568.

G., I., 1614.

Gager, William (1555–1622: Clergyman), 1582, 1583(2), 1584, 1592(2), Supp. II, j.

Garfield, Benjamin (Unknown), 1650.

Garnett, Jasper (Lancashire Schoolmaster), 1621.

Garter, Bernard (*fl.* 1565–1580: Poet), 1578.

Garter, Thomas (poss. same as above), 1569.

Gascoigne, George (*c.* 1539–1578: Courtier), 1566(2), 1572, 1575(3).

Gayton, Edmund (1608–1666: Scholar), 1655.

Geoffrey, of Gorham (d. 1146: Abbot of St Albans), 11th cent.

Gildon, Charles (1665–1724: Author), 1696, 1698, 1700; for later plays, *see* Nicoll, pp. 332–3, 437.

Glapthorne, Henry (1610–a.1643: Poet), 1634, 1635(3), 1636, 1637, 1638(2), 1639(2), 1640.

Godolphin, Sidney, 1st Earl of Godolphin (1645–1712), 1663.

Goffe, John, *see* Gough, John.

Goffe, or Gough, Thomas (*c.* 1591–1629: Clergyman), 1617, 1618(2), 1619(2).

Q

Hopkins, Charles (1665?–1700?: Poet), 1695, 1696, 1697, 1699.

Horden, Hildebrand (1668–1696: Actor), 1696.

Horne, John (born 1654: Oxford M.A., 1677), 1684.

Howard, Edward (1624–1712: Dramatist), 1664, 1667(2), 1670, 1671, 1678.

Howard, Sir George (Master of the Armoury), 1553.

Howard, Henry (brother of Edward and Sir Robert), 1661.

Howard, James (brother of Edward and Sir Robert), 1663, 1664, 1667.

Howard, Sir Robert (1626–1698: Statesman), 1660, 1662(2), 1664(2), 1668, 1669, 1670; adapt., 1695.

Howell, James (1594?–1666: Politician), 1654.

Hughes, John (1677–1720: Scholar), 1696; for later plays, *see* Nicoll, pp. 337–8, 439.

Hughes, Thomas (d. a. 1618: Gray's Inn Lawyer), 1588.

Hunnis, William (d. 1597: Master of Chapel), 1554, 1568, 1575.

Hutton, or Hutten, Leonard (*c.* 1557–1632: Clergyman), 1582.

Hutton, Matthew, Archbishop of York (1529–1606), 1555.

Ingelend, Thomas (Unknown), 1560.

J., B., 1593.
J., F., 1627.
James I, King (1566–1625), 1588, 1594.
Jaques, Francis (Unknown), 1642.
Jeffere, John (Unknown), 1564.
Jevon, Thomas (1652–1688: Actor), 1686.
Johns, William (1644–*c.* 1700: Schoolmaster), 1678.

Johnson, Laurence (Jesuit Martyr, d. 1582; conjectural identification of 'Laurentius Barjona'), 1570.

Johnson, Nathaniel (Unknown), 1651.

Johnson, Patrick (Linlithgow Player and, perhaps, Playwright of late 15th cent.).

Johnson, William (*c.* 1611–1667: Clergyman), 1638.

Jones, John (Unknown), 1635.

Jonson, Benjamin (1572–1637: Playwright), 1587, 1596, 1597, 1598(2), 1599(3), 1601(2), 1602, 1603(2), 1604(2), 1605(2), 1606(3), 1607(2), 1608(2), 1609(2), 1610(2), 1611(3), 1612, 1613(3), 1614(1), 1615, 1616(5), 1617(2), 1618(3), 1619, 1620(3), 1621, 1622, 1623, 1624(2), 1625, 1626, 1629, 1631(2), 1632, 1633(2), 1634, 1637(2); adapt., 1662, 1685.

Jonson, 'Young' (Unknown), 1623.

Jordan, Thomas (*c.* 1620–1685?: Actor), 1635, 1640, 1641, 1654, 1657, 1659(2), 1660(2), 1661, 1671, 1672, 1673, 1674, 1675, 1676, 1677, 1678, 1679, 1680, 1681, 1682, 1683, 1684.

Jordan, William (Cornish Priest?), 1611; trans., 1693.

Joyner, William (1622–1706: Oxford Fellow), 1670.

Katherine of Sutton (Abbess of Barking), 14th cent.

Keigwyn, John (1641–1716: Scholar), 1693, 1695.

Kempe, William (d. b. 1608: Actor), 1589, 1592, 1595(3).

Key, or Caius, Thomas (d. 1572: Scholar), 1550.

Killigrew, Henry (1613–1700: Clergyman), 1635.

Killigrew, Thomas (1612–1683: Courtier and Playhouse Manager), 1635, 1636(2), 1641, 1646, 1650, 1652, 1654, Supp. II, j; adapt., 1677, 1681.

Killigrew, Sir William (1606–1695: Courtier), 1662, 1663, 1664, 1665, 1669.

Kinwelmershe, Francis (d. 1580: Lawyer), 1566.

Kirke, John (*fl.* 1629–1642?: Actor?), 1635, 1642.

Kirkham, R. (Unknown), 1659.

Kirkman, Francis (*c.* 1632–a.1680: Printer), 1661(2), 1662, 1673.

Knevet, Ralph (1600–1671: Clergyman), 1631.

Kornyshe, William, *see* Cornish, William.

Kyd, Thomas (1558–1594: Playwright), 1587, 1589, 1590, 1591, 1594(2), Supp. II, k.

Kyffin, Maurice (d. 1599: Poet), 1588(2).

Kynaston, Sir Francis (1587–1642: Virtuoso), 1636.

Kynder, Philip (1597–a.1665: Physician), 1615.

Lacy, John (d. 1681: Actor), 1665, 1667, 1669, 1682.

Laingby, Robert (d. 1455: Clergyman), 15th cent.

Lancaster, John (Gray's Inn Lawyer), 1588.

Lane, Philip (Unknown), Supp. II, m.

Lansdowne, Lord, *see* Granville, George.

Lateware, Richard (1560–1601: Scholar), 1588.

Lauder, William (1520?–1573: Poet Priest), 1554, 1558.

Leanerd, John (Unknown), 1677, 1678(2).

Montgomery, or Montgomerie, Alexander (*c.* 1556–*c.* 1610: Scottish Poet Laureate), 1603.

Moore (?), — (Unknown), 1636.

More, Sir Thomas (1478–1535: Lord Chancellor), 1495.

Morrell, Roger (*c.* 1556 ?–1624: Clergyman), 1597.

Motteux, Peter Anthony (1663–1718: Librettist), 1695, 1696(2), 1697(2), 1698, 1699; for later works, *see* Nicoll, pp. 345–6, 441.

Mountfort, Walter (*fl.* 1615–1635: Officer in East India Co.), 1633.

Mountfort, William (1664 ?–1692: Actor), 1686, 1688, 1689, 1690(3), 1691, 1692(2).

Mulcaster, Richard (*c.* 1530–1611: Schoolmaster), 1575.

Munday, Anthony (1560–1633: Actor), 1582, 1584, 1589, 1594, 1595, 1598(6), 1599, 1600(3), 1601, 1602(4), 1605, 1609, 1610, 1611, 1614, 1615, 1616, 1618, 1621.

Murgetrode, or Murgetroid, Michael, Archbishop (1551–1608), 1582.

N., N., 1681.

Nabbes, Thomas (*c.* 1605–1641: Playwright), 1633, 1634, 1635, 1637(2), 1638(2), 1639; adapt., 1680.

Naile, Robert (Unknown), 1613.

Nashe, Thomas (1567–1601: Nobleman's Retainer), 1586, 1587, 1592, 1597.

Neale, Thomas (1614–1646 ?: Gentleman), 1637.

Nedham, Marchmont (1620–1678: Journalist), 1647.

Nelson, Thomas (*fl.* 1582–1592: Printer), 1590.

Neville, Alexander (1544–1614: Secretary), 1563.

Neville, Henry (*c.* 1620–1694: Politician), 1659.

Neville, Robert (*c.* 1641–1694: Clergyman), 1662.

Newcastle, Duchess of, *see* Cavendish, Margaret.

Newcastle, Duke of, *see* Cavendish, William.

Newman, Thomas (Schoolmaster of St Paul's ?), 1627(2).

Newton, Thomas (*c.* 1542–1607: Clergyman and Physician), 1581.

Niccols, [Richard ?] (1584–1616 ?: Poet ?), 1612.

Noel, Henry (d. 1597: Courtier), 1566.

Norton, Richard (d. 1732), 1696.

Norton, Thomas (1532–1584: Lawyer), 1562.

Nuce, Thomas (*c.* 1541–1617: Clergyman), 1567.

Ogilby, John (1600–1676: Geographer, Irish Master of Revels, etc.), 1661, 1662.

Oldisworth, Gyles (1619–1678: Clergyman), 1638.

Oldmixon, John (1673–1742: Historian), 1697, 1698, 1700; for later plays, *see* Nicoll, pp. 347, 442.

Orrery, Earl of, *see* Boyle, Roger.

Otway, Thomas (1652–1685: Playwright), 1675, 1676, 1677, 1678, 1679, 1680(2), 1682, 1683.

Owen, Corbet (1646–1671: Latin Poet), Supp. II, h.

Oxford, Earl of, *see* De Vere, Edward.

Pallin, John (Chancellor of Lincoln Church), Supp. I.

Palsgrave, John (*c.* 1483 ?–1554: Clergyman), 1540.

Parfre, John (d. a. 1512: Scribe), 15th cent.

Parkhurst, Ferdinando (*fl.* 1653–1662: Translator), 1662.

Parkinson, — (Unknown), 1603.

Parsons, Philip (1594–1653: Col. Principal, Oxford), 1612.

Paten (Mercurius, *fl.* 1565–1611, Herald ?), 1575.

Payne, Henry Nevil (1648 ?–1705 ?: Jacobite Agent), 1672(2), 1674.

Peaps, [William ?] (Graduate of Eton), 1634.

Peele, George (1556–1596: Playwright), 1579, 1581, 1585, 1586, 1587, 1588(3), 1589, 1590(2), 1591(4), 1592, 1594, 1595.

Pembroke, Countess of, *see* Herbert, Mary.

Penkethman, William (d. 1725), 1699.

Penroodock, or Penrudock, William (Gray's Inn Reader), 1588.

Pepys, Samuel (1633–1703: Naval Administrator), 1653.

Percy, William (1575–1648: Poet), 1601(2), 1602(2), 1603, 1632.

Perrin, Pierre (Writer for visiting French troupe), 1674.

Pestell, Thomas, Jr (1613–1690: Clergyman), 1632.

Pett, [Peter ?] (d. 1600: Tutor), 1600.

Philips, Joan (Poetess), 1678.

Philips, Katherine (1632–1664: Poetess), 1663, 1668.

Phillip, John (b. 1570–b. 1626: Author), 1559.

Phillips, Augustine (d. 1605: Actor), 1595.

Phillips, or Philips, Capt. William (d. 1734: Irish Playwright), 1698(2), 1700; for later plays, *see* Nicoll, p. 349.

Pickering, John (same as Sir John Puckering, 1544–1596, Lord Keeper ?), 1567.

Pitcairne, Archibald (1652–1713: Physician), 1690.

Pix, *née* Griffith, Mary (1666–1709: Playwright), 1696, 1697(2), 1698, 1699, 1700; for later plays, *see* Nicoll, pp. 349–50, 442.

Polwhele, Elizabeth (Unknown), 1671.

Popple, William (1638–1708: Merchant), 1691, 1692.

Pordage, Samuel (1633–1691 ?: Poet), 1660, 1673, 1677.

Porter, Henry (d. 1599: Playwright), 1588, 1598(2), 1599(3).

Porter, Thomas (1636–1680: Man about Town), 1662, 1663(2), 1677.

Pound, Thomas (1538 ?–1616 ?: Lawyer), 1566(2).

Powell, George (1659–1714: Actor), 1690(2), 1693, 1695, 1696(2), 1697, 1698.

Preston, Thomas (Unknown: prob. not the Cambridge Scholar, 1537–1598), 1561, 1570.

Prestwich, Edmund (Unknown), 1651, 1656.

Price, Daniel (1581–1631: Clergyman), 1610.

Puttenham (George, d. 1590, or Richard, d. *c.* 1601, or neither ?), 1580(3).

Quarles, Francis (1592–1644: Poet), 1641.

Quarles, William (Unknown), 1604.

R., N., Supp. I.

R., T., 1638.

R., T., 1654.

Radcliffe, Ralph (1519 ?–1559: Schoolmaster), 1546(4).

Randolph, Thomas (1605–1635: Poet), 1626, 1627(3), 1629(3), 1630(2), 1632, 1638(2); adapt., 1682, 1684.

Rankins, William (*fl.* 1587–1601: Playwright), 1598, 1601(3).

Rant, Humphrey (same as Humphrey Rant of Cambridge and Gray's Inn, *c.* 1640–1726?, or H. R. of Yelverton, d. 1681 ?), 1674.

Rastell, John (*c.* 1475–1536: Printer), 1510, 1517, 1522, 1527(3).

Ravenscroft, Edward (*c.* 1643–1707: Playwright), 1672, 1673, 1676, 1677(3), 1679, 1681, 1683, 1694, 1696, 1697.

Rawlins, — (Unknown), 1676, 1678.

Rawlins, Thomas (*c.* 1618–1670: Engraver), 1636.

Redford, John (d. 1547: Master of Paul's Boys), 1539.

Revet, Edward (Unknown), 1671.

Reymes, William (1629–1660), 1659.

Reynolds, Henry (*fl.* 1627–1632: Critic), 1628.

Rho, John, *see* Roo, John.

Rhodes, Richard (*c.* 1641 ?–1668: Poet), 1663.

Richards, Nathanael (*fl.* 1631–1641: Poet), 1635.

Richards, Thomas (*c.* 1553–1620: Schoolmaster), 1570.

Richards, William (1643–1705: Lecturer at St Andrew's, Newcastle), 1660.

Rickets, John (*c.* 1606–a.1646: Clergyman), 1633.

Rider, W[illiam ?] (Master of Arts), 1635.

Ritwise, or Rightwise, John (1490–*c.* 1532: Schoolmaster), 1527(2).

Rivers, Antony (*fl.* 1615: Jesuit), 1692.

Roberts, Henry (*fl.* 1585–1616: Miscellanist), 1606(2).

Roberts, John (Unknown), 1574.

Robinson, — (Unknown), 1602.

Robinson, Nicholas, Bishop of Bangor (*c.* 1528 ?–1585), 1553.

Roche-Guilhen, Mlle de la (Writer for visiting French troupe), 1677.

Rochester, Earl of, *see* Wilmot, John.

Rollinson, Francis (born *c.* 1575 ?: Clergyman), 1597, 1606.

Roo, or Rho, John (*fl.* 1506–1526: Gray's Inn Sergeant at Law), 1526.

Rowe, Nicholas (1674–1718: Playwright), 1700; for later plays, *see* Nicoll, pp. 351–3, 443.

Rowley, Samuel (d. a. 1624: Actor), 1586, 1591, 1592, 1601, 1602(2), 1604, 1623(2), 1624, 1626.

Rowley, William (d. 1626: Actor), 1599, 1607, 1608(2), 1609(3), 1612, 1613(2), 1617, 1618(2), 1619, 1620, 1621, 1622(2), 1623(3), 1624(3), 1625(2), 1626; adapt., 1662, 1690.

Rudd, Anthony (1549 ?–1615: Clergyman), 1570.

Ruggle, George (1575–1622: Cambridge Fellow), 1599(2), 1615; trans., 1662(2); adapt., 1677.

Rutter, Joseph (Tutor), 1634, 1637, 1638.

Rymer, Thomas (1641–1713: Critic), 1677.

S., J., 1642.

S., J., 1651.

S., S., 1615.

S., W., 1600, 1606, Supp. II, j.

Sackville, Charles, 6th Earl of Dorset (1638–1706), 1663.

Sackville, Edward (d. 1646: brother of following), 1636, 1637, 1638.

Sackville, Richard, 5th Earl of Dorset (1622–1677), 1637, 1638.

Sackville, Thomas, 1st Earl of Dorset (1536–1608), 1562.

Sadler, Anthony (1610–1685?: Clergyman), 1660.

Sadler, John (1615–1674: Master of Magdalen Col., Oxford), 1640.

St Serfe, [Sir?] Thomas (*fl.* 1658–1672: Soldier and Author), 1667.

Salisbury, Earl of, *see* Cecil, Sir Robert.

Salterne, George (born 1568: Lawyer), 1590.

Salusbury, Sir Thomas (*c.* 1605–1643: Politician), 1641.

Sampson, William (*c.* 1600–a.1656: Playwright), 1622, 1625(2).

Sandys, George (1578–1644: Colonist), 1640.

Sansbury, or Sandsbury, John (1576–1610: Clergyman), 1607, 1608(4).

Saunders, Charles (1663–1684: Student), 1681.

Savile, John (Unknown), 1603.

Scogan, John (*fl.* 1480: Court Fool), Supp. II, j.

Scott, Thomas (born 1674: Secretary), 1695, 1697.

Sedley, Sir Charles (1639–1701: Courtier), 1663, 1668, 1677, 1687.

Selby, William, *see* Banister, William.

Sempill, Robert (*c.* 1530–1595: Scottish Ballad Writer), 1603.

Settle, Elkanah (1648–1724: Playwright), 1671, 1673, 1674, 1675, 1676(2), 1679, 1680(2), 1682, 1690, 1691, 1692(2), 1693(2), 1694(2), 1695(2), 1697, 1698, 1699, 1700; for later plays, *see* Nicoll, pp. 353–4, 443–4.

Shadwell, Thomas (1641 or 1642–1692: Playwright), 1667, 1668, 1669(2), 1670, 1672(2), 1674(2), 1675(2), 1676, 1678(2), 1679, 1681, 1687, 1688, 1689, 1690(2), 1692.

Shakespeare, William (1564–1616: Playwright), 1591(2), 1592(2), 1593(2), 1594(2), 1595(4), 1596(2), 1597(2), 1598(2), 1599(3), 1600(2), 1601, 1602(2), 1604(2), 1605, 1606, 1607(2), 1608(2), 1609, 1610, 1611, 1613(6), Supp. II, k; lost plays, 1598, 1613(4)?, 1624(2)?; Apocrypha, 1590(3), 1591(2), 1595, 1599, 1600, 1602, 1604, 1606(2), 1608, 1613; adapt., 1623, 1661(2), 1662(3), 1664(3), 1667(2), 1673, 1674, 1678, 1679(3), 1680(2), 1681(3), 1682, 1692, 1698, 1699, 1700(2).

Shank, or Shanks, John (d. 1636: Actor), 1624.

Sharpe, Lewis (Unknown), 1639.

Sharpham, Edward (1576–1608), 1606, 1607.

Shaw, or Shaa, Robert (d. 1603: Actor), 1603.

Shaw, Samuel (1635–1696: Clergyman), 1678, 1691.

Sheppard, Samuel (*c.* 1624–1655?: Pamphleteer), 1647(2), 1651.

Sherburne, Sir Edward (1618–1702: Ordnance Expert), 1648, 1679, 1700.

Sherman, Thomas (Unknown), 1671.

Shipman, Roger (*c.* 1621–a.1663: Clergyman), 1641.

Shipman, Thomas (1632–1680: Poet), 1672, 1678.

Shirley, Henry (d. 1627: Playwright), 1618, 1623(4), 1628.

Shirley, James (1596–1666: Playwright), 1613, 1619, 1625(2), 1626(3), 1628, 1629, 1631(4), 1632(3), 1633(3), 1634(3), 1635(2), 1636, 1637, 1638(2), 1639(3), 1640(3), 1641(3), 1642(2), 1646, 1653, 1658(2); adapt., 1662(2), 1667, 1692.

Sidnam, Jonathan (Unknown), 1630(2).

Sidney, Sir Philip (1554–1586: Poet), 1578, 1580.

Simons, Joseph, *vere* Lobb, Emmanuel (1594–1671: St Omers Teacher), 1623(2), 1624(2), 1626, 1627, 1631; adapt., 1669.

Singer, John (*fl.* 1583–1603: Actor), 1603.

Singleton, Thomas (1621–a. 1689: Schoolmaster), 1689.

Skelton, John (1460?–1529: Poet), 1504, 1515(4), 1533.

Smith, — (same as Wentworth, or Will., or W. Smith?), 1623.

Smith, Henry (of Clifford's Inn), 1699.

Smith, John (*c.* 1620–1683), 1677.

Smith, W. (same as Wentworth, or Will. Smith?), 1602, 1614.

Smith, Wentworth (*fl.* 1601–1605: Playwright), 1601(4), 1602(9), 1603(3), 1614.

Smith, Will. (Unknown), 1623.

Smythe, or Smith, John (1563–1616: Clergyman), 1584.

Smythe, John (born 1662: School Usher), 1691.

Snelling, Thomas (born 1614: Latin Poet), 1640.

Southby, — (Unknown), 1697.

Southerne, Thomas (1660–1746: Playwright), 1682, 1684, 1690, 1691, 1692, 1693, 1694, 1695, 1700; for later plays, *see* Nicoll, pp. 355–6.

Southland, Thomas (Gentleman), 1663, 1664.

Sparrow, Thomas (born *c.* 1614?: Bishop Williams Scholar), 1634.

Speed, John (1595–1640: Physician), 1635, 1637.

Spencer, — (Priest, turned Actor), 1539.

Spenser, Edmund (1552–1599: Poet), presumed author of 'nine English comedies' – closet plays of unknown title composed before 1580; but plays poss. contemplated only, never written: *see* A. Gilbert, *Mod. Lang. Notes*, LXXIII (1958), 241–3.

Wedderburn, James (1495 ?–1553: Merchant), 1540(2).

Westmorland, Earl of, *see* Fane, Mildmay.

Weston, John (Unknown), 1667.

Wever, R. (Unknown), 1550.

Wharton, *née* Lee, Anne (1632 ?–1685: Poetess), 1685.

Whetstone, George (1544 ?–1587 ?: Adventurer), 1578.

Whitaker, William (Unknown), 1680.

White, Robert (Schoolmaster at Ladies' Hall ?), 1617.

Wiburne, Wibarn, or Wilbourne, Nathaniel (*c.* 1573 ?–1613: Clergyman), 1597.

Wild, Robert (1615 or 1616–1679: Clergyman), 1641.

Wilde, George, Bishop of Derry (1610–1665), 1635, 1636, 1637.

Wilkins, George (*fl. c.* 1604–1608: Pamphleteer), 1604, 1606(2), 1607, 1608.

Willan, Leonard (*fl.* 1649–1670), 1651, 1658.

Williams, Joseph (*fl.* 1673–1700: Actor), 1694.

Wilmot, John, 2nd Earl of Rochester (1647–1680), 1670, 1678(2); adapt., 1684.

Wilmot, Robert (*fl.* 1566–1608: Clergyman), 1566.

Wilson, Arthur (1595–1652: Secretary), 1630, 1631, 1633.

Wilson, John (1627–1696: Lawyer), 1643, 1663, 1664(2), 1677.

Wilson, Robert (*fl.* 1572–1600: Actor; perhaps a synthesis of the careers of two men is here represented), 1579, 1581, 1588, 1590(2), 1592, 1598(10), 1599(2), 1600(3).

Winchilsea, Countess of, *see* Finch, Anne.

Wingfield, Anthony (*c.* 1550–1615: Cambridge Proctor), 1581.

Wood, Ra[lph ?] (Unknown), Supp. II, g(2).

Woodes, Nathaniel (born *c.* 1550 ?: Norwich Clergyman), 1572.

Worseley, Ralph (d. 1590: Lawyer), 1555.

Wotton, Sir Henry (1568–1639: Diplomatist), 1586.

Wren, Christopher, Sr (1591–1658: Clergyman), 1609.

Wright, Abraham (1611–1690: Clergyman), 1631.

Wright, James (1643–1713: Antiquary), 1700.

Wright, John (Middle Temple Lawyer ?), 1674.

Wright, Thomas (Theatre Mechanic), 1693.

Wyatt, Ralph (Unknown), 1575.

Wycherley, William (1640–1715: Playwright), 1671, 1672, 1675, 1676.

Wylley, Thomas (Clergyman), 1537(4).

Yarington, Robert (Unknown), 1594.

Yelverton, Sir Christopher (*c.* 1535–1612: Judge), 1588.

Zouche, Richard (1590–1661: Oxford Professor), 1631.

(Titleless plays and unidentified MS fragments are listed in Supplementary List I.)

Albion Knight, 1537.

Albion Queens, The, or The Death of Mary Queen of Scotland, *see* Island Queens, The, 1684.

Albion's Triumph, 1632.

Albovine King of the Lombards, The Tragedy of, 1628.

Albumazar, 1615.

Alcamenes and Menalippa, 1698.

Alcestis, 1543; *see also* Supp. I.

Alchemist, The, 1610; *adapt.*, 1662.

Alcibiades, 1675.

Alcmaeon, 1573.

Alderman No Conjurer, An, *see* Cuckolds Haven, 1685.

Alderman's Bargain, An, *see* Lucky Chance, The, 1686.

Aleumista, Supp. II, m.

Alexander, Campaspe, and Diogenes, *see* Campaspe, 1584.

Alexander VI, The Tragedy of Pope, *see* Devil's Charter, The, 1607.

Alexander and Lodowick, 1597.

Alexander et Aristobulus, Supp. II, l.

Alexander the Great, The Death of, *see* Rival Queens, The, 1677.

Alexandraean Tragedy, The, 1607.

Alexius Imperator, *see* Andronicus Comnenus, 1618.

Alexius (*or* Alexis, *or* Alexias), or The Chaste Gallant, *see* Alexius, 1639.

Alexius, or The Chaste Lover, 1639.

Alfonso, *see* Alphonsus Emperor of Germany, 1594.

Alfred, or Right Re-enthroned, 1659.

Alfredus, *see* Aluredus, 1619.

Alice and Alexis, Supp. I.

Alice Pierce, 1597.

Alimony Lady, The, *see* Lady Alimony, 1659.

All Fools, 1604.

All Fools but the Fool, 1599.

All for Love, or The World Well Lost, 1677.

All for Money, 1577.

All Is Not Gold That Glisters, 1601; *see also* Supp. II, m.

All Is True, *see* Henry VIII, 1613.

All Manner Weathers, A New and Very Merry Interlude of, *see* Play of the Weather, The, 1528.

All Mistaken, or The Mad Couple, 1667.

All Plot, or The Disguises, 1665.

All without Money, *see* Novelty, The, 1697.

All's Lost by Lust, 1619; *adapt.*, 1690.

All's One, or One of the Four Plays in One, *see* Yorkshire Tragedy, A, 1606.

All's Well That Ends Well, 1602.

Allot, The Pageant for John, 1590.

Almains, A Mask of, 1543.

Almains, A Mask of, 1549.

Almains and Palmers, A Mask of, 1559.

Almains and Spaniards, 1510.

Almains, Pilgrims, and Irishmen, A Great Mask of, 1557.

Almanac, The, 1611.

Almanzor and Almahide, *see* II Conquest of Granada by the Spaniards, The, 1671.

Aloysius sive Saeculi Fuga, Supp. II, l.

Alphonso King of Naples, 1690.

Alphonsus Emperor of Germany, The Tragedy of, 1594.

Alphonsus King of Aragon, The Comical History of, 1587; *see also* Supp. II, k.

Altemira, *see* General, The, 1662.

Althorp, A Particular Entertainment of the Queen and Prince Their Highness at, 1603.

Alucius, The History of, 1579.

Aluredus sive Alfredus, 1619.

Amalasont Queen of the Goths, or Vice Destroys Itself, 1696.

Amazon Queen, The, or The Amours of Thalestris to Alexander the Great, 1667.

Amazon Queen of Denmark, The, *see* Landgartha, 1683.

Amazonians' Mask, The, Supp. II, i.

Amazons, A Mask of, 1579.

Amazons, The Mask of, or The Ladies' Mask, 1618.

Amazons Women of War, A Mask of, 1551.

Ambitio Infelix sive Absalom, 1622.

Ambitio Infelix, *see* Zeno, 1631.

Ambitious Brother, The, Supp. II, m.

Ambitious Father, The, *see* Injured Lovers, The, 1688.

Ambitious Politic, The, *see* Lovesick Court, The, 1639.

Ambitious Queen, The, *see* Siege of Memphis, The, 1676.

Ambitious Slave, The, or A Generous Revenge, 1694.

Ambitious Statesman, The, or The Loyal Favourite, 1679.

Ambitious Step-Dame, The, *see* Roxolana, Supp. II, m.

Ambitious Stepmother, The, 1700.

Aphrodisial, The, or Sea Feast, 1602.

Apocryphal Ladies, The, 1658.

Apollo and Daphne, *see* Pleasant Dialogues and Dramas, 1635.

Apollo, the Nine Muses, and Lady Peace, A Mask of, 1572.

Apollo et Musae Exules, 1561.

Apollo Shroving, 1627.

Apothecary Turned Doctor, The, *see* Physic Lies a-Bleeding, 1697.

Appius and Virginia ('R.B.'), 1564.

Appius and Virginia (Webster), 1624; *adapt.*, 1669.

Appius and Virginia, 1669.

Apprentice's Prize, The, 1634.

Aqua Triumphalis, 1662.

Ara Fortunae, *see* Christmas Prince, The, 1607.

Arabia Sitiens, or A Dream of a Dry Year, 1601.

Arcades, 1633.

Arcadia, The, 1640.

Arcadia Reformed, *see* Queen's Arcadia, The, 1605.

Arcadian Virgin, 1599.

Archer, The, *see* Honourable Entertainments, 1621.

Arches of Triumph, 1604.

Archipropheta, 1547.

Arcules with Mariners, A Mask of, 1554.

Arden of Feversham, 1591.

Are Mask, Supp. II, i.

Argalus and Parthenia, 1638.

Argus, A Mask of, 1551.

Ariadne, 1654.

Ariadne, or The Marriage of Bacchus, 1674.

Ariodante and Genevora, 1583.

Ariosto, *see* Supposes, The, 1566.

Aristippus, or The Jovial Philosopher, 1626.

Aristomenes, or The Royal Shepherd, 1690.

Armenian Queen, The, 1676.

Arraignment, The, *see* Poetaster, 1601.

Arraignment of London, The, 1613.

Arraignment of Paris, The, 1581.

Arsenius, *see* Magister Bonus, 1614.

Artaxerxes, Supp. I.

Artenice, L', 1626.

Arthur, The Marriage of Prince, 1501.

Arthur, *see* Misfortunes of Arthur, The, 1588.

Arthur, King, or The British Worthy, 1691.

Arthur and His Knights, *see* Corpus Christi Procession (Dublin), 15th cent. add.

Arthur King of England, The Life of, 1598.

Arthur's Knights, King, 1539.

Arthur's Show, *see* Arthur King of England, 1598.

I Arviragus and Philicia, 1636.

II Arviragus and Philicia, 1636.

As Merry as May Be, 1602.

As Plain as Can Be, 1567.

As You Like It, 1599.

Ascanius, Supp. I.

Ashby, The Entertainment at, 1607.

Assembly, The, or Scotch Reformation, 1690.

Assignation, The, or Love in a Nunnery, 1672.

Assumption or Coronation of the Virgin, The, 15th cent.; *see also* Lincoln Plays, 15th cent.

Astiages, 1598.

Astraea, Supp. II, l.

Astraea, or True Love's Mirror, 1651.

Astronomers, A Mask of, 1559.

Atalanta, 1612.

Athanasius sive Infamia, 1547.

Atheist, The, or The Second Part of the Soldier's Fortune, 1683.

Atheist's Tragedy, The, or The Honest Man's Revenge, 1609.

Athenians' Reception of Phocion, The, 1656.

Attowell's Jig, 1593.

Augurs, The Mask of, 1622.

Augusta's Triumph, *see* Brutus of Alba, 1696.

Augustus Caesar, 1687.

Augustus Caesar, The Court of, *see* Gloriana, 1676.

Aulae Byzantinae Vota, *see* Andronichus, 1664.

Auld Man and His Wife, *see* Satire of the Three Estates, 1540.

Aureng-Zebe, 1675.

B. Ignatius Societatis Jesu Fundator, *see* Haeresis Triumphata, Supp. II, l.

Babions, A Mask of, 1552.

Bacchides, Supp. I.

Bacchus, 1528.

Bacchus, The Marriage of, *see* Ariadne, 1674.

Bacchus' Festival, or A New Medley, 1660.

Bacon, *see* Friar Bacon, 1699.

Bacon in Virginia, The History of, *see* Widow Ranter, The, 1689.

Bad Beginning Makes (*or* May Have) a Good Ending, A, 1612.

Bad May Amend, *alternative title for* II Worse (A)feared Than Hurt, 1598?

Baggs Seneca, Supp. II, d.

Bagpipes, A Mask of, 1553.

Baiting of the Jealous Knight, The, *see* Fair Foul One, The, 1623.

Belphegor, or The Marriage of the Devil, 1677.

Belyn Dun, The Life and Death of, *see* Bellendon, 1594.

Bendo (*or* Byndo) and Richardo, 1599 add.

Benefice, The, 1641.

Bergeries, Les, *see* Artenice, L', 1626.

Berowne, *see* Biron, 1602.

Berwick, Speech to King James I at, 1603.

Best Words Wear the Garland, The, *see* Two Merry Milkmaids, The, 1619.

Better Late Than Never, *see* Bear a Brain, 1599.

Better Late Than Never, *see* Inconstant Lady, The, 1630.

Beverley Plays, 14th cent.

Bilboe's the Best Blade, *see* Hard Shift for Husbands, 1623.

Bird in a Cage, The, 1633.

Biron, 1602.

Birth of Hercules, The, 1604.

Birth of Merlin, The, or The Child Hath Found His Father, 1608.

Birthday of the Nymph Oenone, The, *see* Rural Sports, 1653.

Bisham, The Entertainment at, 1592.

Bishop of Rome, A Tragedy or Dialogue of the Unjust Usurped Primacy of the, *previously included in* Annals; *not dramatic.*

Bishopswood, A Mumming at, 15th cent.

I Black Bateman of the North, 1598.

II Black Bateman of the North, 1598.

I Black Dog of Newgate, The, 1603.

II Black Dog of Newgate, The, 1603.

Black Joan, 1597.

Black Lady, The, 1622.

Black Man, The, 1653.

Black Prince, The, 1667.

Black Prince, The Death of the, Supp. II, h.

Black Wedding, The, Supp. II, b.

Blackfriars, The Entertainment at, 1620.

Blackfriars Mask, Supp. II, i.

Blackness, The Mask of, 1605.

Blacksmith's Daughter, The, 1578.

Blazing World, The, 1665.

Blind Beggar of Alexandria, The, 1596.

I Blind Beggar of Bednal Green, The, 1600.

II Blind Beggar of Bednal Green, The, 1601.

III Blind Beggar of Bednal Green, The, 1601.

Blind Eats Many a Fly, The, 1603.

Blind Lady, The, 1660.

Bloody Banquet, The, 1639.

Bloody Brother, The, 1619; *adapt.*, 1662.

Bloody Duke, The, or The Adventures for a Crown, 1690.

Blurt Master Constable, or The Spaniard's Night Walk, 1601.

Boadicea Queen of Britain, 1697.

Boarding School, The, *see* Love for Money, 1691.

Bold Beauchamps, The, 1606.

Bolsover, Love's Welcome at, 1634.

Bondman, The, 1623.

Bonduca, The Tragedy of, 1613; *adapt.*, 1695.

Bonduca, or The British Heroine, 1695.

Bondwoman, The, Supp. II, b.

Bonos Nochios, 1609.

Book of Sir Thomas More, The, 1595.

Boot and Spur, 1612.

Boss of Billingsgate, The, 1603.

Both Marriages of the King, Upon, 1537.

Bottom the Weaver, The Merry Conceited Humours of, 1661; *see also* 1673.

Botzarius, *see* Ancient Roman, An, Supp. II, k.

Bouncing Knight, The, or The Robbers Robbed, 1662.

Bourbon, *see* Burbon, 1599 add.

Boys, A Mask of, 1577.

Braggadocio, The, or The Bawd Turned Puritan, 1691.

Brandimer, 1599 add.

Branhowlte, 1597.

Brazen Age, The, 1611.

Brennoralt, or The Discontented Colonel, 1639.

Brennus, *see* Belinus, 1610.

Bretbie, A Mask Presented at, 1640.

Bridals, The, 1665.

Bride, The, 1638.

Bridegr[oom], The, 1619.

Bridegroom and the Madman, The, *see* Bridegr[oom], The, 1619.

Bristol, The Entertainment at, 1613.

Bristow, The Queen's Entertainment at, 1574.

Bristow Merchant, The, 1624.

Bristow Tragedy, 1602.

Britannia Triumphans, 1638.

Britanniae Primitiae sive S. Albanus Protomartyr, Supp. I.

Britannia's Honour, 1628.

Britannicus, or The Man of Honour, 1695.

British Heroine, The, *see* Bonduca, 1695.

British Worthy, The, *see* Arthur, King, 1691.

Broken Heart, The, 1629.

Brome Abraham and Isaac, 14th cent.

Broom-Man, The, 1595.

Cardenno, *see* Cardenio, 1613.

Cardinal, The, 1641.

Cardinal Wolsey, *see* Wolsey, 1601.

Cardinal's Conspiracy, The, 1639.

Cards, The Play of, *see* Game of the Cards, A, 1582.

Careless Lovers, The, 1673.

Careless Shepherdess, The, 1619.

Cariclea, *see* Theagenes and Chariclea, 1572.

Carnival, The, 1663.

Carwidgeon, The, *see* Hengist King of Kent, 1618.

Case Is Altered, The, 1597.

Castara, or Cruelty without Hate, Supp. II, b.

Castle Dangerous, The, 1512.

Castle of Perseverance, The, 15th cent.

Castle of Security, The, 1570.

Cataclysm, The, or General Deluge of the World, *see* Noah's Flood, 1679.

Catchpole, The, *see* Roaring Girl, The, 1640.

Catherine, Queen, *see* Queen Catherine, 1698.

Catilina, Supp. II, l.

Catilina Triumphans, Supp. II, h.

Catiline, *see* Catiline's Conspiracy, 1598.

Catiline, *see* Short and Sweet, 1579.

Catiline, *see* Sylla Dictator, 1588.

Catiline His Conspiracy, 1611.

Catiline's Conspiracies, 1578.

Catiline's Conspiracy, 1598.

Cats, A Mask of, 1553.

Cautious Coxcomb, The, *see* Sir Salomon, 1670.

Cawsome, The Entertainment at, 1613.

Cecil House, The Entertainment at, 1602.

Celestina, 1598.

Celestina, *see* Calisto and Melebea, 1527.

Celestina, *see* Spanish Bawd, The, 1631.

Celinde and Sedea, Supp. II, k.

Cenofalles, The History of the, *see* Cynocephali, The, 1577.

Censure of the Judges, The, or The Court Cure, *see* Mercurius Britannicus, 1641.

Cephalus et Procris, 1627.

Ceres, 1528.

Certain Devices and Shows Presented to Her Majesty at Greenwich, *see* Misfortunes of Arthur, The, 1588.

Chabot Admiral of France, The Tragedy of, 1622.

Challenge at Tilt, A, 1613.

Challenge for Beauty, A, 1635.

Chambermaid Turned Quaker, The, *see* Country Innocence, The, 1677.

Chance Medley, 1598.

Chances, The, 1625; *adapt.*, 1667.

Chances, The, 1667.

Change, The, 1642.

Change Is No Robbery, or The Bearing Down of the Inn, *see* Cuckqueans and Cuckolds Errants, The, 1601.

Change of Crowns, The, 1667.

Change of Government, The, *see* Conspiracy, The, 1680.

Changeling, The, 1622.

Changes, or Love in a Maze, 1632.

Chaos of the World, The, Supp. II, j.

Character of a Mountebank, The, *see* News out of the West, 1647.

Chariclea, 1572.

Chariclea, *see* Queen of Ethiopia, The, 1578.

Charity Triumphant, or The Virgin Show, 1655.

Charlemagne, or The Distracted Emperor, 1600.

Charles Duke of Bourbon, 1641.

Charles Duke of Burgundy, Supp. II, k.

Charles Duke of Byron, 1608.

Charles His Entertainment and London's Loyalty, King, 1641.

Charles I, The Entertainment of King, *see* Edinburgh, The Entertainment of King Charles into, 1633.

Charles I, The Famous Tragedy of King, 1649.

Charles I, The Martyrdom of the Late King, *see* Tragical Actors, The, 1660.

Charles II, The Coronation Entertainment for, *see* Coronation, The Relation of . . ., 1661.

Charles II, *see* Presentation for the Prince on His Birthday, A, 1638.

Charles V, The Welcome for Emperor, 1522.

Charles VIII of France, The History of, or The Invasion of Naples by the French, 1671.

Chaste Gallant, The, *see* Alexius, 1639.

Chaste Lady, The, *see* Erminia, 1661.

Chaste Lady, The, *see* Toy to Please Chaste Ladies, A, 1595.

Chaste Lover, The, *see* Alexius, 1639.

Chaste Maid in Cheapside, A, 1611.

Chaste Nymph, The, *see* Calisto, 1675.

Chaste Virgin, The, 1658.

Chaste Woman against Her Will, The, Suppl. II, e.

Chastity and Time, 1564.

Cheater and the Clown, The, *see* Hengist King of Kent, 1618.

Cheater Cheated, The, 1673.

Cheaters Cheated, The, 1660.

Cheaters' Holiday, The, *see* Drinking Academy, The, 1629.

Cheats, The, 1663.

Cheats of Scapin, The, *see* Titus and Berenice, 1677.

Chelmsford Play, 15th cent. add.

Chester Corpus Christi Play, 15th cent. add.

Chester Plays, 14th cent.

Chester Tragedy, *see* Randall Earl of Chester, 1602.

Chester's Triumph, 1610.

Chief Promises of God unto Man, A Tragedy or Interlude Manifesting the, *see* God's Promises, 1538.

Child Hath Found His Father, The, *see* Birth of Merlin, The, 1608.

Chinon of England, 1596.

Chirke Castle, The Entertainment at, 1634.

Chiswick, The Entertainment at, 1602.

Chloridia: Rites to Chloris and Her Nymphs, 1631.

Christ and the Doctors, 1536.

Christ Jesus Triumphant (Day, J. & R.) *not dramatic*.

Christ's Burial and Resurrection, *see* Burial and Resurrection of Christ, The, 15th cent.

Christ's Passion (Anon.), 1618.

Christ's Passion (Sandys), 1640.

Christ's Resurrection, *see* Resurrection of Our Lord, The, 1545.

Christabella, Supp. II, k.

Christi Descensus ad Inferos, 15th cent.

Christian Turned Turk, A, or The Tragical Lives and Deaths of the Two Famous Pirates, Ward and Dansiker, 1610.

Christiana Fortitudo, *see* Vitus, 1623.

Christianetta, or Marriage and Hanging Go by Destiny, 1633.

Christmas Comes but Once a Year, 1602.

Christmas His Mask, 1616.

Christmas His Show, *see* Christmas His Mask, 1616.

'Christmas Messe, A', 1619.

Christmas Ordinary, The, 1660.

Christmas Prince, The, 1607 *and* 1608.

Christmas Tale, A, or The Knight and the Cobbler, Supp. II, m.

Christus Nascens, 1540.

Christus Redivivus, 1540.

Christus Triumphans, 1556.

Chrysanaleia: The Golden Fishing, or Honour of Fishmongers, 1616.

R

Chryso-Thriambos, 1611.

Cicero, Marcus Tullius, That Famous Roman Orator His Tragedy, 1651.

I Cicilia and Clorinda, or Love in Arms, 1650.

II Cicilia and Clorinda, or Love in Arms, 1650.

I Cid, The, 1637.

II Cid, The, 1638.

Cid, The, 1691.

Cinna, Supp. I.

Cinthia and Endimion, A New Opera Called, or The Loves of the Deities, 1696.

Cinthia, *see also* Cynthia.

Circe, 1677.

Circe and Ulysses, *see* Ulysses and Circe, 1615.

Citizen Turned Gentleman, The, 1672.

City, The, 1619.

City Bride, The, or The Merry Cuckold, 1696.

City Cozener, The, *see* Ordinary, The, 1635.

City Gallant, The, *see* Greene's Tu Quoque, 1611.

City Heiress, The, or Sir Timothy Treat-all, 1682.

City Honest Man, The, 1633.

City in Jollity and Splendour, The, *see* London Triumphant, 1672.

City Lady, The, or Folly Reclaimed, 1697.

City Madam, The, 1632; *adapt.*, 1675.

City Match, The, 1637.

City Nightcap, The, or Crede Quod Habes et Habes, 1624.

City Pageant, 1606.

City Politiques, 1683.

II City Shuffler, The, 1633.

City Wit, The, or The Woman Wears the Breeches, 1630.

I Civil Wars of France, The, 1598.

II Civil Wars of France, The, 1598.

III Civil Wars of France, The, 1598.

Civil Wars of France, The First Introduction of the, 1599.

Civitatis Amor, 1616.

Claracilla, 1636.

Clarasilla, *see* Claracilla, 1636.

Claricilla, *see* Claracilla, 1636.

Claudius Tiberius Nero, 1607.

Cleander, The Tragedy of, 1634.

Cleander, *see* Wandering Lovers, The, 1623.

Cleodora, *see* Queen of Aragon, The, 1640.

Cleomenes the Spartan Hero, 1692.

Cleopatra, Supp. II, c.

Cleopatra, The Tragedy of, 1593.

Cleopatra Queen of Egypt, The Tragedy of, 1626.

Cleopatra, *see also* Antony and Cleopatra.

Cleophilus, 1700.

Clerico et Puella, Interludium de, 14th cent.

Clever Thief, The, Supp. II, k.

Cloridon and Radiamanta, 1572.

Clorys and Orgasto (i.e. Ergasto), 1599 add.

Cloth Breeches and Velvet Hose, A Moral of, 1600.

Clouds, The, 1655.

Cloudy Queen and Singing Moor, The, Supp. II, m.

Clowns, A Mask of, 1560.

Club Law, 1599.

Club-Men, The, 1662.

Clyomon and Clamydes, 1570; see also Supp. II, k.

Clytophon, 1625.

Cobbler (of Queenhithe), The, 1597.

Cobbler's Prophecy, The, 1590.

Cock, The, see Honourable Entertainments, 1621.

Cockle de Moye, see Dutch Courtesan, The, 1604.

Coelum Britannicum, 1634.

Coffee-House, The, see Knavery in All Trades, 1664.

Coffee-House, The, see Tarugo's Wiles, 1667.

Cola's Fury, or Lirenda's Misery, 1645.

Coleoverton, A Mask Presented at, 1618.

College of Canonical Clerks, The, 1567.

Collier, The History of the, 1576.

Colonel, The, see Siege, The, 1629.

Columbus, *a title now believed to be a Collier forgery.*

Combat of Caps, The, see School Moderator, 1647.

Combat of Love and Friendship, The, 1638.

Combat of the Tongue and Five Senses for Superiority, The, see Lingua, 1607.

Come See a Wonder, 1623.

Come to My Country House, see Cra[fty?] Merchant, The, 1623.

Comedy in Disguises, A, see Welsh Ambassador, The, 1623.

Comedy of Errors, The, 1592.

Comedy of Humours, The, see Humorous Day's Mirth, An, 1597.

Comical Hash, The, 1658.

Comical Revenge, The, or Love in a Tub, 1664.

Comical Transformation, A, see Devil of a Wife, The, 1686.

Committee, The, 1662.

I Committee-Man Curried, The, 1647.

II Committee-Man Curried, The, 1647.

Common Conditions, 1576.

Commonwealth of Women, A, 1685.

'Comoedia, Adoptivus', 1699.

Comoedia Sex Anglo-Latinae, 1663.

'Comoediae', Supp. II, j.

'Comoediae aliquot Sacrae', Supp. II, j.

'Comoediolae', 1495.

Complaint of the Satyrs, see Althorp, A Particular Entertainment . . . at, 1603.

Comus, 1634.

Comus the Great Sir of Feasts, see Honourable Entertainments, 1621.

Concealed Fancies, The, 1645.

Concealed Royalty, The, or The May Queen, 1674.

Conceited Cuckold, The, see Politic Whore, The, 1680.

Conceited Duke, The, 1639.

Conceited Pedlar, The, 1627.

Conceits, The, Supp. II, b.

Concessus Animalium, see Synedrii, 1555.

Concordia Regularis, see Regularis Concordia, 10th cent.

Conference between a Gentleman Huisher and a Post, A, *probably part of* Cecil House, The Entertainment at, 1602.

Confessor, 1634.

Conflict of Conscience, The, 1572.

Conjuratis Papistica, see Talpae, 1689.

Connan Prince of Cornwall, 1598.

Conquerors, A Mask of, 1559.

Conqueror's Custom, The, or The Fair Prisoner, 1626.

I Conquest of Brute, with the First Finding of the Bath, The, 1598.

II Conquest of Brute, The, 1598.

Conquest of China by the Tartars (Howard), The, 1670.

Conquest of China by the Tartars (Settle), The, 1675.

I Conquest of Granada by the Spaniards, The, 1670.

II Conquest of Granada by the Spaniards, The, 1671.

Conquest of Ireland, The, see Royal Flight, The, 1690.

Conquest of Lady Scorn, The, 1522.

Conquest of Mexico by the Spaniards, The, see Indian Emperor, The, 1665.

Conquest of Queen Judith, The, see Prince's Ball, The, 1682.

Conquest of Spain by John of Gaunt, The, 1601.

Conquest of the West Indies, The, 1601.

Conspiracy, The, 1635.

Corpus Christi Procession (Norwich), 15th cent.

Corpus Christi Procession (Coventry), 15th cent.

Corpus Christi Procession (Dublin), 15th cent. add.

Corruptiones Legum Divinarum, see Three Laws of Nature, Moses, and Christ, A Comedy Concerning, 1538.

Cosmo, The Comedy of, 1599 add.

Costly Whore, The, 1620.

Council of Bishops, The, 1536.

Count of Angiers, The, Supp. II, k.

Counter Scuffle, The, the Second Part, see New Droll, A.

Counterfeit Bridegroom, The, or The Defeated Widow, 1677.

Counterfeits, The, 1678.

Country Captain, The, 1640.

Country Court, The, 1640.

Country Gentleman, The, 1669.

Country Gentleman, The, Supp. I.

Country Girl, The, 1632; adapt., 1677.

Country House, The, 1698.

Country Innocence, The, or The Chambermaid Turned Quaker, 1677.

Country Justice, The, see Friar Bacon, 1699.

Country Knight, The, 1675.

Country Revel, The, or The Revel of Aldford, 1671.

Country Tragedy in Vacunium, A, or Cupid's Sacrifice, 1602.

Country Wake, The, 1696.

Country Wife, The, 1675.

Country Wit, The, 1676.

Countryman, The, 1657.

Countryman, The, Supp. II, a.

Courage, Kindness, Cleanness, 1539.

Courage of Love, The, see Love and Honour, 1634.

Courageous Turk, The, or Amurath I, 1618.

Coursing of a Hare, The, or The Madcap, 1633.

Court Beggar, The, 1640.

Court Cure, The, see Mercurius Britannicus, 1641.

Court of Augustus Caesar, The, see Gloriana, 1676.

Court of Comfort, The, 1578.

Court Purge, A, Supp. II, m.

Court Secret, The, 1642.

Courtship à la Mode, 1700.

Covent Garden, 1633.

Covent Garden Weeded, The, see Weeding of the Covent Garden, The, 1632.

Coventry Hock-Tuesday Play, see Princely Pleasures at Kenilworth, The, 1575.

Coventry Plays, 14th cent.

Covetous Men, A Mask of, 1552.

Cowdray, The Speeches and Entertainment of the Queen at, 1591.

Cox of Collumpton, 1599.

Coxcomb, The, 1609.

Crack Me This Nut, 1595.

Cradle of Security, The, see Castle of Security, The, 1570.

Craft upon Subtlety's Back, 1570 add.

I Crafty Cromwell, or Oliver Ordering Our New State, 1648.

II Crafty Cromwell, or Oliver in His Glory as King, 1648.

Cra[fty ?] Merchant, The, or Come to My Country House, 1623.

Creation of Eve with the Expelling of Adam and Eve out of Paradise, The, see Norwich Plays, 15th cent.

Creation of Prince Henry, The, 1610.

Creation of the World, The, Supp. II, j.

Creation of the World, The, see Origo Mundi, 14th cent.

Creation of the World with Noah's Flood, The, 1611; trans., 1693.

Creation of the World with Noah's Flood, The, 1693.

Creation of White Knights of the Order of Aristotle's Well, The, see Christmas Prince, The, 1608.

Crede Quod Habes et Habes, see City Nightcap, The, 1624.

Credulous Cuckold, The, see Debauchee, The, 1677.

Creed Play (York), 15th cent.

Cripple of Fenchurch, The, see Fair Maid of the Exchange, The, 1602.

Crispin and Crispinianus, 1528.

Critics, The, 1687.

Croesus, 1604.

Cromwell, Thomas Lord, 1600.

Cromwell's Conspiracy, 1660.

Croxton Play of the Sacrament, The, see Sacrament, The Play of the, 15th cent.

Cruel Brother, The, 1627.

Cruel Debtor, The, 1565.

Cruel War, The, 1643.

Cruelties of the Dutch to the English Merchants, The, see Amboyna, 1672.

Cruelty of a Stepmother, The, 1578.

Cruelty of the Spaniards in Peru, The, 1658.

De Humfredo Aulico Confessionem Repudiante, 1602.

De Imposturis Thomae Becketi, *see* Impostures of Thomas Becket, The, 1538.

De Ioanne Anglorum Rege, *see* I & II John, King, 1538.

De Ioannis Huss Bohemie Noti Condemnatione, 1546.

De Iobi Iusti Afflictionibus, 1546.

De Iona a Deo ad Niniuitas Ablegati Defectione, 1546.

De Iudith Bethuliensis Incredibili Fortitudine, 1546.

De Lazaro a Diuitis aedibus Abacto, 1546.

De Lazaro Resuscitato, *see* Raising of Lazarus, The, 1536.

De Magnis Dei Promissionibus, *see* God's Promises, 1538.

De Melibaeo Chauceriano, *see* Melibeus of Chaucer, The, 1546.

De Meretrice Babylonica, 1548.

De Papatu, 1539.

De Passione Christi, *see* I & II Passion of Christ, The, 1536.

De Predicatione Ioannis, *see* John Baptist's Preaching in the Wilderness, 1538.

'De Puerorum in Musicis Institutione', 1547.

De Pugna Animi, 1650.

De Sectis Papisticis, *see* I & II On Sects among the Papists, 1537.

De Septem Peccatis, *see* On the Seven Sins, 1536.

De Sepultura et Resurrectione, *see* I & II Burial and Resurrection, The, 1536.

De Simone Leproso, *see* Simon the Leper, 1536.

De Sodomo et Gomorre Incendio, 1546.

De Susanne per Iudices Iniquos ob Lese Pudicitie Notam Diuini Liberatione, 1546.

De Titi et Gisippi Firmissima Amicitia, *see* Most Firm Friendship of Titus and Gisippus, The, 1546.

De Virtute, *see* Virtue, 1515.

Dead Man's Fortune, The, 1590.

Death, The Triumph of, *see* Four Plays or Moral Representations in One, 1612.

Death of Alexander the Great, The, *see* Rival Queens, The, 1677.

Death of Dido, Supp. II, i.

Death of Marc Antony, The, *see* Antony and Cleopatra, 1677.

Death of Mary Queen of Scotland, The, *see* Island Queens, The, 1684.

Death of Richard III, The, *see* English Princess, The, 1667.

Death of Robert Earl of Huntingdon, The, 1598.

Death of the Black Prince, The, Supp. II, h.

Death of the Duke of Guise, The, *see* Massacre at Paris, The, 1593.

Death of the Lady Jane Grey, The, *see* Innocent Usurper, The, 1694.

Death of the Lord of Kyme, The, 1601.

Deaths of the Apostles, The, 1528.

Debauched Hypocrite, The, *see* Trick for Trick, 1678.

Debauchee, The, or The Credulous Cuckold, 1677.

Deceiver Deceived, The, 1697.

Defeated Widow, The, *see* Counterfeit Bridegroom, The, 1677.

Defiance of Fortune, A, *a romance sometimes listed as a play.*

Delight, A Comedy Called, 1580.

Deliverance of the Pope, The, *see* Heretic Luther, 1527.

Deliverer Set Forth in His Proper Colours, The, *see* Belgic Hero Unmasked, The, 1686.

Delphrygus and the King of Fairies, 1570 add.

Deluge, The, *see* Noah's Flood, 1679.

Demetrius and Enanthe, *see* Humorous Lieutenant, The, 1619.

Demetrius and Marina (*or* Marsina), or The Imperial Impostor and Unhappy Heroine, Supp. II, g.

Denmark, The Welcome of the King of, etc., 1606.

Deorum Dona, 1647.

Deorum Judicium, *non-dramatic dialogue in* Pleasant Dialogues and Dramas, 1635.

Deposing of Richard II, The, *see* Richard II, 1595.

Depositio Crucis (Winchester), 10th cent.

Depositio Crucis (Barking), 14th cent.

Depositio Crucis (Dublin), 14th cent.

Depositum, *see* Reparatus, 1619.

Derry Defended, *see* Piety and Valour, 1692.

Descensus Astraea, 1591.

Deserving Favourite, The, 1629.

Destruction of Constantinople, The, Supp. II, k.

Destruction of Jerusalem (Legge), The, 1584.

Destruction of Jerusalem (Smythe), The, 1584.

I Destruction of Jerusalem by Titus Vespasian, The, 1677.

II Destruction of Jerusalem by Titus Vespasian, The, 1677.

Destruction of Sodom, The, *see* Fire and Brimstone, 1675.

Divorce, The, Supp. II, b.

Doctor Dodypoll, *see* Wisdom of Doctor Dodypoll, The, 1599.

Doctor Faustus, The Tragical History of, 1592; *see also* Supp. II, k.

Doctor Faustus with the Humours of Harlequin and Scaramouche, The Life and Death of, 1686.

Doctor Lamb and the Witches, 1634.

Doctors of Dull-Head College, The, 1662.

Doge and the Dragon, The, 1641.

Dolorous Castle, The, 1512.

Don Carlos Prince of Spain, 1676.

Don Horatio, 1599 add.

Don Japhet of Armenia, 1657.

Don Pedro the Cruel King of Castile, Supp. I.

Don Phoebo's Triumph, 1645.

I Don Quixote, The Comical History of, 1694.

II Don Quixote, The Comical History of, 1694.

III Don Quixote with the Marriage of Mary the Buxom, The Comical History of, 1695.

Don Quixote, The History of, or The Knight of the Ill-Favoured Face, Supp. II, e.

Don Sebastian King of Portugal, 1689.

Doolittle, Mr, 1683.

Double Dealer, The, 1693.

Double Discovery, The, *see* Spanish Friar, The, 1680.

Double Falsehood, or The Distressed Lovers, *see* Cardenio, 1613.

Double Marriage, The, 1620.

Double Mask, A, 1572.

Doublet, Breeches, and Shirt, 1620.

Doubtful Heir, The, 1638.

Downfall of the Pope, The, *see* Coronation of Queen Elizabeth, The, 1680.

Downfall of Robert Earl of Huntingdon, The, 1598.

Drake, *see* Sir Francis Drake, 1658.

Dream of a Dry Year, A, *see* Arabia Sitiens, 1601.

Drinking Academy, The, or The Cheaters' Holiday, 1629.

Droichis [Dwarf's] Part of the Play, The, 1503.

Drunken Couple, The, *see* Love Lost in the Dark, 1680.

Drunken Mask, A, 1552.

Dublin Abraham and Isaac, 15th cent.

Duchess of Fernandina, The, 1639.

Duchess of Malfi, The, 1614.

Duchess of Suffolk, The, 1624.

Duke, The, *see* Humorous Courtier, The, 1631.

Duke and No Duke, A, 1684.

Duke Humphrey, 1613.

Duke Moraud, *see* Dux Moraud, 14th cent.

Duke of Ferrara, The, Supp. II, k.

Duke of Florence and a Nobleman's Daughter, A, Supp. II, k.

Duke of Guise (Shirley), The, 1623.

Duke of Guise (Dryden & Lee), The, 1682.

Duke of Lerma, The, *see* Great Favourite, The, 1668.

Duke of Lerma, *see also* Spanish Duke of Lerma, The, 1623.

Duke of Mantua and the Duke of Verona, The, Supp. II, k.

Duke of Milan, The, 1621.

Duke of Milan and the Marquis of Mantua, The, 1579.

Duke's Mistress, The, 1636.

Dumb Bawd, The, 1623; *see also* 1628.

Dumb Bawd of Venice, The, 1628.

Dumb Knight, The, 1608; *see also* Supp. II, k.

Dumb Lady, The, or The Farrier Made Physician, 1669.

Duns Furens, 1586.

Durance Mask, Supp. II, i.

Dutch Courtesan, The, 1604; *adapt.*, 1673, 1680.

Dutch Cruelties at Amboyna, with the Humours of the Valiant Welshman, The, 1672.

Dutch Lover, The, 1673.

Dutch Painter, and the French Branke, The, 1622.

Dux Moraud, 14th cent.

Dyccon of Bedlam, *see* Gammer Gurton's Needle, 1553.

I Earl Godwin and His Three Sons, 1598.

II Earl Godwin and His Three Sons, 1598.

Earl of Essex, The, *see* Unhappy Favourite, The, 1681.

Earl of Gloucester, *see* Gloucester.

Earl of Hertford, The, 1602.

Easter Play (Kingston-on-Thames), 15th cent. add.

Easter Play (Morebath), 15th cent. add.

Easter Play, *see also* Quem Quaeritis.

Eastward Ho, 1605; *adapt.*, 1685.

Ebrauk with All His Sons, King, 1589.

Eclogue or Representation in Four Parts, An, 1659.

Edgar, or The English Monarch, 1677.

Edgar and Alfreda, King, 1677.

Edinburgh, The Entertainment of King Charles into, 1633.

Edinburgh Entertainment for Queen Mary, The, 1554.

Entertainment at Sir Francis Jones's at Christmas, The, *see* Honourable Entertainments, 1621.

Entertainment at Sir Francis Jones's at Easter, The, *see* Honourable Entertainments, 1621.

Entertainment at Sir Francis Jones's Welcome, The, *see* Honourable Entertainments, 1621.

Entertainment at Sir William Cokayne's in Easter Week, The, *see* Honourable Entertainments, 1621.

Entertainment at Sir William Cokayne's upon Simon and Jude's Day, The, *see* Honourable Entertainments, 1621.

Entertainment at the Conduit Head, The, *see* Honourable Entertainments, 1621.

Entertainment at the Theatre Royal at the Drawing of the Lottery, *see* Wheel of Fortune, The, 1698.

Entertainment at Wanstead, The, *see* Lady of May, The, 1578.

Entertainment at —, *see also under next word in such titles.*

Entertainment for Queen Mary, The, 1554.

Entertainment for the General Training, The, *see* Honourable Entertainments, 1621.

Entertainment of the Ambassadors, The, 1510.

Entertainment of the Emperor's Ambassadors, The, 1521.

Entertainment of the French Ambassadors, The, 1518.

Entertainment of the Hostages, The, 1519.

Entertainment of the Lords of the Council by Sheriff Allen, The, *see* Honourable Entertainments, 1621.

Entertainment of the Lords of the Council by Sheriff Ducie, The, *see* Honourable Entertainments, 1621.

Entertainment of the Scottish Ambassadors, The, 1524.

Entertainment of the Two Kings of Great Britain and Denmark, The, 1606.

Entertainments, Early Tudor, 1510, 1518, 1519, 1521, 1522, 1524.

Epicoene, or The Silent Woman, 1609.

Epidicus, 1694.

Epiphany Mask, An, 1512.

Epithalamion on the Marquis of Huntly's Marriage, An, 1588.

Epsom Wells, 1672.

Equal Match, An, 1662.

Erasmus, *see* St Erasmus.

Erga Momos et Zoilos, *see* I & II Against Momi and Zoili, 1537.

Erminia, or The Fair and Virtuous Lady, 1661.

Error, The History of, 1577.

Errors, *see* Comedy of Errors, The, 1592.

Escapes of Jupiter, The, *see* Calisto, 1627.

Essex, The Earl of, *see* Unhappy Favourite, The, 1681.

Essex Antic Mask, Supp. II, i.

Essex Entertainment, The, *see* Love and Self-Love, 1595.

Eteocles and Polynices, The Contention between, *see* Destruction of Thebes, The, 1569.

Eumorphus sive Cupido Adultus, 1635.

Eunuch, The, 1627.

Eunuch, The (Tragedy), Supp. II, a.

Eunuch, The, *see* Fatal Contract, The, 1639.

Eunuch, The, *see* Terence's Comedies Made English, 1694.

Eunuchus (Kyffin?), 1588.

Eunuchus (Bernard), 1598.

Eunuchus (Lister), 1700.

Eunuchus, *see* Comoedia Sex Anglo-Latinae, 1663.

Euribates Pseudomagus, 1616.

Euriolus (i.e. Euryalus) and Lucretia, *sometimes incorrectly listed as a play.*

Europe's Revels for the Peace and His Majesty's Happy Return, 1697.

Evangelical Tragedy, An, or A Harmony of the Passion of Our Lord, *sometimes incorrectly listed as a play.*

Evening Adventure, An, or A Night's Intrigue, *probably a ghost title.*

Evening's Love, An, or The Mock Astrologer, 1668.

Every Act a Play, *see* Novelty, The, 1697.

Every Man, *see* Summoning of Every Man, The, 1495.

Every Man in His Humour, 1598.

Every Man out of His Humour, 1599.

Every Woman in Her Humour, 1607.

Everyone in Their Way, *see* Cure of Pride, The, 1675.

Evoradanus Prince of Denmark, *a romance sometimes listed as a play.*

Example, The, 1634.

Excellency of Her Sex, The, *see* Queen, The, 1628.

Exchange Ware at the Second Hand, *see* Band, Cuff, and Ruff, 1615.

Excidium Trojae, 1699.

Excommunicated Prince, The, or The False Relique, 1679.

Exposure, The, 1663.

Fatal Embarrassment, The, *see* Labyrinth, The, 1664.

Fatal Error, The, *see* Orgula, 1658.

Fatal Friendship, 1698.

Fatal Friendship, The, 1646.

Fatal Jealousy, The, 1672.

Fatal Love, or The Forced Inconstancy, 1680.

Fatal Love, The, *see* Charlemagne, 1600.

Fatal Marriage, The, or The Innocent Adultery, 1694.

Fatal Marriage, The, or A Second Lucretia, Supp. I.

Fatal Mistake, A, or The Plot Spoiled, 1692.

Fatal Union, The, *see* Sicily and Naples, 1640.

Fatal Wager, The, *see* Injured Princess, The, 1682.

Fate of Capua, The, 1700.

Fate of Disobedience, The, *see* False Friend, The, 1699.

Father of Heaven, The, *see* Love and Riches, 1527.

Father's Own Son, *see* Monsieur Thomas, 1615.

Fatum Vortigerni, 1619.

Fault in Friendship, A, 1623.

Faustus, *see* Doctor Faustus, 1592 *and* 1686.

Fawn, The, *see* Parasitaster, 1605; *also* Supp. II, k.

Feast, The, 1665.

Fedele and Fortunio, 1584.

Feigned Astrologer, The, 1668.

Feigned Courtesans, The, or A Night's Intrigue, 1679.

Feigned Friendship, or The Mad Reformer, 1699.

Feigned Innocence, The, *see* Sir Martin Mar-all, 1667.

Felix and Philiomena, 1585.

Felix Concordia Fratrum sive Joannes et Paulus, 1651.

Felmelanco, 1602.

Female Academy, The, 1658.

Female Prelate, The, Being the History of the Life and Death of Pope Joan, 1680.

Female Rebellion, The, 1659.

Female Victor, The, *see* Witty Combat, A, 1663.

Female Virtuosos, The, 1693.

Female Warrior, The, *see* Friendship Improved, 1699.

Female Wits, The, or The Triumvirate of Poets at Rehearsal, 1697.

Female Wits, The, *see* Sociable Companions, The, 1665.

Ferdinandus Rex Castellae, Supp. II, l.

Ferrar, A History of, 1583.

Ferrex and Porrex, 1600.

Ferrex and Porrex, *see* Gorboduc, 1562.

Festival of Light, The, *see* Luminalia, 1638.

Fickle Fair One, The, *see* Fortune's Task, 1684.

Fida Pastora, La, 1658.

Fidele and Fortunatus, *see* Fedele and Fortunio, 1584.

Field of Happiness, The, *see* London's Tempe, 1629.

Field of the Cloth of Gold, The, 1520.

Fig for a Spaniard, A, 1591.

Filli di Sciro, 1657.

Filli di Sciro, or Phillis of Scyros, 1630.

Fine Companion, A, 1633; *adapt.*, 1685.

Finding of Troth, The, 1514.

Fire and Brimstone, or The Destruction of Sodom, 1675.

First Anti-Mask of Mountebanks, The, 1618.

First Day's Entertainment at Rutland House, The, 1656.

First Introduction of the Civil Wars of France, The, 1599.

'Fisher Play', 15th cent. add.

Fisherman a Prince, A, *see* I & II Massaniello, 1699.

Fishermen and Fruitwives, A Double Mask of, 1572.

Fisherman, Fishwives, and Marketwives, A Mask of, 1559.

Five Most Noble Speeches, 1641.

Five Plays in One, 1585.

Five Plays in One, 1597.

Five Witty Gallants, The, *see* Your Five Gallants, 1605.

Flattery, Deceit, and Falsehood Mislead King Humanity, *see* Satire of the Three Estates, 1540.

Fleer, The, 1606.

Floating Island, The, 1636.

Flora's Figgaries, *see* Flora's Vagaries, 1663.

Flora's Servants, *see* Honourable Entertainments, 1621.

Flora's Vagaries, 1663.

Flora's Welcome, *see* Honourable Entertainments, 1621.

Florence, The Great Duke of, 1627.

Florentine Friend, The, Supp. II, b.

Florentine Ladies, The, 1659.

Florimene, The Pastoral of, 1635.

Flowers, The Mask of, 1614.

Flowers for Latin Speaking (Udall), *phrases from Terence, included in previous edition of* Annals, *but non-dramatic.*

French Zealot, The, *see* Tartuffe, 1670.

Friar Bacon, or The Country Justice, 1699.

Friar Bacon and Friar Bungay, 1589; *for* II Friar Bacon, *see* John of Bordeaux, 1592.

Friar Fox and Gillian of Brentford, 1599.

Friar Francis, 1599 add.

Friar Rush and the Proud Woman of Antwerp, 1601; *see also* Supp. II, k.

Friar Spendleton, 1597.

Friendship Improved, or The Female Warrior, 1699.

Friendship in Fashion, 1678.

Friendship, Prudence, and Might, 1522.

Frightful Dream to Lucina, *see* Mask, A, 1684.

Frolic, The, or The Lawyer Cheated, 1671.

Fruitless Revenge, A, *see* Unhappy Kindness, The, 1697.

Fucus sive Histriomastix, 1623.

Fucus Histriomastix, *see* Fucus, 1623.

Fuimus Troes, 1625.

I Fulgens and Lucrece, 1497.

II Fulgens and Lucrece, 1497.

Fulgens, Senator of Rome, *see* Fulgens and Lucrece, 1497.

Fulgius and Lucrell, *probably same as* Fulgens and Lucrece.

Funeral of Richard Cœur de Lion, The, 1598.

Funestum Corporis et Animae Duellum, *see* Homo Duplex, 1655.

Furies' Mask, The, Supp. II, i.

Furor Impius sive Constans Fratricida, *see* Sanguis Sanguinem, Supp. I.

Galfrido and Bernardo, *a forged title.*

Galiaso, 1594.

Gallant Cavaliero Dick Bowyer, This, *see* Trial of Chivalry, The, 1601.

Gallathea, 1585.

Gallomyomachia, Supp. I.

Game at Chess, A, 1624.

Game of the Cards, A, 1582.

Gamester, The, 1633.

Gammer Gurton's Needle, 1553.

Garden of Esperance, The, 1517.

Garden of Pleasure, The, 1511.

Garlic, 1612.

Geaner et Hamarte, Supp. II, l.

Geminus Alcides, Supp. II, l.

Gemitus Columbae, Supp. I.

General (Anon.), The, 1638.

General (Boyle), The, 1662.

General Deluge of the World, *see* Noah's Flood, 1679.

Generous Choice, The, 1700.

Generous Enemies, *see* Humorous Lieutenant, The, 1619.

Generous Enemies, The, or The Ridiculous Lovers, 1671.

Generous Lovers, The, *see* St Stephen's Green, 1700.

Generous Mistress, The, *see* Lucky Chance, The, 1686.

Generous Portugal, The, *see* Island Princess, The, 1669.

Generous Portuguese, The, *see* Island Princess, The, 1699.

Generous Revenge, A, *see* Ambitious Slave, The, 1694.

Genius, The, *see* Theobalds, The Entertainment of the King and Queen at, 1607.

Gentle Craft, The, *see* Shoemakers' Holiday, The, 1599.

Gentleman and a Husbandman, A Proper Dialogue between a, *included in previous edition of* Annals, *but not dramatic.*

Gentleman and a Priest, A Dialogue between a, *included in previous edition of* Annals, *but not dramatic.*

Gentleman Dancing-Master, The, 1672.

Gentleman No Gentleman, a Metamorphosed Courtier, A, Supp. II, m.

Gentleman of Venice, The, 1639.

Gentleman of Venice, The, *see* Renegado, The, 1624.

Gentleman Quack, The, *see* Justice Busy, 1700.

Gentleman Usher, The, 1602.

I Gentleness and Nobility, 1527.

II Gentleness and Nobility, 1527.

Genus Humanum, 1553.

George a Greene, the Pinner of Wakefield, 1590.

George Scanderbarge, The True History of, 1601.

German Princess, The, 1664.

Gesta Grayorum, 1594.

Ghismonda, Supp. I.

Ghost, The, or The Woman Wears the Breeches, 1640.

Ghosts, The, 1665.

Gigantomachia, or Work for Jupiter, 1613.

Gillian of Brentford and Friar Fox, *see* Friar Fox, 1599.

Giraldo the Constant Lover, 1623.

Gripsius and Hegio, or The Passionate Lovers, 1647.

Griselda, *see* Rare Patience of Chaucer's Griselda, The, 1546.

Grobiana's Nuptials, 1641.

Grove, The, or Love's Paradise, 1700.

Guardian (Massinger), The, 1633.

Guardian (Cowley), The, 1642.

Guardian, The, *see* Cutter of Coleman Street, 1661.

Guelphs and Ghibellines, Supp. II, j.

Guido, 1597.

Guido Varvicensis, Supp. II, l.

Guiltless Adulteress, The, or Judge in His Own Cause, Supp. II, j.

Guise, *see* Duke of Guise, The, 1623 *and* 1682.

Guise, The, 1615.

Guise, The, *see* Massacre at Paris, The, 1593.

Guise, The Fall of the, *see* Henry III of France, 1672.

Gull upon Gull, *see* Hengist King of Kent, 1618.

Gunpowder Treason under the Parliament House, Conspiracy of, Supp. II, j.

Gustavus King of Sweden, 1631; *see also* Supp. II, k.

Guthlac, St, *see* Cutlack, 1599 add.

Guy Earl of Warwick, The Tragical History of, 1593.

Guy of Warwick, The Life and Death of, 1620.

Guzman, 1669.

Gynaecocratia, 1580.

Gypsies, The Mask of the, *see* Gypsies Metamorphosed, The, 1621.

Gypsies Metamorphosed, The, 1621.

Gypsies' Mask, The, Supp. II, i.

Gypsies' Metamorphosis, The, *see* Gypsies Metamorphosed, The, 1621.

Haddington's Marriage, The Mask at Lord, 1608.

Haeresis Triumphata sive B. Ignatius Societatis Jesu Fundator, Supp. II, l.

Hague, The, *see* Jeweller of Amsterdam, The, 1617.

Haliblud Play, *see* Aberdeen Plays, 15th cent.

Haman and Esther, Supp. II, k.

Hamlet, 1589.

Hamlet Prince of Denmark, The Tragedy of, 1601; *adapt.*, 1661, 1662; Supp. II, k.

Hamlet Prince of Denmark, The Tragedy of, 1661.

Hampton Court, The Royal Mask at, *see* Vision of the Twelve Goddesses, The, 1604.

Hampton Court Mask, Supp. II, i.

Hannibal, Supp. I.

I Hannibal and Hermes, 1598.

II Hannibal and Hermes, *see* II Worse (A)feared Than Hurt, 1598.

Hannibal and Scipio (Hathway & Rankins), 1601.

Hannibal and Scipio (Nabbes), 1635.

Hannibal's Overthrow, *see* Sophonisba, 1675.

Hans Beer-Pot, 1618.

Happy Change, The, *see* Late Revolution, The, 1690.

Hard Shift for Husbands, or Bilboe's the Best Blade, 1623.

Hardicanute, 1599 add.

Harefield, The Entertainment at, 1602.

Harlequin and Scaramouche, *see* Doctor Faustus, 1686.

Harrowing of Hell, The, 13th cent.

Harry of Cornwall, 1599 add.

Hatfield Mask for the Princess Elizabeth, The, 1556.

Have at All, or The Midnight Adventures, 1694.

Hay's, The Mask at Lord, *see* Lovers Made Men, 1617.

Hay's Marriage, The Mask at Lord, 1607.

Haymakers' Mask, The, Supp. II, i.

Health and Prosperity, The Triumphs of, 1626.

Heautontimorumenus, 1598.

Heautontimorumenus, *see* Comoedia Sex Anglo-Latinae, 1663.

Heautontimorumenus, *see* Terence's Comedies Made English, 1694.

Heaven's Blessing and Earth's Joy, 1613.

Heaven's Late Revenge, *see* Andronicus, 1643.

Hector of Germany, The, or The Palsgrave Prime Elector, 1614.

Hectors, The, or The False Challenge, 1656.

Hecyra, 1598.

Hecyra, *see* Comoedia Sex Anglo-Latinae, 1663.

Hecyra, *see* Terence's Comedies Made English, 1694.

Hedon Plays, 14th cent.

Hegge Plays, *see* Ludus Coventriae, 15th cent.

Heildebrand, The Tragedy of, Supp. II, f.

Heir, The, 1620.

Heir of Morocco with the Death of Gayland, The, 1682.

Heiress, The, 1669.

Heliogabalus, The Life and Death of, 1594.

Hell's Higher Court of Justice, or The Trial of the Three Politic Ghosts, viz. Oliver Cromwell, King of Sweden, and Cardinal Mazarin, 1661.

S

Highgate, The Entertainment of the King and Queen at, 1604.

Highway to Heaven, The, 1570 add.

Himatia-Poleos: The Triumphs of Old Drapery, or The Rich Clothing of England, 1614.

Hippolytus (Studley), 1567.

Hippolytus (Anon.), 1604.

Hippolytus (Prestwich), 1651.

Hippolytus (Sherburne), 1700.

Hispanus, 1597.

Historia de Daniel Repraesentanda, see Daniel, 12th cent.

History of Love and Fortune, The, see Rare Triumphs of Love and Fortune, The, 1582.

History of the Cenofalles, see Cynocephali, The, 1577.

Histriomastix, see Fucus, 1623.

Histriomastix, or The Player Whipped, 1599.

Hit Nail o' the Head, 1570 add.

Hob, see Country Wake, The, 1696.

Hobbinol, The Humour of, 1662.

Hock-Tuesday Play, see Princely Pleasures at Kenilworth, The, 1575.

Hocus-Pocus, 1638.

Hoffman, The Tragedy of, or A Revenge for a Father, 1602.

Hog Hath Lost His Pearl, The, 1613.

Holland's Leaguer, 1631.

Hollander, The, 1636.

Holofernes, 1564.

Holophernes, The Play of, 1556.

Homo, 1618.

Homo Duplex, sive Funestum Corporis et Animae Duellum, 1655.

Honest Lawyer, The, 1615.

Honest Man's Fortune, The, 1613.

Honest Man's Revenge, The, see Atheist's Tragedy, The, 1609.

I Honest Whore, The, with the Humours of the Patient Man and the Longing Wife, 1604.

II Honest Whore, The, with the Humours of the Patient Man, the Impatient Wife, 1605.

Honoria and Mammon, 1658.

Honour, The Triumph of, see Four Plays or Moral Representations in One, 1612.

Honour and Industry, The Triumphs of, 1617.

Honour and Virtue, The Triumphs of, 1622.

Honour in the End, 1624.

Honour of Fishmongers, see Chrysanaleia, 1616.

Honour of Wales, For the, 1618.

Honour of Women, The, 1628.

Honour of Young Ladies, The, see Lovesick Maid, The, 1629.

Honour Triumphant (by J. Ford, 1606), not dramatic.

Honour's Academy, or The Famous Pastoral of the Fair Shepherdess Julietta, sometimes incorrectly listed as a play.

Honourable Entertainment of the King of Denmark, 1606.

Honourable Entertainments, 1621.

Horace (Cotton), 1665.

Horace (Denham & Philips), 1668.

Horatius, 1656.

Horestes, see Vice, A New Interlude of, 1567.

Hot Anger Soon Cold, 1598.

Hours, The, see Entertainment of the Two Kings of Great Britain and Denmark, The, 1606.

House is Haunte[d], The, 1619.

How a Man May Choose a Good Wife from a Bad, 1602.

How a Man May Please His Wife, see Way ot Content All Women, The, 1624.

How to Learn of a Woman to Woo, 1604.

Hue and Cry after Cupid, The, see Haddington's Marriage, The Mask at Lord, 1608.

Huff, Suff, and Ruff, 1561.

Hugh Aston's Mask, 1581.

Humanity and Sensuality, see Satire of the Three Estates, 1540.

Humorists, The, 1670.

Humorous Courtier, The, 1631.

Humorous Day's Mirth, An, 1597.

Humorous Earl of Gloucester with His Conquest of Portugal, The Honourable Life of the, 1601.

Humorous Lieutenant, The, 1619; adapt., 1662.

Humorous Lovers, The, 1667.

Humour of Roaring, The, see Amends for Ladies, 1611.

Humour of —, see under next word in such titles.

Humour out of Breath, 1608.

Humours, The Comedy of, see Humorous Day's Mirth, An, 1597.

Humours of Dublin, The, see Hic et Ubique, 1663.

Humours of Teague, The, see Irish Evidence, The, 1682.

Humours Reconciled, see Magnetic Lady, The, 1632.

Humphrey, Duke, 1613; see also Gloucester.

Hungarian Lion, The, 1623.

Hungarians, A Mask of, 1559.

Katherine and Pasquil, *see* Jack Drum's Entertainment, 1600.

Katherine of Aragon, The Welcome for, 1502.

Keep the Widow Waking, *see* Late Murder in White Chapel, The, 1624.

Kendal Corpus Christi Play, 15th cent. add.

Kenilworth, The Princely Pleasures at, 1575.

Kentish Fair, The, or The Parliament Sold to Their Best Worth, 1648.

Key to the Cabinet of Parliament, A, 1648.

Kind Keeper, The, or Mr Limberham, 1678.

King Alfred, King John, *etc.*, *see* Alfred, John, *etc.*

King and No King, A, 1611.

King and the Subject, The, 1638.

King Arthur's Knights, 1539.

King Louis and King Frederick of Hungary, Supp. II, k.

King of Aragon, *see* Alphonsus, 1587.

King of Aragon, The, Supp. II, k.

King of Cyprus and the Duke of Venice, A, Supp. II, k.

King of Denmark and the King of Sweden, The, Supp. II, k.

King of Denmark's Welcome, The, 1606.

King of England and the Goldsmith's Wife, The, Supp. II, k.

King of England and the King of Scotland, The, Supp. II, k.

King of Fairies, The, 1570 add.

King of Numidia, *see* Jugurth, 1600.

King of Scots, The Tragedy of the, 1568.

King of Spain and the Portuguese Ambassador, The, Supp. II, k.

King of Sweden, *see* Gustavus, 1631.

'King Play' (Hascombe), 15th cent. add.

King Robert of Sicily (Lincoln), 15th cent.

King Robert of Sicily (Chester), 15th cent. add.

King Robert of Sicily, 1623.

King's Entertainment at Welbeck, The, 1633.

King's Mistress, The, Supp. II, a.

King's Son of England and a King's Daughter of Scotland, A, Supp. II, k.

Kings of Cologne (Reading), 15th cent. add.

Kitchen Stuff Woman, The, 1595.

Knack to Know a Knave, A, 1592.

Knack to Know an Honest Man, A, 1594.

Knave in Grain New Vamped, The, 1639.

Knave in Print, A, or One for Another, 1613.

Knaveries of Thomas Becket, The, 1538.

Knavery in All Trades, or The Coffee-House, 1664.

Knavery in All Trades, *see* Knave in Grain New Vamped, The, 1639.

I Knaves, The, 1613.

II Knaves, The, 1613.

Knight and the Cobbler, The, *see* Christmas Tale, A, Supp. II, m.

'Knight cleped Florence, A', 15th cent.

Knight in the Burning Rock, The, 1579.

Knight of Malta, The, 1618.

Knight of Rhodes, The, *mentioned in* Merry Conceited Jests of Peele, 1627; *probably a fictitious title.*

Knight of the Burning Pestle, The, 1607; *adapt.*, 1662.

Knight of the Golden Shield, *see* Clyomon and Clamydes, 1570.

Knight of the Ill-Favoured Face, The, *see* Don Quixote, The History of, Supp. II, e.

Knights, A Mask of, 1579.

Knights of India and China, A Mask of the, 1604.

Knights of the Helmet, A Mask of, *see* Gesta Grayorum, 1594.

Knot of Fools, A, 1623.

Knot of Fools, The, 1612.

Knot of Knaves, A, *see* Histriomastix, 1599.

Knot of Knaves, A, *see* Scots Figgaries, The, 1652.

Knowsley, A Mask at, 1641.

Kynes Redux, Supp. II, j.

Labyrinth, The, 1664.

Labyrinthus, 1603.

Ladies à la Mode, The, 1668.

Ladies and Boys, A Mask of, 1583.

Ladies' Mask, The, *see* Amazons, The Mask of, 1618.

Ladies' Privilege, The, 1637.

Ladrones, or The Robber's Island, 1658.

Lady Alimony, or The Alimony Lady, 1659.

Lady Amity, 1604.

Lady Barbara, 1571.

Lady Contemplation, The, 1658.

Lady Errant, The, 1637.

Lady in Fashion, The, *see* Woman's Wit, 1696.

I Lady Jane, 1602.

II Lady Jane, 1602.

Lady Jane Grey, The Death of, *see* Innocent Usurper, The, 1694.

Lady Lucy's Mask, The, Supp. II, i.

Lady Mother, The, 1635.

'Locus, Corpus, Motus', *etc.*, 1605.

Lodovick Sforza, The Tragedy of, 1628.

Londini Artium et Scientiarum Scaturigo, or London's Fountain of Arts and Sciences, 1632.

Londini Emporia, or London's Mercatura, 1633.

Londini Sinus Salutis, or London's Harbour of Health and Happiness, 1635.

Londini Speculum, or London's Mirror, 1637.

Londini Status Pacatus, or London's Peaceable Estate, 1639.

Londinium Triumphans, 1663.

London, A Mumming at, 15th cent.

London against the Three Ladies, 1581.

London Chanticleers, The, 1659.

London Cuckolds, The, 1681.

I London Florentine, The, 1603.

II London Florentine, The, 1603.

London Gentleman, The, 1667.

London in Its Splendour, 1673.

London in Lustre, 1679.

London Maid, The, *see* Thorney Abbey, Supp. I.

London Merchant, The, 1624.

London Prodigal, The, 1604; *see also* Supp. II, k.

London Triumphant, or The City in Jollity and Splendour, 1672.

London Triumphing, *see* Troia Nova Triumphans, 1612.

London's Anniversary Festival, 1688.

London's Annual Triumph, 1685.

London's Fountain of Arts and Sciences, *see* Londini Artium et Scientiarum Scaturigo, 1632.

London's Glory, 1680.

London's Glory Represented by Time, Truth, and Fame, 1660.

London's Great Jubilee, 1689.

London's Harbour of Health and Happiness, *see* Londini Sinus Salutis, 1635.

London's Joy, 1681.

London's Jus Honorarium, 1631.

London's Love to Prince Henry, 1610.

London's Mercatura, *see* Londini Emporia, 1633.

London's Mirror, *see* Londini Speculum, 1637.

London's Peaceable Estate, *see* Londini Status Pacatus, 1639.

London's Resurrection to Joy and Triumph, 1671.

London's Royal Triumph, 1684.

London's Tempe, or The Field of Happiness, 1629.

London's Triumph, 1656.

London's Triumph, 1659.

London's Triumph, 1662.

London's Triumph, or The Goldsmiths' Jubilee, 1687.

London's Triumph, Presented by Industry and Honour, 1658.

London's Triumphs, 1657.

London's Triumphs, 1661.

London's Triumphs, 1664.

London's Triumphs, 1676.

London's Triumphs, 1677.

London's Triumphs, *see* Goldsmiths' Jubilee, The, 1674.

London's Yearly Jubilee, 1686.

Long Meg of Westminster, 1595.

Longbeard, *see* William Longbeard, 1599.

Longer Thou Livest the More Fool Thou Art, The, 1559.

Longshanks, 1595.

Longsword, *see* William Longbeard, 1599.

Look about You, 1599.

Look on Me and Love Me, or Marriage in the Dark, Supp. II, m.

Look to the Lady, 1619.

Looking Glass for London and England, A, 1590.

Looking Glass, the Bachelor, or the Hawk, The, *see* Mull Sack, Supp. II, m.

Lord Governance and Lady Public Weal, 1526.

Lord Mayor's Show, The, 1535.

Lord Mayor's Show, The, 1682.

Lord Mendall, The, *see* Peaceable King, The, 1623.

Lord's Supper and Washing the Feet, The, 1536.

Lords' Mask, The, 1613.

Lost Lady, The, 1637.

Lost Lover, The, or The Jealous Husband, 1696.

Lost Muse, A Mask of the, 1600.

Lost Recovered, The, *see* Captives, The, 1624.

Lot Debauched, 1661.

Louis XI King of France, The History of, Supp. II, e.

Louis and King Frederick of Hungary, King, Supp. II, k.

Love, A Play of, 1533.

Love, The Triumph of, *see* Four Plays or Moral Representations in One, 1612.

Love a Cheat, 1653.

Love à la Mode, 1663.

Love above Ambition, *see* Aristomenes, 1690.

Love and a Bottle, 1698.

Love and Antiquity, The Triumphs of, 1619.

Love and Beauty, The Triumph of, 1514.

Lover's Holiday, The, Supp. II, m.

Lover's Holiday, The, or The Bear, Supp. II, m.

Lover's Luck, The, 1695.

Lover's Melancholy, The, 1628.

Lover's Stratagem, The, or Virtue Rewarded, Supp. I.

Lovers Made Men, 1617.

Lovers of Ludgate, The, Supp. II, g.

Lovers' Hospital, *see* Love's Hospital, 1636.

Lovers' Progress, The, *see* Wandering Lovers, The, 1623.

Loves of Mars and Venus, The, 1696.

Loves of Oroondates and Statira, The, *see* Rival Kings, The, 1676.

Loves of the Deities, The, *see* Cinthia and Endimion, 1696.

Lovesick Court, The, or The Ambitious Politic, 1639.

Lovesick King, The, 1617.

Lovesick Maid, The, or The Honour of Young Ladies, 1629.

Loving Enemies, The, 1680.

Loyal Brother, The, or The Persian Prince, 1682.

Loyal Brother, The, *sometimes erroneously cited as alternative title for* Revenger's Tragedy, The, 1606.

Loyal Citizens, The, 1662.

Loyal Favourite, The, *see* Ambitious Statesman, The, 1679.

Loyal General, The, 1679.

Loyal Lovers, The, 1652.

Loyal Subject, The, 1618.

Loyalty and Beauty, 1579.

Loyola, 1623.

Lucina's Rape, or The Tragedy of Valentinian, 1678.

Lucius Junius Brutus, Father of His Country, 1680.

Luck's All, *see* Fools Have Fortune, 1680.

Lucky Chance, The, or An Alderman's Bargain, 1686.

Lucky Extravagant, The, *see* Sham Lawyer, The, 1697.

Lucky Younger Brother, The, *see* Beau Defeated, The, 1700.

Lucretia, 1605.

Lud, King, 1599 add.

Ludi Domini Regis, 14th cent.

Ludlow Castle, The Mask at, *see* Comus, 1634.

Ludus Coventriae, 15th cent.

Ludus de Bellyale, *see* Belial, 15th cent.

Ludus de Sancta Katerina, *see* St Katherine, 11th cent.

Ludus Filiorum Israelis, 14th cent.

Ludus super Iconia Sancti Nicolai, *see* St Nicholas, 12th cent.

Luminalia, or The Festival of Light, 1638.

Lusiuncula, Supp. I.

Lust's Dominion, or The Lascivious Queen, 1600; *adapt.*, 1676.

Lusty Juventus, 1550.

Lusty London, 1580.

Luther, *see* Heretic Luther, 1527.

Macbeth, 1664.

Macbeth, The Tragedy of, 1606; *adapt.*, 1664.

Machiavel, 1599 add.

Machiavel and the Devil, 1613.

Machiavellus, 1597.

Mack, The, 1595.

Macro Morals, *see* Castle of Perseverance, The; Mankind; Mind, Will, and Understanding.

Mad Amyntas, *see* Wavering Nymph, The, 1684.

Mad Couple, The, *see* All Mistaken, 1667.

Mad Couple Well Matched, A, 1639; *adapt.*, 1677.

Mad Lover, The, 1617.

Mad Priest of the Sun, The, 1587.

Mad Reformer, The, *see* Feigned Friendship, 1699.

Mad Tom of Bedlam, or The Distressed Lovers, with the Comical Humours of Squire Numskull, 1696.

Mad Wooing, The, or A Way to Win and Tame a Shrew, 1698.

Mad World My Masters, A, 1606.

Madam Fickle, or The Witty False One, 1676.

Madcap, The, 1624.

Madcap, The, *see* Coursing of a Hare, The, 1633.

Madman's Morris, The, 1598.

Madon King of Britain, The History of, 1606.

Maenander's Ecstasy, *see* Cynthia's Revenge, 1613.

Magister Bonus sive Arsenius, 1614.

Magnetic Lady, The, or Humours Reconciled, 1632.

Magnificence, a Goodly Interlude, 1515.

Magnificent Entertainment Given to King James, The, 1604.

Mahomet, 1599 add.; *see also* Turkish Mahomet, The, 1588.

Mahomet and Hiren, *see* Turkish Mahomet, The, 1588.

Mock Duellist, The, or The French Valet, 1675.

Mock Marriage, The, 1695.

Mock Marriage, The, see English Moor, The, 1637.

'Mock Mass', 1564.

Mock Pompey, 1674.

Mock Tempest, The, or The Enchanted Castle, 1674.

Mock Testator, The, see Sexton, The, 1662.

Mock Thyestes, see Thyestes, 1674.

Modish Lovers, The, see Mall, The, 1674.

Modish Wife, The, see Tom Essence, 1676.

Moll Cutpurse, see Roaring Girl, The, 1608.

Money Is an Ass, 1635.

Monsieur D'Olive, 1604.

Monsieur Galliard, The Humours of, 1662.

Monsieur Raggou, see Old Troop, The, 1664.

Monsieur Thomas, 1615; adapt., 1662, 1678.

Montacute, The Mask for Lord, 1572.

Montague Mask, The, see Montacute, The Mask for Lord, 1572.

Montezuma sive Mexici Imperii Occasus, Supp. I.

Monuments of Honour, 1624.

Moor's Mask, The, see Moore's Mask, 1636.

Moor's Revenge, The, see Abdelazer, 1676.

Moore's Mask, 1636.

Moors, A Mask of, 1559.

Moors and Amazons, A Mask of, 1551.

More, The Book of Sir Thomas, 1595.

More Dissemblers Besides Women, 1615; adapt., 1678.

More Than Nine Days Wonder: Two Constant Women, Supp. II, m.

Morning Ramble, The, or The Town Humours, 1672.

Morris Mask, A, 1579.

Mors Comoedia, 1619.

Mors Valentiniani Imperatoris, Supp. II, l.

Mortimer His Fall, 1637.

Morus, Supp. I; see also Thomas Morus, 1612.

Most Firm Friendship of Titus and Gisippus, The, 1546.

Most Virtuous and Godly Susanna, The, 1569.

Most Votes Carry It, The, see Love at a Loss, 1700.

Mostellaria, Supp. I.

Mother Bombie, 1589.

Mother in Fashion, The, see Disappointment, The, 1684.

Mother Redcap, 1598.

Mother Rumming, Supp. II, d.

Mother Shipton, The Life of, 1670.

Motions, Supp. II, j.

Mountebanks, The First Anti-Mask of, 1618.

Mourning Bride, The, 1697.

Mucedorus (and Amadine), 1590; see also Supp. II, k.

Much Ado about Nothing, 1598; adapt., 1662.

Mulberry Garden, The, 1668.

Mull Sack, or The Looking Glass, the Bachelor, or the Hawk, Supp. II, m.

Mulleasses the Turk, see Turk, The, 1607.

Mulmutius Dunwallow, 1598.

Muly Molloco, 1599 add.

Mumming at —, see under next word in such titles.

Mumming before the Great Estates of the Land, A, see London, A Mumming at, 15th cent.

Mumming for the Goldsmiths of London, A, 15th cent.

Mumming for the Mercers of London, A, 15th cent.

Mundus et Infans, see World and the Child, 1508.

Mundus Plumbeus, 1525.

Murder Will Out, see Politic Queen, The, 1623.

Murderous Michael, The History of, 1579.

Muse of Newmarket, The, or Mirth and Drollery, a collection of three drolls listed under 1680.

Muses' Looking Glass, The, 1630.

I Music, or A Parley of Instruments, 1676.

Mustapha, 1596; see also Supp. II, m.

Mustapha, Son of Solyman the Magnificent, 1665; see also Supp. II, m.

Mutius Scaevola, The History of, 1577.

Myngs, see Mingo, 1577.

Mystère d'Adam, Le, see Adam, 12th cent.

N. Town Plays, see Ludus Coventriae, 15th cent.

Naamen, Supp. I.

Narcissus, The Play of, 1572.

Narcissus, a Twelfth Night Merriment, 1603.

Nativity Play, see Aberdeen Plays, 15th cent.

Nativity Play, see also Quem Quaeritis, Stella, Pastores.

Nativity Play and Resurrection Play, 15th cent. add.

Natura Naturata, see Nature of the Four Elements, The, 1517.

Natural Magic, see Novelty, The, 1697.

I Nature, A Goodly Interlude of, 1495.

II Nature, A Goodly Interlude of, 1495.

Nature of the Four Elements, The, 1517.

Nature Will Prevail, see Love Triumphant, 1694.

Nature's Three Daughters, Beauty, Love, and Wit, 1658.

Noble Friend, The, Supp. II, f.

Noble Gentleman, The, 1626; *adapt.*, 1688.

Noble Grandchild, The, 1614.

Noble Husbands, The, 1635.

Noble Ingratitude, The, 1659.

Noble Ravishers, The, Supp. II, b.

Noble Servant, The, *see* Osmond the Great Turk, 1637.

Noble Soldier, The, or A Contract Broken Justly Revenged, *see* Noble Spanish Soldier, The, 1626.

Noble Spanish Soldier, The, 1626.

Noble Stranger, The, 1639.

Noble Trial, The, 1635.

Nobleman, The, 1612.

Nobody and Somebody, with the True Chronicle History of Elydure, 1605; *see also* Supp. II, k.

Noctroff's Maid Whipped, *see* Presbyterian Lash, The, 1661.

Nonesuch, The, 1623.

Nonpareilles, The, or The Matchless Maids, *see* Love and Honour, 1634.

Norfolk and Suffolk, The Entertainment in, 1578.

Northern Castle, The, 1667.

Northern Lass, The, 1629.

Northward Ho, 1605.

Norwich, The Entertainment at, 1578.

Norwich Plays, 15th cent.

Nothing Impossible to Love, 1634.

Nottingham Castle, Devices for, 1562.

Nottola, Supp. I.

Novella, The, 1632.

Novelty, The, Every Act a Play, 1697.

Nugize, *see* New Custom, 1571.

Nuptials of Peleus and Thetis, The, 1654.

Nurture and Kind, Dialogue between, *previously included in* Annals; *not dramatic.*

Nusquams with Turkish Commoners, A Mask of, 1559.

Oberon the Fairy Prince, 1611.

Oberon the Second, *see* Fairy Knight, The, 1638.

Obstinate Lady, The, 1639.

Octavia (Nuce), 1566.

Octavia (Anon.), 1591.

Odoardus Varvici Comes, Supp. II, l.

Oedipus (Neville), 1563.

Oedipus (Gager), 1584.

Oedipus (Dryden & Lee), 1678.

Oedipus, Supp. I.

Oedipus, A Tragedy Called, Supp. I.

Oenone, 1673.

Oenone, *see* Rural Sports, 1653.

Officium Pastorum, *see* Pastores.

Officium Peregrinorum, *see* Peregrini.

Officium Resurrectionis, *see* Quem Quaeritis (of Easter), *or* Visitatio Sepulchri.

Old Antic Mask, The, Supp. II, i.

Old Bachelor, The, 1693.

Old Christmas, or Good Order, 1533.

Old Couple, The, 1636.

Old Custom, 1533.

Old Drapery and Clothing of England, The, *see* Himatia-Poleos, 1614.

Old Fools Will Be Meddling, *see* Win Her and Take Her, 1691.

Old Fortunatus, 1599; *see also* Supp. II, k.

Old Joiner of Aldgate, The, 1603.

Old Law, The, or A New Way to Please You, 1618.

Old Man's Lesson and a Young Man's Love, An, 1605, *a dialogue by N. Breton.*

Old Proculus, Supp. II, k.

Old Troop, The, or Monsieur Raggou, 1664; *adapt.*, 1681.

Old Wives Tale, The, 1590.

I Oldcastle, Sir John, 1599.

II Oldcastle, Sir John, 1600.

Oliver in His Glory as King, *see* II Crafty Cromwell, 1648.

Oliver Ordering Our New State, *see* I Crafty Cromwell, 1648.

Olympio and Heugenyo, *see* Seleo and Olympio, 1595.

I On Sects among the Papists, 1537.

II On Sects among the Papists, 1537.

On the Seven Sins, 1536.

Once a Lover Always a Lover, *see* She Gallants, The, 1695.

One for Another, *see* Knave in Print, A, 1613.

One of the Four Plays in One, *see* Yorkshire Tragedy, A, 1606.

Opportunity, The, 1634; *adapt.*, 1662.

Orator, The, 1635.

Ordinary, The, or The City Cozener, 1635.

Ordo Prophetarum, *see* Rubum Quem Viderat, 15th cent.

Orestes, *see* Horestes, 1567.

Orestes, The Tragedy of, 1617.

Orestes Furious, *see* Orestes' Furies, 1599.

Orestes' Furies (*or* Furens), 1599.

Orgula, or The Fatal Error, 1658.

Origin of the World, The, *see* Origo Mundi, 14th cent.

T

Passion Play, *see* Aberdeen Plays, 15th cent.

Passion Play *and* Resurrection Play (New Romney), 15th cent.

I Passionate Lover(s), The, 1638.

II Passionate Lover(s), The, 1638.

Passionate Lovers, The, *see* Gripsius and Hegio, 1647.

Passionate Madman, The, *see* Nice Valour, The, 1616.

Passions Calmed, *see* Floating Island, The, 1636.

Pastor Fido (Sidnam), Il, 1630.

Pastor Fido (Digby), Il, 1635.

Pastor Fido (Fanshawe), Il, 1647.

Pastor Fido, Il, or The Faithful Shepherd (Dymock?), 1601.

Pastor Fido, or The Faithful Shepherd (Settle), 1676.

Pastor Fidus, 1604.

'Pastor Stapilton', *see* Royal Choice, The, 1653.

Pastoral, *see* Royal Choice, The, 1653.

Pastoral, A, 1645.

Pastoral Dialogue, *see* Dialogue between Two Shepherds, A, 1580.

Pastoral Mask, A, 1636.

Pastoral Tragedy, A, 1599.

Pastores (Lichfield), 12th cent.

Pastores (York), 13th cent.

Pastores, *see* Shrewsbury Fragments, 14th cent.

Pastorum Secunda, *see* Wakefield Plays, 14th cent.

Pater, Filius, et Uxor, or The Prodigal Son, 1530; *see also* Supp. II, k.

Pater Noster Play (Lincoln), 14th cent.

Pater Noster Play (York), 14th cent.

Pater Noster Play (Beverley), 15th cent.

Pater Noster Play, 1536.

Pathomachia, or The Battle of Affections, 1617.

Patient and Meek Grissil, The Comedy of, 1559.

Patient Grissil, 1600; *see also* Supp. II, k.

Patient Grizill, 1667.

Patriarchs, A Mask of, 1560.

Pattern of Piety, The, 1638.

Paulo Giordano Ursini, The Tragedy of, *see* White Devil, The, 1612.

Paulus Japonensis, Supp. II, l.

Pausanious the Betrayer of His Country, 1696.

Peaceable King, The, or The Lord Mendall, 1623.

Pearce His Mask, Supp. II, i.

Pedantius, 1581.

Pedlar, The, *see* Conceited Pedlar, The, 1627.

Pedlar's Mask, The, 1574.

Pedlar's Prophecy, The, 1561.

Pelopaea and Alope, *see* Pleasant Dialogues and Dramas, 1635.

Pelopidarum Secunda, Supp. I.

Pen Combatants, The, *see* Invisible Smirk, 1662.

Penates, The, *see* Highgate, The Entertainment . . . at, 1604.

Penelope's Wooers, *see* Christmas Prince, The, 1608.

Peregrini (Lichfield), 12th cent.

Peregrini (Lincoln), 14th cent.

Peregrini, *see* Shrewsbury Fragments, 14th cent.

Perfidus Hetruscus, Supp. I.

Periander, *see* Christmas Prince, The, 1608.

Pericles Prince of Tyre, 1608.

Perjured Husband, The, or The Adventures of Venice, 1700.

Perjured Nun, The, *see* Lovesick King, The, 1617.

Perkin Warbeck (Anon.), 1619.

Perkin Warbeck (Ford), 1633.

Perseus and Andromeda, 1574.

Perseus et Demetrius sive Discordia Omnis Pessima Imperii Lues, 1664.

Persian Prince, The, *see* Loyal Brother, The, 1682.

Petronius Maximus, The Famous History of, Supp. II, j.

Phaedra, 1700.

Phaeton, 1598.

Phaeton, or The Fatal Divorce, 1698.

Phanatique Play, A, 1660.

Pharamus sive Libido Vindex, *see* Thibaldus, 1640.

Pharaoh's Daughter, Supp. II, j.

Phedrastus, 1574.

Phigon and Lucia, 1574.

Philander King of Thrace, 1628.

Philaster, or Love Lies a-Bleeding, 1609; *adapt.*, 1662, 1686, 1695.

Philaster, or Love Lies a-Bleeding, 1695.

Philemon and Philecia, 1574.

Philenzo and Hypollita, 1620.

Philetis and Constantia, 1653.

Philip of Macedon, Supp. II, m.

Philip of Spain, 1602.

Philipo and Hippolito, 1594; *see also* Philenzo and Hypollita, 1620.

Phillis and Amyntas, 1591.

Phillis of Scyros, *see* Filli di Sciro, 1630.

Philoctetes, 1543.

Philole and Mariana, Supp. II, k.

Philomathes, *see* Christmas Prince, The, 1608.

Philomathes' Dream, 1584.

Philomathes' Second Dream, 1586.

Philomela, or Tereus and Progne, *see* Christmas Prince, The, 1607.

Philosophaster, 1606.

Philosopher, The, *see* Wit's Triumvirate, 1635.

Philotas (Lateware), 1588.

Philotas (Daniel), The Tragedy of, 1604.

Philotus, 1603.

Phocas, 1619.

Phocas (C. Wren, Sr.), *previously included in Annals; ghost entry.*

Phocasse, 1596.

Phoebus's Knights, *see* Hay's Mask, 1607.

Phoenissae, 1619.

Phoenix, Supp. II, l.

Phoenix, The, 1604.

Phoenix in Her Flames, The, 1639.

Phormio (Bernard), 1598.

Phormio (Rant), 1674.

Phormio, *see* Comoedia Sex Anglo-Latinae, 1663.

Phormio, *see* Terence's Comedies Made English, 1694.

Phyllida and Corin, 1584.

Physic Lies a-Bleeding, or The Apothecary Turned Doctor, 1697.

Physician against His Will, The, 1667.

Physiponomachia, 1609.

Picture, The, 1629.

Pierce, Alice, 1597.

Pierce of Exton, 1598.

Pierce of Winchester, 1598.

Pietas Coronata, *see* Mercia, 1624.

Piety and Valour, or Derry Defended, 1692.

Pilgrim (Fletcher), The, 1621; *adapt.*, 1700.

Pilgrim (Killigrew), The, 1646.

Pilgrim (Vanbrugh), The, 1700.

Pilgrim Prince, The, *see* Religious Rebel, The, 1671.

Pilgrimage to Parnassus, The, 1599.

Pinner of Wakefield, The, *see* George a Greene, 1590.

Pirate, The, 1626.

Piscator sive Fraus Illusa, 1539.

Piso's Conspiracy, 1675.

Pity the Maid, Supp. II, b.

Place Perilous, The, 1515.

Placidas, alias Sir Eustace, 1534.

Placidas, Sir, *a Collier forgery.*

Plain Dealer, The, 1676.

Plantation of Virginia, A Tragedy of the, 1623.

Platonic Lovers, The, 1635.

Plautus His Trinummi Imitated, 1693.

Plautus's Comedies: Amphitryon, Epidicus, and Rudens Made English, 1694.

Play of Love, A, 1533.

Play of Plays and Pastimes, The, 1582; *see also* Delight, 1580.

Play of the Weather, The, 1528.

Player Whipped, The, *see* Histriomastix, 1599.

Playhouse to Be Let, The, 1663.

Pleasant Adventures at Brussels, The, *see* Campaigners, The, 1698.

Pleasant and Merry Humour of a Rogue, A, 1658; *see also* Triumphant Widow, The, 1674.

Pleasant Dialogues and Dramas, 1635.

Pleasure Reconciled to Virtue, 1618.

Plenum Reconciled to Kulum, *error for* Pleasure Reconciled to Virtue, 1618.

Plot and No Plot, A, 1697.

Plot Discovered, A, *see* Venice Preserved, 1682.

Plot Spoiled, The, *see* Fatal Mistake, A, 1692.

Plotting Sisters, The, *see* Fond Husband, A, 1677.

Pluto Furens et Vinctus, or The Raging Devil Bound, 1669.

Plutophthalmia Plutogamia, A Pleasant Comedy Entitled, 1627.

Plutus the God of Wealth, *see* World's Idol Plutus, The, 1659.

Poet, Painter, and Musician, *see* Mitcham, The Entertainment at, 1598.

Poet Stutter, *see* Wit for Money, 1691.

Poet's Revenge, A, *see* Wits Led by the Nose, 1677.

Poetaster, or The Arraignment, 1601.

Poetess, The, 1667.

Poetical Squire, The, *see* Sir Hercules Buffoon, 1682.

Poikilo-Phronesis, or The Different Humours of Men, 1691.

Polanders, A Mask of, 1552.

Polichinello, *see* Punchinello, 1666.

Policy and Piety, A Dialogue between, 1635.

Politic Bankrupt, The, or Which Is the Best Girl?, Supp. II, a.

Politic Father, The, *see* Brothers, The, 1641.

Politic Queen, The, or Murder Will Out, 1623.

Politic Whore, The, or The Conceited Cuckold, 1680.

Politician, The, 1639.

Politician, The, or Sir Popular Wisdom, 1677.

Politician Cheated, The, 1663.

Politique Father, The, *see* Brothers, The, 1641.

Polyeuctes, or The Martyr, 1655.

Polyhymnia, 1590.

Polyphemus, The Tragedy of, *see* Troy's Revenge, 1599.

Pompae Deorum in Nuptiis Mariae, 1565.

Pompae Deorum Rusticorum, 1566.

Pompae Equestres, 1565.

Pompey, 1663.

Pompey, A Story of, 1581.

Pompey and Caesar, The Wars of, *see* Caesar and Pompey, 1605.

Pompey the Great, 1663.

Pompey the Great His Fair Cornelia's Tragedy, *see* Cornelia, 1594.

Pontius Pilate, 1597.

Poor, The Part of, 1618.

Poor Man and the Pardoner, The, *see* Satire of the Three Estates, 1540.

Poor Man's Comfort, The, 1617.

Poor Man's Paradise, The, 1599.

Poor Northern Man, The, *a Collier forgery*.

Poor Scholar, The, 1662.

Pope Alexander VI, The Tragedy of, *see* Devil's Charter, The, 1607.

'Pope, Cardinals, Friars', 1598.

Pope Joan, 1599 add.

Pope Joan, *see* Female Prelate, The, 1680.

Pope's Councillors, *see* Against the Pope's Councillors, 1537.

Port or Harbour of Piety, The, *see* Porta Pietatis, 1638.

Porta Pietatis, or The Port or Harbour of Piety, 1638.

Portia, 1594.

Portio and Demorantes, 1580.

Practice of Parasites, The, *see* Jew, The, 1578.

Praeludium, 1629.

Pragmatical Jesuit New Leavened, The, 1661.

Praise at Parting, 1577.

Predor and Lucia, 1573.

Presbyterian Lash, The, or Noctroff's Maid Whipped, 1661.

Presence, The, 1665.

Presentation for the Prince on His Birthday, A, 1638.

Presentation of Bushell's Rock, The, 1636.

Prester John, A Mask of, 1547.

Pretenders, The, or The Town Unmasked, 1698.

Pretestus, 1574.

Pride of Life, The, 14th cent.

Priest the Barber, Supp. I.

Prince D'Amour, The Triumphs of the, 1636.

Prince in Conceit, A, 1662.

Prince of Prigs' Revels, The, 1651.

Prince of Tarent, The, *see* Very Woman, A, 1634.

Prince's Ball, The, or The Conquest of Queen Judith, 1682.

Prince's Mask, The, Supp. II, i.

Princely Pleasures at Kenilworth, The, 1575.

Princeps Rhetoricus, *see* School Moderator, 1647.

Princess, The, or Love at First Sight, 1636.

Princess of Cleve, The, 1681.

Princess of Parma, The, 1699.

Princess of Persia, The, *see* Distressed Innocence, 1690.

Princess of Poland, The, *see* Juliana, 1671.

Priscianus Vapulans, Supp. II, j.

Prisoner[s] (Massinger), The, 1640.

Prisoners (Killigrew), The, 1635.

Processus Satanae, 1575.

Prodigal Child, The, *see* Histriomastix, 1599.

Prodigal Scholar, The, 1629.

Prodigal Son, The, Supp. II, k.

Prodigal Son, The, *see* Pater, Filius, et Uxor, 1530.

Prodigality, 1567.

Proditiones Papistarum, *see* I & II On Sects among the Papists, 1537.

Progne, 1566.

Progress to Parnassus, The, *see* II Return from Parnassus, The, 1603.

Projector Lately Dead, A, 1636.

Projectors, The, 1664.

I Promos and Cassandra, The History of, 1578.

II Promos and Cassandra, The History of, 1578.

Prophetess, The, 1622; *adapt.*, 1690.

Prophetess, The, or The History of Diocletian, 1690.

Proteus and the Rock Adamantine, A Mask of, *see* Gesta Grayorum, 1594.

Protomartyr, 1547.

Proud Heart and a Beggar's Purse, A, *see* Histriomastix, 1599.

Proud Maid's Tragedy, The, 1612.

Proud Woman of Antwerp, A, Supp. II, k.

Proud Woman of Antwerp, The, *see* Friar Rush, 1601.

Provoked Wife, The, 1697.

Proxy, The, *see* Love's Aftergame, 1634.

Prudentius, *see* Floating Island, The, 1636.

Pseudolus, Supp. I.

Pseudomagia, 1626.

Psyche, 1675.

Psyche Debauched, 1675.

Rebellion, The, 1636.

Rebellion of Naples, The, or The Tragedy of Massenello, 1649.

Reception of Henry V Returning from France, The, 15th cent.

Reception of Henry VI Returning from France, The, 15th cent.

Recital, The, see Rehearsal, The, 1671.

Recovery, The, 1673.

Rectory, The, see Recovery, The, 1673.

Red Knight, The, 1576.

Reformation (Wright), The, 1631.

Reformation (Arrowsmith), The, 1673.

Reformed Wife, The, 1700.

Regale Excambium, see Byrsa Basilica, 1633.

Regicidium, 1665.

Regularis Concordia, 10th cent.

Regulus, 1692.

Rehearsal, The, 1671.

Rehearsal at Whitehall, The, see Battle, The, 1686.

Rehearsal of Kings, The, 1692.

Relapse, The, or Virtue in Danger, 1696.

Religion, Peace, and Justice, 1528.

Religious, The, 1658.

Religious Rebel, The, or The Pilgrim Prince, 1671.

Renegado, The, 1662.

Renegado, The, or The Gentleman of Venice, 1624; adapt., 1662.

Reparatus sive Depositum, 1619.

Repraesentatio Adae, see Adam, 12th cent.

Respublica, 1553.

Restoration, The, or Right Will Take Place, 1686.

Résurrection du Sauveur, La, see Seinte resureccion, La, 13th cent.

Resurrection of Our Lord, The, 1545.

Resurrection Play, 15th cent. add.

Resurrexio Domini, see Origo Mundi, 14th cent.

I Return from Parnassus, The, 1600.

II Return from Parnassus, The, or The Scourge of Simony, 1603.

Reunited Britannia, The Triumphs of, 1605.

Revel of Aldford, The, see Country Revel, The, 1671.

'Revels called a Maskalyn', 1519.

Revenge, The, Supp. II, j.

Revenge, The, or A Match in Newgate, 1680.

Revenge for a Father, A, see Hoffman, The Tragedy of, 1602.

Revenge for Honour, 1640.

Revenge of Bussy D'Ambois, The, 1610.

Revengeful Queen, The, 1698.

Revenger's Tragedy, The, 1606.

Reverent Receiving of the Sacrament, A, 1537.

Review, The, Supp. I.

Revolution, The, see Timoleon, 1697.

Reward of Loyalty, The, see False Favourite Disgraced, The, 1657.

Rewards of Virtue, The, 1661; adapt., 1669.

Rex Oswius, Supp. II, l.

Rhodon and Iris, 1631.

Rich Man, The, Supp. II, k.

Rich Man's Misery, The, see Dives' Doom, 1675.

Rich Mount, The, 1513.

Richard II, 1611.

I Richard II, or Thomas of Woodstock, 1592.

Richard II, The History of King, 1680.

Richard II, The Tragedy of, 1595; adapt., 1680.

Richard II, The Visit to, 14th cent.

Richard II's Reconciliation with the City of London, 14th cent.

Richard III, The Death of, see English Princess, The, 1667.

Richard III, A Tragedy of, or The English Profit, 1623.

Richard III, The Tragedy of King, 1593; adapt., 1699.

Richard III, The Tragical History of King, 1699.

Richard III, The True Tragedy of, 1591.

Richard Crookback, 1602.

Richard Duke of York, and the Death of Good King Henry VI, with the Whole Contention between the Two Houses Lancaster and York, The True Tragedy of, see III Henry VI, 1591.

Richard the Confessor, 1599 add.

Richard Whittington, The History of, 1605.

Richardus Tertius, 1580.

Riches and Youth, 1552.

Richmond, The King and Queen's Entertainment at, 1636; adapt., 1673.

Richmond Heiress, The, or A Woman Once in the Right, 1693.

Ridiculous Lovers, The, see Generous Enemies, The, 1671.

Right Re-enthroned, see Alfred, 1659.

Right Use of Plays, The, see Soul's Warfare, The, 1672.

Right Will Take Place, see Restoration, The, 1686.

Right Woman, A, 1615.

Rinaldo and Armida, 1698.

Ring, The, 1632.

Rising of Cardinal Wolsey, The, 1601.

Risus Anglicanus, 1620.

Royal Mischief, The, 1696.

Royal Oak, The, 1660.

Royal Penitents, The, *see* Innocence Distressed, 1695.

Royal Shepherd, The, *see* Aristomenes, 1690.

Royal Shepherdess, The, 1669.

Royal Shepherdess, The, *see* Love's Labyrinth, 1660.

Royal Slave, The, 1636.

Royal Union, The, *see* Love's Triumph, 1678.

Royal Voyage, The, or The Irish Expedition, 1690.

Royal Widow of England, The History of a, 1602.

Royalist, The, 1682.

Rubum Quem Viderat, 15th cent.

Rude Commonalty, A, 1537.

Rudens, 1694.

Ruff, Cuff, and Band, 1646; *see also* Band, Cuff, and Ruff, 1615.

Rufus (i.e. Henry) I with the Life and Death of Belyn Dun, The True Tragical History of King, *see* Bellendon, 1594.

Ruins of Love, The, *see* Queen Catherine, 1698.

Rule a Wife and Have a Wife, 1624; *adapt.*, 1662.

Rule of St Benedict, 10th cent.

Rump, The, or The Mirror of the Late Times, 1660.

'Running' (*or* Travelling) Mask, 1620.

Running Stream Entertainment, The, *see* New River, The Entertainment at the Opening of the, 1613.

Rural Sports, or The Birthday of the Nymph Oenone, 1653; *adapt.*, 1662, 1673.

Russet Coat and a Knave's Cap, A, *see* Histrio-mastix, 1599.

Rutland House, The First Day's Entertainment at, 1656.

Rycote, The Entertainment at, 1592.

Sabine War, The, *see* Romulus and Hersilia, 1682.

Sackful of News, The, 1557.

Sacrament, The Play of the, 15th cent.

Sacrament of the Altar, The, 1539.

Sacrifice, The, 1686.

Sad One, The, 1637.

Sad Shepherd, The, or A Tale of Robin Hood, 1637.

Saeculi Fuga, *see* Aloysius, Supp. II, l.

Sailors' Mask, The, Supp. II, i.

St Albans, The Tragedy of, 1625.

S. Albanus Protomartyr, *see* Britanniae Primitiae, Supp. I.

St Ambrose and Emperor Theodosius, *see* Nectar et Ambrosia, 1578.

St Andrew (Braintree), 15th cent. add.

S. Augustinus Angliae Apostolus, Supp. II, l.

St Austin, The Life of, *see* England's First Happiness, 1641.

St Cecily, or The Converted Twins, 1666.

St Christian (Coventry), 15th cent. add.

St Christina (Bethersden), 15th cent. add.

St Christopher, 1609.

St Clara (Lincoln), 15th cent.

St Clotilda, 15th cent.

S. Damianus, 1626.

St Dionysius, 15th cent.

S. Edoardus Confessor sive Mites Terram Possidebunt, 1653.

St Erasmus (Aberdeen), 15th cent. add.

St Erasmus, 1518.

St Eustace (Braintree), 15th cent. add.

S. Franciscus Xaverius, Supp. I.

St George (Norwich), 15th cent.

St George (Lydd), 15th cent.

St George, 1511.

St George and the Castle, 15th cent.

St George and the Dragon, 1686.

St George for England, 1623.

St George Pageant (Dublin), 15th cent. add.

St George Procession (Norwich), 15th cent.

St George Riding (York), 15th cent. add.

St James (Lincoln), 15th cent. add.

St James's Park, *see* Love in a Wood, 1671.

S. Justus et S. Pastor, Supp. II, l.

St Katherine (Dunstable), 11th cent.

St Katherine (London), 14th cent.

St Katherine (Coventry), 15th cent.

S. Kenelmus Rex, Supp. II, l.

St Laurence (Lincoln), 15th cent.

St Mary Magdalene, *see* Mary Magdalene.

St Meriasek Bishop and Confessor, The Life of, 1504.

St Nicholas (France), 12th cent.

St Nicholas Day Ride, *see* Aberdeen Plays, 15th cent.

St Nicholas Play, 13th cent.

St Obert (Perth), 15th cent. add.

St Olave's Play, 15th cent. add.

I St Patrick for Ireland, 1639.

St Paul, *see* Conversion of St Paul, The, 15th cent.

St Paul's Old Testament Plays, 14th cent.

S. Pelagius Martyr, 1623.

S. Sigismundus, Supp. II, l.

Sedgemoor Fight, The Farce upon, *see* Battle, The, 1686.

Seinte resureccion, La, 13th cent.

Sejanus His Fall, 1603.

Seleo and Olympio, 1595.

Self-Interest, or The Belly Wager, 1659.

Self-Love, 1552.

I Selimus, The Tragical Reign of, 1592.

Selindra, 1662.

Senile Odium, 1631.

Senilis Amor, 1636.

Serenade, The, or The Disappointment, 1669.

Sermon of Folly, The, *see* Satire of the Three Estates, 1540.

Sertorius, The Tragedy of, 1679.

Set at Maw, The, 1594.

Set at Tennis, The, 1602.

Seven Champions of Christendom, The, 1635.

I Seven Days of the Week, The, 1595.

II Seven Days of the Week, The, 1596.

Seven Days of the Week, The, *see* Christmas Prince, The, 1608.

I Seven Deadly Sins, The, *see* Five Plays in One, 1585.

II Seven Deadly Sins, The, *see* Three Plays in One, 1585.

Seven Dialogues (Sun and the Moon, *etc.*), *dialogues previously included in* Annals; *not dramatic.*

Seven Ladies, A Mask of, 1574.

Seven Sins, On the, 1536.

Seven Warriors, A Mask of, 1574.

Seven Wise Masters, The, 1600.

Several Affairs, The, 1658.

Several Wits: The Wise Wit, the Wild Wit, the Choleric Wit, the Humble Wit, 1658.

Sexton, The, or The Mock Testator, 1662.

Sforza, The Tragedy of Lodovick, 1628.

Sham Doctor, The, *see* Anatomist, The, 1696.

Sham Lawyer, The, or The Lucky Extravagant, 1697.

Shank's Ordinary, 1624.

She Gallants, The, 1695.

She Saint, The, 1614.

She Ventures and He Wins, 1695.

She Would if She Could, 1668.

She's Jealous of Herself, 1670.

Shearmen and Tailors' Pageant, *see* Coventry Plays, 14th cent.

Shepherd's Holiday, The, 1651.

Shepherd's Paradise, The, 1633.

Shepherd's Song, The, 1613.

Shepherds' Holiday, The, 1634.

Shepherds' Holiday, The, *see* Pan's Anniversary, 1620.

Shepherds' Mask, The, Supp. II, i.

Ship, The, 1611.

Ship of Fame, The, 1511.

Shipmen and Country Maids, A Mask of, 1559.

Shoemaker a Gentleman, A, 1608.

Shoemaker Returned to His Trade, The, *see* Hewson Reduced, 1661.

Shoemakers' Holiday, The, or The Gentle Craft, 1599.

Shore, The Book of [Jane], 1603.

Short and Sweet, 1579.

Shrewsbury Fragments, 14th cent.

Shrewsbury Plays, 15th cent. add.

Shuffling, Cutting, and Dealing in a Game of Picquet, 1659.

Sicelides, 1615.

Sicilian Usurper, The, *see* Richard II, The History of King, 1680.

Sicily and Naples, or The Fatal Union, 1640.

Siderothriambos, or Steel and Iron Triumphing, 1618.

Siege, The, 1629.

Siege, The, or Love's Convert, 1638.

Siege and Surrender of Mons, The, 1691.

Siege of Antwerp, The, *see* Larum for London, A, 1599.

Siege of Babylon, The, 1677.

Siege of Constantinople, The, 1674.

Siege of Croya, The, Supp. I.

Siege of Derry, The, 1692.

Siege of Dunkirk with Alleyn the Pirate, The, 1603.

Siege of Edinburgh Castle, The, 1571.

Siege of London, The, 1599 add.

Siege of Memphis, The, or The Ambitious Queen, 1676.

Siege of Namur, The, 1698.

I Siege of Rhodes, The, 1656.

II Siege of Rhodes, The, 1659.

Siege of Urbin, The, 1665.

Sight and Search, *see* Time's Triumph, 1643.

Sigibertus, Supp. II, l.

Sigward the Famous King of Norway, *see* Landgartha, 1683.

Silent Woman, The, *see* Epicoene, 1609.

Silvanus, 1597.

Silvanus, *see* Princely Pleasures at Kenilworth, The, 1575.

Somebody, Avarice, and Minister, 1550.

Somerset's Marriage, The Mask at the Earl of, 1613.

Somnium Fundatoris, *see* Christmas Prince, The 1608.

Son of Pope Alexander VI, *see* Caesar Borgia, 1679.

Sophister, The, 1631.

Sophomorus, 1620.

Sophompaneas, or Joseph, 1652.

Sophonisba, or Hannibal's Overthrow, 1675.

Sophonisba, The Tragedy of, *see* Wonder of Women, The, 1605.

Sophy, The, 1641.

Soul's Warfare, The, 1672.

Southampton Wedding Mask, The, 1566.

Spaniard's Night Walk, The, *see* Blurt Master Constable, 1601.

Spanish Bawd, The, 1631.

Spanish Comedy, *see* Don Horatio, 1599 add.

Spanish Contract, The, 1624.

Spanish Curate, The, 1622; *adapt.*, 1662.

Spanish Duke of Lerma, The, 1623.

Spanish Fig, The, 1602.

Spanish Friar, The, or The Double Discovery, 1680.

Spanish Gypsy, The, 1623.

Spanish Lovers, The, 1639.

Spanish Maze, The Tragedy of the, 1605.

Spanish Moor's Tragedy, The, 1600.

Spanish Preferment, Supp. II, m.

Spanish Purchase, The, Supp. II, g.

Spanish Revolution, The, *see* Rape Revenged, The, 1690.

Spanish Rogue, The, 1673.

Spanish Tragedy, The, 1587; *see also* Supp. II, k.

Spanish Tragedy [of Petrus Crudelis], A, 1636.

Spanish Viceroy, The, 1624.

Spanish Wives, The, 1696.

Sparagus Garden, The, 1635.

Spartan Ladies, The, 1634.

Spartan Lady, The, *see* Spartan Ladies, The, 1634.

Speech Made to His Excellency (Monk) . . . at Drapers' Hall, A, 1660, *previously included in Annals; not dramatic.*

Speech Made to His Excellency . . . at Fish-mongers' Hall, A, 1660, *see above.*

Speech Made to His Excellency . . . at Goldsmiths' Hall, A, 1660, *see above.*

Speech Made to His Excellency . . . at Skinners' Hall, A, 1660, *see above.*

Speech Made to the Lord General Monk at Cloth-workers' Hall, A, 1660, *see above.*

Speech to King James I at Berwick, 1603.

Spencers, The, 1599.

Spiteful Sister, The, 1667.

Spoiling of Lady Verity, The, *see* Somebody, Avarice, and Minister, 1550.

I Sport upon Sport, *see* I Wits, The, 1662.

II Sport upon Sport, *see* II Wits, The, 1673.

Spring's Glory, The, 1637.

Spurius, 1617.

Squire of Alsatia, The, 1688.

Squire Oldsapp, or The Night Adventurers, 1678.

Squire, Proteus, Amphitrite, and Thamesis, Dialogue between the, *see* Gesta Grayorum, 1594.

Squires, The Mask of, *see* Somerset's Marriage, The Mask at the Earl of, 1613.

Stallion, The, 1662.

Standing Mask, The, Supp. II, i.

Stanislaus Fuga Victor, *see* Fratrum Discordia Felix, Supp. II, l.

Staple of News, The, 1626.

Stark Flattery, *see* Sturgflaterey, 1598.

State Mountebank Administering Physic to a Sick Parliament, The, *see* Disease of the House, The, 1649.

State of Innocence and Fall of Man, The, 1677.

State of Ireland, The, 1553.

Steel and Iron Triumphing, *see* Siderothriambos, 1618.

Stella (Salisbury), 13th cent.

Stella, or Tres Reges (York), 13th cent.

Stella, or Tres Reges (Lincoln), 14th cent.

Stephen, The History of King, 1613.

Stepmother, The, 1663.

Stepmother's Tragedy, The, 1599.

Stirling Revels, *see* Three Christians, The, 1594.

Stock Jobbers, The, *see* Volunteers, The, 1692.

Stoicus Vapulans, 1618.

Stonehenge, 1635.

Stonyhurst Pageants, 1617.

Strange Discovery, The, 1640.

Strange Flattery, *see* Sturgflaterey, 1598.

Strange News out of Poland, 1600.

Strollers, The, 1698.

Strowd, Tom, *see* I, II, & III Blind Beggar of Bednal Green, The, 1600, 1601.

Strylius, 1553.

Stuart, The Marriage Entertainment for Lord James, 1562.

Stukeley, *see* Captain Thomas Stukeley, 1596.

Terentius Christianus, Supp. I.

Tereus and Progne, *see* Christmas Prince, The, 1607.

Tereus with a Pastoral, Supp. II, m.

Terminus et Non Terminus, 1586.

Tes Irenes Trophoea, or The Triumphs of Peace, 1620.

Testy Lord, The, 1662.

Tethys' Festival, or The Queen's Wake, 1610.

That Will Be Shall Be, 1596.

Theagenes and Chariclea, *see* Chariclea, 1572.

Theatre of Apollo, The, 1625.

Thebais (Browne), 1558.

Thebais (Forsett), 1581.

Thenot and Piers in Praise of Astraea, 1592.

Theobalds, The Entertainment at, 1603.

Theobalds, The Entertainment of the King and Queen at, 1607.

Theobalds, The Entertainment of the Two Kings at, *see* Entertainment of the Two Kings of Great Britain and Denmark, The, 1606.

Theobalds, Queen Elizabeth's Welcome at, 1591.

Theobalds, The Queen's Entertainment at, 1594.

Theoctistus sive Constans in Aula Virtus, 1624.

Theodosius, or The Force of Love, 1680.

Theomachia, 1618.

Thersites, A New Interlude Called, 1537.

Thibaldus sive Vindictae Ingenium, 1640.

Thierry and Theodoret, 1617.

This Gallant Cavaliero Dick Bowyer, *see* Trial of Chivalry, The, 1601.

Thomas Lord Cromwell, 1600.

Thomas Merry, 1599.

Thomas Morus, 1612.

Thomas of Woodstock, *see* I Richard II, 1592.

Thomas Randolph's Salting, 1627.

I Thomaso, or The Wanderer, 1654; *adapt.*, 1677.

II Thomaso, or The Wanderer, 1654; *adapt.*, 1681.

Thorney Abbey, or The London Maid, Supp. I.

Thracian Wonder, The, 1599.

Three (*or* Two) Brothers, The, 1602.

Three Christians, The, 1594.

Three Dorothies, The, or Jodelet Boxed, 1657.

Three Dukes of Dunstable, The, *see* Fool's Preferment, A, 1688.

Three Estates, Ane Pleasant Satire of the, 1540.

Three Kings of Cologne (Canterbury), 15th cent. add.

Three Kings of Cologne (Holbeach), 15th cent. add.

Three Kings of Cologne, *see* Shrewsbury Plays, 15th cent. add.

Three Ladies of London, The, 1581.

Three Laws of Nature, Moses, and Christ Corrupted by the Sodomites, Pharisees, and Papists, A Comedy Concerning, 1538.

Three London Prentices, The, *see* Four London Prentices, The, 1591.

Three Lords and Three Ladies of London, The, 1588.

Three Merry Boys, The, 1662.

Three Plays in One, 1585.

Three Sisters of Mantua, The, 1578.

Three Vices Overcome Truth and Chastity, The, *see* Satire of the Three Estates, 1540.

Thyestes, 1560.

Thyestes, 1680.

Thyestes, Supp. I.

Thyestes, *and* Mock Thyestes, 1674.

Thyrsander, 1663.

Thyrsis, *see* Novelty, The, 1697.

Tide Tarrieth No Man, The, 1576.

Tilbury, The Queen's Visit to, 1588.

Time, The Triumph of, *see* Four Plays or Moral Representations in One, 1612.

Time and the Almanac-Makers, *see* Presentation for the Prince on His Birthday, A, 1638.

Time Triumphant, *see* Welcome into England, The, 1603.

Time Triumphant, The, 1604.

Time Vindicated to Himself and to His Honours, 1623.

Time's Complaint, The Comedy of, *see* Christmas Prince, The, 1608.

Time's Trick upon the Cards, 1642.

Time's Triumph, 1643.

Time's Triumph and Fortus (i.e. Fortune's?), 1599 add.

Timoclea at the Siege of Thebes by Alexander, 1574.

Timoleon, or The Revolution, 1697.

Timon, 1586.

Timon of Athens, The Life of, 1607; *adapt.*, 1678.

Timon of Athens the Man-Hater, The History of, 1678.

Tinker of Totness, The, 1596.

'Tis Better Than It Was, 1664.

'Tis Good Sleeping in a Whole Skin, 1563.

'Tis No Deceit to Deceive the Deceiver, 1598.

'Tis Pity She's a Whore, 1632.

Triumph at Calais and Boulogne, The, 1532.

Triumph of All the Founders of Colleges in Oxford, The, *see* Christmas Prince, The, 1608.

Triumph of Amity, The, *see* Friendship, Prudence, and Might, 1522.

Triumph of Beauty, The, 1646.

Triumph of Death, The, *see* Four Plays or Moral Representations in One, 1612.

Triumph of Honour, The, *see* Four Plays or Moral Representations in One, 1612.

Triumph of Innocence, The, Supp. II, m.

Triumph of Love, The, *see* Four Plays or Moral Representations in One, 1612.

Triumph of Love and Beauty, The, 1514.

Triumph of Peace, The, 1634.

Triumph of Temperance, The, *see* Honourable Entertainments, 1621.

Triumph of the Cross, The, 1613.

Triumph of Time, The, *see* Four Plays or Moral Representations in One, 1612.

Triumphant Widow, The, or The Medley of Humours, 1674.

Triumphs of Ancient Drapery, The, *see* Metropolis Coronata, 1614.

Triumphs of Fame and Honour, The, 1634.

Triumphs of Gold, The, *see* Chryso-Thriambos, 1611.

Triumphs of Health and Prosperity, The, 1626.

Triumphs of Honour and Industry, The, 1617.

Triumphs of Honour and Virtue, The, 1622.

Triumphs of Integrity, The, 1623.

Triumphs of London, The, 1675.

Triumphs of London, The, 1678.

Triumphs of London, The, 1683.

Triumphs of London, The, 1691.

Triumphs of London, The, 1692.

Triumphs of London, The, 1693.

Triumphs of London, The, 1694.

Triumphs of London, The, 1695.

Triumphs of London, The, 1699.

Triumphs of London, The, 1700.

Triumphs of London Revived, *see* Glory's Resurrection, 1698.

Triumphs of Love and Antiquity, The, 1619.

Triumphs of Love and Innocence, The, 1688.

Triumphs of Old Drapery, The, *see* Himatia-Poleos, 1614.

Triumphs of Peace, The, *see* Tes Irenes Trophoea, 1620.

Triumphs of Reunited Britannia, The, 1605.

Triumphs of the Prince D'Amour, The, 1636.

Triumphs of Truth, The, 1613.

Triumphs of Virtue, The, 1697.

Triumvirate of Poets at Rehearsal, The, *see* Female Wits, The, 1697.

Troades, 1660.

Troades, or The Royal Captives, 1679.

Troas, 1559.

Troas, 1686.

Troia Nova Triumphans, 1612.

Troilus and Cressida (Chettle & Dekker), 1599.

Troilus and Cressida (Shakespeare), The Tragedy of, 1602; *adapt.*, 1679.

Troilus and Cressida (Anon.), Supp. I.

Troilus and Cressida, or Truth Found Too Late, 1679.

Troilus and Pander, The Story of, 1516.

Troilus ex Chaucero, *see* Troilus, from Chaucer, 1547.

Troilus, from Chaucer, 1547.

Troubles of Queen Elizabeth, The, *see* I If You Know Not Me, 1604.

Troubles of Great Hermenia, The, *see* Sophister, The, 1631.

Troublesome Reign and Lamentable Death of Edward II, King of England, with the Tragical Fall of Proud Mortimer, The, 1592.

I Troublesome Reign of King John, The, 1588.

II Troublesome Reign of King John, The, 1588.

Troy, 1596.

Troy's Revenge, with the Tragedy of Polyphemus, 1599.

True Coventry Plays, *see* Coventry Plays, 14th cent.

True Love's Mirror, *see* Astraea, 1651.

True Tragedy of Richard III, The, 1591.

True Tragedy of Richard Duke of York, The (i.e. II Contention betwixt the Two Famous Houses of York and Lancaster, The), *see* III Henry VI, 1591.

True Tragicomedy [of Robert Carr and Francis Howard], The, 1654.

True Trojans, The, *see* Fuimus Troes, 1625.

True Widow, A, 1678.

Truth, The Triumphs of, 1613.

Truth, Faithfulness, and Mercy, 1574.

Truth Found Too Late, *see* Troilus and Cressida, 1679.

Truth's Supplication to Candlelight, 1600.

Truth's Triumphs, 1635.

Try before You Trust, Supp. I.

Tryphon, 1668.

Tu Quoque, *see* Greene's Tu Quoque, 1611.

Tumblers, A Mask of, 1553.

Tunbridge Wells, or A Day's Courtship, 1678.

Turk, The, 1607.

Turk, The, Supp. II, k.

Turk's Too Good for [Him ?], A, 1619.

Turkish Mahomet and Hiren the Fair Greek, The, 1588.

Turks, A Mask of, 1559.

Turks Magistrates with Turks Archers, A Mask of, 1555.

Turmoils of Love, The, *see* Hypochondriac, The, Supp. I.

Turnholt, 1599.

Turnmill Street against Rosemary Lane, *see* New Brawl, The, 1654.

Twelfth Night, or What You Will, 1600.

Twelfth Night's Revels, The, *see* Blackness, The Mask of, 1605.

Twelve Labours of Hercules, The, 1570 add.

Twelve Months, The Mask of the, 1611.

Twins, The, 1635.

Twins' Tragedy, The, 1612.

I Two Angry Women of Abingdon, The, 1588.

II Two Angry Women of Abingdon, The, 1599.

Two Brothers, The, *see* Three Brothers, The, 1602.

Two Famous Pirates Ward and Dansiker, The Tragical Lives and Deaths of the, *see* Christian Turned Turk, A, 1610.

Two Fools Well Met, *see* Fortune Hunters, The, 1689.

Two Gentlemen of Verona, The, 1593; *see also* Supp. II, k.

Two Italian Gentlemen, *see* Fedele and Fortunio, 1584.

Two Kings in a Cottage, 1623.

Two Lamentable Tragedies, 1594.

Two Maids of More-Clacke, The, 1608.

Two Merry Milkmaids, The, or The Best Words Wear the Garland, 1619; *adapt.*, 1662.

Two Merry Women of Abingdon, 1599.

Two Noble Kinsmen, The, 1613; *adapt.*, 1664.

Two Noble Ladies and the Converted Conjurer, The, 1622.

Two Shapes, *see* Caesar's Fall, 1602.

Two Shepherds, A Dialogue between, 1580.

Two Sins of King David, The, 1562.

Two Socias, The, *see* Amphitryon, 1690.

Two Spanish Gentlemen, The, Supp. II, m.

Two Supposed Heads, The, *see* Necromantes, 1632.

U

Two the Most Faithfullest Friends, *see* Damon and Pithias, 1565.

Two Tragedies in One, *see* Two Lamentable Tragedies, 1594.

Two Wise Men and All the Rest Fools, 1619.

Tyrannic Love, or The Royal Martyr, 1669.

Tyrannical Government Anatomized, or A Discourse Concerning Evil Counsellors, 1643.

Tyrant, The, 1628.

Tyrant King of Crete, The, *an adaptation of H. Killigrew's* Pallantus and Eudora, *included in Sedley's* Works, 1722.

Tyrant of Sicily, The, *see* Richard II, The History of King, 1680.

Ultio Divina, *see* Leo Armenus, 1627.

Ulysses and Circe, 1615.

Ulysses Redux, 1592.

Unfaithful Wife, The, Supp. II, m.

Unfortunate Couple, The, *see* Novelty, The, 1697.

Unfortunate Fortunate, The, 1650.

Unfortunate General, The, 1603.

Unfortunate Kindness, The, *see* Unhappy Kindness, The, 1697.

Unfortunate Lovers, The, 1638.

Unfortunate Mother, The, 1639.

Unfortunate Piety, The, 1631.

Unfortunate Shepherd, The, 1685.

Unfortunate Usurper, The, 1663.

Ungrateful Favourite, The, 1664.

Unhappy Conqueror, The, *see* Neglected Virtue, 1696.

Unhappy Fair Irene, The Tragedy of the, 1658.

Unhappy Favourite, The, or The Earl of Essex, 1681.

Unhappy Kindness, The, or A Fruitless Revenge, 1697.

Unhappy Marriage, The, 1694.

Unhappy Marriage, The, *see* Orphan, The, 1680.

United Kingdoms, The, 1661.

Universal Motion, *see* Encyclochoria, 1663.

University Pedlar, The, *see* Conceited Pedlar, The, 1627.

Unjust Judge, *see* Appius and Virginia, 1669.

Unjust Usurped Primacy of the Bishop of Rome, A Tragedy or Dialogue of the, *previously included in* Annals; *not dramatic.*

Unnatural Brother, The, 1697.

Unnatural Combat, The, 1626.

Unnatural Mother, The, 1697.

Unnatural Tragedy, The, 1658.

Untrussing of the Humorous Poet, The, *see* Satiromastix, 1601.

I Upon Both Marriages of the King, 1537.

II Upon Both Marriages of the King, 1537.

Usurper, The, 1664.

Usurping Tyrant, The, *see* Second Maiden's Tragedy, The, 1611.

Usury Put to Use, *see* Devil of Dowgate, The, 1623.

Uther Pendragon, 1597.

Valentine and Orson (Anon.), 1595.

Valentine and Orson (Hathway & Munday), 1598.

Valentinian, 1614; *adapt.*, 1678, 1684.

Valentinian, 1684.

Valentinian, *see* Lucina's Rape, 1678.

Valentinian, or Rape's Revenge, Supp. II, m.

Valentinianus, Supp. II, l.

Valetudinarium, 1638.

Valiant Cid, The, *see* I Cid, The, 1637.

Valiant Scholar, The, 1622.

Valiant Scot, The, 1637.

Valiant Welshman, The, or The True Chronicle History of the Life and Valiant Deeds of Caradoc the Great, 1612.

Vallia (and Antony), *see* Antony and Vallia, 1599 add.

Valteger, *see* Vortigern, 1596.

Variety, The, 1641; *adapt.*, 1662.

Vayvode, 1598.

Venetian Comedy, The, 1594.

Venetian Senators, A Mask of, 1554.

Venice Preserved, or A Plot Discovered, 1682.

Venus and Adonis (Holland), 1656.

Venus and Adonis (Blow), 1682.

Venus and Adonis, or The Maid's Philosophy, 1653.

Venus and Mars, *see* Cupid, Venus, and Mars, 1553.

Venus, Cupid, Six Damsels, and Six Old Men, A Mask of, 1527.

Venus, the White Tragedy or the Green Knight (by Philips), *mentioned* 1599 *by Nashe in* Lenten Stuff, *and possibly a play or plays.*

Venuses with Cupids, A Mask of, 1554.

Verily, *see* Re Vera, 1599.

Versipellis, 1632.

Vertumnus, *see* Alba, 1605.

Vertumnus sive Annus Recurrens, 1605.

Very Good Wife, A, 1693.

Very Woman, A, or The Prince of Tarent, 1634.

Vestal, The, 1639.

Vestal Virgin, The, or The Roman Ladies, 1664.

Vice, A New Interlude of, 1567.

Vice Destroys Itself, *see* Amalasont Queen of the Goths, 1696.

Vices, The Mask of, Supp. II, i.

Victim, The, or Achilles and Iphigenia in Aulis, *see* Achilles, 1699.

Victoria, 1582.

Victorious Love, 1698.

Vienna Besieged, 1686.

Villain, The, 1662.

Vincentio and Margaret, *see* Gentleman Usher, The, 1602.

Vincentius et Anastasius, Supp. II, l.

Vindicta, *see* Adrastus Parentans, 1622.

Vindictae Ingenium, *see* Thibaldus, 1640.

Vintner Tricked, The, *see* Revenge, The, 1680.

Violence of Love, The, *see* Rival Sisters, The, 1695.

Viper and Her Brood, The, 1606.

Virgil's Eclogues, Supp. II, d.

Virgin Martyr, The, 1620; *see also* Supp. II, k.

Virgin Sacrifice, The, *see* Jephtha's Rash Vow, 1698.

Virgin Show, The, *see* Charity Triumphant, 1655.

Virgin Widow, The, 1641.

Virtue, 1515.

Virtue and Beauty Reconciled, *see* Fortunate Isles and Their Union, The, 1625.

Virtue and Delight, *listed by Hazlitt as an 'allegory' by John Bellenden*, 1536.

Virtue Betrayed, or Anna Bullen, 1682.

Virtue in Danger, *see* Relapse, The, 1696.

Virtue Rewarded, *see* Lover's Stratagem, The, Supp. I.

Virtue's Triumph, 1644.

Virtuoso, The, 1676.

Virtuous Octavia, The, 1598.

Virtuous and Godly Susanna, The Comedy of the Most, 1569.

Virtuous Wife, The, or Good Luck at Last, 1679.

Vision of Delight, The, 1617.

Vision of the Twelve Goddesses, The, 1604.

Visit of Henry VIII to Wolsey, The, 1527.

Visit to Richard II, The, 14th cent.

Visitatio Sepulchri (Winchester), 10th cent.

Visitatio Sepulchri (Lichfield), 12th cent.

Visitatio Sepulchri (Dublin), 14th cent.

Visitatio Sepulchri (Barking), 14th cent.

Visitatio Sepulchri, *see* Shrewsbury Fragments, 14th cent.

Visitatio Sepulchri, *see also* Quem Quaeritis.

Vitam D. Ioannis Baptistae, *see* John the Baptist, The Life of, 1536.

Vittoria Corombona, *see* White Devil, The, 1612.

Vitus sive Christiana Fortitudo, 1623.

Volpone, or The Fox, 1606.

Volunteers, The, or The Stock Jobbers, 1692.

Vortigern, 1596.

Votum, *see* Jephthes, 1542.

Vow and a Good One, A, 1623.

Vow Breaker, The, or The Fair Maid of Clifton, 1625.

Vulcan, 1528.

Wakefield Plays, 14th cent.

Walks of Islington and Hogsdon with the Humours of Wood-Street-Compter, The, 1641.

Wallenstein, *see* Albertus Wallenstein, 1634.

I Wanderer, The, *see* I Thomaso, 1654.

II Wanderer, The, *see* II Thomaso, 1654.

Wandering Jew, The, Supp. II, m.

Wandering Ladies, The, *see* Mulberry Garden, The, 1668.

Wandering Lover, The, 1658.

Wandering Lovers, The, 1623.

Wandering Lovers, The, or The Painter, *see* Dutch Painter and the French Branke, The, 1623.

Wandering Whores' Complaint, The, 1663.

Wanstead, The Entertainment of Her Majesty at, *see* Lady of May, The, 1578.

Wanton Wife, The, *see* Amorous Widow, The, 1670.

War Hath Made All Friends, *see* Edmond Ironside, 1595.

War of Grammar, The, 1666.

War without Blows and Love without Suit (*or* Strife), 1599.

Warbeck, *see* Perkin Warbeck.

Ward, The, 1637.

Ward and Dansiker, *see* Christian Turned Turk, A, 1610.

Warlamchester, 1599 add.

Warning for Fair Women, A, 1599.

Warriors, A Mask of, 1619.

Wars of Cyrus King of Persia against Antiochus King of Assyria, with the Tragical End of Panthaea, The, 1588.

Wars of Pompey and Caesar, The, *see* Caesar and Pompey, 1605.

Wary Widow, The, or Sir Noisy Parrot, 1693.

Wasp, The, 1630.

Water Nymph, The, *see* Honourable Entertainments, 1621.

Wavering Nymph, The, or Mad Amyntas, 1684.

Way of the World, The, 1700.

Way to Content All Women, The, or How a Man May Please His Wife, 1624.

Way to Life, The, 1556.

Way to Make a Knave Honest, A, Supp. II, m.

Way to Win and Tame a Shrew, A, *see* Mad Wooing, The, 1698.

Weakest Goeth to the Wall, The, 1600.

Wealth and Health, 1554.

Wealth Outwitted, *see* Money Is an Ass, 1635.

Weather, The Play of the, 1528.

Weavers' Pageant, *see* Coventry Plays, 14th cent.

Wedding, The, 1626.

Wedding Mask for Sir Philip Herbert, The, 1604.

Weeding of the Covent Garden, The, or The Middlesex Justice of Peace, 1632.

Welbeck, The King's Entertainment at, 1633.

Welcome for Emperor Charles V, The, 1522.

Welcome for James VI, The, 1579.

Welcome for Katherine of Aragon, The, 1502.

Welcome for Margaret of Anjou, The, 15th cent.

Welcome for Marie de Lorraine, The, 1538.

Welcome for Princess Margaret, The, 1503.

Welcome for Queen Anne, The, 1590.

Welcome for Queen Margaret, The, 1511.

Welcome for Queen Mary, The, 1561.

Welcome from the Isle of Ree, A, *see* In Duc Reducem.

Welcome into England, The, 1603.

Wells Plays, 14th cent.

Welsh Ambassador, The, or A Comedy in Disguises, 1623.

Welsh Traveller, The, 1622.

Welshman, The, 1599 add.

Welshman's Prize, The, *see* Famous Wars of Henry I and the Prince of Wales, The, 1598.

Westward Ho, 1604.

What Mischief Worketh in the Mind of Man, 1578.

What Will Be Shall Be, *see* That Will Be Shall Be, 1596.

What You Please, *see* Whisperer, The, 1641.

What You Will, 1601.

What You Will, *see* Twelfth Night, 1600.

Wheel of Fortune, The, *see* Fool's Expectation, The, 1698.

When You See Me You Know Me, 1604.

When Women Go to Law the Devil Is Full of Business, *see* Devil's Law Case, the, 1617.

Whibble, The, *see* Hengist King of Kent, 1618.

Which Is the Best Girl ?, *see* Politic Bankrupt, The, Supp. II, a.

Whimsies of Señor Hidalgo, The, or The Masculine Bride, Supp. I.

Whirligig, The, *see* Hengist King of Kent, 1618.

Whisperer, The, or What You Please, 1641.

White Devil, The, 1612.

White Ethiopian, The, 1650.

White Moor, The, 1629.

White Witch of Westminster, The, or Love in a Lunacy, Supp. II, m.

Whitsun Plays, *see* Chester Plays, 14th cent., *and* Norwich Plays, 15th cent.

Who Would Have Thought It, *see* Law Tricks, 1604.

Whole Contention, The, *see* II & III Henry VI, 1591.

Whore in Grain, The, 1624.

Whore New Vamped, The, 1639.

Whore of Babylon, The, 1606.

Whore of Babylon, The, *see* De Meretrice Babylonica, 1548.

Whore of Babylon, the Devil and the Pope, The, 1685.

Widkirk Plays, *see* Wakefield Plays, 14th cent.

Widow (Middleton), The, 1616.

Widow (Boyle ?), The, 1665.

Widow Captain, The, Supp. II, m.

Widow of Watling Street, The, *see* Puritan, The, 1606.

Widow Ranter, The, or The History of Bacon in Virginia, 1689.

Widow's Apron Strings, The, *see* Histriomastix, 1599.

Widow's Charm, The, 1602.

Widow's Prize, The, or The Woman Captain, 1625.

Widow's Tears, The, 1605.

Wife for a Month, A, 1624; *see also* Unhappy Kindness, The, 1697.

Wife for Any Man, A, 1696.

Wild Gallant, The, 1663.

Wild Goose Chase, The, 1621.

Wild Goose Chase, The, *see* Hengist King of Kent, 1618.

Wild Knight and the Black Lady, The Joust of the, 1507.

Wild Men, *see* Place Perilous, The, 1515.

Will of a Woman, The, *an error for* Ill of a Woman, The; *see* Fount(ain) of New Fashions, The, 1598.

William Cartwright, 1602.

William Longbeard, 1599.

William Longsword, *see* William Longbeard, 1599.

William the Conqueror, 1599 add.

Wiltshire Tom, 1673.

Wily Beguiled, 1602.

Win Her and Take Her, or Old Fools Will Be Meddling, 1691.

Winchester, Prince Henry's Welcome to, 1603.

Winchester Troper, *see* Quem Quaeritis, 10th cent.

Windsor, A Mumming at, 15th cent.

Wine, Beer, Ale, and Tobacco Contending for Superiority, *see* Wine, Beer, and Ale Together by the Ears, 1625.

Wine, Beer, and Ale Together by the Ears, 1625.

Winter's Tale, The, 1610; *see also* Supp. II, k.

Wisdom of Doctor Dodypoll, The, 1599.

Wisdom That Is Christ, The, *see* Mind, Will, and Understanding, 15th cent.

Wise and Foolish Virgins, A Mask of, 1561.

Wise Man of West Chester, The, 1594.

Wise Woman of Hogsdon, The, 1604.

Wit à la Mode, 1672.

Wit above Crowns, *see* Love's Martyr, 1685.

Wit and Folly, *see* Witty and Witless, 1533.

Wit and Science, 1539.

Wit and Science, *see* Marriage of Wit and Science, The, 1568.

Wit and Will, 1568.

Wit and Wisdom, *see* Marriage between Wit and Wisdom, A Contract of a, 1579.

Wit at Several Weapons, 1609.

Wit for Money, or Poet Stutter, 1691.

Wit in a Constable, 1638.

Wit in a Madness, 1637.

Wit of a Woman, The, 1604.

Wit without Money, 1614.

Wit's Triumvirate, or The Philosopher, 1635.

Witch, The, 1615.

Witch of Edmonton, The, 1621.

Witch of Islington, The, 1599 add.

Witch Traveller, The, *an error for* Welsh Traveller, The, 1622.

Wits, The, 1634.

I Wits, The, or Sport upon Sport, 1662.

II Wits, The, or Sport upon Sport, 1673.

Wits Led by the Nose, or A Poet's Revenge, 1677.

Wits' Cabal, The, 1658.

Witten, A Mask at, 1640.

Witty and Witless, 1533.

Witty Combat, A, or The Female Victor, 1663.

Xerxes, 1699.
Xerxes, King, 1575.

Year's Funeral, The, *see* Honourable Entertainments, 1621.
York House, The Mask at, 1623.
York House Mask, Supp. II, i.
York Plays, 14th cent.; *see also* Wakefield Plays, 14th cent.
Yorkshire Gentleman, The, Supp. II, h.
Yorkshire Gentlewoman and Her Son, A, 1613.
Yorkshire Tragedy, A, 1606.
Young Admiral, The, 1633.
Young King, The, or The Mistake, 1679.
Young Moors, A Mask of, 1548.
Younger Brother, The, 1617.
Younger Brother, The, or Male Courtesan, Supp. II, m.

Younger Brother, The, or The Amorous Jilt, 1696.
Your Five Gallants, 1605.
Youth, The Interlude of, 1520.
Youth's Comedy, or The Soul's Trials and Triumph, *previously included in* Annals; *not dramatic.*
Youth's Glory and Death's Banquet, 1658.
Youth's Tragedy, 1671.
Yuletide, *see* Christmas Prince, The, 1608.

Zabeta, *see* Princely Pleasures at Kenilworth, The, 1575.
Zelmane, or The Corinthian Queen, 1692.
Zelotypus, 1606.
Zeno sive Ambitio Infelix, 1631; *adapt.*, 1669.
Zenobia, 1599 add.
Zoroastres, 1676.
Zulziman, *see* Soliman and Perseda, 1590.

6 · INDEX OF FOREIGN PLAYWRIGHTS

(The intention here is to list only those foreign playwrights one or more of whose plays were translated or frankly adapted by English playwrights, and to exclude those whose plays simply furnished an occasional scene or a 'source'. The distinction may not be consistently maintained, because it is not always maintained by my authorities.)

GREEK

Aeschylus (525–456 B.C.), 1663.

Aristophanes (c. 444–c. 380 B.C.), 1627, 1655, 1659.

Euripides (480–406 B.C.), 1543(2), 1550, 1558, 1579, 1602, Supp. I.

Sophocles (495–406 B.C.), 1543, 1564, 1581, 1649.

LATIN

Plautus, Titus Maccius (c. 254–184 B.C.), 1555, 1577, 1592, 1604, 1665, 1694, Supp. I.

Seneca, Lucius Annaeus (4 B.C. ?–A.D. 65), 1558, 1559, 1560, 1561, 1563, 1566, 1567, 1581, 1648, 1651, 1660, 1674, 1679, 1686, 1700, Supp. I.

Terentius Afer, Publius (c. 190–159 B.C.), 1520, 1588(2), 1598, 1613, 1627(2), 1663, 1674, 1687, 1694, Supp. I.

NEO-LATIN

Birck, Sixt, or Xystus Betulius (1501–1554), 1560, 1566.

Corraro, Gregorio (1411–1464), 1566.

De Groot, Hugo, or Hugo Grotius (1583–1645), 1640, 1652.

Kirchmayer, Thomas, or Naogeorgus (1511–1578), 1538.

Schoepper, Jacob (c. 1514–1554), 1547.

Tissier de Ravisy, Jean, or J. Ravisius Textor (c. 1480–1524), 1530, 1537.

Van Langeveldt, George, or Macropedius (c. 1475–1558), 1550.

Van Schoon, Cornelius, or C. Schonaeus (c. 1540–1611), 1595, Supp. I.

Volder, Wilhelm de, or Gnaphaeus, or Fullonius 1493–1568), 1540.

ITALIAN

Ariosto, Lodovico (1474–1533), 1566.

Bassano, Francesco Negri di (1500–c. 1560), 1550, 1568, 1635.

Bonarelli della Rovere, Guido (1563–1608), 1613, 1630, 1657.

Dolce, Lodovico (1508–1568), 1566.

Grazzini, Antonfrancesco, or Il Lasca (1503–1583), 1564.

Groto, Luigi, or Il Cieco d'Adria (1541–1585), 1592, 1626.

Guarini, Giovanni Battista (1537–1612), 1601, 1604, 1630, 1635, 1647, 1676.

Pasqualigo, Luigi (fl. 1563–1581), 1582, 1584.

Porta, Giovanni Battista della (1538–1615), 1599, 1603, 1615.

Salviati, Leonardo (1540–1589), 1612.

Secchi, Niccolò (fl. c. 1549), 1659.

Tasso, Torquato (1544–1595), 1591, 1628, 1635, 1660, 1698.

SPANISH

Calderón de la Barca, Pedro (1600–1681), 1663, 1664(2).

Coello y Ochoa, Antonio (1611–1652), 1663.

Mendoza, Antonio Hurtado de (c. 1590–1644), 1654.

Moreto y Cabaña, Agustin (c. 1600–1669), 1667.

Rojas de Montalvan, Fernando (15th cent.), 1527, 1580, 1598, 1631.

FRENCH

Beza, Theodore (1519–1605), 1575.

Boisrobert, François le Metel de (1592–1662), 1651.

Bueil, Honorat de, Seigneur de Racan (1589–1670), 1626.

Corneille, Pierre (1606–1684), 1637, 1655, 1656, 1661, 1663(2), 1664(2), 1668, 1670, 1684, 1691, Supp. I, Supp. II, h.

Corneille, Thomas (1625–1709), 1654, 1664(2), 1665, 1668.

Dancourt, Florent Carton (1661–1725), 1698, 1700.

Desfontaines, — (*fl.* 1637–1647), 1638.
Estienne, Charles (1504 or 1505–1564), 1595.
Garnier, Robert (1534–1590), 1590, 1594(2).
Molière, or Jean Baptiste Poquelin (1622–1673), 1663, 1667(3), 1669(2), 1670(3), 1672, 1677, 1693, 1700, Supp. I.
Quinault, Philippe (1635–1688), 1659, 1660, 1667, 1669, 1698.

Racine, Jean (1639–1699), 1674, 1677.
Scarron, Paul (1610–1660), 1657(2), 1668, 1669.

DUTCH
Dorlant, Peter, or Peter Dorlandus (1454–1507), 1495.

LOW-GERMAN
Niclaes, Heinrich (*c.* 1502–a. 1565), 1574.

(See note to preceding index.)

Maison rustique, La, 1698.
Malade imaginaire, Le, 1700, Supp. I.
Marc-Antoine, 1590.
Medea (Euripides), 1543, 1602, Supp. I.
Medea (Seneca), 1566, 1648, Supp. I.
Médecin malgré lui, Le, 1667, 1669.
Mejor está que estaba, 1664.
Menaechmi, 1577, 1592, Supp. I.
Menteur, Le, 1661, 1684.
Mercator, Supp. I.
Miles Gloriosus, Supp. I.
Mostellaria, Supp. I.

Naamen, Supp. I.
Nehemiah, Supp. I.
Nicomède, 1670.
No puede ser guarda una mujer, 1667.
No siempre lo peor es cierto, 1663.

Octavia, 1566.
Oedipus, 1563, Supp. I.
Oresteia, 1663.

Pammachius, 1538.
Pastor fido, Il, 1601, 1604, 1630, 1635, 1647, 1676.
Pentimento amoroso, Il, 1626.
Peor está que estaba, 1664.
Persians, The, 1663.
Phaedra, *see* Hippolytus.
Phaeton, 1698.
Philoctetes, 1543.
Phoenissae, *see* Thebais.
Phormio, 1598, 1663, 1674, 1694.
Plutus, 1627, 1659.
Polyeucte, 1655.

Pompée, La Mort de, 1663(2).
Porcie, 1594.
Précieuses ridicules, Les, 1667.
Progne, 1566.
Prometheus Bound, 1663.
Pseudolus, Supp. I.
Pyrandre et Lisimène, 1651.

Querer por solo querer, 1654.

Rare en tout, 1677.
Rebelles, 1550.
Rudens, 1694.

Sacrifice, Le, *see* Abusez, Les, 1595.
Sacrifice d'Abraham, 1575.
Sapientia Salomonis, 1560, 1566.
Saul, Supp. I.
Seven against Thebes, 1663.
Sganarelle, 1663.
Sophomphaneas, 1652.
Spiritata, La, 1564.
Suppliants, The, 1663.
Suppositi, I, 1566.

Tartuffe, 1669, 1670.
Terentius Christianus, Supp. I.
Thebais, 1558, 1581.
Thersites, 1537.
Thyestes, 1560, 1674, Supp. I.
Tobit, Supp. I.
Troades, 1559, 1660, 1679, 1686.
Trois Dorotées, Les, ou le jodelet souffleté, 1657.

Vraie suite du Cid, La, 1638.

8 · INDEX OF DRAMATIC COMPANIES

(Companies whose repertories are wholly unknown or include no new play are omitted from this index. Such companies, all minor ones and for the most part purely provincial, are treated in John Tucker Murray, *English Dramatic Companies*, 2 vols., 1910. See also G. E. Bentley, *Jacobean and Caroline Stage* (1941), I, 260–9, for an account of the King and Queen of Bohemia's Company, not previously recognized; the repertory of this company, which was active between 1626 and 1631, and which probably played at the Fortune Theatre, is wholly unknown. For the English actors in Germany, see Supplementary List II, k.)

ADMIRAL'S MEN, 1587–1589, 1592, 1594–1599, 1599 add., 1600–1603
  Active: 1585–1603, and one of the two leading companies 1594–1603. *Patron:* Charles Howard, 2nd Baron Howard of Effingham, Earl of Nottingham, Lord High Admiral (1536–1624). *Principal Actor:* Edward Alleyn (1566–1626). *Landlord and Financier:* Philip Henslowe (d. 1616). *Theatres:* the Theatre, 1590–1591; Newington Butts, *c.* 1591 (?); Rose, 1594–1600; Fortune, 1600–1603. Continued after 1603 as Prince Henry's Men.

BATH'S MEN, 1578
  Active: 1542–1579 intermittently. *Patrons:* John and William Bourchier, Earls of Bath. A provincial company.

BEESTON'S BOYS, 1637–1641
  Active: 1637–1642. *Patrons:* Charles I and Henrietta Maria. *Managers:* Christopher and (afterwards) William Beeston, 1637–1640; William Davenant, 1640–1641; William Beeston, 1641–1642. *Theatre:* Cockpit. A troupe of boy actors (with several adults) otherwise called the King and Queen's Young Company.

BERKELEY'S MEN, 1578
  Active: 1578–1610 intermittently. *Patron:* Henry Fitzharding Berkeley, Baron Berkeley (d. 1611). A provincial company.

BETTERTON'S COMPANY, 1695–1700
  Active: 1695–a. 1700. *Manager:* Thomas Betterton. *Theatre:* Lisle's Tennis Court in Lincoln's Inn Fields. A company formed of the actors who seceded from the United Company.

CHAMBERLAIN'S MEN, 1582 (as Hunsdon's), 1589, 1594(?), 1595–1599, 1599 add., 1600–1602
  Active: 1564–1590 chiefly in provinces as Lord Hunsdon's Men; 1594–1603 newly organized and one of the chief London companies. *Patrons:* Henry Carey, 1st Lord Hunsdon, Lord Chamberlain (d. 1596); George Carey, 2nd Lord Hunsdon, Lord Chamberlain (1547–1603). *Chief Playwright:* William Shakespeare. *Chief Actor:* Richard Burbage (d. 1619). *Theatres:* Newington Butts, 1594; the Theatre, 1594–*c.* 1597; Curtain, 1597–1599; Globe, 1599–1603. Continued after 1603 as King's Men.

CHAPEL ROYAL (Gentlemen of the Chapel) 1547, 1553, (Chapel Boys) 1514, 1516, 1560, 1565, 1567, 1568, 1572, 1577, 1579, 1581, 1582, 1587, 1601, 1602, (Oxford's Boys) 1584
  Active: b. 1501–1603 intermittently, the gentlemen and choir boys of the royal establishment of the chapel together before 1553, the boys alone under various masters after 1553. *Theatres:* 1st Blackfriars, 1577–1580 (with Windsor Boys); 1st Blackfriars, 1583–1584 (with Windsor

and Paul's Boys under the name of 'Oxford's Boys'); 2nd Blackfriars, 1600–1603. Continued after 1603 as Queen's Revels.

CLINTON'S MEN, 1574

Active: 1566–1577, and as a provincial company 1599–1609 intermittently. *Patrons:* Edward Fiennes de Clinton, 1st Earl of Lincoln (d. 1585); Henry Fiennes de Clinton, 2nd Earl of Lincoln (d. 1616).

COURT INTERLUDERS, 1514, 1552, 1599

Active: b. 1493–1559, and thereafter intermittently in the provinces until 1573. An adult company forming before *c.* 1559 a part of the royal household.

I DERBY'S MEN, 1580, 1582

Active: 1563–1570 in provinces as Strange's Men; 1574–1582 in London and provinces. *Patron:* Henry Stanley, 4th Earl of Derby, Lord Strange (d. 1593).

II DERBY'S MEN, 1593, 1599, 1601

Active: 1594–1618 chiefly in the provinces. *Patron:* William Stanley, 6th Earl of Derby, Lord Strange (d. 1642).

DUDLEY'S MEN, *see* LEICESTER'S MEN

DUKE'S MEN, 1661–1665, 1667–1682

Active: 1660–1682. *Patron:* James, Duke of York, afterwards King James II. *Managers:* Sir William Davenant, Lady Mary Davenant, Charles Davenant (with aid of Thomas Betterton). *Theatres:* Cockpit, 1660 (during temporary amalgamation with King's Men); Salisbury Court, 1660–1661; Lisle's Tennis Court in Lincoln's Inn Fields, 1661–1671; Dorset Garden, 1671–1682. After 1682 merged with King's Men to form United Company.

ELECTOR PALATINE'S MEN, *see* PALSGRAVE'S MEN

ETON BOYS, 1537, 1539

Students of The King's College of Our Lady of Eton beside Windsor. There are records of isolated performances under Udall before Cromwell, 1538–1539, and at Court, 1573.

HOWARD'S MEN, 1576–1578

Active: 1576–1579. *Patron:* Charles Howard, 2nd Baron Howard of Effingham, later Earl of Nottingham and Lord High Admiral, patron of Admiral's Men.

HUNSDON'S MEN, *see* CHAMBERLAIN'S MEN

KING AND QUEEN'S YOUNG COMPANY, *see* BEESTON'S BOYS

I KING'S MEN, 1603–1642

Active: 1603–1642. *Patrons:* King James I (d. 1625), King Charles I (d. 1649). *Theatres:* Globe, 1603–1642; 2nd Blackfriars, 1608–1642. Company a continuation of Chamberlain's Men.

II KING'S MEN, 1661–1665, 1667–1682

Active: 1660–1682. *Patron:* King Charles II. *Manager:* Thomas Killigrew. *Theatres:* Cockpit, 1660 (during temporary amalgamation with Duke's Men); Red Bull, 1660; Gibbon's Tennis Court, 1660–1663; Theatre Royal in Bridges Street, 1663–1672; Lisle's Tennis Court in

Lincoln's Inn Fields, *c.* 1672–1673; Theatre Royal in Drury Lane, 1674–1682. After 1682 merged with Duke's Men to form United Company.

KING'S REVELS (Boys), 1607, 1608; *see also* 1602
  Active: c. 1607–1608. *Manager:* Martin Slater. *Theatre:* Whitefriars, 1608.

KING'S REVELS (Men), 1630–1636
  Active: 1629–1637. *Patron:* King Charles I. *Theatres:* Salisbury Court, 1629–1631; Fortune, 1631–1634(?); Salisbury Court, 1634–1636. Merged into Queen's Company, 1637.

LADY ELIZABETH'S MEN, 1611–1615, 1622–1625
  Active: 1611–1616 in London, and 1616–1622 in provinces; reorganized 1622, active in London 1622–1625. The company was revived in 1628 as the Queen of Bohemia's Players, and in existence until *c.* 1641. *Patron:* Lady Elizabeth, daughter of King James I and afterwards Queen of Bohemia (1596–1662). *Theatres:* Whitefriars, 1613–1614; Hope, 1614–1615; Porter's Hall, 1615(?) (in combination with Prince's Men and Queen's Revels?); Swan, 1611–*c.* 1615; Cockpit, 1622–1625.

LANE'S MEN, 1571, 1572
  Active: 1570–1572. *Patron:* Sir Robert Lane (born *c.* 1528).

LEICESTER'S MEN, 1573, 1574, 1576–1580, 1583
  Active: c. 1559–1588. *Patron:* Robert Dudley, Earl of Leicester (*c.* 1532–1588). *Theatre:* the Theatre, 1576–1583.

LINCOLN'S MEN, *see* CLINTON'S MEN

MERCHANT TAYLORS BOYS, 1574, 1583
  Students of the Merchant Taylors Grammar School (founded 1561) performed occasionally at Court under the first headmaster, Richard Mulcaster, who resigned 1586.

NURSERY COMPANY, 1669
  Active: c. 1661–1682(?). *Manager:* George Jolly and others. *Theatres:* see under Nursery Theatres in List of Theatres. A company of young actors in training maintained by the King's Men and the Duke's Men as a subsidiary, and permitted to give public performances.

I & II OGILBY'S COMPANY, DUBLIN, 1638–1640, 1662, 1663, 1669, 1670, 1700
  Active: 1637–1641 under sponsorship of the Earl of Strafford, reorganized 1661 and active thereafter. *Manager:* John Ogilby, 1637–1641, 1661–1676, succeeded by Joseph Ashbury, who had long acted as his deputy. *Theatres:* Werburgh Street, 1637–1641; Smock Alley, 1662–a. 1700.

OPERA COMPANY, 1656, 1658, 1659
  Active: 1656–*c.* 1659. *Manager:* Sir William Davenant. *Theatres:* Rutland House, 1656–1658; Cockpit, 1658–1659; and possibly others.

OXFORD'S BOYS, 1584
  Active: c. 1583–1584. *Patron:* Edward de Vere, 17th Earl of Oxford (1550–1604). *Managers:* Henry Evans and John Lyly(?). *Theatre:* 1st Blackfriars. Probably a temporary amalgamation of Paul's, Chapel, and Windsor Boys.

OXFORD'S MEN, 1600, 1601

Active: 1547–1563 intermittently in provinces; 1580–1602 intermittently in London and provinces. *Patrons:* John de Vere, 15th Earl of Oxford (d. 1562), Edward de Vere, 17th Earl of Oxford (d. 1604). *Theatre:* Boar's Head, 1602.

PALSGRAVE'S MEN, 1623, 1624

Active: 1613–1625. *Patron:* Frederick, Count Palatine of the Rhine, afterwards King of Bohemia (1596–1632). *Theatre:* Fortune, 1613–1621, 1623–1625. This company, otherwise called Palatine's Men, was a continuation of Prince Henry's Men. Remnants of it joined the King and Queen of Bohemia's Company in 1626.

PATENT COMPANY, 1695–1700

Active: 1695–a. 1700. *Patrons:* the company held both patents, King's and Duke's, and was nominally under the patronage of the royal household. *Manager:* Christopher Rich. *Theatres:* Theatre Royal in Drury Lane and, occasionally, Dorset Garden. The remnants of United Company after Betterton seceded.

PAUL'S BOYS, 1527, 1528, 1539, 1560, 1571, 1573, 1577, 1579–1581, 1584 (as Oxford's Boys, with Windsor and Chapel Boys), 1588–1590, 1599–1606

Active: b. 1500–1606. Boys of the song school and, occasionally, of the grammar school of St Paul's Cathedral, London, performed plays intermittently; notably under the master of the grammar school John Ritwise, 1522–1532, and the following masters of the song school: John Redford, c. 1539–1540; Sebastian Westcott, b. 1577–1582; Thomas Giles, 1584–b. 1590; Edward Pearce, c. 1599–c. 1606; and with Windsor and Chapel Boys as Oxford's Boys, 1584. *Theatres:* 1st Blackfriars, 1583–1584; otherwise their own song school near St Paul's.

PEMBROKE'S MEN, 1592–1594, 1597, 1599 add.

Active: c. 1592–1600. *Patron:* Henry Herbert, 1st Earl of Pembroke (d. 1601). *Theatre:* Swan, 1597.

PRINCE CHARLES'S MEN, 1631, 1633–1635, 1639, 1642

Active: 1631–1642. *Patron:* Prince Charles, afterwards King Charles II. *Theatres:* Salisbury Court, 1631–b. 1634; Red Bull, 1634–1640; Fortune, 1640–1642.

PRINCE HENRY'S MEN, 1604–1606, 1608, 1611

Active: 1603–1612. *Patron:* Henry, Prince of Wales (1594–1612). *Theatre:* Fortune, 1603–1612. A continuation of Admiral's Men. Continued as Palsgrave's Men.

PRINCE'S MEN, 1612, 1613, 1617, 1619, 1620, 1621, 1623–1625

Active: 1608–1625, at first in provinces as Duke of York's Men. *Patron:* Charles, Duke of York, who became Prince of Wales at his elder brother Henry's death in 1612; afterwards King Charles I. *Theatres:* Porter's Hall, 1615(?) (with Lady Elizabeth's Men and Queen's Revels?); Hope, 1615–1617; Red Bull, 1617–1619(?); Cockpit, 1619–1622; Curtain, 1622–1623; Red Bull, 1623–1625.

QUEEN ANNE'S MEN, 1604, 1605, 1607–1612, 1615–1618

Active: 1603–1619, and its provincial subsidiary until 1625. *Patron:* Queen Anne, Consort of King James I (1574–1619). *Theatres:* Boar's Head, 1603–1606; Curtain, 1603–c. 1606; Red Bull, c. 1606–1617; Cockpit, 1617–1619. A continuation of Worcester's Men. Continued after 1619 as Red Bull (Revels) Company in London and as Late Queen's Men in provinces.

QUEEN HENRIETTA'S MEN, 1625–1629, 1631–1636; *see also* 1612, 1621, 1630
Active: 1625–1636. *Patron:* Queen Henrietta Maria. *Manager:* Christopher Beeston. *Theatre:* Cockpit, 1625–1636.

QUEEN OF BOHEMIA'S COMPANY, *see* LADY ELIZABETH'S MEN

QUEEN'S MEN, 1546
Various provincial companies so-called were active 1509–1582.

QUEEN'S MEN, 1584–1586, 1588, 1590–1592, 1595, 1599 add.
Active: 1583–1594. *Patron:* Queen Elizabeth. *Chief Actor:* Richard Tarlton (d. 1588). *Theatres:* Bull Inn and Bell Inn, 1583 and perhaps until 1588; Bel Savage Inn, 1588; the Theatre, 1583–1591; Curtain, 1585–1592(?); Rose, 1594. The chief company before the rise of the Admiral's Men and the Chamberlain's Men.

QUEEN'S MEN, 1637–1639
Active: 1637–1642. *Patron:* Queen Henrietta Maria. (For her first company, see above.) *Manager:* Richard Heton. *Theatre:* Salisbury Court, 1637–1642.

QUEEN'S REVELS, 1604–1611, 1613
Active: 1604–*c.* 1615. *Patron:* Queen Anne. *Theatres:* 2nd Blackfriars, 1604–1608; Whitefriars, 1609–1613; Porter's Hall, 1615(?). A boys' company, formerly the Chapel Royal, otherwise known as Blackfriars or Whitefriars Children, or simply Revels Company. Probably merged with Lady Elizabeth's Men in 1615.

RED BULL (REVELS) COMPANY, 1619–1622
Active: 1619–*c.* 1623. *Theatre:* Red Bull, 1619–1623. A remnant of Queen Anne's Men which continued active after the death of their patron in 1619 and later recruited boys.

RED BULL COMPANY, 1638, 1639, 1641
Active: c. 1626–*c.* 1642. *Theatres:* Red Bull, 1625–1634; Fortune, 1634–1640; Red Bull, 1640–1642. A troupe probably formed of the remnant of the Prince's Men, joined to a provincial King's company.

RHODES'S COMPANY, 1659
A company of 'young actors', under the direction of John Rhodes, active at the Cockpit Theatre in 1659–1660.

RICH'S MEN, 1567
Active: 1564–1570. *Patrons:* Richard, 1st Baron Rich (d. 1567); Robert, 2nd Baron Rich (d. 1581).

SALISBURY COURT COMPANY, 1660
A company of unknown personnel occupying Salisbury Court Theatre for a few months in 1660.

SHEFFIELD'S MEN, 1578
Active: 1578–1586. *Patron:* Edmund, Baron Sheffield. A provincial company.

STRANGE'S MEN, 1587–1593, 1599 add.
Active: 1577(?)–1594. *Patron:* Ferdinando Stanley, Lord Strange, 5th Earl of Derby (d. 1594). *Theatres:* Cross Keys Inn, 1589 and 1594, and perhaps in the interim as a winter house; the

Theatre, 1590–1591; Rose, 1592–1593; Newington Butts, 1594. This company is conjectured to have amalgamated with Admiral's intermittently *c.* 1588–1594, and thereafter to have split up into sections merging with Admiral's, Chamberlain's, and II Derby's.

SUSSEX'S MEN, 1574, 1576–1580, 1590, 1594, 1599 add.

Active: c. 1569–1594 intermittently; 1602–1618 intermittently in provinces. *Patrons:* Thomas Radcliffe, 3rd Earl of Sussex (d. 1583); Henry Radcliffe, 4th Earl of Sussex (d. 1593); Robert Radcliffe, 5th Earl of Sussex (d. 1629). *Theatre:* Rose, 1593–1594.

UNITED COMPANY, 1683–1694

Active: 1682–1695. *Patron:* Held both royal patents. *Manager:* Thomas Betterton, until supplanted by Christopher Rich. *Theatres:* Theatre Royal in Drury Lane, and, occasionally, Dorset Garden, 1682–1695.

WARWICK'S MEN, 1576–1580

Active: 1559–1565, 1575–1580, 1592(?). *Patron:* Ambrose Dudley, Earl of Warwick (d. 1590). *Theatre:* the Theatre, 1576–1580. Company transferred its service to Oxford in 1580.

WESTMINSTER BOYS, 1564, 1566, 1572, 1574

The students of the grammar school of the Abbey of Westminster acted plays in early Tudor times, and later performed occasionally before Queen Elizabeth.

WINDSOR BOYS, 1572, 1574, 1575, 1577

Choir boys of the Chapel Royal of Windsor acted plays at Court 1567–1577 under the mastership of Richard Farrant (master, 1564–1580), and perhaps thereafter in combination with Chapel Royal Boys until 1580. May have formed part of the union of boys known as Oxford's Boys in 1584. *Theatre:* 1st Blackfriars, 1577–1580, 1583–1584(?).

WORCESTER'S MEN, 1602, 1603

Active: 1555–1585 intermittently in provinces; 1590–1603 intermittently in provinces and London. *Patrons:* William Somerset, 3rd Earl of Worcester (d. 1589); Edward Somerset, 4th Earl of Worcester (d. 1628). *Theatres:* Boar's Head, 1602; Rose, 1602–1603. Continued after 1603 as Queen Anne's Men.

9 · LIST OF THEATRES

(The theatres mentioned in the preceding index are here listed in the order of their appearance; the list includes all the houses where plays are known to have been professionally presented before 1700.)

BOAR'S HEAD INN

An inn in Aldgate where a play was suppressed in 1557. Probably distinct from the Boar's Head Inn or Theatre listed below.

RED LION INN

An inn in the parish of Stepney (eastern suburbs) where a play (*Samson*) was performed in 1567.

BULL INN

An inn on Bishopsgate Street, London, probably altered for theatrical purposes. It was used for plays from before 1575 until after 1594. The Queen's Men acted here in 1583 and perhaps until 1588.

BELL INN

An inn in Gracious (Gracechurch) Street, London, probably altered for theatrical purposes. It was used for plays from before 1576 until after 1583. The Queen's Men acted here in 1583 and perhaps later.

BEL SAVAGE INN

An inn in Ludgate Hill, probably altered for theatrical purposes. It was used for plays from before 1576 until after 1588. It was occupied by the Queen's Men in 1588.

CROSS KEYS INN

An inn in Gracious (Gracechurch) Street, London, probably altered for theatrical purposes. It was used as a playhouse from before 1579 until some time before 1596. Strange's Men performed here in 1589 and 1594, and perhaps in the interim during the winter seasons.

THEATRE

The first regular theatre. It was built in 1576 in St Leonard's Parish, Shoreditch (northern suburbs), by James Burbage. A circular,* open-air theatre of unknown size, it was occupied by Leicester's Men, Warwick's Men, and others before 1583; by Queen's Men and others, 1583–1591; by Strange's and Admiral's Men, 1590–1591; by Chamberlain's Men, 1594–c. 1597. In 1598–1599 the structure was torn down, and the timbers used in the building of the Globe.

FIRST BLACKFRIARS

The first regular enclosed or so-called 'private' theatre. It was adapted from several chambers in Blackfriars in 1576–1577 by Richard Farrant, Master of Windsor Chapel. The priory buildings formerly in the possession of the Dominican Monks, or Black Friars, were within the city, but not at this time subject to city control. In type a large hall (forming part of one of the priory buildings), the theatre was used by Chapel (and perhaps Windsor) Boys, 1577–1580, and by Oxford's Boys, 1583–1584. It was reconverted into lodgings after 1584.

CURTAIN

Built in 1577 in Moorfields, Shoreditch (near the Theatre in the northern suburbs), by an unknown enterpriser. An open-air, polygonal theatre of unknown size, it was occupied by Arundel's Men, 1584(?); as an 'easer' for the Theatre, 1585–1592, by various companies, probably including the Queen's Men; by Chamberlain's Men, c. 1597–1599; by Queen Anne's Men, 1603–1606; and by Prince's Men, 1622–1623. The structure was still standing in 1627.

* or polygonal

NEWINGTON BUTTS

At some time probably before 1580 an unknown builder had erected, or adapted from a standing building, a theatre of unknown type at Newington (a village one mile south of London Bridge), a section where archery contests were frequently held. This theatre was used by Strange's Men, *c.* 1591(?); and by the Admiral's and the Chamberlain's Men for a time in 1594. It was no longer in use in 1599.

BANQUETING HOUSE

Temporary structures for plays and masks at Court were erected, 1559, 1572, 1581, near Whitehall. The last was used until 1604. A new one, used for Court masks only, was erected in 1608 and used until 1619. A permanent one, also used only for masks, was erected from the designs of Inigo Jones in 1622 and still stands. Usually the professional companies at Court played in a hall in the palace of Whitehall.

ROSE

Built in 1587, in the Clink on the Bankside, by Philip Henslowe (in partnership with John Cholmley). A circular,* open-air theatre of unknown size, it was occupied by Strange's Men, 1592–1593(?); Sussex's Men, 1593–1594; Queen's Men, 1594; Admiral's Men, 1594–1600; Worcester's Men, 1602–1603. It is referred to as 'the late playhouse' in 1606.

SWAN

Built in 1595 or 1596, on the Bankside near Paris Stairs, by Francis Langley. A circular,* open-air theatre of unknown size, it was used by Pembroke's Men in 1597, and by Lady Elizabeth's Men, 1611–*c.* 1615. The structure was still standing in 1632.

SECOND BLACKFRIARS

Adapted in 1597 from the Frater Hall in the precinct of Blackfriars (see First Blackfriars above), by James Burbage. An enclosed hall, 66 by 46 feet, with several galleries, it is the second known 'private' theatre. It was used by the Chapel Royal Boys, 1600–1603; Queen's Revels, 1604–1608; King's Men, 1608–1642. The interior was dismantled in 1655.

GLOBE

Built in 1599, burnt in 1613, rebuilt, and reopened, in 1614. A circular,* open-air theatre on the Bankside built by a syndicate consisting mostly of members of Chamberlain's Men. It was occupied by Chamberlain's Men, 1599–1603, and by King's Men, 1603–1624 (after 1608 intermittently as a summer theatre). It was torn down in 1644.

FORTUNE

Built in 1600 in the Parish of St Giles without Cripplegate (north-west suburbs) by Philip Henslowe and Edward Alleyn. Originally a square, open-air theatre measuring 80 feet on the outsides and 55 feet on the inside auditorium, it burnt down in 1621, was rebuilt in the traditional circular or polygonal shape, and reopened in 1623. It was used by the Admiral's Men, 1600–1603; Prince Henry's Men, 1603–1612; Palsgrave's Men, 1612–1621, 1623–1625; King and Queen of Bohemia's Company, 1626–1631(?); King's Revels, 1631–1634(?); Red Bull Company, 1634–1640; Prince Charles's Men, 1640–1642; and occasionally for surreptitious performances during the Commonwealth period. The structure was 'totally demolished' by 1662.

BOAR'S HEAD

An obscure playhouse, possibly a converted inn, located somewhere in Middlesex, and occupied by Worcester's and Oxford's Men in 1602, and by Queen Anne's Men, 1603–1606.

RED BULL

Built *c.* 1605, in Upper St John's Street, St James, Clerkenwell (north-west suburbs), by Aaron Holland. A circular, open-air theatre, it was renovated and enlarged by 1633, possibly *c.* 1625. Used by Queen Anne's Men, *c.* 1605–1617; Red Bull (Revels) Company, 1619–1623; Prince's Men, 1623–1625; Red Bull Company, 1625–1634; Prince Charles's Men, 1634–1640; Red Bull Company, 1640–1642; occasionally for surreptitious performances during

* or polygonal

the Commonwealth period; Mohun and others, 1660; King's Men for a short time, 1660. The structure was still standing in 1664.

WHITEFRIARS

Built *c.* 1606 by Thomas Woodford co-operating with Michael Drayton. A 'private' theatre on the model of Second Blackfriars, it consisted of a hall, 35 feet by *c.* 85 feet, adapted from the refectory of the former priory of the Carmelites, or White Friars. It was located to the west of Salisbury Court and Blackfriars, and like the latter was not fully subject to city control until 1608. It was used by King's Revels, 1608–*c.* 1609; Queen's Revels, 1609–1613; Lady Elizabeth's Men, 1613–1614. The end of its career as a regular theatre seems to have come about 1614.

COCKPIT, OR PHOENIX

Built in 1609, by John Best, as a cockpit, and converted 1616–1617, by Christopher Beeston, into a theatre of the enclosed or 'private' type. It was located in St Giles in the Fields, adjoining Drury Lane, subsequently the regular theatrical district. Occupied by Queen Anne's Men, 1617–1619; Prince's Men, 1619–1622; Lady Elizabeth's Men, 1622–1625; Queen Henrietta's Men, 1625–1636; Beeston's Boys, 1637–1642; Opera Company, 1658–1659; Rhodes and his actors, 1659–1660; King's and Duke's Men before their division, 1660; Jolly's Troupe at intervals, 1661–1665. The interior had been razed in 1649, but subsequently repaired.

HOPE

Built in 1614, on the Bankside, by Philip Henslowe in partnership with Jacob Meade. It was a circular, open-air theatre with a removable stage so that it could be used for bear-baiting. It was occupied by Lady Elizabeth's Men, 1614–1615; Prince's Men, 1615–1617. The structure was still standing in 1683, but after 1617 had been used exclusively for bear-baiting.

PORTER'S HALL, OR ROSSETER'S PUDDLE WHARF OR BLACKFRIARS

A theatre in the precinct of Blackfriars (see First Blackfriars above) was begun in 1615 by Philip Rosseter. Although left incomplete because of the intervention of the authorities, it appears to have been used for a time in 1615 by Lady Elizabeth's and Prince's Men (in coalition with the disbanded Queen's Revels).

SALISBURY COURT

Built in 1629, near Whitefriars and Salisbury Court, Fleet Street, by Richard Gunnell and William Blagrove. It was a brick enclosed or 'private' theatre on a plot of ground 140 feet by 42 feet. It was occupied by King's Revels, 1629–1631; Prince Charles's Men, 1631–b. 1635; King's Revels, 1635–1636; Queen's Men, 1637–1642; Duke's Men, 1660–1661; Jolly's Troupe, 1661; it was also used irregularly during the Commonwealth period, and by William Beeston in 1663 and 1664. The inside had been razed in 1649 and repaired by Beeston in 1660. The structure was destroyed in the fire of 1666.

COCKPIT-IN-COURT

A cockpit in Whitehall was used occasionally when the actors brought plays to Court in the reign of King James, and *c.* 1632 was converted by Inigo Jones into a regular Court theatre. It was a small, elegant theatre on Italian models.

FRENCH PLAYERS' THEATRE

A temporary theatre for the French company under Josias de Soulas, *alias* Floridor, was fitted up in M. Le Febure's riding school, Drury Lane, and used 1635–1636.

WERBURGH-STREET THEATRE, DUBLIN

Built by John Ogilby in Dublin in 1637, and used for performances between 1637 and 1641 by Ogilby's company. In type it probably resembled contemporary 'private' theatres of London. It fell into decay during the Interregnum.

RUTLAND HOUSE

A nobleman's mansion near Charterhouse Yard was occupied by Sir William Davenant, and a narrow hall in the building was used for entertainments by his Opera Company, 1656–1658.

GIBBON'S TENNIS COURT, OR THEATRE ROYAL IN VERE STREET

Built in 1634 as an enclosed tennis court near Lincoln's Inn Fields, and converted into a theatre in 1660 by Thomas Killigrew. As converted, it probably resembled the Elizabethan 'private' theatres. It was occupied by King's Men, 1660–1663, and by Nursery Company, c. 1669–1671. The structure was burnt down in 1809.

LISLE'S TENNIS COURT, OR DUKE'S HOUSE, OR LINCOLN'S INN FIELDS

Built in 1656 near Lincoln's Inn Fields by Anne Tyler and James Hooker as an enclosed tennis court, and converted into a theatre in 1661 by Sir William Davenant. It is often described as the first modern theatre with a 'picture-frame' stage; it was semi-modern in that it had a scene-room for movable scenery and a proscenium arch, but retained a modification of the platform stage of the older theatres in its 'apron', which extended before the arch into the auditorium. It was used by Duke's Men, 1661–1671; King's Men, 1672–1674; Betterton's Company, 1695–a. 1700. The structure was demolished in 1848.

SMOCK ALLEY THEATRE, DUBLIN

Built in 1662 by John Ogilby, and used by his company and that of his deputy and successor, Joseph Ashbury, 1662–a. 1700. In type it probably resembled Lisle's Tennis Court.

THEATRE ROYAL IN BRIDGES STREET

Built in 1663, near Lincoln's Inn Fields, by Thomas Killigrew and a syndicate. Of the same type as Lisle's Tennis Court, it was used by the King's Men until 1672, when it burnt down.

NURSERY THEATRES

The Nursery Company occupied Gibbon's Tennis Court, c. 1669–1671, and at other times certain houses of which little is known: a theatre or 'booth' in Hatton Garden, b. 1667–1669; another in Bunhill, 1671; and a playhouse of a more elaborate order erected by Lady Mary Davenant in the Barbican in 1671 and occupied until c. 1682.

DORSET GARDEN

Built in 1671, fronting the Thames near the former Salisbury Court Theatre, by Lady Mary Davenant and a syndicate. In type an elaborate theatre (possibly designed by Christopher Wren) on the model indicated by Lisle's Tennis Court. It was occupied by Duke's Men, 1671–1682; United Company, 1682–1695 occasionally; Patent Company, 1695–a. 1700 occasionally. The house was pulled down in 1709.

THEATRE ROYAL IN DRURY LANE

Built in 1674 by Thomas Killigrew and a syndicate. In type resembling Dorset Garden (and also possibly designed by Christopher Wren), but less ambitious and more practical. It was used by King's Men, 1674–1682; United Company, 1682–1694; Patent Company, 1695–a. 1700. It remained in use as a theatre until 1791, when it was demolished and rebuilt.

THE EXTANT PLAY MANUSCRIPTS, 975–1700:
THEIR LOCATION AND CATALOGUE NUMBERS

Titleless manuscripts and unidentified fragments are listed at the end of Supplementary List I, above. The Latin plays in the following list are marked (L), but no further description is offered. For alternative attributions of authorship and other information, see the Chronology and Tabulation above. The major portion of the following catalogue has been previously published in *PMLA*, L (1935), 687–99; LII (1937), 905–7; LIII (1938), 624–9.

AETHELWOLD, BISHOP OF WINCHESTER
Regularis Concordia, containing directions for the *Quem Quaeritis* (*of Easter*), *Depositio Crucis*, and *Elevatio Crucis* (L). (1) Brit. Mus. MS. Cotton Tiberius A. III, f. 177 (dated *c.* 1025). (2) Ibid., Cotton Faustina B. III, ff. 159a–98a (an inferior version dated *c.* 1000).

ALABASTER, WILLIAM
Roxana (L). (1) Camb. Univ. Lib. MS. Ff. 11. 9. (2) Lambeth Palace MS. 838. (3) Emmanuel Col., Camb., MS. III. 1. 17. (4) Trinity Col., Camb., MS. R. 17. 10. (5) Folger Shakespeare Lib. MS. V. b. 222 (Eng. trans.).

ATKINSON, THOMAS
Homo (L). Brit. Mus. MS. Harleian 6925, Art. I.

AUBREY, JOHN
The Country Revel. Bodl. MS. Aubrey 21.

B., H. (Burkhead, or Birkhead, Henry?)
The Female Rebellion. (1) Bodl. MS. Tanner 466, ff. 174 seq. (2) Glasgow Univ. MS. Hunterian 635.

BACON, FRANCIS
Gesta Grayorum. Fragments by Bacon (?) and Francis Davison appear in Brit. Mus. MS. Harleian 541, f. 138; Inner Temple MS. Petyt 583.43, f. 294; Folger Shakespeare Lib. MS. V. a. 190 (Letter of Henry, Prince of Purpoole, to the Great Turk, Dec. 27 —).

BALE, JOHN
King John. Huntington Lib. MS. HM 3.

BANISTER, *vere* SELBY, WILLIAM
Andronichus (L). Brit. Mus. Add. MS. 15204.
Jephte (L). Ibid.
Perseus et Demetrius (L). Ibid.

BARNES, BARNABE
The Battle of Hexham. MS 'sold among Isaac Reed's books in 1807' (Hazlitt, *Manual*, p. 23). Extant?

BARNES, JOSHUA
The Academy. Emmanuel Col., Camb., MS. III. 1. 4 (2 copies).
Englebert. Ibid., III. 1. 2.
Landgartha. Ibid.
Plautus His Trinummi Imitated. Ibid., III. 1. 4.
Sigward, the Famous King of Norway (an earlier draft of *Landgartha*). Ibid.

BAYLIE, SIMON
The Wizard. (1) MS in Durham Cathedral Lib. (2) Brit. Mus. Add. MS. 10306.

BEAUMONT, FRANCIS, *see* FLETCHER, JOHN

BEAUMONT, SIR JOHN
The Theatre of Apollo. Brit. Mus. MS. Royal 18 A. LXX.

BEHN, APHRA
The Younger Brother. Bodl. MS. Rawlinson, poet. 195.

BELLAMY, HENRY
Iphis (L). Bodl. MS. Lat. misc. e. 17 (formerly Malone MS. 43).

BERKELEY, SIR WILLIAM
The Lost Lady. Folger Shakespeare Lib. MS. J. b. 4 (last 298 ll. missing).

BERNARD, RICHARD
The Birth of Hercules. Brit. Mus. Add. MS. 28722.

BERNARD, SAMUEL
Andronicus Comnenus (L). Brit. Mus. MS. Sloane 1767, ff. 18–66.

BLENCOWE, JOHN
Mercurius (L). St John's Col., Oxford, MS. 218.

BLOW, JOHN
Venus and Adonis. (1) Brit. Mus. Add. MS. 22100. (2) MS in Westminster Chapter Lib. (3) MS in Christ Church Lib., Oxford.

BOYLE, ROGER, EARL OF ORRERY
The General (Altemira). (1) MS in Worcester Col., Oxford. (2) MS, present location unknown, printed by Halliwell[-Phillipps] in 1853.
Henry V. (1) Huntington Lib. MS. EL 11642 (from the Bunbury MSS? see *Hist. MSS. Comm.*, III, 241). (2) Ibid., HM 20. (3) Ibid., HM 599. (4) Bodl. MS. Rawlinson, poet. 2. (5) Ibid., poet. 180. (6) Folger Shakespeare Lib. MS. V. b. 133. (7) Ibid., V. a. 220.
Mustapha. (1) Huntington Lib. MS. EL 11641 (from the Bunbury MSS? see *Hist. MSS. Comm.*, III, 241). (2) Brit. Mus. Add. MS. 29280. (3) Bodl. MS. Rawlinson, poet. 5. (4) Ibid., Rawlinson, poet. 27. (5) Folger Shakespeare Lib. MS. V. b. 133. (6) Ibid., V. a. 220.
Tryphon. (1) Bodl. MS. Malone 11. (2) Bodl. MS. Rawlinson, poet. 39.
Zoroastres. Brit. Mus. MS. Sloane 1828, ff. 46a–80b.

BROME, RICHARD
The English Moor. MS in Lichfield Cathedral Lib.

BROOKE, SAMUEL
Adelphe (L). (1) Trinity Col., Camb., MS. R. 3. 9. (2) Ibid., R. 10. 4.
Melanthe (L). Folger Shakespeare Lib. MS. J. a. 2.
Scyros (L). (1) Camb. Univ. Lib. MS. Ee. V. 16. (2) Emmanuel Col., Camb., MS. III. 1. 17. (3) Trinity Col., Camb., MS. R. 3. 9. (4) Ibid., R. 3. 37. (5) Ibid., R. 10. 4. (6) Ibid., R. 17. 10. (7) Ibid., O. 3. 4. (8) MS in Hodgson sale catalogue 89, 29 Mar. 1951.

BROWNE, WILLIAM
Ulysses and Circe. (1) Emmanuel Col., Camb., MS 68. (2) MS in the collection of H. C. Pole-Gell (see Chambers, *E.S.*, IV, 406).

BUCHANAN, GEORGE
Cupid, Chastity, and Time. MS verses sent by Thomas Randolph to Sir William Cecil (see

Keith, *Hist. of the Affairs of Church and State in Scotland*, II, 220).

BURTON, ROBERT
Philosophaster (L). (1) Folger Shakespeare Lib. MS V. a. 315. (2) MS in Harvard College Lib. (3) Harvard Univ. MS. Thr. 10.1, ff. 48–56 (an actor's part).

C., W.
Rape Revenged. Extant? See Hazlitt, *Manual*, p. 191.

CARLELL, LODOWICK
Arviragus and Philicia. (1) Bodl. MS. Eng. misc. d. 11. (2) MS in Lord Leconfield's lib. at Petworth (see *Hist. MSS. Comm.*, VI, 312; also B. M. Wagner, *T.L.S.*, 4 Oct. 1934, p. 675).

CARLETON, R.
The Concealed Royalty. Bodl. MS. Eng. poet. d. 2.
The Martial Queen. (1) Bodl. MS. Rawlinson, poet. 126. (2) Bodl. MS. Eng. poet. d. 2.

CARLETON, THOMAS
Fatum Vortigerni (L). Brit. Mus. MS. Lansdowne 723, ff. 1–42.

CARTWRIGHT, WILLIAM
The Royal Slave. (1) Brit. Mus. Add. MS. 41616 (from the Petworth collection). (2) Bodl. MS. Arch. Seld. B. 26. (3) MS in the lib. of the Duke of Bedford. (4) Folger Shakespeare Lib. MS. V. b. 212. (5) Heber MS. 1043. Extant?

CAVENDISH, JANE, AND ELIZABETH BRACKLEY
The Concealed Fancies. Bodl. MS. Rawlinson, poet. 16.
A Pastoral. Ibid.

CAVENDISH, WILLIAM, DUKE OF NEWCASTLE
The Country Captain. Brit. Mus. MS. Harleian 7650 (formerly Add. 5001).
The Humorous Lovers. Brit. Mus. MS. Harleian 7367, Art. I.
A Pleasant and Merry Humour of a Rogue. MS in the lib. of the Duke of Portland, Welbeck Abbey.
'Various drafts and fragments.' Ibid.

CECIL, ROBERT
The Queen's Entertainment at Theobalds, 1594. Bodl. MS. Rawlinson D. 692, f. 106 (frag.).

CHAPMAN, GEORGE
The Twelve Months. MS formerly in the possession of J. P. Collier, but not now among

his papers in Brit. Mus. MS. Egerton 2623. Extant?

MSS of *The Gentleman Usher* and *Monsieur D'Olive* are mentioned in Hazlitt, *Manual, passim,* but see Chambers, *E.S.,* III, 253.

CHAPPELL, JOHN

Susenbrotus (L). (1) Bodl. MS. Rawlinson, poet. 195, ff. 79 seq. (2) MS at Bridgewater House, London (entitled *Fortunia*).

CHEKE, HENRY

Free-Will. Folger Shakespeare Lib. MS. V. b. 221 (dated 1635).

CHETTLE, HENRY, AND THOMAS DEKKER

Troilus and Cressida. Brit. Mus. Add. MS. 10449, f. 5 ('plot' only).

CHRISTOPHERSON, JOHN

Jephthes (Greek version). (1) Trinity Col., Camb., MS. O. 1. 37. (2) St John's Col., Camb., MS. 287. H. 19.

Jephthes (Lat. version). Bodl. MS. Tanner 466, ff. 126–53.

'CLARETUS, PATER'

Homo Duplex (L). (1) Stonyhurst MS. A. VII. 50 (2), ff. 33–62. (2) English Col., Rome, Archives MS. C. 17 (ii) (frag.).

Innocentia Purpurata (L). Stonyhurst MS. A. VII. 50 (2), ff. 2–31.

CLAVELL, JOHN

The Soddered Citizen. MS in the private collection of Lt.-Col. E. G. Troyte-Bullock, of Zeals House, Mere, Wilts.

CROWTHER, JOSEPH

Cephalus et Procris (L). St John's Col., Oxford, MS. 217 P. 3587.

CRUSO, AQUILA

Euribates (L). Emmanuel Col., Camb., MS. III. I. 17.

DABORNE, ROBERT

The Poor Man's Comfort. Brit. Mus. MS. Egerton 1994, ff. 268–93.

DANIEL, SAMUEL

Hymen's Triumph. Edinburgh Univ. MS. Drummond.

DAVENANT, WILLIAM

Macbeth. MS in Yale University Lib.

II The Siege of Rhodes. Public Lib., Douai, MS. 7.87.

DAVENPORT, ROBERT

A Dialogue between Policy and Piety. (1) Folger Shakespeare Lib. MS. V. a. 313. (2) MS re-ported to be once in the collection of John Withorn of Broomhead (see J. G. McManaway, *Notes and Queries,* CLXX [1936], 295). See also *The Enchanted Lovers* and *The City Nightcap,* below, under Anonymous.

DAVIES, JOHN

The Entertainment at Cecil House, 1602 (*A Conference between a Gentleman Huisher and a Post*). Brit. Mus. MS. Harleian 286, f. 248. (For further fragments, see MS. Hatfield XII. 568.)

The Entertainment at Harefield, 1602. Fragments in Brit. Mus. MS. Harleian 5353, f. 95; Col. of Arms MS. Talbot K, f. 43; Brit. Mus. MS. Birch 4173; Folger Shakespeare Lib. MS. X. d. 172. (See further Chambers, *E.S.,* IV, 68.)

DAVISON FRANCIS, *see* BACON, FRANCIS

DAY, JOHN

The Parliament of Bees. Brit. Mus. MS. Lansdowne 725.

DEKKER, THOMAS

The Welsh Ambassador. MS in the Cardiff Public Lib.

DENNY, SIR WILLIAM

The Shepherd's Holiday. Brit. Mus. Add. MS. 34065.

DERING, SIR EDWARD

Henry IV (Shakespeare's two parts combined into one play). Folger Shakespeare Lib. MS. V. b. 34.

DIGBY, GEORGE

Elvira. MS, item 251, in H. F. House sale at Sotheby's, 21 Jan. 1924.

DIGBY, KENELM

Il Pastor Fido. MS found among papers of Sir Kenelm Digby, once in the possession of Henry Bright (see *Poems from Sir Kenelm Digby's Papers,* 1877, pp. 4–5).

D'OYLEY, E.

Britannicus. Folger Shakespeare Lib. MS. V. b. 219.

DRYDEN, JOHN

The Fall of Angels, and Man in Innocence (*The State of Innocence*). (1) Brit. Mus Add. MS. 37158. (2) Bodl. MS. Rawlinson C. 146. (3) MS in the Harvard College Lib. (4) Huntington Lib. MS. EL 11640. (5) Ibid. (6) Folger Shakespeare Lib. MS. V. a. 225. (7) Ibid., V. b. 235.

The Indian Emperor. (1) Trinity Col., Camb.,

MS. R. 3. 10. (2) Public Lib., Douai, MS. 7.87.

The Indian Queen (altered as an opera, in score by H. Purcell). Brit. Mus. Add. MS. 31449.

DUNBAR, WILLIAM

The Droichis Part of the Play. (1) Auchinleck, Ayrshire, MS. Asloan. (2) Advocates' Lib., Edinburgh, MS. Bannatyne.

EDES, RICHARD

The Second Woodstock Entertainment. Brit. Mus. Add. MS. 41499A, ff. 12–16 (frag.). For further MS fragments, see Chambers, *E.S.*, III, 404.

ELIZABETH I, QUEEN

Hercules Oetaeus. Bodl. MS. E. Museo. 55, f. 48 (frag.).

FANE, MILDMAY, EARL OF WESTMORLAND

Candy Restored. (1) Huntington Lib. MS. HM 771. (2) Brit. Mus. Add. MS. 34221, ff. 1ᵛ–18ᵛ.

The Change. Brit. Mus. Add. MS. 34221, ff. 50ʳ–68ᵛ.

Don Phoebo's Triumph. Huntington Lib. MS. HM 770.

Ladrones. MS, item 1054, in sale at Sotheby's, 17 July 1888.

De Pugna Animi. Brit. Mus. Add. MS. 34221, ff. 124ᵛ–47ʳ.

Raguaillo D'Oceano. Ibid., ff. 107ᵛ–23ʳ.

Time's Trick upon the Cards. Ibid., ff. 19ᵛ–49ᵛ.

Virtue's Triumph. Ibid., ff. 69ᵛ–106ᵛ.

FANSHAWE, SIR RICHARD

To Love Only for Love's Sake. Brit. Mus. Add. MS. 32133.

FINCH, ANNE, COUNTESS OF WINCHILSEA

Aristomenes. Folger Shakespeare Lib. MS. N. b. 3.

Triumphs of Love and Innocence. Ibid.

FLETCHER, JOHN, AND OTHERS

Beggars' Bush. Folger Shakespeare Lib. MS. J. b. 5.

Bonduca. Brit. Mus. Add. MS. 36758.

The Elder Brother. Brit. Mus. MS. Egerton 1994, ff. 2–30.

The Faithful Friends. See below, under ANONYMOUS.

The Honest Man's Fortune. Victoria and Albert Mus. MS. Dyce 9.

The Humorous Lieutenant (*Demetrius and Enanthe*). Lord Harlech MS.

The Woman's Prize. Folger Shakespeare Lib. MS. J. b. 3.

FLETCHER, PHINEAS

Sicelides. (1) Bodl. MS. Rawlinson, poet. 214. (2) Brit. Mus. Add. MS. 4453.

FORD, JOHN

Perkin Warbeck. Bodl. MS. Rawlinson, poet. 122 (*c.* 1700?).

FORSETT, EDWARD

Pedantius (L). (1) Gonville and Caius Col., Camb., MS. 62. (2) Trinity Col., Camb., MS. R. 17. 9. (3) Huntington Lib. MS. EL 34. B. 13.

FOX, RICHARD

The Welcome for Katherine of Aragon. (1) Brit. Mus. MS. Harleian 69, ff. 37 seq. (2) Ibid., Cotton Vitellius C. xi, ff. 117 seq. (3) Ibid., Cotton Vitellius A. xvi, ff. 184 seq. (4) MS printed in *Antiq. Rep.*, II, pp. 248 seq.

FOXE, JOHN

Christus Triumphans (L). Brit. Mus. MS. Lansdowne 1073.

FRAUNCE, ABRAHAM

Hymenaeus (L). (1) St John's Col., Camb., MS. S. 45. (2) Gonville and Caius Col., Camb., MS. 62.

Victoria (L). MS reported in *Hist. MSS. Comm.*, III, 230 (MSS of Lord de L'Isle and Dudley at Penshurst).

FREEMAN, SIR RALPH

Imperiale. Brit. Mus. MS. Egerton 2948.

GAGER, WILLIAM

Dido (L). (1) Brit. Mus. Add. MS. 22583 (frag.). (2) MS at Christ Church, Oxford.

Oedipus (L). Brit. Mus. Add. MS. 22583, ff. 31–34.

GASCOIGNE, GEORGE

Jocasta. Brit. Mus. Add. MS. 34063.

The Queen's Entertainment at Woodstock (*The Tale of Hemetes the Hermit*). (1) Brit. Mus. MS. Royal 18A. XLVII, 27. (2) Ibid., Add. MS. 41499A, ff. 4–5ᵇ (frag.).

GLAPTHORNE, HENRY

The Lady Mother. Brit. Mus. MS. Egerton 1994, ff. 212–45.

GOFFE, THOMAS

The Tragedy of Amurath. (1) MS in lib. of John Leicester-Warren, Esq., Tabley House, Knutsford, Cheshire (*Hist. MSS. Comm.*, I, 49). (2) Harvard Univ. MS. Thr 10.1, ff. 57–71 (an actor's part).

GOLDINGHAM, WILLIAM
 Herodes (L). Camb. Univ. Lib. MS. Mm. I. 24.

GREENE, ROBERT
 John of Bordeaux. MS in the Duke of Northumberland's lib. at Alnwick.
 Orlando Furioso. Dulwich Col. MS. I. 138 (an actor's part).

GREVILLE, FULKE
 Alaham. MS at Warwick Castle, Vol. D.
 Mustapha. (1) MS at Warwick Castle, Vol. D. (2) Camb. Univ. Lib. MS. Ff. 2. 35. (3) Folger Shakespeare Lib. MS. V. b. 223 ('c. 1609').

GRIMALD, NICHOLAS
 Archipropheta (L). Brit. Mus. MS. Royal 12A. XLVI.

HACKET, JOHN
 Loyola (L). (1) Brit. Mus. Add. MS. 26709. (2) Trinity Col., Camb., MS. R. 17. 9. (3) Ibid., R. 17. 10 (imperf.). (4) MS in Durham Cathedral Lib. (5) Folger Shakespeare Lib. MS. V. b. 222 (cast-list only). (6) MS in Hodgson sale catalogue 89, 29 Mar. 1951.

HADTON, 'DOMINUS'
 St Meriasek (Cornish). Hengwrt MS of Mr Wynne at Peniarth.

HAUSTED, PETER
 Senile Odium (L). MS of Marquis of Bath (see *Hist. MSS. Comm.*, III, 200).

HAWKESWORTH, WALTER
 Labyrinthus (L). (1) Bodl. MS. Douce 43315. (2) Lambeth Palace MS. 838. (3) Camb. Univ. Lib. MS. Ee. V. 16. (4) St John's Col., Camb., MS. J. 8. (5) Trinity Col., Camb., MS. R. 3. 9. (6) Warwick County Record Office, Newdigate MS. CR 1631/B 761. (7) MS in Hodgson sale catalogue 89, 29 Mar. 1951.
 Leander (L). (1) Lambeth Palace MS. 838. (2) Camb. Univ. Lib. MS. Ee. V. 16. (3) Bodl. MS. Rawlinson D. 341. (4) St John's Col., Camb., MS. J. 8. (5) Emmanuel Col., Camb., MS. I. 2. 30. (6) Brit. Mus. MS. Sloane 1762 (1602 version). (7) Trinity Col., Camb., MS. R. 3. 8 (1602 version). (8) MS in Hodgson sale catalogue 89, 29 Mar. 1951.

HEYWOOD, JOHN
 Witty and Witless. Brit. Mus. MS. Harleian 367.

X

HEYWOOD, THOMAS
 The Captives. Brit. Mus. MS. Egerton 1994, ff. 52ᵃ–73ᵃ.
 The Escapes of Jupiter (Calisto). Ibid., ff. 74ᵃ–95ᵃ.

HILARIUS
 Daniel. Bibliothèque Nationale, Paris, MS. lat. 11331, XII, 9–10.
 The Raising of Lazarus. Ibid., lat. 11331, XII, 11–12.
 St Nicholas. Ibid., lat. 11331, XII, 12–16.

HOADLEY, SAMUEL
 The War of Grammar. Brit. Mus. Add. MS. 22725.

HOLLAND, SAMUEL
 The Enchanted Grove. MS formerly in Lord Northampton's lib. at Castle Ashby (see A. Watkin-Jones, *T.L.S.*, 15 Nov. 1934, p. 795). Extant?

HORNE, JOHN
 Fortune's Task. Huntington Lib. MS. HM 11.

HOWARD, EDWARD
 The Change of Crowns. MS formerly in the possession of R. A. Austen-Leigh.

HUGHES, JOHN
 Amalasont, Queen of the Goths. MS once in the possession of the Rev. John Duncombe; see Halliwell-Phillipps, *Dict.*, p. 13. Extant?

JAMES I, KING
 'Wedding Masque.' (1) Bodl. MS. 165, ff. 60ʳ–4ᵛ. (2) Brit. Mus. Add. MS. 24195, ff. 52ʳ–55ᵛ.

JAQUES, FRANCIS
 The Queen of Corsica. Brit. Mus. MS. Lansdowne 807, ff. 2–28.

JEFFERE, JOHN
 The Bugbears. Brit. Mus. MS. Lansdowne 807, ff. 57 seq.

JOHNSON, LAURENCE
 Misogonus. Huntington Lib. MS. HM 542.

JOHNSON, WILLIAM
 Valetudinarium (L). (1) Camb. Univ. Lib. MS. Dd. III. 73. (2) St John's Col., Camb., MS. S. 59. (3) Emmanuel Col., Camb., MS. I. 2. 32.

JONSON, BEN
 Christmas His Mask. (1) Folger Shakespeare Lib. MS. J. a. 1. (2) Bodl. MS. Rawlinson, poet. 160, ff. 173–4 (song of Christmas only). (3) Brit. Mus. MS. Harleian 4955, ff. 46–47 (song of Christmas only).
 The Entertainment at the Earl of Newcastle's in

Blackfriars. Brit. Mus. MS. Harleian 4955, ff. 48–52.

The Entertainment of the Two Kings of Great Britain and Denmark. Brit. Mus. MS. Egerton 2877, f. 162b (speech of Eumone, Dice, and Irene).

The Gypsies Metamorphosed. (1) Huntington Lib. MS. HM 741. (2) Brit. Mus. MS. Harleian 4955, ff. 2–30. (3) MS (frag.) in Conway papers in Public Record Office (S.P.D., James I, CXXII, art. 58). (4) Bodl. MS. Tanner 306, f. 252 (frag.). (5) Bodl. MS. Rawlinson, poet. 172, f. 78 (frag.).

The King's Entertainment at Welbeck. Brit. Mus. MS. Harleian 4955, ff. 194–98.

Love's Welcome at Bolsover. Ibid., ff. 199–202.

The Mask of Blackness. Brit. Mus. MS. Royal 17B. XXXI.

The Mask of Queens. Ibid., Royal 18A. XLV.

Pleasure Reconciled to Virtue. MS in Duke of Devonshire's collection at Chatsworth.

The Vision of Delight. Brit. Mus. MS. Harleian 4955, ff. 40–1 (frag.).

Volpone. MS said to be extant by J. S. Farmer in Introduction to *Believe as You List*, but see Chambers, *E.S.*, III, 368.

JORDAN, THOMAS

Cupid His Coronation. Bodl. MS. Rawlinson B. 165, ff. 109–13.

JORDAN, WILLIAM

The Creation of the World, with Noah's Flood (Cornish). (1) Bodl. MS. 219. (2) Bodl. MS. Corn. c. 1 (includes Eng. prose trans.). (3) Brit. Mus. MS. Harleian 1867. (4) MS belonging to J. C. Hotten, bookseller, in 1864 (see Chambers, *M.S.*, II, 435); same as Brit. Mus. Add. MS. 28554?

JOYNER, WILLIAM

The Roman Empress. MS at Worcester Col., Oxford.

KATHERINE OF SUTTON

Quem Quaeritis (*of Easter*), with directions for *Depositio Crucis* and *Elevatio Crucis* (L). University Col., Oxford, MS. 169, XV, 108–9, 119–24.

KEIGWIN, JOHN

The Creation of the World, with Noah's Flood (trans. of Jordan, W.). (1) Bodl. MS. Corn. c. 1. (2) Brit. Mus. MS. Harleian 1867. (3) Brit. Mus. Add. MS. 28554.

Origo Mundi (trans.). Bodl. MS. Corn. e. 3.

KILLIGREW, THOMAS

I and II Cicilia and Clorinda. Folger Shakespeare Lib. MS. V. b. 208–9.

Clarasilla. MS in Castle Howard Lib.

KILLIGREW, SIR WILLIAM

The Siege of Urbin. Bodl. MS. Rawlinson, poet. 29.

KIRKHAM, R.

Alfred. Bodl. MS. Rawlinson, poet. 80.

LEE, SIR HENRY, *see* GASCOIGNE, GEORGE: *The Queen's Entertainment at Woodstock.*

LEE, NATHANIEL

Mithridates, King of Pontus. Public Lib., Douai, MS. 7.87.

Theodosius. MS, item 1322, in Joseph Haselwood's sale, 1833, to Thorpe. Extant?

LEGGE, THOMAS

Richardus Tertius (L). (1) Bodl. Lat. misc. e. 16. (2) Camb. Univ. Lib. MS. Mm. IV. 40. (3) Folger Shakespeare Lib. MS. V. a. 310. (4) Huntington Lib. MS. HM 179. (5) Clare Col., Camb., MS. Kk. 3. 12 (dated Jan. 1583). (6) Gonville and Caius Col., Camb., MS. 125. 62 (dated, prob. erroneously, 1573). (7) Emmanuel Col., Camb., MS. I. 3. 19 (*c.* 1628). (8) Bodl. MS. Tanner 306, f. 42 (Part I only; dated, prob. erroneously, 17 Mar. 1582). (9) Finch-Hatton MS. 320 in Northamptonshire Record Office. (10) Brit. Mus. MS. Harleian 2412 (dated 1588). (11) Ibid., Harleian 6926, Art. I (dated 1586).

LINDSAY, DAVID

A Satire of the Three Estates. (1) Brit. Mus. MS. Reg. 7. C. XVI, ff. 136–9 (descrip. of version of 1540). (2) Advocates' Lib., Edinburgh, MS. Bannatyne, ff. 164ᵃ–210ᵃ (version of 1552).

LISTER, MARTIN

Eunuchus (trans. Terence). Bodl. MS. Lister 23.

LOWER, SIR WILLIAM

Don Japhet of Armenia. Brit. Mus. Add. MS. 28723.

The Enchanted Lovers. See below, under ANONYMOUS.

The Three Dorothies. MS formerly in the collection at Skeffington Hall. Extant?

LUTTREL, NARCISSUS

Love's Metamorphosis. MS from Colbeck, Radford & Co. catalogue cited by Summers, *Playhouse of Pepys*, p. 449.

LYDGATE, JOHN

The Mumming at Bishopswood. Bodl. MS. Ashmolean 59, ff. 62–64.

A Mumming at Eltham. (1) Trinity Col., Camb., MS. R. 3. 20, ff. 37–40. (2) Brit. Mus. Add. MS. 29729, ff. 135^b–6^b.

A Mumming at Hertford. (1) Trinity Col., Camb., MS. R. 3. 20, ff. 40–8. (2) Brit. Mus. Add. MS. 29729, ff. 136^b–40^a.

A Mumming at London (A Mumming before the Great Estates of the Land). (1) Trinity Col., Camb., MS. R. 3. 20, ff. 55–65. (2) Brit. Mus. Add. MS. 29729, ff. 140^a–4^a.

A Mumming at Windsor. (1) Trinity Col., Camb., MS. R. 3. 20, ff. 71–74. (2) Brit. Mus. Add. MS. 29729, ff. 144^a–5^b.

A Mumming for the Goldsmiths of London. (1) Trinity Col., Camb., MS. R. 3. 20, ff. 175–8. (2) Brit. Mus. Add. MS. 29729, ff. 134^a–5^b.

A Mumming for the Mercers of London. (1) Trinity Col., Camb., MS. R. 3. 20, ff. 171–5. (2) Brit. Mus. Add. MS. 29729, ff. 132^b–4^a.

The Reception of Henry VI. Brit. Mus. MS. Cotton. Julius B. II, ff. 89–100.

LYLY, JOHN

The Entertainment at Chiswick. Finch-Hatton MS. 2414.

MABBE, JAMES

The Spanish Bawd. MS, prob. of this play, reported at Alnwick Castle, *Hist. MSS. Comm.*, III, 119.

MAITTAIRE, MICHAEL

Excidium Trojae (L). Bodl. MS. Rawlinson, D. 284.

Dido (L). Ibid.

Inferno Navigatio (L). Ibid.

MANUCHE, COSMO

The Banished Shepherdess. Huntington Lib. MS. EL 8395.

The Feast. MS at Worcester Col., Oxford.

Agamemnon, The Banished Shepherdess, The Captives, The Feast, Lenotius King of Cyprus, The Mandrake, Mariamni, and an unnamed comedy (actor: Hermenigildus) and tragedy (actors: Macrinus, Papinianus, and Ardentius). MSS (lost?) once in Lord Northampton's lib. at Castle Ashby. See *D.N.B.*, First Supplement, III, 138–9, and B. M. Wagner, *T.L.S.*, 4 Oct. 1934, p. 675.

MARLOWE, CHRISTOPHER

The Massacre at Paris. Folger Shakespeare Lib. MS. J. b. 8 (frag.).

MARSTON, JOHN

The Entertainment at Ashby. (1) Huntington Lib. MS. EL 34 B. 9. (2) Brit. Mus. MS. Sloane 848, f. 9 (frag.).

MASSINGER, PHILIP

Believe as You List. Brit. Mus. MS. Egerton 2828.

The Parliament of Love. Victoria and Albert Mus. MS. Dyce 39 (frag.).

Sir John van Olden Barnavelt. Brit. Mus. Add. MS. 18653.

See also *The Cure of Pride* and *The Renegado,* below, under ANONYMOUS, and *Beggars' Bush, The Elder Brother,* and *The Honest Man's Fortune,* above, under FLETCHER, JOHN.

MAY, THOMAS

Cleopatra. Brit. Mus. MS. Royal 18C. VII.

Julius Caesar (L). MS extant? See Hazlitt, *Manual,* p. 124, and Bentley, *J. & C. S.,* IV, 838.

MAYDISTON, RICHARD

Richard II's Reconciliation with the City of London. (1) Bodl. MS. Ashmolean 793. (2) Bodl. MS. E. Museo. 94.

MEASE, PETER

Adrastus Parentans (L). Brit. Mus. Add. MS. 10417.

MERBURY, FRANCIS

A Marriage between Wit and Wisdom. Brit. Mus. Add. MS. 26782.

MEWE, WILLIAM

Pseudomagia (L). (1) Emmanuel Col., Camb., MS. I. 3. 16 (item 3). (2) Trinity Col., Camb., MS. R. 17. 10. (3) Folger Shakespeare Lib. MS. V. b. 222.

MIDDLETON, THOMAS

A Game at Chess. (1) Bodl. MS. Malone 25. (2) Trinity Col., Camb., MS. O. 2. 66. (3) Brit. Mus. MS. Lansdowne 690. (4) Huntington Lib. MS. EL 34 B. 17. (5) Folger Shakespeare Lib. MS. V. a. 231. (6) Ibid., V. a. 342.

Hengist, King of Kent (The Mayor of Queenborough). (1) Folger Shakespeare Lib. MS. J. b. 6. (2) MS. in the lib. of the Duke of Portland, Welbeck Abbey.

An Invention. MS in Conway papers in Public

Record Office (S.P.D., James I, CXXIX, art. 53).

The Witch. Bodl. MS. Malone 12.

MILTON, JOHN

Arcades. MS (frag.) at Trinity Col., Camb.

Comus. (1) MS at Bridgewater House, London. (2) MS at Trinity Col., Camb. (3) Brit. Mus. Add. MS. 11518 (5 songs only).

MITCHELL, FRANCIS

Michael and Francis. MS in Public Record Office, Star Chamber, Proceedings, 5. S. 30/16.

MONTAGUE, WALTER

The Shepherd's Paradise. (1) Brit. Mus. MS. Sloane 3649. (2) Brit. Mus. MS. Stowe 976. (3) Brit. Mus. Add. MS. 41617. (4) Folger Shakespeare Lib. MS. V. b. 203. (5) Ibid., V. b. 204.

MORRELL, ROGER

Hispanus (L). Bodl. MS. Douce 234, ff. 15 seq.

MOTTEUX, PETER

The Island Princess. Brit. Mus. Add. MS. 15318.

MOUNTFORT, WALTER

The Launching of the Mary. Brit. Mus. MS. Egerton 1994, ff. 318 seq.

MUNDAY, ANTHONY

John a Kent and John a Cumber. Huntington Lib. MS. HM 500.

Sir Thomas More. Brit. Mus. MS. Harleian 7368, Art. I.

NEALE, THOMAS

The Ward. Bodl. MS. Rawlinson, poet. 79.

OLDISWORTH, GYLES

The Pattern of Piety. Bodl. MS. Rawlinson C. 422.

PARKHURST, FERDINANDO

Ignoramus. Two copies of close, one of paraphrastical, translation of Ruggle. MS reported in *Hist. MSS. Comm.*, III, 215 (MSS of Marquis of Westminster, Eaton Hall, Chester).

PARKINSON, —

Speech to James I at Berwick, 1603. Folger Shakespeare Lib. MS. V. b. 75.

PARSONS, PHILIP

Atalanta (L). Brit. Mus. MS. Harleian 6924.

PEELE, GEORGE

Anglorum Feriae. Brit. Mus. Add. MS. 21432.

The Battle of Alcazar. Brit. Mus. Add. MS. 10449, f. 3 ('plot' only).

Polyhymnia. St John's Col., Oxford, MS. 216.

PERCY, WILLIAM

Aphrodysial. (1) Huntington Lib. MS. HM 4. (2) Alnwick Castle MS. 509.

Arabia Sitiens. (1) Huntington Lib. MS. HM 4. (2) Alnwick Castle MS. 508. (3) Ibid., 509.

A Country Tragedy in Vacunium. (1) Huntington Lib. MS. HM 4. (2) Alnwick Castle MS. 508 (frag.). (3) Ibid., 509 (dated 1646).

The Cuckqueans and Cuckolds Errants. (1) Huntington Lib. MS. HM 4. (2) Alnwick Castle MS. 508. (3) Ibid., 509.

The Fairy Pastoral. (1) Huntington Lib. MS. HM 4. (2) Alnwick Castle MS. 508. (3) Ibid., 509.

Necromantes. (1) Huntington Lib. MS. HM 4. (2) Alnwick Castle MS. 509.

PHILIPS, KATHERINE

Horace. Folger Shakespeare Lib. MS. V. b. 231.

Pompey. Ibid.

PITCAIRNE, ARCHIBALD

The Assembly. Brit. Mus. Add. MS. 11503.

POLWHELE, ELIZABETH

The Frolic, or The Lawyer Cheated. MS cited by Halliwell-Phillipps, *Dict.*, p. 105. Extant?

POPPLE, WILLIAM

The Cid. Brit. Mus. Add. MS. 8888.

Tamerlane the Beneficent. Ibid.

POUND, THOMAS

Two Mask Orations. Bodl. MS. Rawlinson, poet. 108, ff. 24, 29^v (formerly MS. 14601).

RANDOLPH, THOMAS

Aristippus. Brit. Mus. MS. Sloane 2531, ff. 124^a–40^b.

The Conceited Pedlar. (1) Brit. Mus. Add. MS. 27406. (2) Edinburgh Univ. MS. Laing III. 493. (3) (*The University Pedlar*). MS formerly in the possession of Richard West, then of the Rev. Mr Collins of Knaresborough: *teste* J. Hunter, *Cho. Vatum*, and R. West. Extant?

The Drinking Academy. Huntington Lib. MS. HM 91.

Praeludium. Brit. Mus. Add. MS. 37425, ff. 54–55.

'Thomas Randolph's Salting.' MS, item 1488, in sale at Maggs Brothers, 1944 (Catalogue 598).

RANT, HUMPHREY

Phormio. Brit. Mus. MS. Sloane 1145, ff. 41–84.

REDFORD, JOHN
Courage, Kindness, Cleanness. Brit. Mus. Add. MS. 15233, f. 28 (frag.).
D, G, and T[om]. Ibid., f. 38 (frag.).
Wit and Science. Ibid., ff. 11–27 (frag.).

REYMES, WILLIAM
Self-Interest. Folger Shakespeare Lib. MS. V. b. 128.

RICHARDS, THOMAS, *see* JOHNSON, LAURENCE

RICHARDS, WILLIAM
The Christmas Ordinary. Brit. Mus. MS. Sloane 1458, ff. 36^v–42^r.

RICKETS, JOHN
Byrsa Basilica (L). Bodl. MS. Tanner 207.

RUGGLE, GEORGE
Club Law. St John's Col., Camb., MS. S. 62.
Ignoramus (L). (1) MS at Clare Hall, Camb. (2) Brit. Mus. MS. Egerton 2982, Art. 5 (frag.). (3) Brit. Mus. MS. Harleian 6869, ff. 57 seq. (frag.). (4) Ibid., Harleian 980, Art. 173. (5) Brit. Mus. MS. Sloane 2531. (6) Bodl. MS. Douce 43. (7) Bodl. MS. Tanner 306 (2 copies). (8) Bodl. MS. Rawlinson 1361, ff. 129–76.

SALTERNE, GEORGE
Tomumbeius (L). Bodl. MS. Rawlinson, poet. 75.

SALUSBURY, SIR THOMAS
A Mask at Knowsley. MS in the National Lib. of Wales.

SANSBURY, JOHN
Periander (part of *The Christmas Prince*, for MS of which see, below, ANONYMOUS). Folger Shakespeare Lib. MS. J. a. 1, ff. 134^r–57^v.

SETTLE, ELKANAH
Love and Revenge. Brit. Mus. MS. Harleian 6903, Art. I.
Pastor Fido. Bodl. MS. Rawlinson, poet. 8.

SHADWELL, THOMAS
The Humorists. MS in the lib. of the Duke of Portland, Welbeck Abbey.
The Sullen Lovers. Ibid.

SHAKESPEARE, WILLIAM
Henry IV. See above, under DERING, SIR EDWARD.
Julius Caesar (transcript, with alterations, from MS based on Second Folio). Folger Shakespeare Lib. V. a. 85.
The Merry Wives of Windsor (transcript from Second Folio). (1) Ibid., V. a. 73. (2) Ibid., V. b. 240 (portion of III. 5; IV. 1–5).

Sir Thomas More. See above, under MUNDAY, ANTHONY.
Titus Andronicus. MS in the possession of the Marquis of Bath at Longleat (frag. and illustration).
As You Like It, The Comedy of Errors, Julius Caesar, Macbeth, Romeo and Juliet, and *Twelfth Night* appear in MS. 7.87, a volume dated 1694–1695, Public Lib. of Douai, as do Lee's *Mithridates*, Dryden's *The Indian Emperor*, and Davenant's *The Siege of Rhodes*, Pt. II. All the plays are transcripts from printed texts, or from MSS based on printed texts (the Second Folio for Shakespeare). See B. M. Wagner, *T.L.S.*, 4 Oct. 1934, p. 675, and G. B. Evans, 'The Douai Manuscript – Six Shakespearean Transcripts (1694–95)', *Phil. Quarterly*, XLI (1962), 158–72.

SHIPMAN, ROGER, AND WILLIAM TAYLOR
Grobiana's Nuptials. Bodl. MS. 30, ff. 13 seq. (formerly MS. 27639).

SHIRLEY, JAMES
The Court Secret. Worcester Col., Oxford, MS. 1200.
Cupid and Death (music only). Brit. Mus. Add. MS. 17799.
The Royal Master. MS said to be in the collection of The Players Club, New York. Extant?

SIDNAM, JONATHAN
Il Pastor Fido. Brit. Mus. Add. MS. 29493.

SIDNEY, SIR PHILIP
The Lady of May. MS in collection of A. A. Houghton, Jr., of New York (formerly at Helmingham Hall, Suffolk).

SIMONS, JOSEPH, *vere* LOBB, EMMANUEL
Leo Armenus (L). (1) Camb. Univ. Lib. MS. Ii. VI. 35. (2) St John's Col., Camb., MS. 504. (3) Stonyhurst MS. B. VI. 25.
S. Damianus (L). (1) St John's Col., Camb., MS. 504. (2) Stonyhurst MS. B. VI. 25.
Zeno (L). (1) Camb. Univ. Lib. MS. Ii. VI. 35. (2) Brit. Mus. MS. Harleian 5024, Art. I. (3) Stonyhurst MS. B. VI. 25. (4) St John's Col., Camb., MS. 504.

SINGLETON, THOMAS
Talpae (L). Bodl. MS. Rawlinson D. 288.

SPARROW, THOMAS
Confessor (L). Bodl. MS. Rawlinson, poet. 77.

SPEED, JOHN
The Converted Robber. Brit. Mus. Add. MS. 14047.

STUB, EDMUND
Fraus Honesta (L). (1) Emmanuel Col., Camb., MS. III. 1. 17. (2) Trinity Col., Camb., MS. R. 17. 9. (3) Ibid., R. 17. 10. (4) Brit. Mus. MS. Harleian 2296, f. 151.

SUCKLING, SIR JOHN
Aglaura. (1) Brit. Mus. MS. Royal 18C. XXV. (2) Brit. Mus. MS. Harleian 3889, ff. 28–31ᵛ (I. 1 and part of I. 2).

TALBOT, SIR GEORGE
Filli di Sciro. (1) Bodl. MS. Rawlinson, poet. 130. (2) Brit. Mus. Add. MS. 12128.

TATE, NAHUM
Dido and Aeneas. MS. at St Michael's Col., Tenbury (score).

UDALL, NICHOLAS
The Coronation Triumph of Anne Boleyn. Brit. Mus. MS. Royal 18A. LXIV (frags.).
Respublica. Carl H. Pforzheimer Lib. MS. 40A.

VERNEY, FRANCIS
Antipoe. Bodl. MS. 31041.

VINCENT, THOMAS
Paria (L). (1) Emmanuel Col., Camb., MS. I. 3. 16. (2) Folger Shakespeare Lib. MS. V. b. 222, f. 100.

WARD, ROBERT
Fucus sive Histriomastix (L). (1) Lambeth Palace MS. 828. (2) Bodl. MS. Rawlinson, poet. 21.

WATSON, THOMAS
Absalom (L). Brit. Mus. MS. Stowe 957.

WHARTON, *née* LEE, ANNE
Love's Martyr. Brit. Mus. Add. MS. 28693.

WHITE, ROBERT
Cupid's Banishment. MS sold 'among Mr R. S. Turner's books in 1881' (Hazlitt, *Manual*, p. 55). Present whereabouts unknown.

WIBURNE, NATHANIEL
Machiavellus (L). Bodl. MS. Douce 234.

WILD, ROBERT
The Benefice. (1) Brit. Mus. MS. Lansdowne 807, Art. 4 (frag.). (2) Folger Shakespeare Lib. MS. V. a. 232.

WILDE, GEORGE
Eumorphus (L). Brit. Mus. Add. MS. 14047, ff. 60–96.

Love's Hospital. (1) Brit. Mus. Add. MS. 14047, ff. 1–39ʳ. (2) Folger Shakespeare Lib. MS. J. b. 7 (frags.).

WILMOT, JOHN, EARL OF ROCHESTER
The Conquest of China. (1) Brit. Mus. Add. MS. 28692, ff. 70–5 (one scene). (2) Folger Shakespeare Lib. MS. V. b. 233 (one scene).
Lucina's Rape. (1) Brit. Mus. Add. MS. 28692. (2) Folger Shakespeare Lib. MS. V. b. 233.
Sodom. (1) MS in the Bibliothèque Nationale, Paris; see *Nouvelles acquisitions du département des manuscrits, 1891–1916*, Manuscrits anglais, 1884–1910. (2) Brit. Mus. MS. Harleian 7312. (3) MS in the Hague Lib. (4) MS in the Hamburger Staats-und Universitäts-Bibliothek. (5) Victoria and Albert Mus. MS. Dyce 43.

WILMOT, ROBERT, AND OTHERS
Gismond of Salerne. (1) Brit. Mus. MS. Hargrave 205. (2) Brit. Mus. MS. Lansdowne 786. (3) Folger Shakespeare Lib. MS. V. a. 198 (frag.).

WILSON, ARTHUR
The Corporal. (1) Victoria and Albert Mus. MS. Forster 638 (frag.). (2) Bodl. MS. Douce C. 2 (frag.). (3) Bodl. MS. Rawlinson, poet. 9, f. 45ʳ (title and *dramatis personae* only).
The Inconstant Lady. (1) Bodl. MS. Rawlinson, poet. 9. (2) Ibid., 128. (3) Folger Shakespeare Lib. MS. J. b. 1.
The Swisser. Brit. Mus. Add. MS. 36759.

WILSON, JOHN
Belphegor. Folger Shakespeare Lib. MS. V. b. 109.
The Cheats. MS. at Worcester Col., Oxford.

WORSELEY, RALPH
Synedrium (both versions) (L). Trinity Col., Camb., MS. O. 3. 25.

WREN, CHRISTOPHER, SR
Physiponomachia (L). Bodl. MS. 30, ff. 2 seq. (formerly 27639).

WRIGHT, JAMES
La Mallad (trans.). Folger Shakespeare Lib. MS. V. b. 220.

ZOUCHE, RICHARD
Fallacy. Brit. Mus. MS. Harleian 6869, Art. 2, ff. 24ᵛ–56ᵛ.

ANONYMOUS
Abraham and Isaac (Brome). MS formerly at Brome Manor, Suffolk; now at Ipswich and East Suffolk Record Office, Ipswich.

Abraham and Isaac (Dublin). Trinity Col., Dublin, MS. D. IV. 18.

Absalom (L). See under Watson, Thomas, above.

Adam (Le Mystère d'Adam). Lib. of the City of Tours MS. 927.

Alcestis. See under Buchanan, George, Supp. I.

Alice and Alexis. Bodl. MS. Douce 171, ff. 48^b–70 (frag.).

Ambitio Infelix sive Absalom (L). Stonyhurst MS. A. VII. 50 (2).

Ananias, Azarias, Mesael (L). Stonyhurst MS. B. VI. 10.

Anna Bullen. Huntington Lib. MS. HM 973.

Antipolargesis (L). Stonyhurst MS. A. VII. 50 (1).

Antoninus Bassianus Caracalla (L). (1) Bodl. MS. Rawlinson C. 590. (2) Harvard Univ. MS. Thr 10.1, ff. 8–19 (an actor's part).

Antonio of Ragusa. Bodl. MS. Rawlinson, poet. 93.

Ara Fortunae (L). See *The Christmas Prince*, below.

Artaxerxes (L). Stonyhurst MS. A. VII. 50 (1).

Ascanius (L). Bodl. MS. Add. B. 73.

Bacchides. See under Buchanan, George, Supp. I.

Band, Cuff, and Ruff (Ruff, Band, and Cuff). (1) Brit. Mus. Add. MS. 23723. (2) MS reported in *Hist. MSS. Comm.*, III, 295 (MSS at Ashton Hall, York). (3) Folger Shakespeare Lib. MS. J. a. 2, f. 25^r–25^v.

The Baptist. See under Buchanan, George, Supp. I.

Basilindus (L). Stonyhurst MS. A. VII. 50 (1).

Bila, Ariscancus, etc. (L). Brit. Mus. Add. MS. 27569, f. 1.

Blurt, Master Constable. Folger Shakespeare Lib. 17876 (transcript of H2^r–4^v supplied in defective copy of 1602 Quarto).

Boot and Spur. Folger Shakespeare Lib. MS. J. a. 1, ff. 19^r–23^r.

Britanniae Primitiae (L). (1) Stonyhurst MS. A. VII. 50 (2). (2) Bodl. MS. Rawlinson, poet. 215 (frag.).

The Burial and Resurrection of Christ. Bodl. MS. E. Museo. 160.

Bury St Edmunds Fragment. MS attached to a roll of Rickinghall Manor, Suffolk, formerly property of Abbey of Bury St Edmunds, acquired by Brit. Mus. 1921 (Add. MS. Charter 63481B [roll]).

Caiphas. Brit. Mus. MS. Sloane 2478, f. 43^r.

Cancer (L). Folger Shakespeare Lib. MS. J. a. 2, ff. 26^r–47^r.

Captiva Religio (L). (1) English Col., Rome, Archives MS. Lib. 321. (2) Ibid., C. 17 (iv).

The Castle of Perseverance. Macro MS in the Folger Shakespeare Lib.

Charlemagne. Brit. Mus. MS. Egerton 1994, ff. 119–36.

Chester Plays. (1) MS. Peniarth 399, National Lib. of Wales. (2) Huntington Lib. MS. HM 2 (frag.). (3) Brit. Mus. Add. MS. 10305. (4) Brit. Mus. MS. Harleian 2013. (5) Ibid., 2124. (6) Bodl. MS. 175. (7) MS in Manchester Free Lib. (frag.).

A Christmas Messe. Folger Shakespeare Lib. MS. J. a. 1, ff. 105^r–15^v.

The Christmas Prince. (Contains following Lat. pieces: *Ara Fortunae, Philomela, Philomathes, Saturnalia,* the last poss. by Owen Vertue. Contains also English *Periander,* for another MS of which see SANSBURY, JOHN, above.) St John's Col., Oxford, MS.

Cinna. Oxford MS Exoniensis, saec. XVII.

Clytophon (L) (William Ainsworth 'Scriptor' [transcriber?]). Emmanuel Col., Camb., MS. III. 1. 17.

The Conversion of St Paul. Bodl. MS. Digby 133, ff. 37–50.

The Coronation of King Edward VI. MS 'formerly belonging to William Le Neve Norroy' (see Leland, *Collect.,* IV, pp. 310 seq.).

The Country Gentleman. Folger Shakespeare Lib. MS. V. b. 228.

Crux Vindicata (L). Stonyhurst MS. A. VII. 50 (2).

The Cure of Pride. Huntington Lib. MS. HM 95.

The Cyprian Conqueror. Brit. Mus. MS. Sloane 3709.

The Dead Man's Fortune. Brit. Mus. Add. MS. 10449, f. 1 ('plot' only).

Description of the Pageants Made in the City of London at the Receiving of . . . Charles V and Henry VIII . . . Corpus Christi Col., Camb., MS. 298, No. 8.

Devices to Be Shown before the Queen at Nottingham Castle after the Meeting of the Queen of Scots. Brit. Mus. MS. Lansdowne 5, item 38.

Diana's Grove, or The Faithful Genius. (1) MS cited by M. Summers, *Playhouse of Pepys,* p. 449, from Dobell catalogue of 1918. (2) MS, item 361, in H. F. House sale at Sotheby's, 21 Jan. 1924 (*The Faithful Genius*).

Dick of Devonshire. Brit. Mus. MS. Egerton 1994, ff. 30–52.

The Disloyal Favourite. Bodl. MS. Rawlinson D. 1361, ff. 285–306.

Don Pedro, the Cruel King of Castile (L). MS, item 482, in Sotheby's sale, 13 Dec. 1938.

Dux Moraud. Bodl. MS. Eng. poet. f. 2 (R).

Edmond Ironside. Brit. Mus. MS. Egerton 1994, ff. 96–119.

The Enchanted Lovers (Lower) and *The City Nightcap* (Davenport) adapted and combined. Folger Shakespeare Lib. MS. J. b. 2.

The Entertainment at Chirke Castle. Brit. Mus. MS. Egerton 2623, ff. 20–23 (speeches of Genius, Orpheus, and Winter).

The Entertainment at Mitcham. Brit. Mus. Add. MS. 12497, ff. 253–62ᵛ.

The Essex Entertainment, 1595. Fragments appear in Lambeth Palace MSS. V. 118; VIII, 274; Northumberland MS. Burgoyne 55, ff. 47–53; S.P.D. Elizabeth, CCLIV, 67, 68; Folger Shakespeare Lib. MS. V. b. 213 (speeches for a Squire, Hermit, Soldier, and Secretary).

The Fairy Knight. Folger Shakespeare Lib. MS. V. a. 128.

The Faithful Friends. Victoria and Albert Mus. MS. Dyce 10.

The Faithful Virgins. Bodl. MS. Rawlinson, poet. 195.

The Fatal Marriage. Brit. Mus. MS. Egerton 1994, ff. 136–61.

Felix Concordia Fratrum (L). Stonyhurst MS. A. VII. 50 (2).

Fenisa. MS, item 251, in H. F. House sale at Sotheby's, 21 Jan. 1924.

The First Anti-Mask of Mountebanks. (1) Huntington Lib. MS. HM 21. (2) Brit. Mus. Add. MS. 5956, ff. 72–84. (3) Bodl. MS. Rawlinson D. 1021.

Fool's Fortune. MS in Public Record Office, Star Chamber, Proceedings, 8. 250/31.

Fortunae Ludibrium (L). Stonyhurst MS. A. VII. 50 (2).

'*II Fortune's Tennis*.' MS once identified with this play. Brit. Mus. Add. MS. 10449, f. 4 ('plot' only).

Fraus Pia (L). Brit. Mus. MS. Sloane 1855, ff. 71–84.

Frederick and Basilea. Brit. Mus. Add. MS. 10449, f. 2 ('plot' only).

Furor Impius sive Constans Fratricida (L). Bodl. MS. Rawlinson, poet. 215. (May be same as *Sanguis Sanguinem sive Constans Fratricida*, below.)

Gallomyomachia (Greek). Brit. Mus. MS. Harleian 5664, Art. 5.

Gemitus Columbae (L). Stonyhurst MS. A. VII. 50 (2).

Ghismonda (*Tancred and Ghismonda*). Brit. Mus. Add. MS. 34312, f. 139.

Gigantomachia. Folger Shakespeare Lib. MS. J. a. 1, ff. 186ʳ–200ʳ.

Glausamond and Fidelia. Warwick County Record Office, Newdigate MS. CR 163/B 766.

The Governor. Brit. Mus. Add. MS. 10419.

Gown, Hood, and Cap. Folger Shakespeare Lib. MS. J. a. 2, ff. 43ᵛ–49ʳ.

The Great Cham. Folger Shakespeare Lib. MS. X. d. 259.

Hannibal (L). Bodl. MS. Malone 531 (frag.).

The Harrowing of Hell. (1) Advocates' Lib., Edinburgh, MS. Auchinleck W. 4, 1. (2) Bodl. MS. Digby 86, ff. 119–20. (3) Brit. Mus. MS. Harleian 2253, ff. 55–56.

Hercules Furens. Bodl. MS. Rawlinson, poet. 76.

Heteroclitanomalonomia. Folger Shakespeare Lib. MS. J. a. 1, ff. 119ʳ–33ʳ.

Hierarchomachia. English Col., Rome, Archives MS. C. 17 (i).

The Hypochondriac. Brit. Mus. MS. Sloane 1863, ff. 44ᵃ–69ᵇ (frag.).

Icon Ecclesiastici (L). Brit. Mus. MS. Sloane 1767, ff. 2–17.

The Illustrious Slaves. Brit. Mus. Add. MS. 32094, ff. 274 seq.

Interludium de Clerico et Puella. Brit. Mus. Add. MS. 23986.

Jephthes. See under Buchanan, George, Supp. I.

Joseph. See under Buchanan, George, Supp. I.

Jovis et Junonis Nuptiae (L). Trinity Col., Camb., MS. R. 10. 4.

Judith. National Lib. of Wales MS. Peniarth 508 (frag.).

Judith. See under Buchanan, George, Supp. I.

Jugurtha. Bodl. MS. Rawlinson, poet. 195.

Juli and Julian. Folger Shakespeare Lib. MS. V. a. 159.

Laelia (L). Lambeth Palace MS. 838.

'*Locus, Corpus, Motus*', etc. Bodl. MS. Tanner 306 (frag.).

Love and Self-Love. See *The Essex Entertainment*, above.

Love Feigned and Unfeigned. A fragment written on first and last leaves of J. Herolt's *Sermones Discipuli*, pub. 1492, Brit. Mus. MS. I. B. 2172 (fac.).

Love's Changelings' Change. Brit. Mus. MS. Egerton 1994, ff. 293–318.

Love's Victory. Huntington Lib. MS. HM 600.

The Lover's Stratagem. Bodl. MS. Rawlinson, poet. 18.

Ludus Coventriae. Brit. Mus. MS. Cotton Vespasian D. VIII.

Lusiuncula (L). Extant? See Hazlitt, *Manual*, p. 145.

Magister Bonus sive Arsenius (L). Stonyhurst MS. A. VII. 50 (2).

Mankind. Macro MS in the Folger Shakespeare Lib.

Marcus et Marcellianus (L). Stonyhurst MS. B. VI. 22.

The Marriage of Frederick and Elizabeth. Brit. Mus. Add. MS. 5767.

The Marriage of Prince Arthur. College of Arms MS. 1st M. 13.

Marriage Revived. MS in Harvard Col. Lib.

Mary Magdalene, The Mystery Play of. Bodl. MS. Digby 133, ff. 95–145.

The Masculine Bride. See *The Whimsies of Señor Hidalgo*, below.

A Mask Presented at Coleoverton. Victoria and Albert Mus. MS. Dyce 36.

The Massacre of Innocents. Bodl. MS. Digby 133, ff. 146–57.

Medea. Brit. Mus. MS. Sloane 911, ff. 100–15.

Medea. See under Buchanan, George, Supp. I.

Menaechmi. See under Buchanan, George, Supp. I.

Mercator. See under Buchanan, George, Supp. I.

Mercurius Rusticans (L). Bodl. MS. Wood D. 18.

The Merry Loungers. Brit. Mus. Add. MS. 6402, f. 84.

'*Microcosmus*' (L). Trinity Col., Camb., MS. R. 10. 4 (item 4).

Miles Gloriosus. See under Buchanan, George, Supp. I.

Mind, Will, and Understanding. (1) Macro MS in the Folger Shakespeare Lib. (2) Bodl. MS. Digby 133, ff. 158–69 (large frag.).

Mr Doolittle. (1) Brit. Mus. MS. Sloane 1828, ff. 1–45[b]. (2) Ibid., Sloane 1911–1913, ff. 203–4 (frag.).

Montezuma (L). Stonyhurst MS. B. VI. 10.

Moore's Mask. MS listed by Fleay, *Biog. Chron.*, II, 358. Extant?

Morus (L). Stonyhurst MS. A. VII. 50 (1).

Mostellaria. See under Buchanan, George, Supp. I.

Naamen. See under Buchanan, George, Supp. I.

Narcissus. Bodl. MS. Rawlinson, poet. 212.

Nehemiah. See under Buchanan, George, Supp. I.

Nero, The Tragedy of. (1) Brit. Mus. MS. Egerton 1994, ff. 245–68. (2) Excerpts in Samuel Butler's commonplace book; see item 135 in A. S. W. Rosenbach catalogue, Oct. 1941.

The New Moon. English Col., Rome, Archives MS. Z. 142.

Nottola (L). Bodl. MS. Douce 47.

Oedipus. MS in the possession of Stevens Cox of Dorset.

Oedipus. Bodl. MS. Rawlinson, poet. 76.

Origo Mundi, etc. (1) Bodl. MS. 791. (2) Bodl. MS. Corn., c. 2.

The Part of Poor. Harvard Univ. MS. Thr 10.1, ff. 21–46 (an actor's part).

Parthenia (L). Emmanuel Col., Camb., MS. I. 3. 16.

The Partial Law. Folger Shakespeare Lib. MS. V. a. 165.

Pastor Fidus (L). (1) Camb. Univ. Lib. MS. Ff. 11. 9. (2) Trinity Col., Camb., MS. R. 3. 37.

Pathomachia. (1) Brit. Mus. MS. Harleian 6869, Art. I. (2) Bodl. MS. Eng. misc. e. 5.

Pelopidarum Secunda. Brit. Mus. MS. Harleian 5110, Art. 4.

Perfidus Hetruscus (L). Bodl. MS. Rawlinson C. 787.

The Pilgrimage to Parnassus. Bodl. MS. Rawlinson D. 398.

Preist the Barber. Folger Shakespeare Lib. MS. J. a. 2, ff. 47[v]–48[r].

The Pride of Life. MS in the Public Record Office, Dublin.

'*Processus Satanae.*' MS in the lib. of the Duke of Portland at Welbeck Abbey (an actor's part).

Pseudolus. See under Buchanan, George, Supp. I.

Psyche et Filii ejus (L). Bodl. MS. Rawlinson, poet. 171, f. 60.

Publius Cornelius Scipio sui Victor (L). Folger Shakespeare Lib. MS. V. a. 227.

Pygmalion (L). Bodl. MS. Rawlinson D. 317, ff. 190–5.

The Queen's Welcome at Theobalds. (1) MS formerly in the collection of Frederic Ouvry (frag.). Extant? (2) MS formerly in the possession of J. P. Collier (frag.). Extant?

Quem Quaeritis in *Winchester Troper* (L). (1) Bodl. MS. 775. X, 17 (dated 978–980?). (2) Christ's Col., Camb., MS. 473. XI, 26 (dated *c.* 1050).

Quem Quaeritis (*of Easter*) of the Church of St John the Evangelist, Dublin (L). (1) Bodl. MS. Rawlinson, Liturg. d. IV. XIV, 68–70, 85–86, 127–32. (2) Lib. of Archbishop Marsh, Dublin, MS. Z. 4. 2. 20.

Quem Quaeritis. See also under Aethelwold, and Katherine of Sutton.

The Renegado. Bodl. MS. Rawlinson, poet. 20.

The Resurrection of Our Lord. Folger Shakespeare Lib. MS. V. b. 192.

I The Return from Parnassus. Bodl. MS. Rawlinson D. 398.

II The Return from Parnassus (*The Progress to Parnassus*). Folger Shakespeare Lib. MS. V. a. 355 (the Halliwell-Phillipps MS).

The Review (prob. after 1700). Folger Shakespeare Lib. MS. W. a. 114.

I Richard II. Brit. Mus. MS. Egerton 1994, ff. 161–86.

Risus Anglicanus (L). Folger Shakespeare Lib. MS. J. a. 1, ff. 24^r–43^v.

Robin Hood and the Sheriff of Nottingham. MS at Trinity Col., Camb. (frag.).

Rodogune. Folger Shakespeare Lib. MS. V. b. 227.

Roffensis (L). English Col., Rome, Archives MS. Lib. 321.

Romanus. Brit. Mus. MS. Harleian 4628, Art. 14, ff. 272–82^v (frag.).

Romeus et Julietta (L). Brit. Mus. MS. Sloane 1775, f. 242 (frag.).

Rowland's Godson. Bodl. MS. Rawlinson, poet. 185, ff. 15^v–19^r.

Sacrament, The Croxton Play of the. Trinity Col., Dublin, MS. F. IV. 20.

S. Edoardus Confessor (L). Magdalen Col., Oxford, MS. C. 2. 22.

S. Franciscus Xaverius (L). Stonyhurst MS. B. VI. 10.

S. Pelagius Martyr (L). Stonyhurst MS. B. VI. 10.

S. Thomas Cantuariis (L). English Col., Rome, Archives MS. Lib. 321.

Sanguis Sanguinem sive Constans Fratricida (L). Stonyhurst MS. A. VII. 50 (2). (May be same as *Furor Impius sive Constans Fratricida*, above.)

Sapientia Solomonis (L). (1) Brit. Mus. Add. MS. 20061. (2) Folger Shakespeare Lib. MS. V. a. 212.

Saul. See under Buchanan, George, Supp. I.

The Second Maiden's Tragedy. Brit. Mus. MS. Lansdowne 807, ff. 28–56.

La Seinte resureccion (Anglo-Norman). (1) Bibliothèque Nationale, Paris, MS. fr. 902 (frag.). (2) Brit. Mus. Add. MS. 45103 (frag.).

Senilis Amor (L). Bodl. MS. Rawlinson, poet. 9, ff. 46–81.

II The Seven Deadly Sins. Dulwich Col. MS. XIX ('plot' only).

Shrewsbury Fragments (Lat. and Eng.). Shrewsbury School MS. Mus. III. 42.

The Siege of Croya. Bodl. MS. Rawlinson, poet. 119.

Silvanus (L). Bodl. MS. Douce 234.

Sisigambis, Queen of Syracuse. Bodl. MS. Rawlinson, poet. 167.

Solymannidae (L). Brit. Mus. MS. Lansdowne 723.

Sophomoros comoedia (L). MS, item 240, in Robinson sale catalogue 76.348, 3 May 1946.

Stonyhurst Pageants. Stonyhurst MS. A. VI. 33.

The Telltale. Dulwich Col. MS. XX.

Thomas Morus (L). English Col., Rome, Archives MS. Lib. 321. (Same play as *Morus*, above?)

Thyestes. Bodl. MS. Rawlinson, poet. 76.

Time's Triumph. Brit. Mus. MS. Egerton 1994, ff. 212–45.

Timon. Victoria and Albert Mus. MS. Dyce 52.

Tobit. See under Buchanan, George, Supp. I.

Towneley Plays. See *Wakefield Plays.*

Tragoedia Miserrima Pyrami et Thisbes fata enuncians. Brit. Mus. Add. MS. 15227, ff. 56^v–61^r.

Troilus and Cressida. National Lib. of Wales MS. Peniarth 106 (formerly Hengwrt 338).

The True Tragicomedy Formerly Acted at Court, etc. Brit. Mus. Add. MS. 25348.

Try before You Trust. Brit. Mus. Add. MS. 37158, f. 17.

The Two Noble Ladies and the Converted Conjurer. Brit. Mus. MS. Egerton 1994, ff. 224–45.

Wakefield Plays. Huntington Lib. MS. HM 1.

The Wasp. MS in the Duke of Northumberland's lib. at Alnwick.

The Welcome for Emperor Charles V. Corpus Christi, Camb., MS. 298 (no. 8), pp. 132 seq.

The Welcome for James VI. Advocates' Lib., Edinburgh, Hist. MSS. 35.4.2, vol. II, f. 524 (Johnston's MS History of Scotland).

The Welcome for Queen Mary. (1) MS formerly in the possession of Sir John Maxwell of Pollock (*Diurnal of Remarkable Occurrents*). (2) Advocates' Lib., Edinburgh, Hist. MSS. 35.4.2, vol. II, f. 356 (Johnston's MS History of Scotland).

The White Ethiopian. Brit. Mus. MS. Harleian 7313, Art. 1.

Wine, Beer, and Ale. Univ. of Edinburgh MS. Laing. III. 493.

Wit's Triumvirate. Brit. Mus. Add. MS. 45865.

The Wooing of Nan. Dulwich Col. MS., Vol. I, f. 272 (no. 139).

York Plays. Brit. Mus. Add. MS. 35290.

Zelotypus (L). (1) Trinity Col., Camb., MS. R. 3. 9. (2) Emmanuel Col., Camb., MS. III. 1. 17. (3) MS in Durham Cathedral Lib.

ADDENDA & CORRIGENDA

ADDENDA

1554. Anon. (Mey, John?). '*Theano*' (Character's name). *c.* 1540–1554. Latin (?) Tragedy. Queens' Col., Cambridge. Lost.

1574. Anon. *A Mask of Hobby-Horses*. Xmas, 1574–1575. Mask. Court. Lost.

1574. Anon. *A Mask of Mariners*. Xmas, 1574–1575. Mask. Court. Lost.

1574. Anon. *A Mask of Pilgrims*. Xmas, 1574–1575. Mask. Court. Lost.

p. 202. *Bila, Ariscancus, etc.* Anon. Lat. play, 15th cent. MS (frag.; ed. J. Bolte, *Hermes*, XXI [1886], 313–18†).

p. 202. *The Captive Lady*. Anon. tragicomedy, 'first half of 17th cent.' MS.

p. 202. *The Lover's Stratagem, or Virtue Rewarded*. Limits: *c.* 1680–1685. Ed.: A. Obertello, 1952†.

p. 203. Brit. Mus. MS. Egerton 2623, ff. 37–38. Ed.: W. W. Greg, *Mod. Lang. Quart.*, VII (1904), 148–55†.

p. 204. 'A fragment of an English play in which the sexton of St Denys Church is a character', 16th–17th cent. National Lib. of Wales MS. Peniarth 403 D (formerly Hengwrt 326).

p. 204. Fragment of a play, '1645–1649'. Among the characters are the King, Prince Rupert, a tailor and apprentices, and True Wit. MS in the collection of James M. Osborn, New Haven, Conn.

p. 209. 32a. C. R. Baskervill, 'William Lyly's Verse for the Entry of Charles V into London', *Huntington Lib. Bull.*, IX, 1–14.

p. 212. 175a. M. J. C. Cavanaugh, ed., *Technogamia* [facs. text, with introd. and notes].

p. 214. 287a. Douglas Grant, ed., *Dryden: Poetry and Plays*.

p. 214. 294a. J. Cadwalader, ed., *King Edward the Third, with the Fall of Mortimer Earl of March, 1691*.

p. 215. 300a. A. N. Wiley, ed., *Rare Prologues and Epilogues, 1642–1700*.

p. 216. *Beggars' Bush*, ed. J. H. Dorenkamp (Univ. of Illinois, 1962).

p. 217. *The Woman's Prize*, ed. G. B. Ferguson (Univ. of Illinois, 1962).

p. 303. Saracen's Head: An Inn in Islington where there is reference to the performance of plays in 1557.

p. 308. Carlell, Lodowick. *Arviragus and Philicia*. See also J. E. Ruoff, *Notes and Queries*, Jan. 1955, pp. 21–22. (3) MS in Sotheby sale catalogue, 1–4 July 1889.

p. 312. Keigwin, John. *The Creation of the World, with Noah's Flood* (trans. of Jordan, W.). (4) National Lib. of Wales MS. Llanstephan 97.

p. 313. Marston, John. *City Pageant*. Brit. Mus. MS. Royal 18A. XXXI.

p. 316. Wilmot, John, Earl of Rochester. *Sodom*. (6) Princeton Univ. Lib. MS. 14401. (7) Ibid. (abridged version).

p. 317. *The Captive Lady*. MS in the collection of James M. Osborn, New Haven, Conn.

p. 318. *Diana's Grove, or The Faithful Genius*. MS. now in the collection of James M. Osborn, New Haven, Conn.

p. 319. *Origo Mundi, etc.* (3) National Lib. of Wales MS. Peniarth 428E (formerly Hengwrt 347; 17th-cent. transcription).

CORRIGENDA

1600. *II Sir John Oldcastle*. Transfer entire entry to 1599.

1641. *The Distracted State*. Transfer entire entry to 1650.

1686. *Doctor Faustus*. Transfer entire entry to 1688.

p. 216. *Edward III*, ed. J. Cadwalader (Univ. of Pennsylvania, 1949). Omit entry.

POSTSCRIPT

The Complete Plays of Christopher Marlowe, ed. I. Ribner (1963), appeared too late to be included in the List of Editions. Unlisted for the same reason are E. M. Waith's edition of *Bartholomew Fair* in the Yale Ben Jonson, and the first titles in the Regents Renaissance Drama series: *Friar Bacon and Friar Bungay*, ed. D. Seltzer; *A King and No King*, ed. R. K. Turner; *Bartholomew Fair*, ed. E. B. Partridge. Several thesis-editions were recorded in *Dissertation Abstracts* after proofs had been corrected, and are therefore absent from the List of Dissertations: *Clyomon and Clamydes*, ed. Betty Jacqueline Littleton (Univ. of Missouri, 1962), *The English Traveller*, ed. R. J. Hudson (New York Univ., 1962), and *The Empress of Morocco* (Settle) and *The Empress of Morocco* (Duffett), ed. Anne Therese Doyle (Univ. of Illinois, 1963).

Shakespeare's *I Henry VI* is probably not to be identified with the 'Harey the vj' acted as new on 3 March 1592 by Strange's men; I would now list *I Henry VI* separately under the year 1590, and give as limits *c.* 1590–1592. *The Militant Couple* and *The Belgic Hero Unmasked*, listed under the year 1686 as doubtful plays of Villiers, are non-dramatic dialogues, and thus should be omitted from the Chronology and tabulation. In the Last Edition column I failed to indicate that *The Ancient Cornish Drama*, ed. E. Norris, and Rickets's *Byrsa Basilica*, ed. R. H. Bowers, include translations. The 'plot' fragment of Chettle and Dekker's *Troilus and Cressida* (1599) was most recently edited by N. H. Hillebrand and T. W. Baldwin, New Variorum Shakespeare *Troilus and Cressida* (1953), pp. 459–61. For one entry in the Chronology, *The Laws of Candy* (1619), I have sacrificed proper alphabetical sequence in order to make a late correction in the Author column.

The Bodleian manuscript of Ford's *Perkin Warbeck* was 'almost certainly' written in 1745, and so should be excluded from the Chronology and from the Appendix (see D. K. Anderson, Jr., 'The Date and Handwriting of a Manuscript Copy of Ford's "Perkin Warbeck" ', *Notes and Queries*, September 1963, pp. 340–1). A lost (?) Latin play by the biblical translator Gregory Martin (d. 1582), *Tragoedia Cyri Regis Persarum*, is said by Pitsius (*De Angliae Scriptoribus*, 1619) to be extant in the library of St John's College, Oxford, where Martin was in residence from 1557 to 1568. For this reference I am obliged to Professor George B. Parks of Queens College, New York.